HTML and CSS Quick Reference

STRUCTURE TAGS

`<!--...-->`	Creates a comment
`<html>...</html>`	Encloses the entire HTML document
`<head>...</head>`	Encloses the head of the HTML document
`<meta />`	Provides general information about the document
`<style>...</style>`	Style information
`<script>...</script>`	Scripting language
`<noscript>...</noscript>`	Alternative content when scripting is not supported
`<title>...</title>`	The title of the document
`<body>...</body>`	Encloses the body (text and tags) of the HTML document

HEADINGS

`<h1>...</h1>`	Heading level 1
`<h2>...</h2>`	Heading level 2
`<h3>...</h3>`	Heading level 3
`<h4>...</h4>`	Heading level 4
`<h5>...</h5>`	Heading level 5
`<h6>...</h6>`	Heading level 6

PARAGRAPHS

`<p>...</p>`	A plain paragraph

LINKS

`<a>...</a>`	Creates a link or anchor; includes common attributes
`href="..."`	The URL of the document to be linked to this one
`name="..."`	The name of the anchor
`target="..."`	Identifies the window or location in which to open the link
`rel="  "`	Defines forward link types
`rev="..."`	Defines reverse link types
`accesskey="..."`	Assigns a hotkey to this element
`shape="..."`	Is for use with object shapes
`coords="..."`	Is for use with object shapes
`tabindex="..."`	Determines the tabbing order
`onClick`	Is a JavaScript event
`onMouseOver`	Is a JavaScript event
`onMouseOut`	Is a JavaScript event

LISTS

`<ol>...</ol>`	An ordered (numbered) list
`<ul`	An unordered (bulleted) list
`<me`	...ms
`<d`	
`<l`	
`<c`	...ossary list
`<d...`	
`<dd>...</dd>`	...ing definition to a definition term

CHARACTER FORMATTING

`<em>...</em>`	Emphasis (usually italic)
`<strong>...</strong>`	Stronger emphasis (usually bold)
`<code>...</code>`	Code sample
`<kbd>...</kbd>`	Text to be typed
`<var>...</var>`	A variable of placeholder for some other value
`<samp>...</samp>`	Sample text
`<dfn>...</dfn>`	A definition of a term
`<cite>...</cite>`	A citation
`<b>...</b>`	Boldfaced text
`<i>...</i>`	Italic text
`<tt>...</tt>`	Typewriter font
`<u>...</u>`	Underlined text
`<pre>...</pre>`	Preformatted text

OTHER ELEMENTS

`<hr />`	A horizontal rule
` `	A line break
`<blockquote>...</blockquote>`	Used for long quotes or citations
`<address>...</address>`	Signatures or general information about a document's author
`<font>...</font>`	Change the size, color, and typeface of the font
`size="..."`	The size of the font from 1 to 7
`color="..."`	The font color
`face="..."`	The font type
`<basefont />`	Sets the default size of the font for the current page
`size="..."`	The default size of the font from 1 to 7

SAMS Teach Yourself — *When you only have time for the answers™*

HTML and CSS Quick Reference

IMAGES

`<img />`	Inserts an inline image into the document; includes common attributes
`usemap="..."`	A client-side imagemap
`src="..."`	The URL of the image
`alt="..."`	A text string that will be displayed in browsers that cannot support images
`align="..."`	Determines the alignment of the given image
`height="..."`	Is the suggested height in pixels
`width="..."`	Is the suggested width in pixels
`vspace="..."`	The space between the image and the text above and below it
`hspace="..."`	The space between the image and the text to its left and right

CSS TEXT AND FONT STYLE PROPERTIES

`color`	Sets the color of text
`direction`	Sets the direction of text, as in left-to-right or right-to-left
`font`	A shorthand property that allows you to set all the font properties in one declaration
`font-family`	A prioritized list of font family names and/or generic family names for an element
`font-size`	Sets the size of a font
`font-style`	Sets the style of the font
`font-variant`	Displays text in a small-caps font or a normal font
`font-weight`	Sets the weight (boldness) of a font
`letter-spacing`	Increase or decrease the space between characters of text
`text-align`	Aligns the text within an element
`text-decoration`	Applies a decoration to text
`text-indent`	Indents the first line of text in an element
`text-transform`	Controls the capitalization of letters of text
`white-space`	Establishes the handling of white space within an element
`word-spacing`	Increases or decreases the space between words

TABLES

`<table>...</table>`	Creates a table
`background="..."`	Background image for the table
`bgcolor="..."`	Background color of the table
`border="..."`	Width of the border in pixels
`cols="..."`	Number of columns
`cellspacing="..."`	Spacing between cells
`cellpadding="..."`	Spacing in cells
`width="..."`	Table width
`<caption>...</caption>`	The caption for the table
`<tr>...</tr>`	A table row
`align="..."`	The horizontal alignment of the contents of the cells within this row; possible values are `left`, `right`, `center`, `justify`, and `char`
`bgcolor="..."`	Background color for the row
`valign="..."`	The vertical alignment of the contents of the cells within this row; possible values are `top`, `middle`, `bottom`, and `baseline`
`<th>...</th>`	A table heading cell
`align="..."`	The horizontal alignment of the contents of the cell
`valign="..."`	The vertical alignment of the contents of the cell
`bgcolor="..."`	Background color for the cell
`rowspan="..."`	The number of rows this cell will span
`colspan="..."`	The number of columns this cell will span
`nowrap="..."`	Turns off text wrapping in a cell
`<td>...</td>`	Defines a table data cell
`align="..."`	The horizontal alignment of the contents of the cell
`valign="..."`	The vertical alignment of the contents of the cell
`bgcolor="..."`	Background color for the cell
`rowspan="..."`	The number of rows this cell will span
`colspan="..."`	The number of columns this cell will span
`nowrap="..."`	Turns off text wrapping in a cell

SAMS
Teach
Yourself

HTML and CSS

Dick Oliver and
Michael Morrison

in **24** Hours

SEVENTH EDITION

SAMS   800 East 96th Street, Indianapolis, Indiana, 46240 USA

Sams Teach Yourself HTML and CSS in 24 Hours, Seventh Edition

International Standard Book Number: 0-672-32841-0

Library of Congress Catalog Card Number: 2005927446

Printed in the United States of America

First Printing: December 2005

08   07   06   4   3

Trademarks

All terms mentioned in this book that are known to be trademarks or service marks have been appropriately capitalized. Sams Publishing cannot attest to the accuracy of this information. Use of a term in this book should not be regarded as affecting the validity of any trademark or service mark.

Warning and Disclaimer

Every effort has been made to make this book as complete and as accurate as possible, but no warranty or fitness is implied. The information provided is on an "as is" basis.

Bulk Sales

Sams Publishing offers excellent discounts on this book when ordered in quantity for bulk purchases or special sales. For more information, please contact

U.S. Corporate and Government Sales
1-800-382-3419
corpsales@pearsontechgroup.com

For sales outside of the U.S., please contact

International Sales
international@pearsoned.com

Acquisitions Editor
Linda Bump Harrison

Development Editor
Damon Jordan

Managing Editor
Charlotte Clapp

Project Editor
George E. Nedeff

Copy Editor
Cheri Clark

Indexer
Erika Millen

Proofreader
Linda Seifert

Technical Editor
Michelle Jones

Publishing Coordinator
Vanessa Evans

Book Designer
Gary Adair

Page Layout
Kelly Maish

Contents at a Glance

Table of Contents

About the Author

Michael Morrison is a writer, developer, toy inventor, and author of a variety of computer technology books and interactive web-based courses. In addition to his primary profession as a writer and freelance nerd for hire, Michael is the creative lead at Stalefish Labs, an entertainment company he co-founded with his wife, Masheed. The first web-based project for Stalefish Labs is an online music game called *Guess That Groove* (http://www.guessthat-groove.com/). When not glued to his computer, playing hockey, skateboarding, or watching movies with his wife, Michael enjoys hanging out by his koi pond while he daydreams about new web creations. You can visit Michael on the Web and discuss this book at http://www.michaelmorrison.com/.

Dedication

To my hockey and skateboarding buddies, who so generously offered their photos and other personal information for some of the examples in this book.

Acknowledgments

Thanks to Linda Harrison, George Nedeff, Damon Jordan, Cheri Clark, and the rest of the gang at Pearson for keeping me on track and helping to make this a successful project. I also owe a big thanks to Michelle Jones for her expert technical assistance. My wife, Masheed, deserves perhaps the biggest thank-you for tolerating my night-owl writing schedule. And finally, I want to thank you, the reader, for deciding to learn HTML and help make the Web a better and more interesting place tomorrow than it is today.

We Want to Hear from You!

As the reader of this book, *you* are our most important critic and commentator. We value your opinion and want to know what we're doing right, what we could do better, what areas you'd like to see us publish in, and any other words of wisdom you're willing to pass our way.

You can email or write me directly to let me know what you did or didn't like about this book—as well as what we can do to make our books stronger.

Please note that I cannot help you with technical problems related to the topic of this book, and that due to the high volume of mail I receive, I might not be able to reply to every message.

When you write, please be sure to include this book's title and author as well as your name and phone or email address. I will carefully review your comments and share them with the author and editors who worked on the book.

E-mail: webdev@samspublishing.com

Mail: Mark Taber
           Associate Publisher
           Sams Publishing
           800 East 96th Street
           Indianapolis, IN 46240 USA

Reader Services

For more information about this book or another Sams Publishing title, visit our website at www.samspublishing.com. Type the ISBN (excluding hyphens) or the title of a book in the Search field to find the page you're looking for.

Introduction

Put Your HTML Page Online Today

In 2005, it is estimated that approximately 900 million people will have accessed the Internet, including 188 million in the U.S. alone. Throw in 58 million Japanese users, 45 million German users, 35 million British users, 18 million Russian users, and 17 million Canadians, and you can see the meaning of the word "world" in "World Wide Web." Along with all of these people who use the Internet, there are also quite a few people cranking out new content for the Web. Although accurate measurements of the total number of web pages are difficult to come by, the popular search engine Google reports having indexed more than 4 billion web pages as of late 2005.

In the next 24 hours, tens of thousands of new web pages will be posted in publicly accessible areas of the Internet. At least as many pages will be placed on private intranets, where they will be viewed by businesspeople connected to local networks. Every one of those pages—like the 4 billion pages already online—will use Hypertext Markup Language, or HTML.

If you read on, your web pages will be among those that appear on the Internet in the next 24 hours. This will also be the day that you acquire one of the most valuable skills in the world today: mastery of HTML.

Can you really learn to create top-quality web pages yourself, without any specialized software, in less time than it takes to schedule and wait for an appointment with a highly paid HTML wizard? Can this thin, easy-to-read book really enable you to teach yourself state-of-the-art web page publishing?

Yes. In fact, within two hours of starting this book, someone with no previous HTML experience at all can have a web page ready to place on the Internet's World Wide Web.

How can you learn the language of the Web so fast? By example. This book breaks HTML down into simple steps that anyone can learn quickly, and shows you exactly how to tackle each step. Every HTML example is pictured directly above the web page it will produce. You see it done, you read a brief, plain-English explanation of how it works, and you immediately do the same thing with your own page. Ten minutes later, you're on to the next step.

The next day, you're marveling at your own impressive pages on the Internet.

Beyond HTML

This book isn't just about HTML because HTML isn't the only thing you need to know to create web pages today. My goal is to give you all the skills you need in order to create a stunning, state-of-the-art web site in just 24 short, easy lessons. I've received literally thousands of email messages from readers telling me that the earlier editions of this book achieved that goal better than any other book available.

Go ahead and scan the bookstore shelves. You'll discover that the book you're holding now is the only one on the market that covers all the following key skills and technologies in plain English that even beginners will understand:

▶ XHTML (Extended Hypertext Markup Language) and XML (eXtensible Markup Language) are the new standards for web page creation. Every example in this book (and on the accompanying web site) is fully XHTML and XML compatible, so you won't have to relearn anything as XHTML and XML replace old-fashioned HTML.

By the Way

Do you have existing web pages that you need to bring up-to-date so that they're compatible with the new standards? If so, Appendix D, "Migrating from HTML to XHTML," gives you complete, easy-to-follow instructions for converting HTML pages into XHTML.

▶ At the same time, all the examples you'll learn here have been tested for compatibility with the latest version of every major web browser. That includes Microsoft Internet Explorer, Mozilla Firefox, Opera, and Safari. You'll learn from the start to be compatible with the past, yet ready for the future.

▶ There is extensive coverage of Cascading Style Sheets (CSS), which allow you to carefully control the layout, fonts, colors, and formatting of every aspect of your web pages, including both text and images. When it comes to creating eye-popping web pages, CSS goes far beyond what traditional HTML pages could do by themselves. For example, did you know that CSS allows you to specifically tailor the information on a page just for printing, in addition to normal web viewing?

▶ Hours 7 through 10 teach you to design and create your own web page graphics (including animations) using industry-standard software you can download and try free. Creating graphics is the single most important part of producing a great-looking site—and one that most HTML books leave out.

▶ Along with HTML and CSS, you'll learn how to use JavaScript, Dynamic HTML (DHTML), and embedded multimedia in Hours 17 through 19. Your web pages will be interactive and enchanting, not static and unresponsive.

▶ Have you ever wished you could create a really slick item listing on eBay using HTML? Hour 20 shows you how to use your newfound HTML and CSS knowledge to create visually stunning eBay auction listings that will help you get maximum dollars for your auction sales.

▶ You've probably heard about the blogging craze that has hit the Internet by storm. Hour 21 teaches you how to create your own blog and connect it to your personal web site. You'll be a bona fide blogger in no time!

▶ The technical stuff is not enough, so I also include the advice you need when setting up a web site to achieve your real-world goals. Key details—designing an effective page layout, posting your page to the Internet with FTP software, organizing and managing multiple pages, and getting your pages to appear high on the query lists at all the major Internet search sites—are all covered in enough depth to get you beyond the snags that often trip people up.

▶ You may be aware that graphical web site editors such as Microsoft FrontPage and Macromedia DreamWeaver make web design accessible to people who don't know anything about HTML—but these tools also make it more necessary than ever to understand HTML yourself so you can create pages that do exactly what you want and are easy to read and maintain. Throughout the book, I include notes telling you when the what-you-see-is-what-you-get editors are helpful and when you're better off coding the HTML yourself.

Many of these essentials are what made the first six editions of this book nonstop best-sellers. For this edition, I've continued to incorporate the email feedback of thousands of readers to make every lesson easy, fast, and foolproof. I've also revised and updated the hands-on examples for you to experience online and modify to suit your own purposes—nearly 300 sample pages in all. The color quick-reference sheets and updated reference appendixes are sure to keep this volume at your side long after you've become an experienced webmaster.

How to Use This Book

There are several ways to go through this book, and the best way for you depends on your situation. Here are five recommended options. Pick the one that matches your needs:

1. *"I need to get some text on the Internet today. Then I can worry about making it look pretty later."*

   . Read Hour 1, "Understanding HTML and XHTML."

   . Read Hour 2, "Create a Web Page Right Now."

   . Read Hour 4, "Publishing Your HTML Pages."

   . Put your first page on the Internet!

   (Total work time: 2–4 hours)

   . Read the rest of the book, and update your pages as you learn more HTML.

2. *"I need a basic web page with text and graphics on the Internet as soon as possible. Then I can work on improving it and adding more pages."*

   . Read Hour 1, "Understanding HTML and XHTML."

   . Read Hour 2, "Create a Web Page Right Now."

   . Read Hour 7, "Creating Your Own Web Page Graphics."

   . Read Hour 8, "Putting Graphics on a Web Page."

   . Read Hour 4, "Publishing Your HTML Pages."

   . Put your first page on the Internet!

   (Total work time: 4–8 hours)

   . Read the rest of the book, and update your pages as you learn more HTML.

3. *"I need a professional-looking business web site with an order form right away. Then I can continue to improve and develop my site over time."*

   . Read all four hours in Part I, "Your First Web Page."

   . Read Hour 17, "Web Page Scripting for Nonprogrammers."

   . Read Hour 18, "Gathering Information with HTML Forms."

   . Read Hour 7, "Creating Your Own Web Page Graphics."

   . Read Hour 8, "Putting Graphics on a Web Page."

   . Read Hour 9, "Custom Backgrounds and Colors."

   . Put your pages and order form on the Internet!

   (Total work time: 8–12 hours)

   . Read the rest of the book, and update your pages as you learn more HTML.

4. *"I need to develop a creative and attractive 'identity' web site on a tight schedule. Then I need to develop many pages for our corporate intranet as well."*

   - Read all four hours in Part I, "Your First Web Page."

   - Read all six hours in Part II, "Building Practical Web Pages with HTML."

   - Read all seven hours in Part III, "Creative Web Page Design."

   - Put your pages on the Internet and your intranet!

     (Total work time: 12–18 hours)

   - Read the rest of the book, and update your pages as you learn more HTML.

5. *"I need to build a cutting-edge interactive web site or HTML-based multimedia presentation—fast!"*

   - Read this whole book.

   - Put your pages on the Internet and/or CD-ROM!

     (Total work time: 18–24 hours)

   - Review and use the techniques you've learned to continue improving and developing your site.

It may take a day or two for an Internet service provider to set up a host computer for your pages, as discussed in Hour 4. If you want to get your pages online immediately, read Hour 4 now so that you can have a place on the Internet all ready for your first page.

No matter which of these approaches you take, you'll benefit from the unique presentation elements that make this book the fastest possible way to learn HTML.

Visual Examples

Every example in this book is illustrated in two parts. The text you type in to make an HTML page is shown first, with all HTML and CSS code highlighted. The resulting web page is shown as it will appear to people who view it with the world's most popular web browsers: Microsoft Internet Explorer, Mozilla Firefox, or Opera. You'll often be able to adapt the example to your own pages without reading any of the accompanying text at all.

All the examples in this book work with Mozilla Firefox and Microsoft Internet Explorer, as well as Opera and Safari. I often alternate between browsers in the figures throughout the book just to clarify that well-designed web pages should have a consistent look across all browsers. In the event that a page uses a special feature that isn't supported by a major browser, I make sure to point out the browser limitation.

Special Highlighted Elements

As you go through each hour, sections marked "Try It Yourself" guide you in applying what you just learned to your own web pages at once.

Whenever a new term is used, it is clearly highlighted. No flipping back and forth to the Glossary!

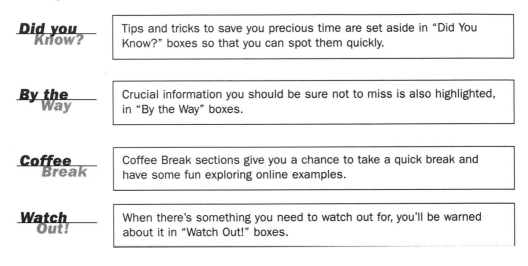

Did you Know? — Tips and tricks to save you precious time are set aside in "Did You Know?" boxes so that you can spot them quickly.

By the Way — Crucial information you should be sure not to miss is also highlighted, in "By the Way" boxes.

Coffee Break — Coffee Break sections give you a chance to take a quick break and have some fun exploring online examples.

Watch Out! — When there's something you need to watch out for, you'll be warned about it in "Watch Out!" boxes.

Q&A, Quiz, and Exercises

Every hour ends with a short question-and-answer session that addresses the kind of "dumb questions" everyone wishes they dared to ask. A brief but complete quiz lets you test yourself to be sure you understand everything presented in the hour. Finally, one or two optional exercises give you a chance to practice your new skills before you move on.

The Sams Publishing Website

Every sample page illustrated in this book, plus more web pages designed to reinforce and expand your knowledge of HTML, can be found at the Sams Publishing website (www.samspublishing.com). I built files at the website especially to provide readers of this book with oodles more examples and reusable HTML pages than I could ever picture in a compact book.

You'll also get to have some fun with whimsical "edutainment" pages and break-time surprises, plus an extensive hotlist of links to a wide variety of Internet resources to help you produce your own web pages even faster. See you there!

PART I

Your First Web Page

HOUR 1

Understanding HTML and XHTML

Before you begin creating your own web pages with HTML, you need a little background knowledge about what web pages are, how to view and edit them, and what you can expect to achieve with them. It might also help to have a basic understanding of how HTML differs from XHTML, and why there are two different languages designed to do the same thing—create web pages. This hour provides a quick summary of HTML and XHTML basics, and gives some practical tips to make the most of your time as a web page author and publisher. It's not all theory, however; you do get to see a real web page and the HTML code behind it.

▼ Try It Yourself

Here's a review of what you need to do before you're ready to use the rest of this book:

1. Get a computer. I used a computer with Windows XP to test the sample web pages and capture the figures in this book, but you can use any Windows, Macintosh, or UNIX machine to create and view your web pages. The speed of the computer itself doesn't matter much for accessing web pages; the speed of the computer's modem or network interface card (NIC), however, should be at least 56Kbps, and faster is better. If you have access to broadband Internet access via a cable modem, DSL modem, or wireless access point, that's even better!

2. Get a connection to the Internet. You can either dial up an Internet service provider (ISP) by using the modem in your computer or connect through the local network of your school or business. Most ISPs now offer dial-up Internet service for under $20 per month. If you don't mind spending a little more, a cable or DSL Internet service can dramatically improve the browsing experience, thanks to the speed and "always on" connection. The ISP, school, or business that provides your Internet connection can help you with the details of setting it up properly. Many public spaces such as airports, bookstores, and libraries also now offer free wireless Internet service that you can use if you have a laptop computer with Wi-Fi network support. ▼

Not sure how to find an ISP? The best way is to comparison-shop online (using a friend's computer that's already connected to the Internet). You'll find a comprehensive list of national and regional ISPs at http://thelist.internet.com/.

3. Get web browser software. This is the software your computer needs in order to retrieve and display HTML web pages. The most popular browser programs are currently Microsoft Internet Explorer, Netscape, Mozilla Firefox, Opera, and Safari (Macintosh only). It's not a bad idea to install several of these browsers so that you can experiment and make sure that your web pages look consistent across them all; you don't want to assume anything about the browsers other people are using. Web browsers are available at software retailers, or you can download them free over the Internet at www.microsoft.com/, browser.netscape.com/, www.getfirefox.com/, www.opera.com/, and www.apple.com/safari/.

Although all web browsers process and handle information in the same general way, there are some specific differences among them that result in things not always looking the same in different browsers. Be sure to check your web pages in multiple browsers to make sure that they look reasonably consistent.

4. Explore! Use a web browser to look around the Internet for web pages that are similar in content or appearance to those you'd like to create. Note what frustrates you about some pages, what attracts you and keeps you reading others, and what makes you come back to some pages over and over again. If there is a particular topic that interests you, consider searching for it using a popular search engine such as Google (www.google.com/).

If you plan to put your HTML pages on the Internet (as opposed to publishing them on CD-ROM or a local intranet), you'll need to transfer them to a computer that is connected to the Internet 24 hours a day. The same company or school that provides you with Internet access may also let you put web pages on their computer; if not, you may need to pay another company to host your pages.

You can start learning HTML with this book right away and wait to find an Internet host for your pages when they're done. However, if you want to have a place on the Internet ready for your very first page as soon as it is finished, you may want to read Hour 4, "Publishing Your HTML Pages," before you continue.

What Is a Web Page?

Once upon a time, back when there weren't any footprints on the moon, some far-sighted folks decided to see whether they could connect several major computer networks together. I'll spare you the names and stories (there are plenty of both), but the eventual result was the "mother of all networks," which we call the Internet.

Until 1990, accessing information through the Internet was a rather technical affair. It was so hard, in fact, that even Ph.D.-holding physicists were often frustrated when trying to swap data. One such physicist, the now-famous Tim Berners-Lee, cooked up a way to easily cross-reference text on the Internet through "hypertext" links. This wasn't a new idea, but his simple Hypertext Markup Language (HTML) managed to thrive while more ambitious hypertext projects floundered.

Hypertext originally meant text stored in electronic form with cross-reference links between pages. It is now a broader term that refers to just about any object (text, images, files, and so on) that can be linked to other objects.

Hypertext Markup Language is a language for describing how pages of text, graphics, and other information are organized and linked together.

By 1993, almost 100 computers throughout the world were equipped to serve up HTML pages. Those interlinked pages were dubbed the *World Wide Web (WWW)*, and several web browser programs had been written to allow people to view web pages. Because of the popularity of the Web, a few programmers soon wrote web browsers that could view graphics images along with the text on a web page. One of these programmers was Marc Andressen; he went on to become rich and famous, selling one of the world's most popular web browsers, Netscape Navigator.

Today, HTML pages are the standard interface to the Internet. They can include animated graphics, sound and video, complete interactive programs, and good old-fashioned text. Millions of web pages are retrieved and viewed each day from thousands of web server computers around the world. Incidentally, the term "web" arose from the fact that web pages are linked together in such a way that they form a massive web of information, roughly akin to a spider's web. This is also why you sometimes hear the term "crawler," which refers to a program that wanders around the Web gathering information on web pages.

Just in case you have it in your head that a web server must be some huge computer that runs off coal and causes the lights to dim when a page gets served up, allow me to introduce you to the world's smallest web server. A University of Massachusetts graduate student built a web server at a cost of less than $1 that is about the size of a match head. To learn more about this impressive technological feat, visit http://www-ccs.cs.umass.edu/~shri/iPic.html.

Coffee Break

The Web is rapidly becoming a mass-market medium, as high-speed Internet connections through TV cables, modernized phone lines, direct satellite feeds, and both public and private wireless networks become increasingly commonplace. You can already browse the Web using a small box attached to your television instead of using your computer, with the cost of such devices likely to fall sharply over the next few years. In other words, it may not be necessary to rely on a computer for web browsing in the near future.

Yet the Internet is no longer the only place you'll find HTML. Most private corporate networks (called *intranets*) now use HTML to provide business information to employees and clients. HTML is now the interface of choice for publishing presentations on CD-ROM and the very popular high-capacity digital versatile disk (DVD) format. Microsoft has even integrated HTML directly into the Windows operating system, allowing every storage folder in your computer to be associated with an HTML page and hypertext links to other folders and pages.

In short, HTML is everywhere. Fortunately, you're in the right place to find out how HTML web pages work and how to create them.

By the Way

There are actually two flavors of HTML. One is called HTML 4 and the other is called XHTML 1.1. The X stands for eXtensible, and you'll find out later in this lesson why it isn't called HTML 5. You'll also find out what all this has to do with another new language called XML.

The most important thing to know from the outset is that all the examples in this book are compatible with both HTML 4 and XHTML (as well as XML) and should be fully compatible with future versions of any software that interprets any web page language.

If you have other books on creating web pages, the sample HTML in those books may look slightly different from what you see in this one. Even though the old-fashioned format shown in those books will work in the current crop of web browsers, I strongly recommend that you use the more modern approach shown in this book; this will ensure that your pages remain usable as far into the future as possible.

How Web Pages Work

When you are viewing web pages, they look a lot like paper pages. At first glance, the process of displaying a web page is simple: You tell your computer which page you want to see, and the page appears on your screen. If the page is stored on a disk inside your computer, it appears almost instantly. If it is located on some other computer, you might have to wait for it to be retrieved.

Of course, web pages can do some very convenient things that paper pages can't. For example, you can't point to the words "continued on page 57" in a paper magazine and expect page 57 to automatically appear before your eyes. Nor can you tap your finger on the bottom of a paper order form and expect it to reach the company's order fulfillment department five seconds later. You're not likely to see animated pictures or hear voices talk to you from most paper pages either (newfangled greeting cards aside). All these things are commonplace on web pages.

But there are some deeper differences between web pages and paper pages that you'll need to be aware of as a web page author. For one thing, what appears as a single page on your screen may actually be an assembly of elements located in many different computer files. In fact, it's possible (though uncommon) to create a page that combines text from a computer in Australia with pictures from a computer in Russia and sounds from a computer in Canada.

Figure 1.1 shows a typical page as shown by Microsoft Internet Explorer, currently the world's most popular software for viewing web pages. The page in Figure 1.1 would look roughly the same if viewed in Netscape, Firefox, or some other web browser. I say "roughly" because web browsers don't always interpret web pages exactly the same, even though in theory they should. For the sake of simplicity, let's for now assume that all the major web browsers display pages without any major differences.

> Although Internet Explorer is currently the number-one web browser in terms of user base, Mozilla Firefox is hot on its heels, and stands a realistic chance of unseating the giant at some point. Firefox is currently in second place in the latest round of browser wars, far ahead of Opera and Apple's Safari browser. Runner-up browser vendors have largely done a better job than Microsoft in adhering to web standards and addressing security issues, which is why browsers such as Firefox and to a lesser extent Opera are rapidly gaining in popularity.

By the Way

A web browser such as Internet Explorer does much more than just retrieve a file and put it on the screen. It actually assembles the component parts of a page and arranges those parts according to commands hidden in the text by the author. Those commands are written in HTML.

A **web browser** is a computer program that interprets HTML commands to collect, arrange, and display the parts of a web page.

FIGURE 1.1
A web browser
assembles sep-
arate text and
image files to
display them as
an integrated
page.

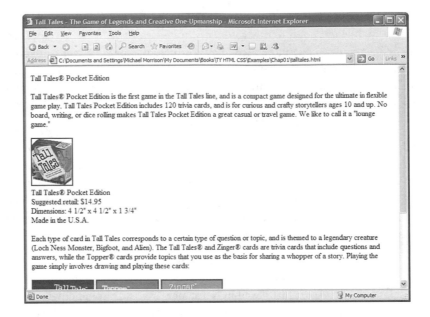

Listing 1.1 shows the text, including the HTML commands, I typed to create the
page shown in Figure 1.1. This text file can be read and edited with any word
processor or text editor. It looks a bit strange with all those odd symbols and code
words, but the text file itself doesn't include any embedded images, boldface text, or
other special formatting. The words between < and > are HTML tags.

LISTING 1.1   Text Used to Create the Page Shown in Figure 1.1

```
<?xml version="1.0" encoding="UTF-8"?>
<!DOCTYPE html PUBLIC "-//W3C//DTD XHTML 1.1//EN"
  "http://www.w3.org/TR/xhtml11/DTD/xhtml11.dtd">

<html xmlns="http://www.w3.org/1999/xhtml" xml:lang="en">
  <head>
    <title>Tall Tales - The Game of Legends and Creative One-Upmanship</title>
  </head>

  <body>
    <p>
      Tall Tales&reg; Pocket Edition
    </p>
    <p>
      Tall Tales&reg; Pocket Edition is the first game in the Tall Tales line,
      and is a compact game designed for the ultimate in flexible game play.
      Tall Tales Pocket Edition includes 120 trivia cards, and is for curious
      and crafty storytellers ages 10 and up. No board, writing, or dice
      rolling makes Tall Tales Pocket Edition a great casual or travel game.
      We like to call it a "lounge game."
    </p>
    <p>
```

LISTING 1.1   Continued

```
      <a href="ttpe_box_pic.jpg"><img src="ttpe_box_sm.gif"
      alt="Tall Tales&reg; Pocket Edition" />
      </a><br />
      Tall Tales&reg; Pocket Edition<br />
      Suggested retail: $14.95<br />
      Dimensions: 4 1/2" x 4 1/2" x 1 3/4"<br />
      Made in the U.S.A.
    </p>
    <p>
      Each type of card in Tall Tales corresponds to a certain type of question
      or topic, and is themed to a legendary creature (Loch Ness Monster,
      Bigfoot, and Alien). The Tall Tales&reg; and Zinger&reg; cards are trivia
      cards that include questions and answers, while the Topper&reg; cards
      provide topics that you use as the basis for sharing a whopper of a story.
      Playing the game simply involves drawing and playing these cards:
    </p>
    <p>
      <a href="pg_games_ttcard_lg.gif"><img src="pg_games_ttcard_sm.gif"
      alt="Tall Tales&reg; Example Card" /></a>
      <a href="pg_games_topcard_lg.gif"><img src="pg_games_topcard_sm.gif"
      alt="Topper&reg; Example Card" /></a>
      <a href="pg_games_zngcard_lg.gif"><img src="pg_games_zngcard_sm.gif"
      alt="Zinger&reg; Example Card" /></a>
    </p>
    <p>
      To learn more about Tall Tales, visit the Tall Tales Web site at <a
      href="http://www.talltalesgame.com/">www.talltalesgame.com</a>.
    </p>
  </body>
</html>
</body></html>
```

Internet Explorer reads the commands in the HTML code shown in Listing 1.1 and then displays all the images and text you see in Figure 1.1. The coded HTML commands in the text instruct the browser to look for separate image files and display them along with the text. Other commands tell it how to break up the lines of text on the page. Although there is certainly some code in the listing that looks a bit strange to the untrained HTML eye, you can still pick through the code and make out much of the content that appears on the page.

To see the HTML commands for any page on the Web, click with the right mouse button (or hold down the Control key while clicking if you're using a Macintosh computer), and then select View Source from the pop-up menu in Internet Explorer, or View Page Source in Firefox. This is a great way to get an intuitive idea of how HTML works and learn by others' examples. Some web sites may have the right mouse button disabled, in which case you can rely on the Source (Internet Explorer) and Page Source (Firefox) commands from the View menu.

Did you Know?

Some web pages use an advanced feature called frames to display more than one HTML page at the same time. In most web browsers, you can view the HTML commands for any frame by right-clicking it and selecting View Frame Source.

Regardless of how you go about viewing the source for existing web pages, keep in mind that many commercial web pages use complex HTML code that can be difficult to read and understand. So don't get discouraged if you view the source of a popular web site and the code is more complex than you had imagined.

The web page shown in Figure 1.1 and listed in Listing 1.1 was deliberately designed with very little formatting so that the code would be less cluttered. HTML is obviously capable of much more, and I thought it was worth demonstrating how the application of a little formatting can dramatically affect the appearance of a web page. Figure 1.2 contains the same web page with some additional formatting applied, including a background image and some font tweaks.

FIGURE 1.2
You can dramatically change the look of a web page by styling the page, without even altering the content.

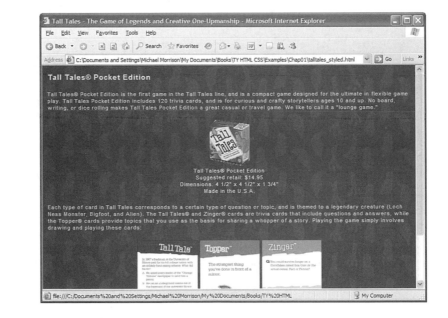

The styled version of the page contains the same content (text and images) as the unstyled version, but the end result is considerably different. Throughout the book you learn how to apply styles to HTML code to achieve dramatic visual effects.

The Pieces and Parts of a Web Page

You'll learn how to understand and write HTML commands soon. The important point to note right now is that creating a web page is just a matter of typing some text. You can type and save that text with any word processor or text editor you have on hand. You then open the text file with any HTML-compatible software (web browser) to see it as a web page.

I encourage you not to try creating your first HTML page with Microsoft Word, or any other HTML-compatible word processor; most of these programs attempt to rewrite your HTML for you in strange ways, potentially leaving you totally confused. It's fine to use a web development tool such as Microsoft FrontPage or Macromedia Dreamweaver, but be sure to switch the view so that you're editing the raw HTML code.

Watch Out!

When you want graphics, sound, animations, video, and interactive programming to appear on a web page, you don't insert them into the text file directly, as you would if you were creating a document in most print-oriented page layout programs, such as Microsoft Word and Adobe Acrobat. Instead, you type HTML text commands telling the web browser where to find the media files. The media files themselves remain separate, even though the web browser makes them *look* as if they're part of the same document when it displays the page.

For example, the HTML document in Listing 1.1 directly references four separate graphics images. Figure 1.3 shows these four image files being edited in the graphics program Microsoft Photo Editor, which ships standard with Microsoft Office.

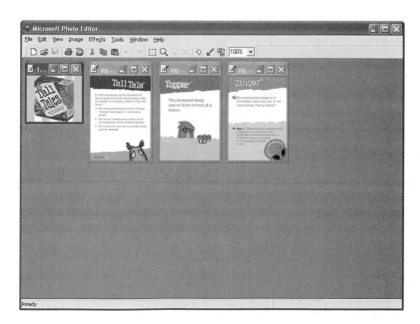

FIGURE 1.3
Although text and graphics appear integrated in Figure 1.1 and Figure 1.2, the graphics files are actually stored, and can be edited, separately.

You could use any graphics program you like to modify or replace these images at any time, even the simple Paint program that comes standard with all versions of Windows. Changing the graphics can make a big difference in how the page looks, even if you don't make any changes to the HTML text file. You can also use the same image on any number of pages while storing only one copy of the graphics file. You'll learn much more about incorporating graphics files into web pages in Part III, "Creative Web Page Design."

There are two basic approaches to making an HTML page: You can type the text and HTML commands yourself with a text editor, or you can use graphical software that generates the HTML commands for you.

You will be able to follow along with this book and learn HTML much more easily if you work with an editor that shows the actual HTML text. Any word processor or text editor you already have—even the Windows Notepad or Macintosh TextEdit editor—will do nicely. In fact, I encourage you to use a simple text editor starting out, just to keep things simple—word processors like to include formatting information that can be tricky to remove if you aren't careful.

For now, I recommend that you do not use a graphical, what-you-see-is-what-you-get (WYSIWYG) web page editor such as Microsoft FrontPage or Macromedia Dreamweaver unless you commit to using a view within the tool that allows you to edit the code directly. You'll likely find it easier and more educational to start out with a simple text editor while you're just learning HTML, and then progress to visual tools after you have a better understanding of what's going on under the hood of your web pages. But as I said, most visual tools also offer a code view that serves as a text editor within the visual tool, which is certainly okay to use.

The Many Faces of HTML

It's important to understand that a single web page can take on many different appearances, depending on who views it and what they view it with. Figure 1.4 is the same web page pictured earlier in Figure 1.1, as seen in Microsoft's Mobile Explorer emulator, which you can use to test web pages for mobile devices. Most mobile phones have screens less than 200 pixels in width and height, which limits them considerably when it comes to displaying web pages.

As you can see, the mobile phone view on the web page is considerably different from its desktop counterpart. In fact, the page is displayed purely as text with no images because there is not enough screen space to accommodate images. This distinction in web page views is important to grasp early in your HTML education because it hammers home the point that you don't have a whole lot of control over how your pages are viewed. Or, more accurately, you don't have much control over the size of the area in which your pages are viewed. Beyond that, browsers are reasonably consistent in rendering the actual content on your pages, as well as deciding what is most important (text) and what can be overlooked (images) if screen space is limited.

FIGURE 1.4
The page from Figure 1.1 looks very different in the Pocket PC version of Internet Explorer.

Although mobile phones typically have very small screens, there are larger "smart-phones" such as Pocket PCs, Treo devices, and BlackBerry devices. The screens on these handheld devices are typically in the range of 240×320 in size, which is considerably larger than normal mobile phones but still much smaller than the 640×480, 800×600, and higher resolution screens that most desktop PCs use these days.

By the Way

What this means is that most web pages will look the same across major desktop web browsers, and they will also look the same on PCs, Macintoshes, and UNIX machines. The page in Figure 1.1, for example, would look the same on any of these machines as long as the size of the viewing window, fonts, and program settings were the same on each machine.

Now for the bad news. Even users of the same version of the same web browser can alter how a page appears by choosing different display options and/or changing the size of the viewing window. All the major web browsers allow users to override the background and fonts specified by the web page author with those of their own choosing. Screen resolution, window size, and optional toolbars can also change how much of a page someone sees when it first appears. The mobile phone example in Figure 1.4 illustrates this point quite clearly.

Earlier in the lesson I introduced you to the world's tiniest web server. Because we're now on the subject of screen size and web pages, it only makes sense to show you the world's tiniest web site. Visit http://www.guimp.com/ to see a fully functioning web site that takes up only 18×18 pixels of screen space. Impressive!

To continue the study of how web pages change with different browsers and display settings, take a look at the page shown in Figure 1.5, which is viewed at 800×600 resolution with a large size font in the Firefox browser. Compare this figure with Figure 1.2, which shows the same page at 800×600 in Internet Explorer with default font settings. Unfortunately, you as a web page author have no direct control over the display settings on a particular computer; each individual who looks at your pages can always choose whatever browser settings he or she prefers. Your job is to design pages so that they look as consistent as possible across major browsers with their default settings.

FIGURE 1.5
The page from Figure 1.2, displayed by Mozilla Firefox with larger fonts.

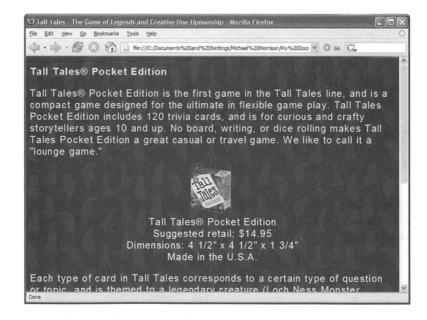

You can't even assume that people will be viewing your web pages on a computer screen. The page in Figures 1.1, 1.2, and 1.5 might also be read on a low-resolution television screen or a high-resolution paper printout (see Figure 1.6).

FIGURE 1.6
Web browsers usually change the background to white when sending pages to a printer.

As you learn to make your own web pages, remember how many different forms they can take when people view them. Some web page authors fall into the trap of trying to make pages appear "perfect" on their computer and are sorely disappointed the first time they discover that it looks different on someone else's screen. (Even worse, some authors put silly messages on their pages demanding that everyone change the size of their viewing window and font settings to match the author's computer, or proclaiming, "This page is best viewed by such-and-such." If you've ever encountered such messages, I'm sure you ignored them just like everyone else does.)

In Part III, "Creative Web Page Design," you'll find many tips and tricks for ensuring that your pages look great in the widest variety of situations.

> In this book you encounter many sample web pages. At the accompanying *Sams Publishing* website (http://www.samspublishing.com/), you'll find all those examples in living color, along with many more sample pages to explore.

By the Way

The Scoop on HTML, XML, and XHTML

As you learned earlier in the lesson, HTML in its early days was great because it allowed scientists to share information over the Internet in an efficient and relatively structured manner. It wasn't until later that web browsers caught on and HTML started being used to code more than scientific papers. HTML quickly went from a tidy little markup language for researchers to a full-blown online publishing language. And after it was established that HTML could be jazzed up for graphical browsing, the creators of web browsers pretty much went crazy by adding lots of nifty features to the language. Although these new features were neat at first, they compromised the simple design of HTML and introduced lots of inconsistencies when it came to how browsers displayed web pages. The problem was that most new features worked on only one browser or another, and you were out of luck if you happened to be running the wrong browser. HTML had started to resemble a bad remodeling job on a house that really should've been left alone. As it turns out, some of the browser-specific features that turned up during this time have now been adopted as standards and others have been dropped completely.

As with most revolutions, the birth of the Web was very chaotic, and the modifications to HTML reflected that chaos. In the past few years a significant effort has been made to reel in the inconsistencies of HTML and attempt to restore some order to the language. The problem with disorder in HTML is that it results in web browsers having to guess at how a page is to be displayed, which is not a good thing. Ideally, a web page designer should be able to define exactly how a page is to look and have it look the same regardless of what kind of browser or operating system someone is using. Better still, a designer should be able to define exactly what a page *means*, and have it look consistent across different browsers and platforms. This utopia is still off in the future somewhere, but a language called XML (Extensible Markup Language) is playing a significant role in leading us toward it.

XML is a language used to create markup languages, such as HTML, that describe structured information.

XML is a general language used to create specific languages such as HTML. I know this sounds a little strange, but it really just means that XML provides a basic structure and set of rules to which any markup language must adhere. Using XML, you can create a unique markup language to describe just about any kind of information, including web pages. Knowing that XML is a language for creating other markup languages, you could create your own version of HTML using XML. You could even create a markup language called BCCML (Bottle Cap Collection Markup Language), for example, which you could use to create and manage your extensive collection of rare bottle caps. The point is that XML lays the ground rules for organizing information in a consistent manner, and that information can be anything from web pages to bottle caps.

You might be thinking that bottle caps don't have anything to do with the Web, so why mention them? The reason is that XML is not entirely about web pages. XML is actually broader than the Web in that it can be used to represent any kind of information on any kind of computer. If you can visualize all the information whizzing around the globe among computers, mobile phones, handheld computers, televisions, and radios, you can start to understand why XML has much broader ramifications than just cleaning up web pages. However, one of the first applications of XML is to restore some order to the Web, which is why XML is relevant to your learning HTML.

If XML describes data better than HTML, does it mean that XML is set to upstage HTML as the markup language of choice for the Web? No. XML is not a replacement for HTML, or even a competitor of HTML; XML's impact on HTML has to do with cleaning up HTML. HTML is a relatively unstructured language that could benefit from the rules of XML. The natural merger of the two technologies results in HTML's adherence to the rules and structure of XML. To accomplish this merger, a new version of HTML was formulated that follows the stricter rules of XML. The new XML-compliant version of HTML is known as XHTML. Fortunately for you, you'll actually be learning XHTML throughout this book since it is really just a cleaner version of HTML.

XHTML (Extensible Hypertext Markup Language) is a version of HTML that is compliant with the stricter rules of XML.

Earlier in the lesson, I referred to HTML as HTML 4, which is the latest version of HTML. XML and XHTML also have versions, with XML 1 being the latest version of XML, and XHTML 2 being the latest version of XHTML. XHTML 2 is very new and has yet to be supported in any major web browsers, so this book sticks with teaching you XHTML 1.1. You'll learn more details about XHTML 1.1, HTML 4, and their relationship with each other as you progress through the book and create working web pages.

By the Way

Summary

This hour introduced the basics of what web pages are and how they work. You learned that coded HTML commands are included in the text of a web page, but images and other media are stored in separate files. You also learned why typing HTML text yourself is often better than using a graphical editor to create HTML commands for you, especially when you're starting out learning HTML. You saw that a single web page can look very different, depending on what software and hardware are used to display it. Finally, you learned about XML and XHTML, and how they relate to HTML.

Q&A

Q *I'm stuck on my first page. It didn't work. What did I do wrong?*

A That first page is always the hardest. For a step-by-step analysis of what might have gone wrong and how to fix it, refer to Appendix A, "Readers' Most Frequently Asked Questions." (You'll find that appendix handy anytime you have a question that doesn't seem to be answered elsewhere in the book.)

Q *I'm still not quite sure what the difference between a "web page" and an "HTML page" is. And how are these different from a "home page" or a "web site"?*

A If you want to get technical, I suppose a "web page" would have to be a page located on the Internet instead of a disk on your own computer. But in practice, the terms "web page" and "HTML page" are used interchangeably. A "web site" is one or more pages that are created together and related in content, like the pages of a book. "Home page" usually means the first page people visit when they look at a web site, though some people use "home page" to mean any web page. Others use "home page" to mean a personal page, as opposed to a corporate web site.

Q *I've looked at the HTML "source" of some web pages on the Internet, and it looks frighteningly difficult to learn. Do I have to think like a computer programmer to learn this stuff?*

A Although complex HTML pages can indeed look daunting, learning HTML is several orders of magnitude easier than learning other computer languages such as BASIC, C++, and Java. You don't need any experience or skill as a computer programmer to be a very successful HTML author. The reason the HTML code for many commercial web pages looks complicated is because it was likely created by a visual web design tool, as opposed to being hand-coded; visual tools have a knack for making code difficult to read! Keep in mind that the apparent complexity in large pages could also be the natural result of changes and improvements over a long period; every web page is built a piece at a time.

Q *Do I need to be connected to the Internet constantly while I create HTML pages?*

A No. In fact, you don't need any Internet connection at all if you only want to produce web pages for publication on a CD-ROM, Zip or floppy disk, or local network. You also don't need a connection while you're developing pages that you aren't ready to publish online. In fact, I've spent months creating entire web sites offline on my hard disk before placing them on the Internet. Hour 2, "Create a Web Page Right Now," gives more detailed instructions for working with web pages offline.

Workshop

The workshop contains quiz questions and activities to help you solidify your understanding of the material covered. Try to answer all questions before looking at the "Answers" section that follows.

Quiz

1. Define the terms *Internet*, *web page*, and *World Wide Web*.

2. How many files would you need to store on your computer to make a web page with some text and two images on it?

3. Can you create web pages with Microsoft Word or a similar word processor?

Answers

1. The Internet is the "network of networks" that connects millions of computers around the globe.

   A web page is a text document that uses commands in a special language called HTML to add formatting, graphics and other media, and links to other pages.

   The World Wide Web is a collective name for all the web pages on the Internet.

2. At least three files: one for the web page itself, which includes the text and the HTML commands, and one for each of the two graphics images. In some cases, you might need more files to add a background pattern, sound, or interactive features to the page.

3. Yes. In fact, you can create web pages with any application on any computer as long as the application will save plain-text or ASCII files. Just keep in mind that word processors usually save files with extra formatting information by default, which is why you have to save the file as plain-text for it to work as a web page. It's a little simpler to just stick with a pure text editor such as Windows Notepad or TextEdit for the Macintosh.

Exercises

At the end of each hour in this book, you'll find some suggestions for optional exercises to reinforce and expand what you learned in the hour. However, because you're undoubtedly eager to get started learning HTML, let's skip the warm-up calisthenics for Hour 1 and dive right into Hour 2.

HOUR 2

Create a Web Page Right Now

This hour guides you through the creation of your first web page. The best way to follow along with this hour is to actually create a web page as you read and model it after the sample pages developed here in the book. If you're a little nervous about jumping right in, you might want to read this hour once to get the general idea and then go through it again at your computer while you work on your own page. But I encourage you to throw caution aside and dive right in!

As mentioned in Hour 1, "Understanding HTML and XHTML," you can use any text editor or word processor to create HTML web pages. Although you may eventually want to use an editor especially designed for HTML, for this hour I recommend that you use Windows Notepad or the Macintosh TextEdit editor that came with your computer. That way you won't have to learn a new software program at the same time you're learning HTML.

Try It Yourself ▼

Before you begin working with this hour, you should start with some text that you want to put on a web page:

1. Find (or write) a few paragraphs of text about yourself, your family, your company, your softball team, or some other subject in which you're interested.

2. Be sure to save it as plain, standard ASCII text. Notepad and most simple text editors always save files as plain-text, but you may need to choose this file type as an option (after selecting File, Save As) if you're using another program.

3. As you go through this hour, you will add HTML commands (called *tags*) to the text file, making it into a web page. Use Notepad or some other simple text editor to do this; don't use Word or WordPad!

4. Always give files containing HTML tags a name ending in .html when you save them. This is important: If you forget to type the .html at the end of the filename when you save the file, most text editors will give it some other extension (such as .txt or .doc). If that happens, you may not be able to find it when you try to look at it with a web browser. In other words, web browsers expect web pages to have a file extension of .html; you may also encounter web pages with a file extension of

▼

▼

.htm, which is also acceptable. There are also other file extensions used on the Web such as .asp (Microsoft Active Server Pages) and .php (PHP: Hypertext Preprocessor), but they are typically related to technologies beyond the scope of HTML.

By the Way

If you're using TextEdit on a Macintosh computer, the steps for creating a web page are a little different than for Windows Notepad. You must first select Make Plain Text from the Format menu and then change the preferences under the Saving header by unchecking the box for Append '.txt' Extension to Plain Text Files. Also, the default preferences are set to show .html documents as they would appear in a browser, which won't allow you to edit them. To fix this, check Ignore Rich Text Commands in HTML Files under the Rich Text Processing header.

▲

Getting Started with a Simple Web Page

Listing 2.1 shows the text you would type and save to create a simple HTML page. If you opened this file with a web browser such as Internet Explorer, you would see the page shown in Figure 2.1. Every web page you create must include the <html>, <head>, <title>, and <body> tags.

LISTING 2.1   The <html>, <head>, <title>, and <body> Tags

```
<?xml version="1.0" encoding="UTF-8"?>
<!DOCTYPE html PUBLIC "-//W3C//DTD XHTML 1.1//EN"
  "http://www.w3.org/TR/xhtml11/DTD/xhtml11.dtd">

<html xmlns="http://www.w3.org/1999/xhtml" xml:lang="en">
  <head>
    <title>The First Web Page</title>
  </head>

  <body>
    <p>
      In the beginning, Tim created the HyperText Markup Language. The Internet
      was without form and void, and text was upon the face of the monitor and
      the Hands of Tim were moving over the face of the keyboard. And Tim said,
      Let there be links; and there were links. And Tim saw that the links were
      good; and Tim separated the links from the text. Tim called the links
      Anchors, and the text He called Other Stuff. And the whole thing together
      was the first Web Page.
    </p>
  </body>
</html>
```

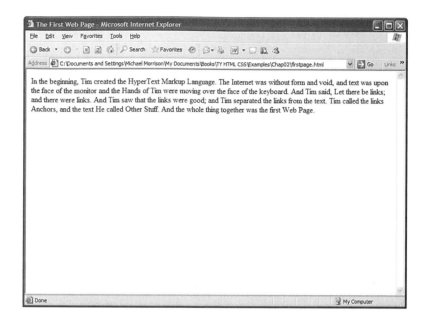

FIGURE 2.1
When you view
the web page in
Listing 2.1 with
a web browser,
only the actual
title and body
text are dis-
played.

In Listing 2.1, as in every HTML page, the words starting with < and ending with >
are actually coded commands. These coded commands are called HTML tags
because they "tag" pieces of text and tell the web browser what kind of text it is.
This allows the web browser to display the text appropriately.

An **HTML tag** is a coded command used to indicate how part of a web page should
be displayed.

The first few lines of code in the web page serve as standard boilerplate code that
you will include in all of your pages. This code actually identifies the page as an
XHTML 1.1 document, which means that technically the web page is an XHTML
page. All the pages developed throughout the book are XHTML 1.1 pages. Because
XHTML is a more structured version of HTML, it's still okay to generally refer to all
the pages in the book as HTML pages. By targeting XHTML 1.1 with your code, you
are developing web pages that adhere to the very latest web standards. This is a
good thing!

Before you learn what the HTML tags in Listing 2.1 mean, you might want to see
exactly how I went about creating and viewing the document itself:

1. Type all the text in Listing 2.1, including the HTML tags, in Windows Notepad
   (or Macintosh TextEdit).

2. Select File, Save As and be sure to select Text Documents as the file type.

3. Name the file `firstpage.html`.

4. Choose the folder on your hard drive where you would like to keep your web pages—and remember which one you choose! Click the Save or OK button to save the file.

5. Now start your favorite web browser. (Leave Notepad running, too. That way you can easily switch back and forth between viewing and editing your page.)

By the Way

You don't need to be connected to the Internet to view a web page stored on your own computer. By default, your web browser tries to connect to the Internet every time you start it, which makes sense most of the time. However, this can be a hassle if you're developing pages locally on your hard drive (offline) and you keep getting errors about a page not being found. If you have a full-time web connection via a LAN, cable modem, or DSL, this is a moot point because the browser will never complain about being offline. Otherwise, the appropriate disciplinary action will depend on your breed of browser:

▶ In Microsoft Internet Explorer for Windows, select Tools, Internet Options; click the General tab and click Use Blank under Home Page. In Internet Explorer under Macintosh OS X, look in the application preferences under the Browser Display set, and click the Use None button in the Home Page cluster.

▶ In Mozilla Firefox, select ToolsTools, Options; click the Use Blank Page button under the General settings.

▶ Other browsers should have a similar setting for changing the default home page so that it doesn't attempt to access the Internet.

This teaches your browser not to run off and fetch a page from the Internet every time it starts. Of course, you'll likely want to restore the default setting after you're finished working locally.

6. In Internet Explorer, select File, Open and click Browse. If you're using Firefox, select File, followed by Open File. Navigate to the appropriate folder and select the `firstpage.html` file. You can also drag and drop the `firstpage.html` file onto the browser window.

Voilà! You should see the page shown in Figure 2.1.

HTML Tags Every Web Page Must Have

The time has come for the secret language of HTML tags to be revealed to you. When you understand this language, you will have creative powers far beyond those of other humans. Don't tell the other humans, but it's really pretty easy.

Before you get into the HTML tags, let's first address the messy-looking code at the top of Listing 2.1. The first line indicates that the HTML document is in fact an XML document:

```
<?xml version="1.0" encoding="UTF-8"?>
```

The version of XML is set to 1.0, which is fairly standard, as is the type of character encoding (UTF-8).

It isn't terribly important that you understand concepts such as character encoding at this point. What is important is that you include the appropriate boilerplate code in your pages so that they adhere to the latest web standards.

The second and third lines of code in Listing 2.1 are even more complicated looking:

```
<!DOCTYPE html PUBLIC "-//W3C//DTD XHTML 1.1//EN"
  "http://www.w3.org/TR/xhtml11/DTD/xhtml11.dtd">
```

Again, the specifics of this code aren't terribly important as long as you remember to include the code at the start of your pages. This code identifies the document as being XHTML 1.1, which then allows web browsers to check and make sure that the code meets all the requirements of XHTML 1.1.

The XML/XHTML boilerplate code isn't strictly required in order for you to create web pages. You can delete the opening lines of code in the example so that the page starts with the <html> tag, and it will still open fine in a web browser. The reason for including the extra code has to do with ensuring that your pages smoothly migrate to the new and improved Web that has already started unfolding. Additionally, the extra code allows you to validate your web pages for accuracy, which you'll learn how to do a bit later in this lesson.

Most HTML tags have two parts: an *opening tag*, which indicates where a piece of text begins, and a *closing tag*, which indicates where the piece of text ends. Closing tags start with a / (forward slash) just after the < symbol. Another type of tag is the *empty tag*, which is unique in that it doesn't involve a pair of matching opening and closing tags. Instead, an empty tag consists of a single tag that starts with a < and ends with a / just before the > symbol. Following is a quick summary of these three tags just to make sure you understand the role each of them plays:

- ▶ An *opening tag* is an HTML tag that indicates the start of an HTML command; the text affected by the command appears after the opening tag. Opening tags always begin with < and end with >, as in <html>.

▶ A *closing tag* is an HTML tag that indicates the end of an HTML command; the text affected by the command appears before the closing tag. Closing tags always begin with </ and end with >, as in </html>.

▶ An *empty tag* is an HTML tag that issues an HTML command without enclosing any text in the page. Empty tags always begin with < and end with />, as in <br />.

For example, the <body> tag in Listing 2.1 tells the web browser where the actual body text of the page begins, and </body> indicates where it ends. Everything between the <body> and </body> tags will appear in the main display area of the web browser window, as you can see if you refer to Figure 2.1, shown earlier.

Web browsers display any text between <title> and </title> at the very top of the browser window, as you can also see in Figure 2.1. The title text is also used to identify the page on the browser's Bookmarks or Favorites menu, depending on which browser you use. It's important to provide a title for your pages so that visitors to the page can properly bookmark it for future reference.

You will use the <body> and <title> tags in every HTML page you create because every web page needs a title and some body text. You will also use the other two tags shown in Listing 2.1, <html> and <head>. Putting <html> at the very beginning of a document simply indicates that this is a web page. The </html> at the end indicates that the web page is over.

Within a page, there is a head section and a body section, each of which is identified by <head> and <body> tags. The idea is that information in the head of the page somehow describes the page but isn't actually displayed by a web browser. Information placed in the body, however, is displayed by a web browser. The <head> tag always appears near the beginning of the HTML code for a page, just after the opening <html> tag.

By the
Way

> You no doubt noticed that there is some extra code associated with the <html> tag in the example. This code consists of two attributes (xmlns and xml:lang), which are used to specify additional information related to the tag. These two attributes are standard requirements of all XHTML web pages.

The <title> tag used to identify the title of a page appears within the head of the page, which means it is placed after the opening <head> tag and before the closing </head> tag. (Upcoming lessons reveal some other advanced header information that can go between <head> and </head>, such as style sheet rules that are used to format the page.)

You may find it convenient to create and save a *bare-bones page* (also known as a *skeleton* page) with just the opening and closing <html>, <head>, <title>, and <body> tags, similar to the document in Listing 2.1. You can then open that document as a starting point whenever you want to make a new web page and save yourself the trouble of typing out all those obligatory tags every time.

The <p> tag used in Listing 2.1 is used to enclose a paragraph of text. It isn't entirely necessary in this example because there is only one paragraph, but it becomes very important in web pages that have multiple paragraphs of text.

Organizing a Page with Paragraphs and Line Breaks

When a web browser displays HTML pages, it pays no attention to line endings or the number of spaces between words. For example, the top version of the poem shown in Figure 2.2 appears with a single space between all words, even though that's not how it's entered in Listing 2.2. This is because extra whitespace in HTML code is automatically reduced down to a single space. Additionally, when the text reaches the edge of the browser window, it automatically wraps down to the next line, no matter where the line breaks were in the original HTML file; in this example, the text all happened to fit on one line.

LISTING 2.2   HTML for the Page Shown in Figure 2.2

```
<?xml version="1.0" encoding="UTF-8"?>
<!DOCTYPE html PUBLIC "-//W3C//DTD XHTML 1.1//EN"
  "http://www.w3.org/TR/xhtml11/DTD/xhtml11.dtd">

<html xmlns="http://www.w3.org/1999/xhtml" xml:lang="en">
  <head>
    <title>The Advertising Agency Song</title>
  </head>

  <body>
    <p>
      When your client's    hopping mad,
      put his picture in the ad.

      If he still should    prove refractory,
      add a picture of his factory.

    </p>

    <hr />

    <p>
      When your client's hopping mad,<br />
      put his picture in the ad.
    </p>
```

LISTING 2.2   Continued

```
  <p>
    If he still should prove refractory,<br />
    add a picture of his factory.
  </p>
 </body>
</html>
```

FIGURE 2.2
When the HTML
in Listing 2.2 is
viewed as a web
page, line and
paragraph
breaks only
appear where
there are

 and <p>
tags.

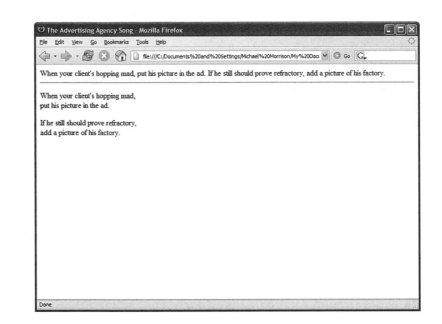

You must use HTML tags if you want to control where line and paragraph breaks actually appear. To skip a line between paragraphs, put a <p> tag at the beginning of each paragraph and a </p> tag at the end. In other words, enclose the text of the paragraph within a pair of matching <p> and </p> tags.

The <br /> tag forces a line break within a paragraph. Unlike the other tags you've seen so far, <br /> doesn't require a closing </br> tag—this is one of those empty tags I was talking about earlier. This is also an example of where XHTML enters the web page picture, because normal HTML doesn't require the / in empty tags. However, the newer XHTML standard does, so it's important for you to stick to the latest standards and create web pages that are coded properly—always code empty tags so that they end with />.

Note that most web pages you see on the Internet today use <br> instead of <br />, and the current crop of web browser software treats them both the same. However, you may save yourself a lot of work rewriting your pages in the future if you get in the habit of using the newer <br /> form of the tag now.

Likewise, the closing </p> tag is always optional in HTML 4 and is often left out by web page authors today. Closing </p> tags are required by the new XHTML standard, so I recommend that you always include them. Developing clean HTML coding habits is a very important part of becoming a successful web page designer.

Watch Out!

The poem in Listing 2.2 and Figure 2.2 shows the <br /> and <p> tags being used to separate the lines and verses of a rhyming advertising agency song. You might have also noticed the <hr /> tag in the listing, which causes a horizontal rule line to appear on the page (see Figure 2.2). Inserting a horizontal rule with the <hr /> tag also causes a line break, even if you don't include a <br /> tag along with it. For a little extra blank space above or below a horizontal rule, you can put a <p> tag before the <hr /> tag and a </p> tag after it, effectively placing the horizontal rule within its own paragraph.

Like <br />, the <hr /> horizontal rule tag is an empty tag and therefore never gets a closing </hr> tag.

Try It Yourself

Take a passage of text and try your hand at formatting it as proper HTML:

1. Add <html><head><title>My Title</title></head><body> to the beginning of the text (using your own title for your page instead of My Title). Also include the boilerplate code at the top of the page that takes care of meeting the requirements of XHTML.

2. Add </body></html> to the very end of the text.

3. Add a <p> tag at the beginning of each paragraph and a </p> tag at the end of each paragraph.

4. Use <br /> tags anywhere you want single-spaced line breaks.

5. Use <hr /> to draw horizontal rules separating major sections of text, or wherever you'd like to see a line across the page.

6. Save the file as mypage.html (using your own filename instead of mypage).

> If you are using a word processor to create the web page, be sure to save the HTML file in plain-text or ASCII format.

7. Open the file in a web browser to see your web page.

8. If something doesn't look right, go back to the text editor to make corrections and save the file again. You then need to click Reload/Refresh in the browser to see the changes you made to the web page.

Calling Out Text with Headings

When you browse through web pages on the Internet, you'll notice that many of them have a heading at the top that appears larger and bolder than the rest of the text. Listing 2.3 is a simple web page containing an example of a heading as compared to normal paragraph text. Any text between <h1> and </h1> tags will appear as a large heading. Additionally, <h2> and <h3> make smaller headings, and so on down the line of heading tags.

> The sample page in Listing 2.3 is part of a larger example that you'll continue to work on as you progress through the book. I thought a practical example would help you get a more applied feel for HTML, so I'll guide you through the development of a web site for a recreational hockey team. In fact, it's the hockey team that I happen to play on, Music City Mafia. My hockey buddies were nice enough to allow me to use their ugly mugs as examples throughout the book!

LISTING 2.3   Heading Tags

```
<?xml version="1.0" encoding="UTF-8"?>
<!DOCTYPE html PUBLIC "-//W3C//DTD XHTML 1.1//EN"
  "http://www.w3.org/TR/xhtml11/DTD/xhtml11.dtd">

<html xmlns="http://www.w3.org/1999/xhtml" xml:lang="en">
  <head>
    <title>Music City Mafia - Terry Lancaster</title>
  </head>

  <body>
    <h1>16 - Terry Lancaster</h1>
    <p>
      <img src="tlancaster.jpg" alt="Terry &quot;Big T&quot; Lancaster" /><br />
      Nickname: Big T<br />
```

LISTING 2.3 Continued

```
      Position: RW<br />
      Height: 6'3"<br />
      Weight: 195<br />
      Shoots: Left<br />
      Age: 40<br />
      Birthplace: Nashville, TN
    </p>
    <hr />
    <p>
      Favorite NHL Player: Brett Hull<br />
      Favorite NHL Team: Nashville Predators<br />
      Favorite Southern Fixin: Skillet Fried Potatoes<br />
      Favorite Meat and Three: Swett's<br />
      Favorite Country Star: Patsy Cline<br />
      Favorite Mafia Moment: "Chet finishing a game with his eyelid completely
      slashed through."
    </p>
  </body>
</html>
```

> **By the Way**
>
> By now you've probably caught on to the fact that HTML code is indented to reveal the relationship between different parts of the HTML document. This indentation is entirely voluntary—you could just as easily run all the tags together with no spaces or line breaks and they would still look fine when viewed in a browser. The indentations are for you so that you can quickly look at a page full of code and understand how it fits together. Indenting your code is a very good web design habit, and ultimately makes your pages easier to maintain.

As you can see in Figure 2.3, the HTML that creates headings couldn't be simpler. In this example, the jersey number and name of the hockey player are made larger and more prominent on the page via the <h1> tag. To create the big level-1 heading, you just put an <h1> tag at the beginning and a </h1> tag at the end. For a slightly smaller level-2 heading, you can use <h2> and </h2>, and for a little level-3 heading, use <h3> and </h3>.

> **By the Way**
>
> I'm admittedly jumping the gun a bit by including an image in this sample page, but sometimes it's worth stepping just outside of your comfort zone to get a desired effect. You'll learn all about creating and using images in web pages in Hour 7, "Creating Your Own Web Page Graphics," and Hour 8, "Putting Graphics on a Web Page," but for now all you need to know is that a tag named <img> is responsible for placing an image on a page.

FIGURE 2.3
The <h1> tag in
Listing 2.3
makes the jer-
sey number and
name of the
hockey player
stand out above
his other infor-
mation.

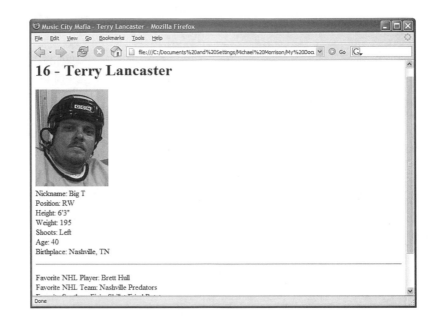

FIGURE 2.3
The <h1> tag in Listing 2.3 makes the jersey number and name of the hockey player stand out above his other information.

Coffee Break

While we're on the subject of hockey and HTML, check out http://www.azhockey.com/unusual.html for some highly entertaining and unusual stories about the sport of hockey. This page is also a good example of how simple a web page can be yet still do a decent job of presenting information to the visitor. I'm not suggesting that this page should get a design award, but it's a good example of understatement on the web, which can be a refreshing change of pace.

Theoretically, you can also use <h4>, <h5>, and <h6> to make progressively less important headings, but nobody uses these very much—after all, what's the point of a heading if it's not big and bold? Besides, most web browsers don't show a noticeable difference between these and the small <h3> headings anyway. In the sample page shown in the figure, it was sufficient to simply use an <h1> heading along with normal paragraph text.

By the Way

On many web pages nowadays, graphical images of ornately rendered letters and logos are often used in place of the ordinary text headings discussed in this hour. You'll discover how to create graphics and put them on your pages in Part II, "Building Practical Web Pages with HTML." However, old-fashioned text headings are still widely used and have the advantage of being transferred and displayed almost instantly, no matter how fast or slow the reader's connection to the Internet is.

It's important to remember the difference between a *title* and a *heading*. These two words are often interchangeable in day-to-day English, but when you're talking HTML, `<title>` gives the entire page an identifying name that isn't displayed on the page itself, but only on the browser window's title bar. The heading tags, on the other hand, cause some text on the page to be displayed with visual emphasis. There can be only one `<title>` per page and it must appear within the `<head>` and `</head>` tags, whereas you can have as many `<h1>`, `<h2>`, and `<h3>` headings as you want, in any order that suits your fancy. Also, unlike the title, headings are always placed in the body.

Don't forget that anything placed in the head of a web page is not intended to be viewed on the page, whereas everything in the body of the page is intended for viewing.

You'll learn to take complete control over the appearance of text on your web pages in Part II. Short of taking exacting control of the size, family, and color of fonts, headings provide the easiest and most popular way to draw extra attention to important text.

Peeking at Other People's Pages

Given the visual and sometimes audio pizzazz present in many popular web pages, you probably realize that the simple pages described in this hour are only the tip of the HTML iceberg. Now that you know the basics, you may surprise yourself with how much of the rest you can pick up just by looking at other people's pages on the Internet. As mentioned in Hour 1, you can see the HTML for any page by right-clicking and selecting View Source in a web browser.

Don't worry if you aren't yet able to decipher what some HTML tags do or exactly how to use them yourself. You'll find out about all those things in the next few hours. However, sneaking a preview now will show you the tags that you do know in action and give you a taste of what you'll soon be able to do with your web pages.

The HTML goodies at the *Sams Publishing* website are especially designed to be intuitive and easy to understand.

Validating Your Pages

I'm going to break tradition and recommend something that few web designers currently bother doing: I'm going to suggest that you validate all of your web pages. Few web designers bother with validation because we're still in the early stages of the rebirth of the Web as a more structured web of consistent pages, as opposed to a cobbled-together jungle of hacked code. It's one thing to design and draw a beautiful set of house plans, but it's quite another for an architect to stamp it as a safe structure suitable for construction. Validating your web pages is a similar process, except in this case the architect is an application instead of a person.

Validation is the process of running your pages through a special application that searches for errors and makes sure that your pages follow the strict XHTML standard.

The good news about web page validation is that it's very easy to do. In fact, the standards body responsible for developing web standards, the World Wide Web Consortium, or W3C for short, offers an online validation tool you can use. Follow this URL to try validating a page: http://validator.w3.org/. The W3C Markup Validation Service is shown in Figure 2.4.

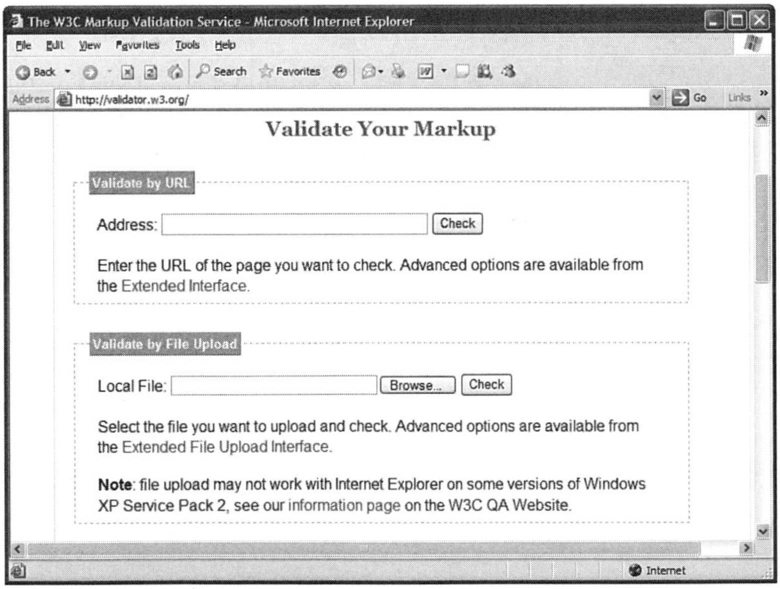

FIGURE 2.4
The W3C
Markup
Validation
Service allows
you to validate
an HTML
(XHTML) docu-
ment to ensure
that it has
been coded
accurately.

If you've already published a page online, you can use the Validate by URL option. Otherwise, use the Validate by File Upload option because it allows you to validate files stored on your local computer file system. Just click the Browse button, browse to the file, and then click the Check button. If all goes well, your page will get a passing report as shown in Figure 2.5.

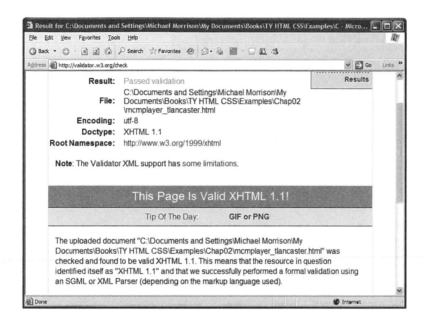

FIGURE 2.5
If a page passes the W3C Markup Validation Service, you know it is ready for prime time.

If the W3C Markup Validation Service encounters an error in your web page, it will provide specific details including the line numbers of the offending code. This is a great way to hunt down problems and rid your pages of buggy code. So not only does document validation allow you to know whether your pages are constructed properly, but it also assists you in finding and fixing problems before you post pages for the world to see.

> Some web development tools include built-in validation features you can use in lieu of the W3C Markup Validation Service.

Did you
Know?

Summary

In this hour you've been introduced to the most basic and important HTML tags. By adding these coded commands to any plain-text document, you can quickly transform it into a bona fide web page.

The first step in creating a web page is to put a few obligatory HTML tags at the beginning and end, including a title for the page. You then mark where paragraphs and lines end and add horizontal rules and headings if you want them. Table 2.1 summarizes all the tags introduced in this hour.

TABLE 2.1   HTML Tags Covered in Hour 2

Tag	Function
`<html>...</html>`	Encloses the entire HTML document.
`<head>...</head>`	Encloses the head of the HTML document.
`<title>...</title>`	Indicates the title of the document. Used within `<head>`.
`<body>...</body>`	Encloses the body of the HTML document.
`<p>...</p>`	A paragraph; skips a line between paragraphs.
` `	A line break.
`<hr />`	A horizontal rule line.
`<h1>...</h1>`	A first-level heading.
`<h2>...</h2>`	A second-level heading.
`<h3>...</h3>`	A third-level heading.
`<h4>...</h4>`	A fourth-level heading (seldom used).
`<h5>...</h5>`	A fifth-level heading (seldom used).
`<h6>...</h6>`	A sixth-level heading (seldom used).

Q&A

Q *I've created a web page, but when I open the file in my web browser I see all the text including the HTML tags. Sometimes I even see weird gobbledygook characters at the top of the page! What did I do wrong?*

A You didn't save the file as plain-text. Try saving the file again, being careful to save it as Text Only or ASCII Text. If you can't quite figure out how to get your word processor to do that, don't stress. Just type your HTML files in Notepad or TextEdit instead and everything should work just fine. (Also, always make sure that the filename of your web page ends in `.html` or `.htm`.)

Q *I have this HTML web page on my computer now. How do I get it on the Internet so that everyone else can see it?*

A Hour 4, "Publishing Your HTML Pages," explains how to put your pages on the Internet as well as how to get them ready for publishing on a local network or CD-ROM.

Q *I want "Fred's Fresh Fish" to appear both at the top of my page and on people's bookmark (or favorites) lists when they bookmark my page. How can I get it to appear both places?*

A Make a heading at the top of your page with the same text as the title, like this:

```
<html>
  <head>
    <title>Fred's Fresh Fish</title>
  </head>

  <body>
    <h1>Fred's Fresh Fish</h1>
    ...the rest of the page goes here...
  </body>
</html>
```

Q *I've seen web pages on the Internet that don't have <html> tags at the beginning. You said pages always have to start with <html>. What's the deal?*

A Many web browsers will forgive you if you forget to put in the <html> tag and will display the page correctly anyway. Yet it's a very good idea to include it because some software does need it to identify the page as valid HTML. Besides, you want your pages to be bona fide XHTML pages so that they conform to the latest web standards.

Workshop

The workshop contains quiz questions and activities to help you solidify your understanding of the material covered. Try to answer all questions before looking at the "Answers" section that follows.

Quiz

1. What four tags are required in every HTML page?

2. Insert the appropriate line-break and paragraph-break tags to format the following two-line poems with a blank line between them:

> Good night, God bless you,
>
> Go to bed and undress you.
>
> Good night, sweet repose,
>
> Half the bed and all the clothes.

3. Write the HTML for the following to appear one after the other:

. A small heading with the words "We are Proud to Present"

. A horizontal rule across the page

. A large heading with the one word, "Orbit"

. A medium-sized heading with the words "The Geometric Juggler"

. Another horizontal rule

4. Write a complete HTML web page with the title "Foo Bar" and a heading at the top that reads "Happy Hour at the Foo Bar," followed by the words "Come on down!" in regular type.

Answers

1. `<html>`, `<head>`, `<title>`, and `<body>` (along with their closing tags, `</html>`, `</head>`, `</title>`, and `</body>`).

2.
```
<p>Good night, God bless you,<br />
Go to bed and undress you.</p>
<p>Good night, sweet repose,<br />
Half the bed and all the clothes.</p>
```

3.
```
<h3>We are Proud to Present</h3>
<hr />
<h1>Orbit</h1>
<h2>The Geometric Juggler</h2>
<hr />
```

4.
```
<?xml version="1.0" encoding="UTF-8"?>

<!DOCTYPE html PUBLIC "-//W3C//DTD XHTML 1.1//EN"
  "http://www.w3.org/TR/xhtml11/DTD/xhtml11.dtd">

<html xmlns="http://www.w3.org/1999/xhtml" xml:lang="en">
  <head>
    <title>Foo Bar</title>
  </head>

  <body>
    <h1>Happy Hour at the Foo Bar</h1>
    <p>Come on Down!</p>
  </body>
</html>
```

Exercises

▶ Even if your main goal in reading this book is to create web pages for your business, you might want to make a personal web page just for practice. Type a few paragraphs to introduce yourself to the world, and use the HTML tags you've learned in this hour to make them into a web page.

▶ You'll be using the HTML tags covered in this hour so often that you'll want to commit them to memory. The best way to do that is to take some time now and create several web pages before you go on. You can try creating some basic pages with serious information you want to post on the Internet, or just use your imagination and make some fun pages. Don't forget to test each page in a browser as you make changes so that you can see the effect of each change.

HOUR 3

Linking to Other Web Pages

In the previous two hours you learned how to use HTML tags to create a web page with some text on it. However, at this point the web page is an island unto itself, with no connection to anything else. To make it a "real" web page, you need to connect it to the rest of the World Wide Web—or at least to your own personal or corporate web of pages.

This hour shows you how to create hypertext links. You'll learn how to create links that go to another part of the same page in Hour 6, "Creating Text Links."

Hypertext links are those words that take you from one web page to another when you click them with your mouse.

Although the same HTML tag you study in this hour is also used to make graphical images into clickable links, graphical links aren't explicitly discussed here. You'll find out about those in Hour 8, "Putting Graphics on a Web Page." For now you'll focus your energy on linking to other pages via words, not graphics.

Linking to Another Web Page

The tag to create a link is called <a>, which stands for "anchor." While the word "anchor" might seem a little obscure when describing links, it has to do with the fact that you can use the <a> tag to identify a particular spot within a web page—an anchor point. Granted, there are certainly better words out there that would make more sense, but we're stuck with "anchor" so just go with it! Within the <a> tag, you put the address of the page to link to in quotes after href=, like the following:

```
<a href="http://www.stalefishlabs.com/products.html">click here!</a>
```

This link displays the words click here! in blue with an underline. When a user clicks those words, she sees the web page named products.html, which is located on the web server computer whose address is www.stalefishlabs.com—just as if she had typed the address into the web browser by hand. (By the way, Internet addresses are also called *Uniform Resource Locators*, or *URLs*, by techie types.)

Getting back to the <a> tag, href stands for "hypertext reference" and is an attribute of the <a> tag. You'll learn more about attributes in Hour 5, "Basic Text Alignment and Formatting."

An **attribute** is an extra piece of information associated with a tag that provides further details about the tag. For example, the href attribute of the <a> tag identifies the address of the page to which you are linking.

As you may know, you can leave out the http:// at the front of any address when typing it into most web browsers. However, you cannot leave that part out when you type an Internet address into an <a href> link on a web page.

One thing you can often leave out of an address is the actual name of the HTML page. Most computers on the Internet automatically pull up the home page for a particular address or directory folder. For example, you can use http://www.stalefishlabs.com to refer to the page located at http://www.stalefishlabs.com/index.html because the server computer knows that index.html is the page you should see first (see Hour 4, "Publishing Your HTML Pages"). Of course, this works only if a main index page exists—otherwise, you should spell out the full web page name.

Listing 3.1 includes a few <a> tags, which show up as underlined links in Figure 3.1. The addresses for the links are given in the href attributes. For example, clicking the words Times Square in Figure 3.1 will take you to the page located at http://www.earthcam.com/usa/newyork/timessquare/ as shown in Figure 3.2.

LISTING 3.1   <a> Tags Can Connect Your Pages to Interesting Locations

```
<?xml version="1.0" encoding="UTF-8"?>
<!DOCTYPE html PUBLIC "-//W3C//DTD XHTML 1.1//EN"
  "http://www.w3.org/TR/xhtml11/DTD/xhtml11.dtd">

<html xmlns="http://www.w3.org/1999/xhtml" xml:lang="en">
  <head>
    <title>You Aren't There</title>
  </head>

  <body>
    <h1>Wonders of the World</h1>
    <p>
      Vacations aren't cheap. But who needs them anymore, with so many live
      cameras connected to the World Wide Web? Pack a picnic, and you can
```

LISTING 3.1 Continued

```
          visit just about any attraction you want without ever spending any gas
          money or boarding a plane. Stop off at
          <a href="http://www.earthcam.com/usa/newyork/timessquare/">Times
          Square</a> in New York City to see a live view of the busy spot. Then
          head south to Atlanta, Georgia and watch the
          <a href="http://www.atlantafalcons.com/fans/article.jsp?id=6947">Atlanta
          Falcons training camp</a> live online. When you're finished watching
          Michael Vick, head out west to one of my favorite destinations and take
          in the incredible red rocks of
          <a href="http://www.earthcam.com/cams/arizona/sedona/">Sedona,
          Arizona</a>.
      </p>
   </body>
</html>
```

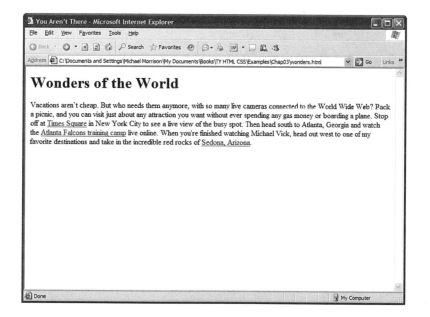

FIGURE 3.1
The HTML in Listing 3.1 produces this page, with links appearing as blue or purple underlined text.

You can easily transfer the address of a page from your web browser to your own HTML page by using the Windows or Macintosh clipboard. Just highlight the address in the Location, Address, Bookmark Properties, or Edit Favorites box in your web browser, and select Edit, Copy (or press Ctrl+C or Command+C on the Mac). Then type <a href=" and select Edit, Paste (Ctrl+V or Command+V) in your HTML (text) editor.

FIGURE 3.2
Clicking the
Times Square
link in Figure
3.1 retrieves
the live Times
Square Earth
Cams page
from the
Internet.

Linking Between Your Own Pages

One exception to the rule earlier about needing to include http:// before each
address specified in the href attribute is when you're dealing with links between
files on the same computer or web server. When you create a link from one page to
another page on the same computer, it isn't necessary to specify a complete Internet
address. In fact, if the two pages are stored in the same folder, you can simply use
the name of the HTML file by itself:

```
<a href="pagetwo.html">click here to go to page 2.</a>
```

As an example, Listing 3.2 and Figure 3.3 show a quiz page with a link to the
answers page in Listing 3.3 and Figure 3.4. The answers page contains a link back
to the quiz page. Because the page in Listing 3.2 links to another page in the same
directory, the filename can be used in place of a complete address.

LISTING 3.2   Linking to Another Page in the Same Directory

```
<?xml version="1.0" encoding="UTF-8"?>
<!DOCTYPE html PUBLIC "-//W3C//DTD XHTML 1.1//EN"
  "http://www.w3.org/TR/xhtml11/DTD/xhtml11.dtd">

<html xmlns="http://www.w3.org/1999/xhtml" xml:lang="en">
  <head>
    <title>History Quiz</title>
  </head>
```

LISTING 3.2   Continued

```
<body>
  <h1>History Quiz</h1>
  <p>
    Complete the following rhymes. (Example: William the Conqueror played
    cruel tricks on the Saxons in... ten sixty-six.)
  </p>
  <p>
    1. Columbus sailed the ocean blue in...<br />
    2. The Spanish Armada met its fate in...<br />
    3. London burnt like rotten sticks in...<br />
    4. Tricky Dickie served his time in...<br />
    5. Billy C. went on a spree in...
  </p>
  <p>
    <a href="answers.html">Click here for answers.</a>
  </p>
</body>
</html>
```

LISTING 3.3   This Is the `answers.html` file; Listing 3.2 Is
`quizzer.html`, to Which This Page Links Back

```
<?xml version="1.0" encoding="UTF-8"?>
<!DOCTYPE html PUBLIC "-//W3C//DTD XHTML 1.1//EN"
  "http://www.w3.org/TR/xhtml11/DTD/xhtml11.dtd">

<html xmlns="http://www.w3.org/1999/xhtml" xml:lang="en">
  <head>
    <title>History Quiz Answers</title>
  </head>

  <body>
    <h1>History Quiz Answers</h1>
    <p>
      1. ...fourteen hundred and ninety-two.<br />
      2. ...fifteen hundred and eighty eight.<br />
      3. ...sixteen hundred and sixty-six.<br />
      4. ...nineteen hundred and sixty-nine.<br />
      5. ...nineteen hundred and ninety-three.
    </p>
    <p>
      <a href="quizzer.html">Click here for the questions.</a>
    </p>
  </body>
</html>
```

Using filenames instead of complete Internet addresses saves you a lot of typing.
More important, the links between your pages will work properly no matter where
the group of pages is stored. You can test the links while the files are still on your
computer's hard drive. You can then move them to a computer on the Internet, or to
a CD-ROM, DVD, or memory card, and all the links will still work correctly. There is

nothing magic about this simplified approach to identifying web pages—it all has to do with web page addressing, which you'll learn about next.

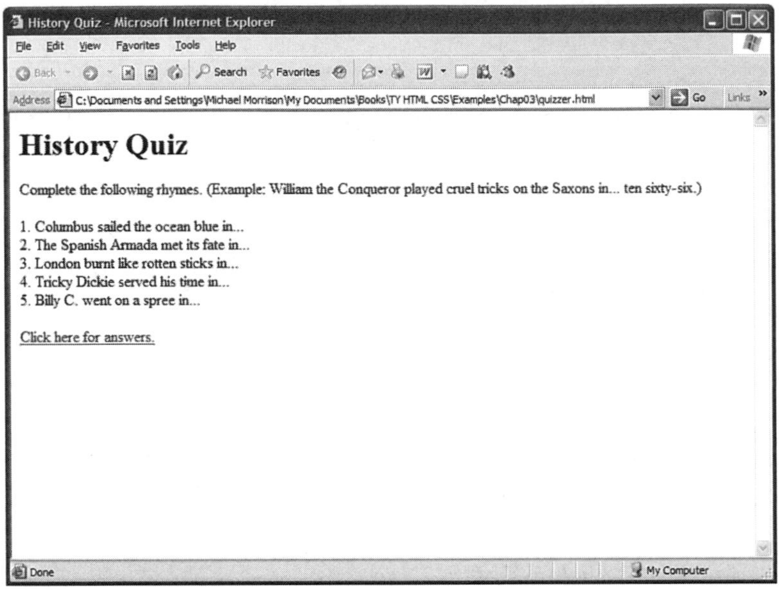

FIGURE 3.3
This is the
quizzer.html
file listed in
Listing 3.2 and
referred to by
the link in
Listing 3.3.

FIGURE 3.4
Click here
for answers in
Figure 3.3 takes
you here. Click
here for the
questions in
this figure takes
you back to
what's shown in
Figure 3.3.

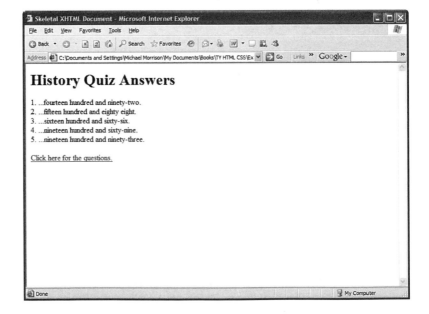

At the *Sams Publishing* website, you'll find some fun sample pages demonstrating hypertext links, including a tour of Indigestible Ingestibles Research sites on the Internet and a light-hearted literary history quiz.

By the Way

Addressing Web Pages

The simplest way to organize web pages for an individual web site is to place them all in the same folder together. When files are stored together like this, you can link to them by simply providing the name of the file in the href attribute of the <a> tag. If you have many pages, you may want to put them in more than one folder for better organization. In that case, you still shouldn't use the full Internet address to link between them. You can use relative addresses, which include only enough information to find one page from another.

A **relative address** describes the path from one web page to another, instead of a full (or **absolute**) Internet address.

For instance, suppose you are creating a page named zoo.html in a directory folder named webpages on your hard drive. You want to include a link to a page named african.html, which is in a subfolder named elephants within webpages. The link would look like the following:

```
<a href="elephants/african.html">learn about african elephants.</a>
```

The / forward slash is always used to separate directory folders in HTML. Don't use the \ backslash normally used in Windows and DOS! I apologize if the reference to DOS was shocking, but believe it or not there are still a few remnants of it in the Windows operating system, such as backslashes.

Watch Out!

The african.html page might contain a link back to the main zoo.html page:

```
<a href="../zoo.html">return to the zoo.</a>
```

The double dot (..) is a special code that indicates the folder containing the current folder—in other words, the parent folder. (The .. means the same thing in Windows, Macintosh, and UNIX.) In truth, specifying a filename by itself is also a form of relative addressing because you're saying that the file resides in the current folder.

If you use relative addressing consistently throughout your web pages, you can move the pages to another folder, disk drive, or web server without changing the links. Or, using the example, everything will work as long as you always put `african.html` inside a subfolder named `elephants`.

Did you Know?

> The general rule surrounding relative addressing (elephants/african.html) versus absolute addressing (http://www.takeme2thezoo.com/elephants/african.html) is that you should use relative addressing when linking to files that are stored together, such as files that are all part of the same web site. Absolute addressing should be used when you're linking to files somewhere else—another computer, another disk drive, or, more commonly, another web site on the Internet.

Relative addresses can span quite complex directory structures if necessary; Hour 22, "Organizing and Managing a Web Site," offers more detailed advice for organizing and linking among large numbers of web pages.

▼ **Try It Yourself**

You probably created a page or two of your own while working through Hour 2, "Create a Web Page Right Now." Now is a great time to add a few more pages and link them together:

- ▶ Use a home page as a main entrance and central hub to which all of your other pages are connected. If you created a page about yourself or your business in Hour 2, use that as your home page. You also might like to make a new page now for this purpose.

- ▶ On the home page, put a list of `<a href>` links to the other HTML files you've created (or plan to create soon). Be sure that the exact spelling of the filename, including any capitalization, is correct in every link.

- ▶ On every other page, include a link at the bottom (or top) leading back to your home page. That makes it simple and easy to navigate around your site.

- ▶ You may also want to include a list of links to sites on the Internet, either on your home page or on a separate hotlist page. People often include a list of their friends' personal pages on their own home page. (Businesses, however, should be careful not to lead potential customers away to other sites too quickly—there's no guarantee they'll come back!)

▼

By the Way

There is one good reason to sometimes use the complete address of your own pages in links. If someone saves one of your pages on his own hard drive, none of the links to your other pages from that page will work unless he downloads all the pages or you've included full addresses.

A good middle-of-the-road solution to this addressing problem involves including a link with the full address of your main home page at the bottom of every page, and using simple filenames or relative addresses in all the rest of the links.

Remember to use only filenames (or relative addressing) for links between your own pages, but full Internet addresses for links to other sites.

Opening a Link in a New Browser Window

Now that you have a handle on how to create addresses for links, I want to share one additional little linking trick that is somewhat controversial. You've no doubt heard of pop-up windows, which are new browser windows that are opened and displayed without the user's approval. Although pop-ups have been used maliciously by some aggressive advertisers, they still serve a valid purpose in some instances when you want to present information in a separate web browser window.

When a linked page is opened in a new browser window, the original page is left open in its original window. To accomplish this feat, you can include an additional attribute in the <a> tag called target. You must set the target attribute to blank for this nifty little trick to work, as the following example shows:

```
<a href="../zoo.html" target="_blank">return to the zoo.</a>
```

When someone clicks the linked text in this example, the zoo.html web page is opened in a completely new browser window. I don't encourage you to use this technique too much because most people don't enjoy new browser windows popping up everywhere. One scenario where I've found it useful is when you link to a page that isn't located on your site. This can be a helpful way to keep your site active in the background so you aren't forgotten when the link is followed!

Now that I've shown you the easy way to open a page in a new browser window, I have to break the bad news to you. In an effort to discourage web designers from using the new window trick, the W3C removed the target="_blank" feature from XHTML. So, you can't use the code I just showed if you want your pages to be valid XHTML documents. But there's a workaround.

By the
~~Way~~

> The W3C was a bit aggressive in throwing out the target="_blank" attribute set-
> ting entirely. There has been a lot of debate about whether web designers should
> force a link to open in a pop-up window. I think as long as you use pop-up win-
> dows sparingly for links that the user clicks, they are perfectly acceptable; a pop-
> up should never appear that isn't prompted by the user.

The workaround to the pop-up window restriction involves using a JavaScript script
to sneakily set the target attribute of all the links on a page. You could argue that
this workaround goes against the intentions of the W3C, and you'd be right. But the
fact remains that pop-ups can be used effectively in some situations. You find out
about one of these situations when you see a new version of the Music City Mafia
hockey player web pages later in the lesson.

If my mentioning of JavaScript scared you, don't worry, because you don't need to
know anything about JavaScript or programming to use an existing script. The
script in this case is stored in a file named external.js. I won't even bother showing you the script code because this book isn't about JavaScript. What I will show
you is how to use the script in a web page. The first step is to import the
external.js script into the page, which is accomplished with a single line of code
in the page header:

```
<script type="text/javascript" src="external.js"></script>
```

With the script imported into the page, all you then must do to create a link so that
it opens in a new window is add the rel="external" attribute to the <a> tag for the
link. The script looks for this attribute and then doctors the link appropriately so
that it opens in a new window. The end result is a link that is opened in a new
browser window but that is still compliant with XHTML.

By the
~~Way~~

> The rel="external" code sounds a bit cryptic, but what it actually means is that
> the **rel**ationship between the link and the current page is **external**. In other words,
> the link should be opened externally, as in a separate browser window.

Linking to Google Maps

If you've never used Google Maps before, stop reading right now and go open
http://maps.google.com in a web browser. Now type in your home or business
address in the search box and click the Search button. Click and drag around on the
map to move it around in real time. You can also click the little "plus" and "minus"

buttons near the left side of the page to zoom in and out of the map. And finally, try switching to a satellite view of the map by clicking the Satellite button, or try "hybrid" mode where you can see a satellite image with streets overlaid. Why am I sidetracking an HTML book with a discussion of Google Maps? Because it's one of the coolest tools on the Web, and you may find it incredibly useful in your own web pages. Figure 3.5 shows Google Maps in action.

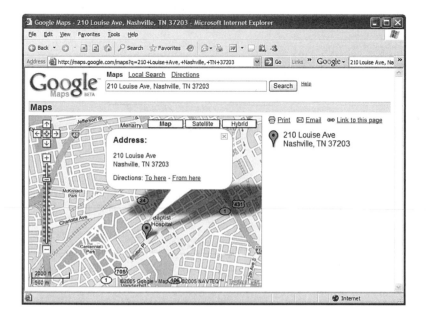

FIGURE 3.5
Google Maps allows you to create links to interactive maps for just about any geographical location.

For the record, I have no affiliation with Google and get no kickbacks for recommending Google Maps. I've just personally found it to be one of the most amazing online tools out there.

Now that you have a feel for how to use Google Maps, I want to show you how to link to a map in your web pages. This could be useful for providing a mapped location of a business, directions to an important event, or any number of other things. The key to providing a Google Maps link lies in the "Link to this page" option visible on the right side of the map screen (see Figure 3.5). Click this option to view a link to the current map in the address bar of the browser. You can then copy and paste this link from the address bar into your HTML code as the value of the href attribute for the <a> tag. And *voilà*, you now have a link to an exact geographical location on Google Maps.

> If you found Google Maps to be an interesting tool, you'll no doubt want to check
> out Google Earth at http://earth.google.com/. Unlike Google Maps, Google Earth
> is an application that you download to your computer. It is considerably more pow-
> erful in terms of its imagery, effectively providing you with an interactive, photoreal-
> istic view of the entire planet.

As an example, the map in Figure 3.5 shows the location of a restaurant (Café
Coco) owned by a friend of mine. If my friend wanted to include a link to a map of
his restaurant location on his web site, all he'd need to do is include the following
HTML code:

```
<a href="http://maps.google.com/maps?q=210+Louise+Ave,+Nashville,+TN+37203">
View map</a>
```

This code uses the text View map as a link to the Google map for Café Coco. This is
a great example of adding a heck of a lot of interesting functionality to a web page
with very little effort.

Adding Links to a Practical Example

Before we leave this lesson, it's worth revisiting the hockey player sample page and
incorporating links into it. In fact, I'm expanding the example to use multiple pages
for different players. This provides a great way to show in practical terms how pages
on the same site link together, along with how to inject useful links to other sites,
including Google Maps.

Listing 3.4 contains the HTML code for the web page of another hockey player on
my recreational hockey team, and in this case the player's interests are linked to
other relevant pages.

**LISTING 3.4   Linking to Other Pages That Provide Additional
                  Information**

```
<?xml version="1.0" encoding="UTF-8"?>
<!DOCTYPE html PUBLIC "-//W3C//DTD XHTML 1.1//EN"
  "http://www.w3.org/TR/xhtml11/DTD/xhtml11.dtd">

<html xmlns="http://www.w3.org/1999/xhtml" xml:lang="en">
  <head>
    <title>Music City Mafia - Donny Sowers</title>
    <script type="text/javascript" src="external.js"></script>
  </head>

  <body>
    <h1>21 - Donny Sowers</h1>
    <p>
      <img src="dsowers.jpg" alt="Donny &quot;The Donger&quot; Sowers" /><br />
      Nickname: The Donger<br />
```

LISTING 3.4   Continued

```
      Position: LW<br />
      Height: 5'9"<br />
      Weight: 175<br />
      Shoots: Rarely<br />
      Age: 42<br />
      Birthplace: God's Country (Texas)
    </p>
    <hr />
    <p>
      Favorite NHL Player: <a
      href="http://www.nhl.com/lineups/player/8458520.html">
      Peter Forsberg</a><br />
      Favorite NHL Team: <a href="http://www.nashvillepredators.com/">Nashville
      Predators </a><br />
      Favorite Southern Fixin: <a href="http://www.jackdaniels.com/">Jack
      Daniels</a><br />
      Favorite Meat and Three: <a href="http://www.judgebeans.com/">Judge Beans
      Bar-B-Q & Steakhouse</a> (<a
      href="http://maps.google.com/maps?q=123+12th+ave+n,+nashville,+tn"
      rel="external">map</a>)
      <br />
      Favorite Country Star: None<br />
      Favorite Mafia Moment: "Any time <a href="mcmplayer_dfirlus.html">Duke</a>
      scores a game-winning goal but we still somehow lose the game."
    </p>
  </body>
</html>
```

Most of the interesting link code takes place in the latter part of the document.
Before attempting to decipher the code, take a look at the end result in Figure 3.6.

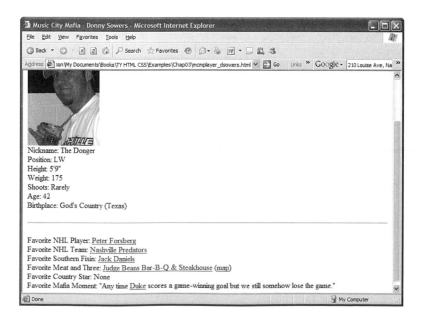

FIGURE 3.6
Several links
are used to pro-
vide additional
information
about the
hockey player's
interests.

By the
Way

In the figure I deliberately scrolled down so that all the links are revealed.

The page doesn't look a whole lot different than the hockey player page you saw in the preceding hour, except in this page there are highlighted links to many of the player's interests. Clicking any of these links takes you to another page. However, the links aren't all created equal. If you take a closer look at the code in Listing 3.4, you'll notice that the last link to the word "Duke" is a link to another player page on the same web site. Contrast this with the link to the word "map," which is an external link (pop-up window) to a Google map. In this case the "map" link provides a map to the player's favorite restaurant, Judge Beans Bar-B-Q & Steakhouse. All the remaining links are normal links to other web sites. Figure 3.7 shows the page that opens if you follow the link to "Duke" on the page.

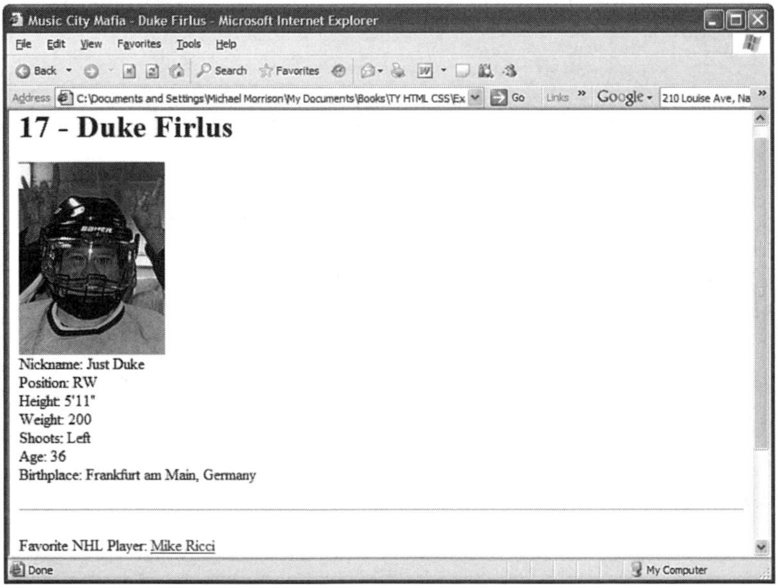

FIGURE 3.7
Linking player pages to each other is done by simply specifying the name of the page by itself in the anchor tag.

The page in the figure is referenced in the HTML code by an anchor tag (<a>) that specifies only the name of the HTML file (mcmplayer_dfirlus.html) in the href attribute. If you recall from earlier in the hour, when you specify only the name or partial path of a web page (relative address), it is assumed to be on the same computer as the page from which it is being linked.

Summary

The <a> tag is what makes hypertext "hyper." With it, you can create clickable links between pages, as well as links to specific anchor points on any page. This hour focused on creating simple links to other pages using either relative or absolute addressing to identify the pages.

You learned that when you're creating links to other people's pages, it's important to include the full Internet address of each page in an <a href> tag. For links between your own pages, include just the filenames and enough directory information to get from one page to another.

Table 3.1 summarizes the <a> tag discussed in this hour.

TABLE 3.1 HTML Tags and Attributes Covered in Hour 3

Tag/Attribute	Function
<a>...</a>	With the href attribute, creates a link to another document or anchor.
Attributes	
href="*address*"	The address of the document or anchor point to link to.
target="_blank"	Opens the linked page in a new browser window but doesn't conform to XHTML requirements (there is a JavaScript workaround).

Q&A

Q *When I make links, some of them are blue and some of them are purple. Why? How come most of the links I see on the Internet aren't blue and purple?*

A By default, a link appears blue to anyone who hasn't recently visited the page to which it points. After you visit a page, any links to it turn purple. These default colors can be (and often are) changed to match any color scheme a web page author wants, so many links you see on the Web won't be blue and purple. You can even change the size, weight, and other font characteristics of links using Cascading Style Sheets (CSS). (Hour 9, "Custom Backgrounds and Colors," tells how to change the colors of text on your web pages using CSS, and Hour 13, "Digging Deeper into Style Sheet Formatting," shows you how to alter the color and appearance of links.)

Q *What happens if I link to a page on the Internet and then the person who owns that page deletes or moves it?*

A That depends on how that person has set up his server computer. Usually, people see a message saying page not found or something to that effect when they click the link. They can still click the Back button to return to your page.

Q *One of my links works fine on my computer, but when I put the pages on the Internet it doesn't work anymore. What's up?*

A These are the most likely culprits:

- *Capitalization problems.* On Windows computers, linking to a file named Freddy.html with <a href="freddy.html"> will work. On most web servers (which are often UNIX machines), the link must be <a href="freddy.html"> (or you must change the name of the file to freddy.html). To make matters worse, some text editors and file transfer programs actually change the capitalization without telling you! The best solution is to stick with all-lowercase filenames for web pages.

- *Spaces in filenames.* Most web servers don't allow filenames with spaces. For example, you should never name a web page my page.html. Instead, call it mypage.html or maybe my_page.html with an underscore instead of a space.

- *Local absolute addresses.* If for some reason you link to a file using a local absolute address, such as C:\mywebsite\news.html, the link won't work when you place the file on the Internet. You should never use local absolute addresses; when this occurs it is usually an accident caused from a temporary link created just to test part of a page. So, be careful to remove any test links like this before publishing a page on the Web.

The next hour explains how to upload files to a web site and how to rename files after they're online so that you can make sure that the spelling and capitalization are perfect.

Workshop

The workshop contains quiz questions and activities to help you solidify your understanding of the material covered. Try to answer all questions before looking at the "Answers" section that follows.

Quiz

1. Your best friend from elementary school finds you on the Internet and says he wants to trade home page links. How do you put a link to his page at www.cheapsuits.com/~billybob/ on your page?

2. Your home page will be at http://www.mysite.com/home.html when you put it on the Internet. Write the HTML code to go on that page so that when someone clicks the words `all about me`, they see the page located at http://www.mysite.com/mylife.html.

3. You plan to publish a CD-ROM disk containing HTML pages. How do you create a link from a page in the `\guide` directory folder to the `\guide\maine\katahdin.html` page?

4. How about a link from `\guide\maine\katahdin.html` to the `\guide\arizona\superstitions.html` page?

Answers

1. Put the following on your page:

```
<a href="http://www.cheapsuits.com/~billybob/">
my buddy billy bob's page of inexpensive businesswear</a>
```

2. `<a href="mylife.html">all about me</a>`

The following would work equally well, though it would be harder to test on your hard drive:

```
<a href="http://www.mysite.com/mylife.html">all about me</a>
```

3. `<a href="maine/katahdin.html">mount katahdin</a>`

4. `<a href="../arizona/superstitions.html">`

`the superstition range</a>`

Exercises

Make a web page consisting of a formatted list of your favorite web sites. You may already have these sites bookmarked in your web browser, in which case you can visit them to find the exact URL in the browser's address bar.

HOUR 4

Publishing Your HTML Pages

Here it is, the hour you've been waiting for! Your web pages are ready for the world to see, and this hour explains how to get them to appear before the eyes of your intended audience, whether it's your circle of friends or co-workers, or the entire online world.

The most obvious avenue for publishing web pages is, of course, the Internet, but you may want to limit the distribution of your pages to a local intranet within your organization instead of making them available to the general public. You may also choose to distribute your web pages on CD-ROMs, DVD-ROMs, USB memory cards, or even good old-fashioned floppy disks. This hour covers all of these options and offers advice for designing your pages to work best with whichever distribution method you choose.

An **intranet** is a private network with access restricted to one organization, but which uses the same technical standards and protocols as the global public Internet.

Try It Yourself ▼

Before you read about publishing your pages, you should give some thought to which methods of distribution you will be using:

▶ If you want your pages to be visible to as many people as possible all over the world, Internet publishing is a must. However, don't rule out other distribution methods; you can easily adapt Internet-based pages for distribution on disks or local networks.

▶ If you want to reach only employees of your organization, publish on your local intranet only.

▶ If you want to provide very large graphics, multimedia, or other content that would be too slow to transfer over even a cable or DSL modem connection, consider publishing on a CD-ROM or DVD-ROM. You can easily offer the CD-ROM from your web site to people who find you through the Internet but want the full experience. Of course, these days you'd really have to design a hog of a web site for it to require a CD-ROM, especially when you look around and see how much multimedia some sites are using.

▼

▼

▲

▶ If you plan to make a presentation at a meeting and would also like to publish related material on the Internet or an intranet, why not use HTML instead
of old-fashioned PowerPoint slides as a visual aid? You can even place the files
on a memory card or burn one-off CD-ROMs if necessary for people to take
home.

Setting Up Web Space on the Internet

To make an HTML page part of the publicly accessible World Wide Web, you need to
put it on a web server. If you run your own web server, this procedure is simply a
matter of copying the file to the right directory folder. However, you may not have
access to a web server that you can use to host your own web site, in which case
you'll need to use a web server run by an Internet service provider (ISP) to host your
pages.

A **web server** is a computer permanently connected to the Internet that uses special
software to deliver web pages upon request by web browsers.

Almost all ISPs that offer Internet access also now offer space in which to place your
own personal web pages for little or no additional cost, though you may have to
pay extra if your site attracts a huge number of visitors or includes very large multimedia files. Be sure to check with the company you're getting Internet access from
to see whether any web space is built into your standard account. This is often a
great way to get started with creating a web site because the space is usually free
and readily available.

*Did you
Know?*

> Even if it's free initially, you don't have to use the same company that provides
> you with Internet access to host your pages, especially if they don't offer
> advanced features such as shopping cart and online merchant services. You may
> also want your own domain name (www.*yourname*.com), which typically requires
> you to use a paid hosting service. And, finally, if you plan on running a high-traffic
> business web site, you may get more features and more reliable service from a
> company that specializes solely in web hosting. To comparison-shop the hosting
> services offered by various Internet service providers, go to the list of ISPs at
> http://thelist.internet.com/.

Web hosting prices for a site start as low as $3 per month, but that price can rise if
lots of people start viewing your pages. For a site with about a hundred different
web pages, I have paid as little as $3 per month when a few thousand people
looked at my pages, and as much as $2,000 per month when hundreds of thou-
sands of people looked at my pages. The pricing ultimately comes down to how

much traffic your site gets from web users, although early on you can probably expect traffic to be fairly light. Keep in mind also that web hosting prices are getting more and more affordable, so you're likely to find a suitable hosting service on the lower end of the range I've mentioned.

Free web hosting services such as Geocities (http://geocities.yahoo.com/), Tripod (http://www.tripod.lycos.com/), and Angelfire (http://www.angelfire.lycos.com/) are very popular with web page authors—and, yes, they really are free—although most such services require that you include advertisements of their choosing on your pages. The other issue with these free services is that they often display pop-up ads to people viewing your pages, which can be annoying. I know that Angelfire offers an in-between option for around $5 per month that is ad free, so that's not a bad trade-off if you're on a tight budget.

One of the most important choices you'll need to make when you set up a web site is the name you want to use as the site's address. If you don't pay to register a unique domain name of your own, which runs around $30 per year, your site's address will include the name of your Internet service provider (http://www.shore.net/~smith/, for example). If you're willing to pay for it and register a name, you can choose any name that isn't already used by another company (http://www.mister-smith.com/, for example).

If your web hosting service doesn't offer domain name registration, you can use a domain service such as http://www.godaddy.com/, http://www.easydns.com/, or http://www.register.com/. Before registering a new name, you must first perform a search to see whether the name is available; each domain name service offers such a search service at no charge. Keep in mind that you can register a domain name even if you aren't ready to publish your web site; this is a good idea if you want to make sure you don't lose the name while you build your site.

By the Way

Transferring Pages to a Web Server

When a web server computer sends web pages to people through the Internet, it uses an information exchange standard called *Hypertext Transfer Protocol (HTTP)*. To upload a page to your web site, however, you usually need software that uses a different communications standard called *File Transfer Protocol (FTP)*.

FTP is the standard that your file transfer software must adhere to when sending files to a web server. After you've published files to a web server using FTP, the server sends those files out to anyone who asks for them using HTTP. Here's an easy way to remember the protocols: FTP is used to upload your HTML files to the web server, and HTTP is used by web browsers to download and view your web pages.

You'll most likely need to get four important pieces of information from your web hosting service before you can put pages up on your web site:

1. Your *account name* (sometimes called a *username* or *user ID*). If the same company provides you with both Internet access and web hosting, the account name for your web site will probably be the same as your email account name.

2. Your *password*. This may also be the same as your email password.

3. The *FTP address* for your site, such as `ftp.yoursite.com`. Note that this address may or may not be the same as the address people go to when they view your web pages in a web browser.

4. The *folder* where your web page files should be placed. You can sometimes place them in the root folder of the web server, which is the topmost folder on the server, but often you need to go into a subdirectory named www or `public`, or the same as your domain name.

Next, you need to decide which software you'll use to send your pages to the web server and maintain your site. This hour covers five options:

- ▶ Microsoft Internet Explorer
- ▶ Mozilla Firefox (fireFTP extension)
- ▶ Microsoft FrontPage (or similar web development software)
- ▶ FTP software (such as SmartFTP, CuteFTP, or FileZilla)
- ▶ Windows Web Publishing Wizard

Which of these do I recommend? It depends on your situation. If you plan to develop a complex web site, you will find that a program such as Microsoft FrontPage or Macromedia Dreamweaver saves you a lot of time by helping manage changing links between pages and automatically keeping track of which pages have changed and need updating. However, for the beginning web page author and anyone who plans to have only a modest site with a few personal or business pages, it's easier to learn and use a simple FTP program such as SmartFTP or CuteFTP. If you just want to get your pages online without bothering to set up any new software at all, you can get the job done with the web browser you already have or with the standard Windows Web Publishing Wizard.

The next few sections cover the details of publishing web pages using each of the previously mentioned approaches. You may end up trying several of the approaches before deciding which technique is best for your needsv.

Using Microsoft Internet Explorer

As you might guess from the name, Microsoft Internet Explorer for Windows was designed to work much like the Windows Explorer file manager that comes with Windows. When you enter an FTP address in the Address bar of Internet Explorer, you can cut, paste, delete, and rename any file or directory folder on the web server just as if it were on your computer's own hard drive.

If you're using the Windows version of Internet Explorer, follow these steps to upload a page you've created on your hard drive so that it will appear on your web site online:

1. Start Microsoft Internet Explorer. Click the Address bar, type My Computer, and press the Enter key, and you will see all the drives and folders available on your computer. Navigate to where the page you created is currently located. Note that going to the folder by selecting File, Open won't work—you have to navigate to the page within Explorer.

If you know that the page is located within the My Documents folder, you can type My Documents in the Address bar to jump straight to that folder.

Did you Know?

---

2. Click once on the file you want to upload to your web site to highlight it. As in any Windows program, you can select multiple files by holding down the Shift or Ctrl key as you click on the files. Be sure to include any graphics files (see Hour 7, "Creating Your Own Web Page Graphics," and Hour 8, "Putting Graphics on a Web Page") that need to go with the HTML file.

3. Select Edit, Copy (see Figure 4.1).

4. Now click the Address bar again in Internet Explorer and enter your web account name, password, and site address in the following format:

   `ftp://myname:mypassword@mywebaddress.com/home/web/wherever/`

   Put your account name and password for accessing the site in place of *myname* and *mypassword*, the FTP address for your site in place of *mywebaddress.com*, and the top-level directory where your web pages go on the server in place of */home/web/wherever/*.

5. Wait until the web server folder is opened in Internet Explorer, and then select Edit, Paste (see Figure 4.2). The file(s) will be transferred from your hard drive to the web server.

6. Test your page by returning to the Address bar and entering the URL of the web page. You're on the Web!

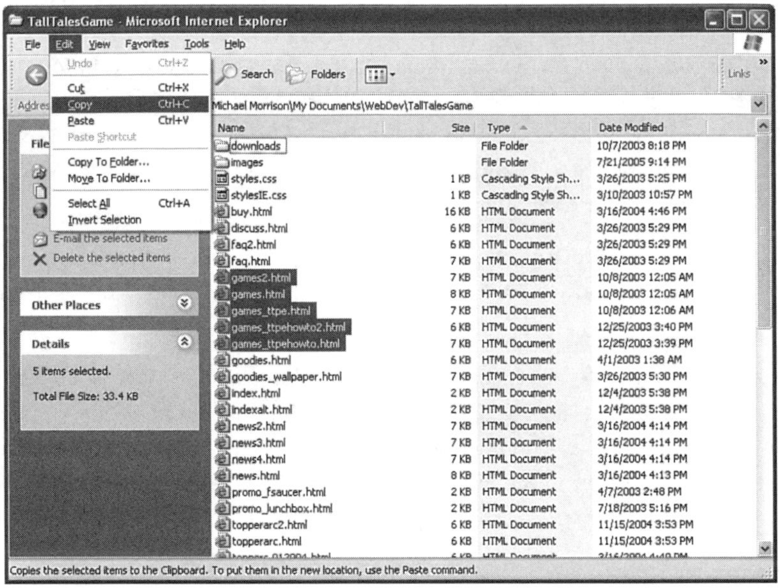

FIGURE 4.1
To upload a
page using
Microsoft
Internet
Explorer, first
navigate to the
folder where the
files are on your
own computer
and select Edit,
Copy.

FIGURE 4.1
To upload a
page using
Microsoft
Internet
Explorer, first
navigate to the
folder where the
files are on your
own computer
and select Edit,
Copy.

To delete or rename a file or folder on the web server, right-click it and select Delete
or Rename, just as you would with local files in a Windows application.

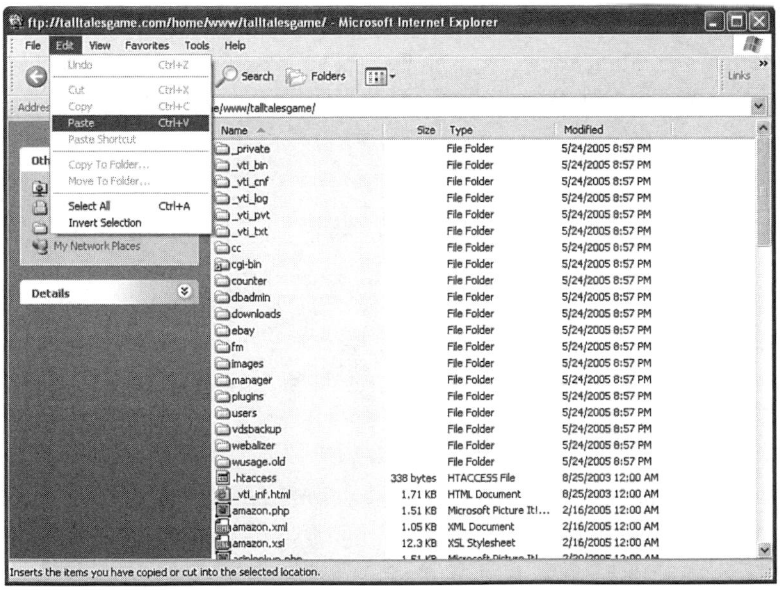

FIGURE 4.2
Microsoft
Internet Explorer
uses the famil-
iar Windows
Explorer inter-
face to paste
files into folders
on a distant
web server
computer.

Did you
Know?

You can follow the first three steps with Windows Explorer instead of Internet Explorer. Another good technique for transferring files in Windows is to drag and drop them from Windows Explorer into Internet Explorer, as opposed to using the copy-and-paste approach.

After you've successfully published the file onto the web server, it's very important that you test it by entering the name of the web page in the Address bar of Internet Explorer, and pressing the Enter key. If you've registered a domain name for the site, you'll probably enter the domain name followed by a forward slash (/) followed by the web page filename. Otherwise, you'll need to enter the exact name of your web server as provided by your web hosting service provider, followed by a slash and the filename.

Watch
Out!

You typically cannot directly transfer a file from one folder on an FTP site to another folder on an FTP site. If you want to do that, you need to transfer the file to your hard drive first and then transfer it back to the new location on the FTP site. This is because most FTP programs are designed for sending files back and forth between your local computer and an FTP site, not between folders on an FTP site.

Using Mozilla Firefox

If you prefer using Mozilla Firefox over Internet Explorer, you can still use your web browser as the basis for uploading files to a web server. However, you'll need to first install a browser extension called fireFTP. The fireFTP extension is available for free download at http://fireftp.mozdev.org/. Be sure to download and install this extension in Firefox before attempting the steps that follow; you must install the fireFTP extension from within Firefox by entering the previously mentioned URL.

An **extension** is a small application, similar to a plug-in, that you can download and install into Firefox to add new features.

You may encounter a warning about Firefox attempting to download software. If so, click Edit Options in the upper-right corner of the browser window, and then click Allow to indicate that it's okay to download the extension. You will likely also see a confirmation about installing the extension, as shown in Figure 4.3. Just click the Install Now button to allow the installation of fireFTP to continue. When the installation finishes, you'll need to close and restart Firefox for the changes to take effect. Then you're ready to fire up fireFTP and start uploading web pages.

FIGURE 4.3
When prompted
to install the
fireFTP browser
extension in
Firefox, just
click Install Now
to confirm the
installation.

Following are the steps required to publish HTML files using Mozilla Firefox and the fireFTP browser extension:

1. Run Firefox from your Mozilla Firefox installation folder, or double-click the icon for it if you have a desktop icon assigned to it.

2. Select Tools followed by FireFTP to start the fireFTP extension. The browser window will change to show somewhat of a file manager view, as shown in Figure 4.4.

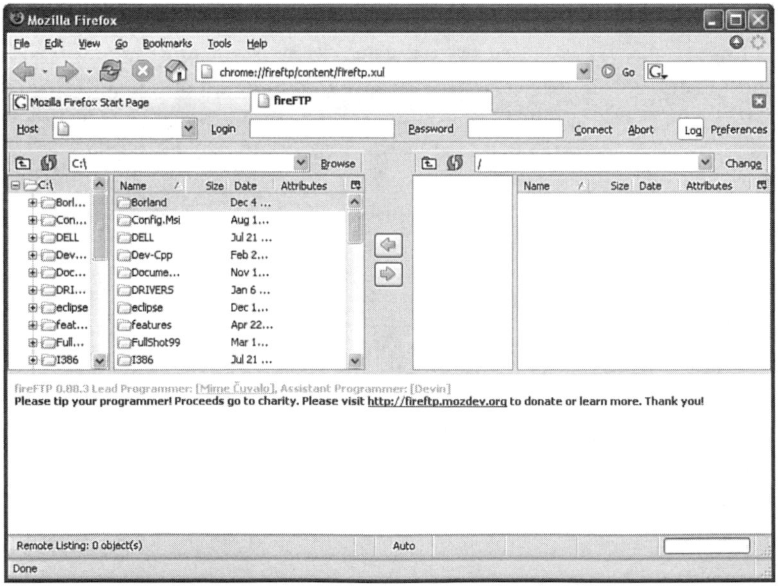

FIGURE 4.4
The user inter-
face for fireFTP
looks somewhat
like a file man-
ager but with
separate panes
for local files
(left pane) and
files on the web
server (right
pane).

3. Enter your web site address, account name, and password in the edit fields along the top of the fireFTP window. The specific fields are named Host, Login, and Password, respectively (see Figure 4.4). After entering this information, click Connect just to the right of the Password field to connect to the web server. If all goes well, you'll see a notification box that confirms the connection—just click OK to proceed.

4. Navigate to the appropriate local folder in the left pane, and then click and drag the pages over to the far-right pane. Wait while the files are transferred.

5. Test your page by entering the URL of the web page in the Address bar.

Even though Firefox can send files to any web server on the Internet, you may elect to use a standalone application such as SmartFTP or CuteFTP. There really is no reason you can't rely on Firefox and fireFTP for all of your web publishing needs, assuming that you're happy with Firefox as your primary web browser. Thanks to fireFTP, Firefox offers a much more feature-rich FTP option than Internet Explorer.

Using Microsoft FrontPage

Although using Internet Explorer or Firefox to publish a few pages is certainly a reasonable approach to consider, there are more advanced options if you're looking for a complete web development software package. One such package is Microsoft FrontPage for Windows, which is also a useful tool for creating web pages after you get a solid handle on HTML. FrontPage turns publishing your entire web site into a one-step, automated process (see Figure 4.5). Whether you've created one or one hundred pages, you can put them all online by selecting File, Publish Web. There are also Macintosh-compatible web development tools for publishing web pages, which you'll learn about in a moment.

FIGURE 4.5
Microsoft FrontPage makes it easy to upload many pages at once—or upload just those pages you've made changes to.

The first time you publish pages to a particular site, you are asked to specify the location of the web server, which simply means to enter the FTP address your web hosting service gave you (or the HTTP address, if the web server has FrontPage extensions installed).

You are then asked to enter your account name and password. FrontPage automatically uploads all pages that you've changed since your last update; it keeps track of which pages you've modified since the last publish. Other web development software, including Macromedia Dreamweaver and Adobe GoLive, also offers similar automated uploading and site management features.

> Be very careful to include the correct subdirectory when you tell FrontPage where to publish the web. For example, the web host `sover.net` requires pages to go in a directory folder named www, which means files must be published to
>
> `ftp.sover.net/www/`
>
> Be careful not to forget the www/ at the end, or FrontPage will place all your pages in the wrong directory.

Using FTP Software

If you don't like any of the preceding options for publishing web pages, or if you just want a little more control over how HTML files and related resources are organized on a web server, you need to consider using FTP software. FTP software allows you to transfer, delete, and rename files on a web server, as well as create, rename, and delete folders. This gives you a great deal of control over how your web sites are organized. There are many FTP programs, most of which are free or require a relatively minimal registration fee. CuteFTP is a popular FTP program for Windows that I've used with success. An evaluation version of CuteFTP is available for free download from the CuteFTP web site at http://www.cuteftp.com/. Figure 4.6 shows CuteFTP in action as it displays files on a web server.

If you aren't using a Windows computer, don't worry, because there are plenty of FTP software packages similar to CuteFTP that you can use on other operating systems such as Macintosh and UNIX systems. Fetch (http://www.fetchsoftworks.com/) and Transit (http://www.panic.com/transmit/) are both popular Macintosh FTP programs, and gFTP is a good option if you're using a computer that runs UNIX (http://gftp.seul.org/). You can also use your favorite search engine to perform a search on "ftp client" or "ftp software" and see what else you find.

> Another popular Windows FTP program is SmartFTP, which is available online at http://www.smartftp.com/. From that site you can download an evaluation version of SmartFTP free, or purchase the full version online. Also, you might want to look into FileZilla, which is an open-source Windows FTP client that is available online at http://filezilla.sourceforge.net/.

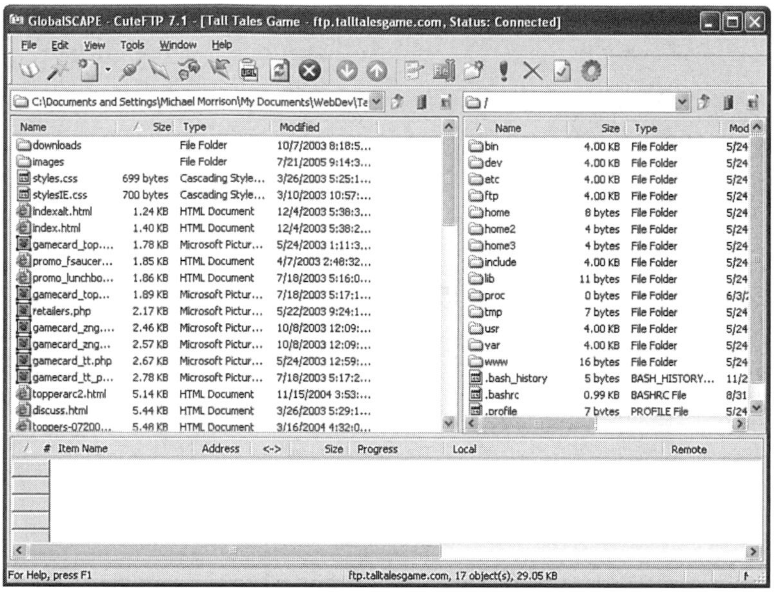

FIGURE 4.6
CuteFTP is a
powerful and
user-friendly FTP
program that
individuals can
use free.

Regardless of what kind of computer you're using and what FTP software you select, the process of publishing web pages is very straightforward. I'll show you steps using CuteFTP as an example, but you should be able to follow along in virtually any FTP program. Just follow these steps:

1. Before you can access the web server, you must tell your FTP program its address, as well as your account name and password (see Figure 4.7). Clicking the tabs along the top of the window allows you to specify additional information about the FTP site.

2. Here's how to fill in each of the items in Figure 4.7:

   . The site label is the name you'll use to refer to your own site. Nobody else will see this name, so enter whatever you want.

   . The FTP host address is the FTP address of the web server to which you need to send your web pages. This usually (but not always) starts with ftp. Notice that it may or may not resemble the address that other people will use to view your web pages. The ISP that runs your web server will be able to tell you the correct address to enter here.

   . The company that runs the web server also issues your username and password. Be aware that CuteFTP (and most other FTP programs) remembers your password automatically, which means that anyone who has physical access to your computer can modify your web site.

. You should set the Login method to Normal unless somebody important tells you otherwise. (The Anonymous setting is for downloading files from public FTP services that don't require user IDs or passwords.)

. Normally, you won't need to change any settings on the other CuteFTP tabs unless you experience problems with your connection. If that happens, have your ISP help you figure out the best settings.

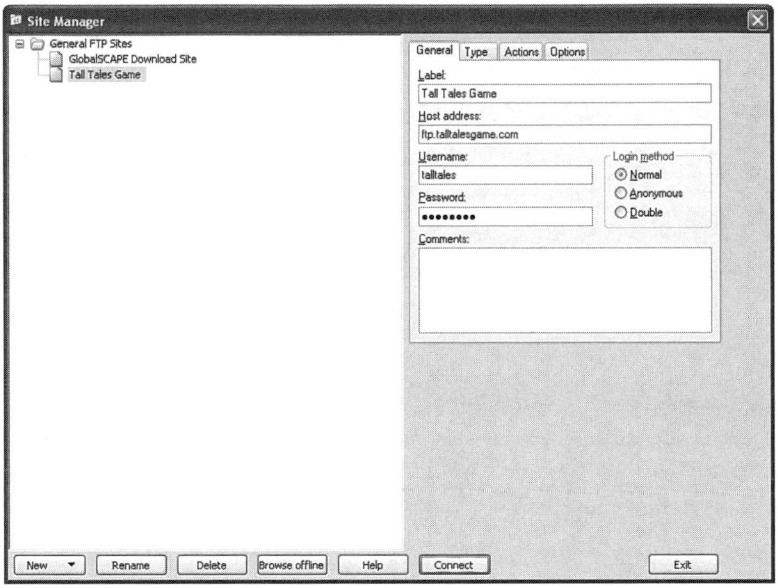

FIGURE 4.7
CuteFTP includes an intuitive FTP site manager, although most web page authors need only a single FTP site entry.

3. When you're finished with the settings, click Connect to establish a connection with the web server computer.

Most server computers issue a short message to everyone who connects to them. Many FTP programs ignore this message, but CuteFTP presents it to you. It seldom says anything important, so just click OK.

4. After you're connected to the server, you'll see two lists of files, as shown earlier in Figure 4.6. The left window pane lists the files on your computer, and the right pane lists the files on the server computer.

To transfer a web page to the server, select the HTML file and any accompanying image files in the left window. (Remember that you can hold down the Ctrl key and click with the mouse to select multiple files in any Windows program.) Then select Transfer, Upload, or click the Upload button on the toolbar. You can also drag and drop files from one pane to the other to transfer files.

CuteFTP also contains commands that delete or rename files (either on your computer or on the server), as well as commands to make and change directory folders.

Most web servers have a special name for the file that should be sent if a user doesn't include a specific filename when he requests a page. For example, if you go to the web site at http://www.talltalesgame.com/, the web server will automatically give you the index.html file. Other web servers use different names for the default file, such as default.html or welcome.html.

Be sure to ask your ISP for the default filename so that you can give your home page that name.

5. You can immediately view the page you just put on the web server by entering the URL of the page in a web browser.

6. When you're finished sending and modifying files on the web server, select File, Disconnect to close the connection.

Most FTP programs remember the settings for each FTP connection you make, so the next time you need to upload web pages, you won't need to fill in all the information in step 2. You can just click Connect, select the pages you want to send, and click the Upload button.

Most web servers are set up so that any documents placed onto them are immediately made available to the entire World Wide Web. However, a few require that users manually change file permission settings, which control who is allowed to access individual files. Your ISP can tell you exactly how to change permission settings on their server and whether it's necessary to do so.

Using the Windows Web Publishing Wizard

Thus far we've kind of moved up the scale of web publishing options from the most simple to the most powerful. Now I'd like to take a step back and show you one last option that is extremely simple, yet admittedly somewhat limited. I'm referring to the Web Publishing Wizard that ships standard with Windows XP (both Home and Professional). The Web Publishing Wizard is extremely easy to use, but it is limited in terms of what kinds of web hosting services it supports. So if you're using a service that isn't supported, you'll have to go with a different approach to publishing your pages.

> One of the default web service providers supported by the Web Publishing Wizard is MSN Groups, which is an online community that is part of MSN (Microsoft Network). You can learn more about MSN Groups at http://groups.msn.com/.

As its name implies, the Web Publishing Wizard uses a familiar wizard interface, which means you publish web pages by answering a series of questions presented in a succession of windows. To publish pages with the Web Publishing Wizard, you must start out in Windows Explorer. Here are the steps to follow:

1. Start Windows Explorer and navigate to the folder containing the HTML file(s) you want to publish. Click Publish This File to the Web in the left side of the Explorer window.

2. The Web Publishing Wizard appears. Click the Next button to get started.

3. The first step in the Web Publishing Wizard allows you to confirm the files in the current folder for publishing, as shown in Figure 4.8. Click Next when you're finished selecting the files.

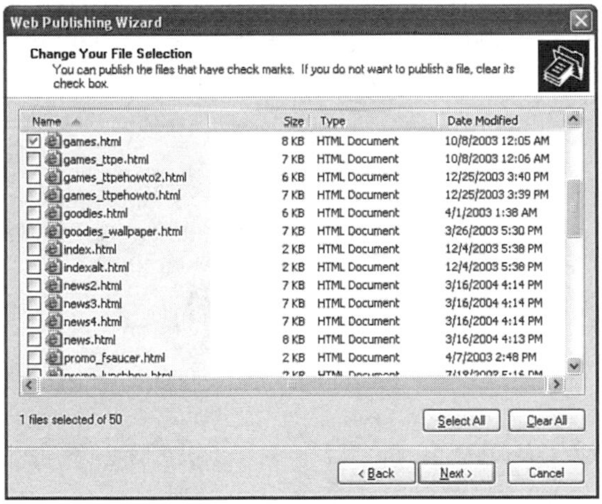

FIGURE 4.8
Click to check the files that you want to publish using the Web Publishing Wizard.

4. Select your web hosting service provider from the list shown in the Web Publishing Wizard (see Figure 4.9). If your provider isn't shown, you may want to skip ahead to the next section and try a different method of uploading your files.

5. Enter the information required of the web hosting service provider you selected. This information varies depending on the specific service provider, so you may want to check with your provider if you aren't sure what the wizard is asking you to enter.

FIGURE 4.9
The Windows
Web Publishing
Wizard provides
a simple
approach to
publishing web
pages as long
as you're using
a supported
web hosting
provider to host
your pages.

6. Proceed through the final step of the wizard, and your pages will be uploaded to the web server. This may take a few minutes if you're uploading a bunch of files or if your Internet connection isn't too speedy.

7. Test your web page by launching your web browser and entering the URL of the page.

Making a File Available for Downloading

Now that you know the scoop about getting your web pages online, it's worth addressing another issue closely related to publishing HTML files. I'm referring to files other than web pages that you want to make available online. Whether it's a ZIP file containing your art portfolio, or an Excel spreadsheet with sales numbers, it's often useful to publish files on the Internet that aren't web pages.

To make a file available on the Web that isn't a web page, just upload the file to your web site as if it were an HTML file, following the instructions earlier in this hour for uploading. After the file is uploaded to the web server, you need to create a link to the file on one of your web pages, as explained in Hour 3, "Linking to Other Web Pages." For example, if the file were called artfolio.zip, the link would look like this:

```
<a href="artfolio.zip">Click here to download my art portfolio.</a>
```

Remember that some web host services charge by the number of bytes sent out, so you need to be careful about posting huge multimegabyte files if a lot of people will be downloading them. For example, if 10,000 people a day download a 2MB file from your site, it might start costing you some serious money and overburden your web server. Of course, short of your creating the next Yahoo! or eBay, that's a lot of traffic for a web site by most normal standards. And at that point you should be cashing in on some advertising revenue if you have that many site visitors!

Other HTML Publishing Options

Publishing HTML pages online is obviously the number-one reason to learn HTML and create web pages. However, there are also situations in which other forms of publishing simply aren't viable. For example, you might want to distribute CD-ROMs or DVD-ROMs at a trade show with marketing materials designed as HTML pages. You may also want to include HTML-based instructional manuals on floppy disks, memory cards, or CD-ROMs for students at a training seminar. These are just two examples of how HTML pages can be used in publishing scenarios that don't involve the Internet. The next couple of sections provide additional information about these publishing options.

Putting Web Pages on an Intranet

Although the approach you learned for publishing pages to the global Internet will often work with private corporate intranets, the internal workings of intranets vary considerably from company to company. In some cases, you may need to use an FTP program to send files to an intranet server. In others, you may be able to transfer files by using the same file management program you use on your own computer. You may also need to adjust permission settings or make special allowances for the firewall that insulates a private intranet from the public Internet.

The best advice I can give regarding publishing to an intranet is to consult with your systems administrator. He or she can help you put your web pages on the company server in a way that best ensures their accessibility and security.

Putting Web Pages on Disks and Memory Cards

Unless you were hired to create documents for a company intranet, you have probably assumed that the Internet is the best way to get your pages in front of the eyes of the world, and for the most part this is true. There are, however, three major incentives for considering distribution on some form of disk instead:

▶ Currently, more people have disk drives and USB ports than Internet connections.

▶ Disks and memory cards can deliver information to the computer screen much faster than people can download it from the Internet.

▶ You can distribute disks and memory cards to a select audience, regardless of whether they are connected to the Internet or any particular intranet.

In the very near future, as web-enabled televisions and high-speed networks become more commonplace, these advantages may diminish considerably. For now, publishing on disk is a viable alternative in situations in which you are dealing with your audience in person. And perhaps more important, you can deliver it to people when Internet access isn't readily available.

For a detailed analysis of all the types of memory cards and what each has to offer, check out the memory card entry on Wikipedia at http://en.wikipedia.org/wiki/Memory_card. There's lots good information here, including an average price per gigabyte (Amazon.com prices) of memory for each card type.

Coffee Break

Publishing on CD-ROM/DVD-ROMs and memory cards is simply a matter of copying files from your hard disk with any file management program. You just need to keep in mind that any links starting with http:// will work only if and when someone reading your pages is also connected to the Internet. The cost associated with CD-ROMs is very small, although DVD-ROMs are a little more expensive. Memory cards are considerably more expensive but you can more easily reuse them.

Never use a drive letter (such as C:) in `<a href>` link tags on your web pages; otherwise, they won't work when you copy the files to a different disk. Refer to Hour 3 for more details on how to make links that will work both on disk and on the Internet.

Watch Out!

Publishing on CD-ROM or DVD-ROM disks requires that you have a drive (and accompanying software) capable of creating the disks, or you can send the files to a disk mastering and duplication company. Costs for CD-ROM duplication are surprisingly low, especially when you consider how much information you can store on a CD-ROM (650MB). DVD-ROM pricing is a little more volatile, and expensive, but it will eventually be similar to that of CD-ROMs. And keep in mind that you can cram a whole lot more on a DVD-ROM, which can hold anywhere from 4.7GB (single sided, single layer) to 17.1GB (double sided, double layer).

> Web browser software is always necessary for reading HTML pages. However, these days almost everyone has a web browser, so you may not need to supply one with your web pages. If you do want to include a browser, you might consider Opera, which includes most of the basic features of Mozilla Firefox and Microsoft Internet Explorer but is small enough to fit on a single 1.44MB floppy disk or small memory card and can be freely distributed in the form of a 30-day evaluation version. (You can download Opera at http://www.operasoftware.com/.)
>
> Microsoft and Netscape are also often willing to allow their browsers to be included on CD-ROMs if you ask nicely in writing or pay them a licensing fee. Never give out copies of Microsoft software without written permission, because they aren't afraid to flex their enormous legal muscles to ensure that you obtain proper licensing.

Memory cards are certainly more expensive to give out to people than CD-ROMs or DVD-ROMs, but they are quite handy and their prices are rapidly falling. They are extremely flexible because you can read and write to them as many times as you want, and their compact size makes them very easy to carry around. Memory cards are available with various hardware interfaces, including USB, MMC (MultiMedia Card), SD (Secure Digital), and CompactFlash. The largest available memory cards are currently in the 32GB range but this number is steadily rising.

Testing Your Web Pages

Whenever you transfer web pages to an Internet site, an intranet server, a disk, or a memory card, you should immediately test every page thoroughly.

The following checklist will help make sure that everything on your pages behaves the way you expected:

1. Before you transfer the pages, follow all of these steps to test the pages while they're on your hard drive. After you transfer the pages to the master disk or web server, test them again—if your pages are on the Internet, consider testing through a 56Kbps modem connection to try them out under a minimal connection speed.

2. Do each of the following steps with the latest version of Mozilla Firefox, the latest Microsoft Internet Explorer, and at least one other browser such as Opera or Safari. Testing with an older version of Netscape Navigator or Internet Explorer isn't a bad idea either because many people still use outdated versions and some pages will appear differently.

3. If possible, use a computer with 800×600 resolution for testing purposes. If pages look good at this resolution, they'll probably look fine at larger resolutions too. (Additional testing at 1,024×768 or 1,600×1,200 resolution can't hurt.) I think we're finally to a point where you don't have to worry about testing at 640×480, because the number of people out there who are still using smaller low-res monitors is very small.

4. Turn off auto image loading in your web browser before you start testing so that you can see what each page looks like without the graphics. Check your `alt` tag messages and then turn image loading back on to load the graphics and review the page carefully again. Hour 8 explains how to place images on a page, along with how the `alt` tag works.

5. Use your browser's font size settings to look at each page in various font sizes, to ensure that your careful layout doesn't fall to pieces.

6. Start at the home page and systematically follow every link. (Use the Back button to return after each link, and then click the next link on the page.)

7. Wait for each page to completely finish loading, and scroll all the way down to make sure that all images appear where they should.

8. If you have a complex site, it may help to make a checklist of all the pages on your site to ensure that they all get tested.

9. Time how long it takes each page to load through a 56Kbps modem, preferably when connected through a different ISP than the one that runs the web server. Is the information on that page valuable enough to keep users from going elsewhere before the page finishes loading? Granted, broadband connections are getting much more common, but it's still a little too soon to ignore dial-up web users.

If your pages pass all those tests, you can be pretty certain that they'll look great to every Internet surfer in the world.

Summary

This hour gave you the basic knowledge you need in order to choose among the most common distribution methods for web pages. It also stepped you through the process of placing web pages on a web server computer by using commonly available file transfer software. Finally, it offered a checklist to help you thoroughly test your web pages after they are in place.

Q&A

Q *When I try to send pages to my web site from home, it works fine. When I try it from the computer at work, I get error messages. Any idea what the problem might be?*

A The company where you work probably has a *firewall*, which is a layer of security protecting their local network from tampering via the Internet. You need to set some special configuration options in your FTP program to help it get through the firewall when you send files. Your company's network administrator can help you with the details.

Q *I don't know which ISP to choose—there are so many!*

A Obviously, you should compare prices of the companies listed at http://thelist.internet.com. You should also ask for the names of some customers with sites about the same size you're planning on having; ask those customers (via email) how happy they are with the company's service and support. Also, make sure that your ISP has at least two major (T3 or bigger) connections to the Internet, preferably provided to them by two different network companies.

Q *All the tests you recommend would take longer than creating my pages! Can't I get away with less testing?*

A If your pages aren't intended to make money or provide an important service, it's probably not a big deal if they look funny to some people or produce errors once in a while. In that case, just test each page with a couple of different window and font sizes and call it a day. However, if you need to project a professional image, there is no substitute for rigorous testing.

Q *I wanted to name my site lizardlover.com but someone beat me to it. Is there anything I can do?*

A Well, if you operated a reptilian pet store and your company was named Lizard Lover, Inc., before the other party registered the domain name, you could always try contacting them and making your case. You could also sue them, but even if you don't have the budget to take on their legal army, you may still be able to register lizardlover.org, lizardlover.net, or possibly even lizardlover.biz (if you aren't scooped again). Also, many domain name registration companies allow you to backorder a name for a small fee, which means that the name is monitored and automatically registered for you if it ever is allowed to expire.

Workshop

The workshop contains quiz questions and activities to help you solidify your understanding of the material covered. Try to answer all questions before looking at the
"Answers" section that follows.

Quiz

1. How do you put a few web pages on a flash memory stick, CD-ROM, or DVD-ROM?

2. Suppose that your ISP tells you to put your pages in the default main directory
   at `ftp.bigisp.net`, that your username is `rastro`, and that your password is
   `rorry_relroy`. Where do you put all that information in CuteFTP so that you
   can get the files on the Internet?

3. What address would you enter in Internet Explorer to view the web pages you
   uploaded in question 2?

4. If the following web page is named `mypage.html`, which files would you need
   to transfer to the web server to put it on the Internet?

```
<html>
  <head>
    <title>My Page</title>
  </head>
  <body background="joy.gif">
    <img src="me.jpg" alt="It's me!" style="text-align:right" />
    <h1>My Web Page</h1>
    <p>Oh happy joy I have a page on the Web!</p>
    <a href="otherpage.html">Click here for my other page.</a>
  </body>
</html>
```

Answers

1. Just copy the directory structure with the HTML and image files from your
   hard drive to the memory card, CD, or DVD. Anyone can then insert the
   media in the appropriate place on his or her computer, start the web browser,
   and open the pages right from the card or disc.

2. Click the New button on the CuteFTP toolbar, and then enter the following
   information:

FIGURE 4.10

3. You can't tell from the information given in question 2. A good guess would be http://www.bigisp.net/~elroy/, but you might choose a completely different domain name, such as http://elroy-and-astro.com/.

4. You need to transfer all three of the following files into the same directory on the web server:

```
mypage.html
joy.gif
me.jpg
```

If you want the link on that page to work, you must also transfer this one, as well as any image files that are referred to in that HTML file:

```
otherpage.html
```

Exercises

Put your pages on the Internet already!

PART II

Building Practical Web Pages with HTML

Basic Text Alignment and Formatting

In the early days of the Web, text was displayed in only one font and in one size. If you've been around computers long enough to remember what it was like before mice and graphical operating systems entered the picture, you know what I'm talking about because text formatting in those days was limited to making sure that you pressed Enter to start a new paragraph! HTML makes it possible to control the appearance of text and how it is aligned and displayed on a web page. This hour starts off with the basics of text alignment and formatting, and eventually guides you through some advanced text tips and tricks. You'll learn to incorporate boldface, italics, superscripts, subscripts, underlining, and strikethrough text into your pages, as well as how to choose typefaces and font sizes.

Another important topic covered in this hour is lists, which provide a means of listing multiple items in HTML. Because lists are so common in web pages, HTML provides tags that automatically indent text and add numbers or bullets in front of each listed item. You'll find out in this hour how to format numbered and bulleted lists, not to mention definition lists, which can be used as a simple way to indent content on a page.

> **By the Way**
>
> There are two completely different approaches to controlling text formatting and alignment in HTML. The approach you'll study in this lesson conforms to the XHTML standard and involves a technology called CSS (Cascading Style Sheets). Even though you won't formally learn about CSS until Hour 12, "Formatting Web Pages with CSS Style Sheets," you'll find out just enough in this lesson to apply styles to text. There is an "old way" of formatting text that I mention briefly at the beginning of this lesson, but there is no sense in spending much time learning it because it is being phased out of HTML. Not only that, but CSS is considerably more powerful.

▼   **Try It Yourself**

You can make the most of this hour if you have some text that needs to be indented, centered, or otherwise manipulated visually in order to be more presentable:

- ▶ Any type of outline, bullet points from a presentation, numbered steps, glossary, or list of textual information from a database will serve as good material to work with.

- ▶ Any text will do, but try to find (or type) some text you want to put onto a web page. The text from a company brochure or from your personal résumé might be a good choice.

- ▶ If the text you'll be using is from a word processor or database program, be sure to save it to a new file in plain-text or ASCII format. You can then add the appropriate HTML tags and style attributes to format it as you go through this lesson.

- ▶ Add the <html>, <head>, <title>, and <body> tags (discussed in Hour 2, "Create a Web Page Right Now") before you use the code introduced in this chapter to format the body text.

▲

The Old Way Versus the New Way

In earlier versions of HTML, special tags were used to format text. For example, to format a word in a bold typeface, you would simply place it inside the <b> and </b> tags. Similarly, there was a <font> tag that could be used to specify a certain font, including its family and size, among other things. Although this system of formatting tags worked reasonably well for basic text formatting, it cluttered up the HTML language by making it difficult to distinguish between content and the code used to format content. It turned out to be bad design to use tags to mark up the information on a web page and the specifics of how that information is formatted.

The solution was to eliminate many of the formatting tags and use a separate technology for web page formatting. This technology is CSS, which stands for Cascading Style Sheets. The technology sounds a bit intimidating, but you're going to find out that it isn't difficult to use to format text. In fact, CSS lets you do a lot more interesting text formatting than you could have ever done with the old tag approach. Even so, it's important to clarify that not all the old tags were eliminated. For example, <b> and <i> are still supported and widely used to format text in bold and italics, respectively.

Although I prefer the style sheet alternatives to pretty much all presentation tags, you can't ignore the tags entirely. For this reason, this hour does double duty in showing both the tag approach and the style rule approach to basic text formatting. You'll dig much deeper into CSS style rules later in the book in Part III, "Creative Web Page Design." In this hour, the emphasis is on presenting you with the alternatives to text formatting when it comes to the old tag approach and the newer style rule approach.

Aligning Text on a Page

It's easy to take for granted the fact that most paragraphs are automatically aligned to the left when you're reading information on the Web. However, there are certainly situations in which you may choose to align content to the right or even the center of a page. HTML gives you the option to align a single HTML element, such as a paragraph of text, or entire sections of a page. Before we get into the details of these two alignment approaches, however, let's briefly recap how attributes work.

In Hour 3, "Linking to Other Web Pages," you briefly learned how attributes are used to provide additional information related to an HTML tag. Attributes are special code words used inside an HTML tag to control exactly what the tag does. They are very important in even the simplest of web pages, so it's important that you get comfortable using them. As an example, attributes are used to determine the alignment of paragraphs. When you begin a paragraph with the <p> tag, you can specify whether the text in that paragraph should be aligned to the left margin, right margin, or center of the page by setting the style attribute.

> The style attribute is actually used for just about all HTML formatting, as you'll learn throughout this lesson and the remainder of the book.

By the Way

Aligning a Paragraph

To align a paragraph to the right margin, you place style="text-align:right" inside the <p> tag at the beginning of the paragraph. To center a paragraph, use <p style="text-align:center">. Similarly, the tag to align a paragraph to the left is <p style="text-align:left">. (For the record, this last alignment setting is seldom used because paragraphs are always aligned to the left by default when you use plain old <p>.) The text-align part of the style attribute is referred to as a *style rule*, which means that it is setting a particular style aspect of an HTML element. There are many style rules you can use to carefully control the formatting of web page content.

Every attribute and style rule in HTML has a default value that is assumed if you don't set the attribute yourself. In the case of the `text-align` style rule of the `<p>` tag, the default value is `left`, so using the bare-bones `<p>` tag has the same effect as using `<p style="text-align:left">`. Learning the default values for common style rules is an important part of becoming a good web page developer.

The `text-align` style rule is not reserved for just the `<p>` tag. In fact, you can use the `text-align` style rule with just about any HTML tag that contains text, including `<h1>`, `<h2>`, the other heading tags, and some tags you will meet later. There are many other style rules besides `text-align`. You will find out how to use them as you learn more HTML tags.

According to the official HTML standard, it doesn't matter whether tags and attributes are in uppercase or lowercase letters. However, the more exacting XHTML standard requires tags and attributes to be lowercase, so it's important to make all of your code lowercase to adhere to XHTML. The XHTML standard also requires quotation marks around attribute values.

For example, the following code is technically acceptable in most popular web browsers:

```
<P STYLE=TEXT-ALIGN:CENTER>
```

However, this code does not conform to the latest standards for how web pages should be designed because it is in uppercase and the `style` attribute value `text-align:center` isn't in quotes. If you want to stay compatible with upcoming standards and software, you should always use the following instead:

```
<p style="text-align:center">
```

Keep in mind that sometimes the same style rule can have different meanings when used with different tags. For instance, you will discover in Hour 8, "Putting Graphics on a Web Page," that `style="text-align:left"` does something quite different when used with the `<img>` image tag than it does when used with the text tags discussed in this hour.

It's worth pointing out that prior to CSS style rules, HTML content was aligned using a special tag named `<align>`. The `<align>` tag functioned much like the `text-align` style rule, but it was eliminated from XHTML by the W3C. It still works in most browsers but you're discouraged from using it.

Aligning an Entire Section of a Page

When you want to set the alignment of more than one paragraph or heading at a time, you can use the text-align style rule with the <div>, or *division*, tag. By itself, <div>, and its corresponding closing </div> tag, actually doesn't do anything at all—which would seem to make it a peculiarly useless tag!

Yet if you include a text-align style rule, <div> becomes quite useful indeed. Everything you put between <div style="text-align:center"> and </div>, for example, is centered. This may include lines of text, paragraphs, headings, images, and all the other things you'll learn how to put on web pages in upcoming lessons. Likewise, <div style="text-align:right"> will right-align everything down to the next </div> tag.

> Later in the book you'll find out that the <div> tag is also useful as a means of organizing text for applying special formatting styles.

By the Way

Listing 5.1 demonstrates the style attribute and text-align style rule with both the <p> and the <div> tags. The results are shown in Figure 5.1. You'll learn many more advanced uses of the <div> tag in Part III.

LISTING 5.1 The text-align Style Rule Used with the style Attribute

```
<?xml version="1.0" encoding="UTF-8"?>
<!DOCTYPE html PUBLIC "-//W3C//DTD XHTML 1.1//EN"
  "http://www.w3.org/TR/xhtml11/DTD/xhtml11.dtd">

<html xmlns="http://www.w3.org/1999/xhtml" xml:lang="en">
  <head>
    <title>Bohemia</title>
  </head>

  <body>
    <div style="text-align:center">
      <h1>Bohemia</h1>
      <h3>by Dorothy Parker</h3>
    </div>
    <p style="text-align:left">
      Authors and actors and artists and such<br />
      Never know nothing, and never know much.<br />
      Sculptors and singers and those of their kidney<br />
      Tell their affairs from Seattle to Sydney.
    </p>
    <p style="text-align:center">
      Playwrights and poets and such horses' necks<br />
      Start off from anywhere, end up at sex.<br />
      Diarists, critics, and similar roe<br />
      Never say nothing, and never say no.
    </p>
```

LISTING 5.1   Continued

```
  <p style="text-align:right">
    People Who Do Things exceed my endurance;<br />
    God, for a man that solicits insurance!
  </p>
 </body>
</html>
```

FIGURE 5.1
The alignment
settings in
Listing 5.1, as
they appear in a
web browser.

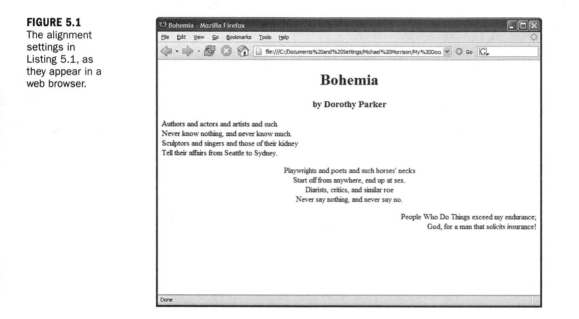

The Three Types of HTML Lists

It's often useful to present information on a web page as a list of items. There are three basic types of HTML lists. All three are shown in Figure 5.2, and Listing 5.2 reveals the HTML to construct them:

- ▶ The numbered list is called an ordered list. It begins with the `<ol>` tag and ends with a closing `</ol>` tag. Numbers and line breaks appear automatically at each `<li>` tag, and the entire list is indented.

- ▶ The bulleted list is called an unordered list. It opens with the `<ul>` tag and closes with `</ul>`. It looks just like an ordered list, except that bullets appear at each `<li>` tag instead of numbers. The "li" in the `<li>` tag stands for "list item."

- ▶ The list of terms and their meanings is called a definition list. It starts with the `<dl>` and ends with `</dl>`. The `<dt>` tag goes in front of each term to be defined, with a <dd> tag in front of each definition. Line breaks and indentations appear automatically.

▶ Ordered lists are indented lists that have numbers or letters in front of each item.

▶ Unordered lists are indented lists with a special bullet symbol in front of each item.

▶ Definition lists are indented lists without any number or symbol in front of each item.

LISTING 5.2   Unordered Lists, Ordered Lists, and Definition Lists

```
<?xml version="1.0" encoding="UTF-8"?>
<!DOCTYPE html PUBLIC "-//W3C//DTD XHTML 1.1//EN"
  "http://www.w3.org/TR/xhtml11/DTD/xhtml11.dtd">

<html xmlns="http://www.w3.org/1999/xhtml" xml:lang="en">
  <head>
    <title>How to be Proper</title>
  </head>

  <body>
    <p>
      Basic Etiquette for a Gentlemen Greeting a Lady Aquaintance
    </p>
    <ul>
      <li>Wait for her acknowledging bow before tipping your hat.</li>
      <li>Use the hand farthest from her to raise the hat.</li>
      <li>Walk with her if she expresses a wish to converse; Never
      make a lady stand talking in the street.</li>
      <li>When walking, the lady must always have the wall.</li>
    </ul>
    <p>
      Recourse for a Lady Toward Unpleasant Men Who Persist in Bowing
    </p>
    <ol>
      <li>A simple stare of iciness should suffice in most instances.</li>
      <li>A cold bow discourages familiarity without offering insult.</li>
      <li>As a last resort: "Sir, I have not the honour of your
      aquaintance."</li>
    </ol>
    <p>
      Proper Address of Royalty
    </p>
    <dl>
      <dt>Your Majesty</dt>
      <dd>To the king or queen.</dd>
      <dt>Your Royal Highness</dt>
      <dd>To the monarch's spouse, children, and siblings.</dd>
      <dt>Your Highness</dt>
      <dd>To nephews, nieces, and cousins of the sovereign.</dd>
    </dl>
  </body>
</html>
```

Basic Etiquette for a Gentlemen Greeting a Lady Aquaintance

- Wait for her acknowledging bow before tipping your hat.
- Use the hand farthest from her to raise the hat.
- Walk with her if she expresses a wish to converse; Never make a lady stand talking in the street.
- When walking, the lady must always have the wall.

Recourse for a Lady Toward Unpleasant Men Who Persist in Bowing

1. A simple stare of iciness should suffice in most instances.
2. A cold bow discourages familiarity without offering insult.
3. As a last resort: "Sir, I have not the honour of your aquaintance."

Proper Address of Royalty

Your Majesty
    To the king or queen.
Your Royal Highness
    To the monarch's spouse, children, and siblings.
Your Highness
    To nephews, nieces, and cousins of the sovereign.

> Remember that different web browsers can display web pages quite differently.
> The HTML standard doesn't specify exactly how web browsers should format lists,
> so people using older web browsers may not see the same indentation you see.
> Software of the future may also format HTML lists differently, though all current
> web browsers now display lists in almost exactly the same way.

Placing Lists Within Lists

Although definition lists are officially supposed to be used for defining terms, many
web page authors use them anywhere they'd like to see some indentation. In practice, you can indent any text simply by putting <dl><dd> at the beginning of it and
</dd></dl> at the end. However, a better approach to indenting text is to use the
<blockquote> tag, which indents content without the presumption of a definition.

You can indent items further by *nesting* one list inside another, like the following:

```
<dl>
  <dd>this item will be indented</dd>
  <dl>
    <dd>this will be indented further</dd>
    <dl>
      <dl>
        <dd>and this will be indented very far indeed</dd>
      </dl>
    </dl>
  </dl>
</dl>
```

> Nesting refers to a tag that appears entirely within another tag, such as the <dd> tag appearing within the <dl> tag in the preceding example. Nested tags are also referred to as child tags of the (parent) tag that contains them. It is a common (but not required) coding practice to indent nested tags so that you can easily see their relationship to the parent tag.

By the Way

Just make sure that you always have the same number of closing </dl> tags as opening <dl> tags. Indenting your code so that the opening and closing tags are aligned can help make sure that you have the correct number of matched tags definition lists.

Ordered and unordered lists can also be nested inside one another, down to as many levels as you want. In Listing 5.3, a complex indented outline is constructed from several unordered lists. You'll notice in Figure 5.3 that Firefox automatically uses a different type of bullet for each of the first three levels of indentation, making the list very easy to read.

LISTING 5.3   Using Lists to Build Outlines

```
<?xml version="1.0" encoding="UTF-8"?>
<!DOCTYPE html PUBLIC "-//W3C//DTD XHTML 1.1//EN"
  "http://www.w3.org/TR/xhtml11/DTD/xhtml11.dtd">

<html xmlns="http://www.w3.org/1999/xhtml" xml:lang="en">
  <head>
    <title>Vertebrates</title>
  </head>

  <body>
    <h2>Vertebrates</h2>
    <ul>
      <li>
        Fish
        <ul>
          <li>Barramundi</li>
          <li>Kissing Gourami</li>
          <li>Mummichog</li>
        </ul>
      </li>
      <li>
        Amphibians
        <ul>
          <li>
            Anura
            <ul>
              <li>Goliath Frog</li>
              <li>Poison Dart Frog</li>
              <li>Purple Frog</li>
            </ul>
          </li>
          <li>
            Caudata
            <ul>
```

LISTING 5.3   Continued

```
                  <li>Hellbender</li>
                  <li>Mudpuppy</li>
               </ul>
            </li>
          </ul>
        </li>
        <li>
          Reptiles
          <ul>
            <li>Nile Crocodile</li>
            <li>King Cobra</li>
            <li>Common Snapping Turtle</li>
          </ul>
        </li>
      </ul>
    </body>
</html>
```

FIGURE 5.3
Multilevel
unordered lists
are neatly
indented and
bulleted for
readability.

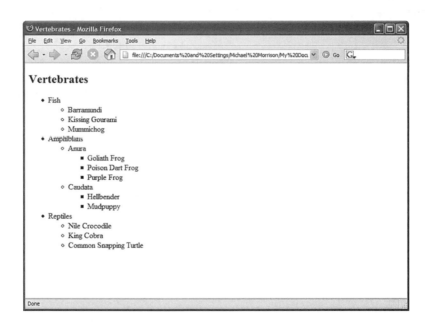

As definition lists shown in Figure 5.3, a web browser will normally use a solid disc for the first-level bullet, a hollow circle for the second-level bullet, and a solid square for all deeper levels. However, you can explicitly choose which type of bullet to use for any level by using <ul style="list-style-type:disc">, <ul style="list-style-type:circle">, or <ul style="list-style-type:square"> instead of <ul>.

You can even change the bullet for any single point within an unordered list by using the list-style-type style rule in the <li> tag. For example, the following would display a hollow circle in front of the words extra and super, but a solid square in front of the word special:

```
<ul style="list-style-type:circle">
  <li>extra</li>
  <li>super</li>
  <li style="list-style-type:square">special</li>
</ul>
```

The list-style-type style rule also works with ordered lists, but instead of choosing a type of bullet, you choose the type of numbers or letters to place in front of each item. Listing 5.4 shows how to use Roman numerals (list-style-type:upper-roman), capital letters (list-style-type:upper-alpha), and lowercase letters (list-style-type:lower-alpha) along with ordinary numbers in a multi-level list. In Figure 5.4, you can see the resulting nicely formatted outline.

Although Listing 5.4 uses the list-style-type style rule only with the <ol> tag, you can also use it for specific <li> tags within a list (though it's hard to imagine a situation in which you would want to). You can also explicitly specify ordinary numbering with list-style-type:decimal, and you can make lowercase Roman numerals with list-style-type:lower-roman.

LISTING 5.4   Using the list-style-type Style Rule with the style Attribute in Multitiered Lists

```
<?xml version="1.0" encoding="UTF-8"?>
<!DOCTYPE html PUBLIC "-//W3C//DTD XHTML 1.1//EN"
  "http://www.w3.org/TR/xhtml11/DTD/xhtml11.dtd">

<html xmlns="http://www.w3.org/1999/xhtml" xml:lang="en">
  <head>
    <title>Advice from the Golf Guru</title>
  </head>

  <body>
    <h2>How to Win at Golf</h2>
    <ol style="list-style-type:upper-roman">
      <li>Training
        <ol>
          <li>Mental prep
            <ol style="list-style-type:upper-alpha">
              <li>Watch PGA on TV religiously</li>
              <li>Get that computer game with Jack whatsisname</li>
              <li>Rent "personal victory" subliminal tapes</li>
            </ol>
          </li>
          <li>Equipage
            <ol style="list-style-type:upper-alpha">
              <li>Make sure your putter has a pro autograph on it</li>
```

LISTING 5.4   Continued

```
            <li>Pick up a bargain bag of tees-n-balls at Costco</li>
          </ol>
        </li>
        <li>Diet
          <ol style="list-style-type:upper-alpha">
            <li>Avoid baseball or football food
              <ol style="list-style-type:lower-alpha">
                <li>No hotdogs</li>
                <li>No pretzels</li>
                <li>No peanuts and Crackerjacks</li>
              </ol>
            </li>
            <li>Drink cheap white wine only, no beer</li>
          </ol>
        </li>
      </ol>
    </li>
    <li>Pre-game
      <ol>
        <li>Dress
          <ol style="list-style-type:upper-alpha">
            <li>Put on shorts, even if it's freezing</li>
            <li>Buy a new hat if you lost last time</li>
          </ol> definition lists
        </li>
        <li>Location and Scheduling
          <ol style="list-style-type:upper-alpha">
            <li>Select a course where your spouse won't find you</li>
            <li>To save on fees, play where your buddy works</li>
          </ol>
        </li>
        <li>Opponent
          <ol style="list-style-type:upper-alpha">
            <li>Look for: overconfidence, inexperience</li>
            <li>Shun: suntan, stethoscope, strident walk, Florida accent</li>
            <li>Buy opponent as many pre-game drinks as possible</li>
          </ol>
        </li>
      </ol>
    </li>
    <li>On the Course
      <ol>
        <li>Tee first, then develop severe hayfever</li>
        <li>Drive cart over opponent's ball to degrade aerodynamics</li>
        <li>Say "fore" just before ball makes contact with opponent</li>
        <li>Always replace divots when putting</li>
        <li>Water cooler holes are a good time to correct any errors in ball
          placement</li>
        <li>Never record strokes taken when opponent is urinating</li>
      </ol>
    </li>
  </ol>
 </body>
</html> definition lists
```

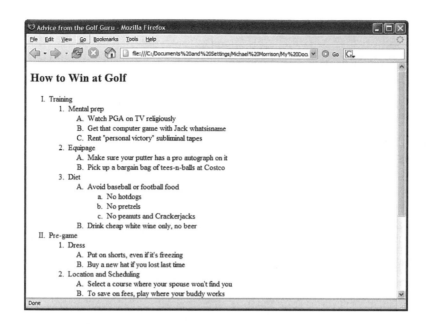

FIGURE 5.4
A well-formatted outline can make almost any plan look more plausible.

By combining ordered, unordered, and definition lists within one another, you can organize the most complex information in a readable and attractive way. To get your creative juices flowing, I've created a list of lists for you to browse through before you begin organizing your own HTML lists.

To check it out, go to the *Sams Publishing* website at http://www.samspublishing.com/.

By the Way

Boldface, Italics, and Special Text Formatting

Way back in the age of the typewriter, we were content with plain-text and an occasional underline for emphasis. Today, **boldface** and *italic* text have become de rigueur in all paper communication. Naturally, you can add bold and italic text to your web pages too. There are several tags and style rules that make text formatting possible.

The tried-and-true approach to adding bold and italic formatting to text involves the <b> and <i> tags. For boldface text, you put the <b> tag at the beginning of the text and </b> at the end. Similarly, you can make any text italic by enclosing it between <i> and </i>. Although this approach still works fine in browsers and is supported by XHTML, it isn't as flexible or powerful as the newer CSS style rule approach to text formatting.

You can *nest* one type of formatting inside another. For instance, if you want some text to be both bold and italic, put <b><i> in front of it and </i></b> after it. To avoid confusing some web browsers, be careful to close the tags in the opposite order in which you opened them in. For example, don't do this:

```
<b>Bold, <i>bold and elegant,</b> or just plain elegant.</i>
```

Instead, do it this way:

```
<b>Bold, <i>bold and elegant,</i></b><i>or just plain elegant.</i>
```

Although you'll learn much more about CSS style rules in Part III, it's worth a little foreshadowing just so you understand the text formatting options. The font-weight style rule allows you to set the weight, or boldness, of a font using a style rule. Standard settings include normal, bold, bolder, and lighter, with normal being the default. Italic text is controlled via the font-style rule, which can be set to normal, italic, or oblique. Style rules can be specified together if you want to apply more than one, as the following example demonstrates:

```
<p style="font-weight:bold; font-style:italic">This paragraph is bold and
italic!</p>
```

In this example, both style rules are specified in the style attribute of the <p> tag. The key to using multiple style rules is that they must be separated by a semicolon (;).

You aren't limited to using font styles in paragraphs, however. The following code shows how to italicize text in a bulleted list:

```
<ul>
  <li style="font-style:italic">Important Stuff</li>
  <li style="font-style:italic">Critical Information</li>
  <li style="font-style:italic">Highly Sensitive Material</li>
  <li>Nothing All That Useful</li>
</ul>
```

Getting back to the traditional <b> and <i> tags, you can code the same bulleted list with those tags instead of using a style rule. You should always close any <b>, <i>, or other formatting tags that occur within an <li> list item or heading before you end the </li>. Most of the <i> and </i> tags in the following list may seem redundant, but adhering to this good form ensures that your pages fully meet the new XHTML standards, which may save you from having to rewrite them in the future:

```
<ul>
  <li><i>Important Stuff</i></li>
  <li><i>Critical Information</i></li>
  <li><i>Highly Sensitive Material</i></li>
  <li>Nothing All That Useful</li>
</ul>
```

You can also use the <b> tag and font-weight style rule within headings, but a heavier font usually doesn't have an effect on headings because they are already bold.

An alternative to style rules when it comes to bold and italic text involves the <strong> and <em> tags. The <strong> tag does the same thing as the <b> tag in most browsers, whereas the <em> tag acts just like the tag <i> by formatting text as italics.

The <strong> and <em> tags are considered by some to be an improvement over <b> and <i> because they imply only that the text should receive special emphasis, rather than dictating exactly how that effect should be achieved. In other words, a browser doesn't necessarily have to interpret <strong> as meaning bold or <em> as meaning italic. This makes <strong> and <em> more fitting in XHTML because they add meaning to text, along with affecting how the text should be displayed. Even so, as long as the <b> and <i> tags are still fully supported, which they are, you shouldn't have any problem using them.

By the Way

In addition to <b>, <i>, <strong>, and <em>, there are several other HTML tags for adding special formatting to text. Table 5.1 summarizes all of them (including the boldface and italic tags), and Listing 5.5 and Figure 5.5 demonstrate each of them in action.

TABLE 5.1   HTML Tags That Add Special Formatting to Text

Tag	Function
<small>	Small text
<big>	Big text
<sup>	Superscript text
<sub>	Subscript text
<em> or <i>	Emphasized (italic) text
<strong> or <b>	Strong (boldface) text
<tt>	Monospaced text (typewriter font)
<pre>	Monospaced text, preserving spaces and line breaks

Watch
Out!

There used to be a <u> tag for creating underlined text, but there are a couple of reasons not to use it now. First off, people expect underlined text to be a link, and may get confused if you underline text that isn't a link. Secondly, the <u> tag is *deprecated*, which means that it has been phased out of the HTML/XHTML language. Along with the <strike> tag for creating strikethrough text, the <u> tag is still supported in web browsers and likely will be for quite a while, but the preferred approach to creating underlined and strikethrough text is style sheets. These topics are covered in more detail in Hour 12, "Formatting Web Pages with CSS Style Sheets," and Hour 13, "Digging Deeper into Style Sheet Formatting."

LISTING 5.5   Special Formatting Tags

```
<?xml version="1.0" encoding="UTF-8"?>
<!DOCTYPE html PUBLIC "-//W3C//DTD XHTML 1.1//EN"
  "http://www.w3.org/TR/xhtml11/DTD/xhtml11.dtd">

<html xmlns="http://www.w3.org/1999/xhtml" xml:lang="en">
  <head>
    <title>The Miracle Product</title>
  </head>

  <body>
    <p>
      New <sup>Super</sup><strong>Strength</strong> H<sub>2</sub>O
      <em>plus</em> will knock out any stain, <big>big</big> or
      <small>small</small>.<br /> Look for new
      <sup>Super</sup><b>Strength</b> H<sub>2</sub>O <i>plus</i>
      in a stream near you.
    </p>
    <p>
      <tt>NUTRITION INFORMATION</tt> (void where prohibited)
    </p>
    <pre>
                Calories   Grams    USRDA
                /Serving   of Fat   Moisture
Regular           3          4       100%
Unleaded          3          2       100%
Organic           2          3        99%
Sugar Free        0          1       110%
    </pre>
  </body>
</html>
```

The <tt> tag usually changes the typeface to Courier New, a monospaced font. (*Monospaced* means that all the letters and spaces are the same width.) However, web browsers let users change the monospaced <tt> font to the typeface of their choice (under Tools, Internet Options, Fonts in Microsoft Internet Explorer, and under ToolsToolsToo, Options, General, Fonts & Colors in Mozilla Firefox). The monospaced font may not even be monospaced for some users, though the vast majority of people stick with the standard fonts that their browsers come set up with.

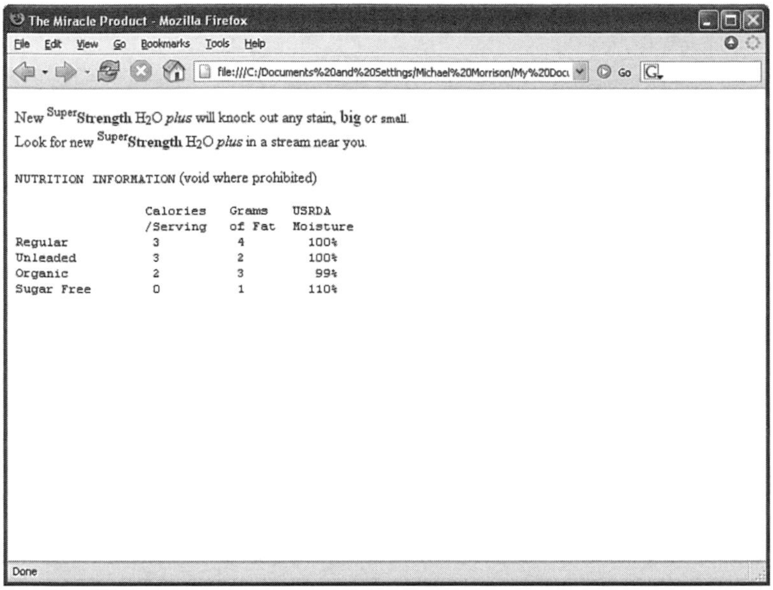

FIGURE 5.5
Here's what all the character formatting from Listing 5.5 looks like.

The <pre> tag causes text to appear in the monospaced font, but it also does something else unique and useful. As you learned in Hour 2, multiple spaces and line breaks are normally ignored in HTML files, but <pre> causes exact spacing and line breaks to be preserved. For example, without <pre>, the text at the end of Figure 5.5 would look like the following:

```
calories grams usrda /serving of fat moisture regular
3 4 100% unleaded 3 2 100% organic 2 3 99% sugar free 0 1 110%
```

Even if you added <br /> tags at the end of every line, the columns wouldn't line up properly. However, when you put <pre> at the beginning and </pre> at the end, the columns line up properly because the exact spaces are kept—no <br /> tags are needed.

There are fancier ways to make columns of text line up, and you'll learn all about them in Part III. The <pre> tag gives you a quick and easy way to preserve the alignment of any monospaced text files you might want to transfer to a web page with a minimum of effort.

By the Way

You can use the <pre> tag as a quick way to insert extra vertical space between paragraphs. For example, to put several blank lines between the words up and down, you could type this:

```
up<pre>
</pre>down
```

Tweaking the Font

The <big>, <small>, and <tt> tags give you some rudimentary control over the size and appearance of the text on your pages. However, there may be times when you'd just like a bit more control over the size and appearance of your text. Before I get into the appropriate way to tinker with the font in XHTML code, let's briefly take a look at how things were done prior to CSS.

Before style sheets entered the picture, the now phased-out <font> tag was used to control the fonts in web page text. For example, the following HTML will change the size and color of some text on a page:

```
<font size="5" color="purple">this text will be big and purple.</font>
```

As you can see, the size and color attributes of the <font> tag made it possible to alter the font of the text without too much effort. Although this approach worked fine, it was replaced with a far superior approach to font formatting thanks to CSS style rules. Following are a few of the main style rules used to control fonts:

▶ font-family—Sets the family (typeface) of the font.

▶ font-size—Sets the size of the font.

▶ color—Sets the color of the font.

By the Way

> You'll learn more about controlling the color of the text on your pages in Hour 9, "Custom Backgrounds and Colors." That lesson also shows you how to create your own custom colors and control the color of text links.

The font-family style rule allows you to set the typeface used to display text. You can and usually should specify more than one value for this style (separated by commas) so that if the first font isn't available on a user's system, the browser can try an alternative. This is important because every user potentially has a different set of fonts installed, at least beyond a core set of common basic fonts (Arial, Times, and so forth). By providing a list of alternative fonts, you have a better chance of your pages gracefully falling back on a known font if your ideal font isn't found. Following is an example of the font-family style used to set the typeface for a paragraph of text:

```
<p style="font-family:arial, sans-serif, 'times roman'">
```

There are several interesting things about this example. First off, arial is specified as the primary font. Case doesn't matter when specifying the font family, so arial is no different from Arial or ARIAL. Another interesting thing about this code is how single quotes are used around the times roman font name because it has a space in it.

The font-size and color style rules are also commonly used to control the size and color of fonts. The font-size style can be set to a predefined size such as small, medium, or large, or you can set it to a specific point size such as 12pt or 14pt. The color style can be set to a predefined color such as white, black, blue, red, or green, or you can set it to a specific hexadecimal color such as #FFB499. Following is the previous paragraph example with the font size and color specified:

```
<p style="font-family:arial, sans-serif, 'times roman'; font-size:14pt;
color:green">
```

> You'll find out what in the world a hexadecimal color is in Hour 9. For now, just understand that it allows you to specify exact colors beyond just saying green, blue, orange, and so forth.

By the Way

The web page given in Listing 5.6 and shown in Figure 5.6 uses these font style rules to improve on one of the earlier hockey-player examples and provide some text formatting. The name and jersey number of the player are displayed in a more exacting font that actually still resembles the original <h1> tag. More important, the remaining player information is displayed in navy blue with the description of each piece of information in bold.

LISTING 5.6 The Hockey Player Sample Page Is Improved with Font Style Rules

```
<?xml version="1.0" encoding="UTF-8"?>
<!DOCTYPE html PUBLIC "-//W3C//DTD XHTML 1.1//EN"
  "http://www.w3.org/TR/xhtml11/DTD/xhtml11.dtd">

<html xmlns="http://www.w3.org/1999/xhtml" xml:lang="en">
  <head>
    <title>Music City Mafia - Terry Lancaster</title>
  </head>

  <body>
    <p style="font-family:verdana, arial; font-size:18pt; font-weight:bold">16
    - Terry Lancaster</p>
    <p style="font-family:verdana, arial; font-size:12pt; color:navy">
      <img src="tlancaster.jpg" alt="Terry &quot;Big T&quot; Lancaster" /><br />
      <span style="font-weight:bold">Nickname:</span> Big T<br />
      <span style="font-weight:bold">Position:</span> RW<br />
      <span style="font-weight:bold">Height:</span> 6'3"<br />
      <span style="font-weight:bold">Weight:</span> 195<br />
      <span style="font-weight:bold">Shoots:</span> Left<br />
      <span style="font-weight:bold">Age:</span> 40<br />
      <span style="font-weight:bold">Birthplace:</span> Nashville, TN
```

LISTING 5.6   Continued

```
    </p>
    <hr />
    <p style="font-family:verdana, arial; font-size:12pt; color:navy">
      <span style="font-weight:bold">Favorite NHL Player:</span> Brett
      Hull<br />
      <span style="font-weight:bold">Favorite NHL Team:</span> Nashville
      Predators<br />
      <span style="font-weight:bold">Favorite Southern Fixin:</span> Skillet
      Fried Potatoes<br />
      <span style="font-weight:bold">Favorite Meat and Three:</span>
      Swett's<br />
      <span style="font-weight:bold">Favorite Country Star:</span>
      Patsy Cline<br />
      <span style="font-weight:bold">Favorite Mafia Moment:</span> "Chet
      finishing a game with his eyelid completely
      slashed through."
    </p>
  </body>
</html>
```

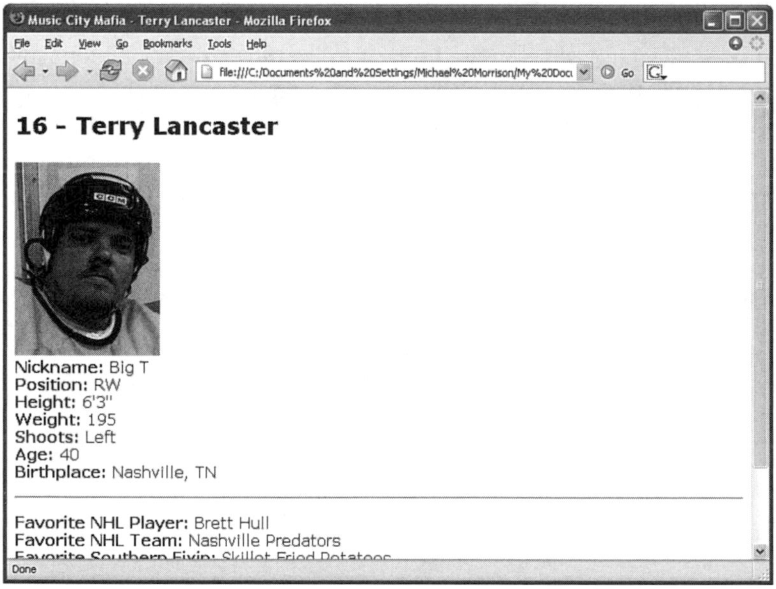

FIGURE 5.6
If you have the Verdana font installed on your computer, it will be used to display the page listed in Listing 5.6.

> You may be wondering about the <span> tag that is used repeatedly throughout this sample code. This tag allows you to apply a set of styles to an inline piece of content, which means that you can isolate individual words or sentences within a paragraph, as opposed to styling a whole block of text using a <div> or <p> tag. You'll learn more about the <span> tag in Hour 12. For now, just understand that it allows you to isolate a chunk of text and apply a font to it.

By the Way

Following is the code to set the typeface used for the player's name and jersey number text in Listing 5.6:

```
<p style="font-family: verdana, arial; font-size:18pt; font-weight:bold">
```

If your web browser can find a font named Verdana on a user's system, that font is used. Otherwise, the browser will look for Arial. Figure 5.7 shows how the page would look on a computer that didn't have Verdana installed but did have the Arial font. If neither of those fonts can be found, the browser will display the text using the default font (usually Times New Roman).

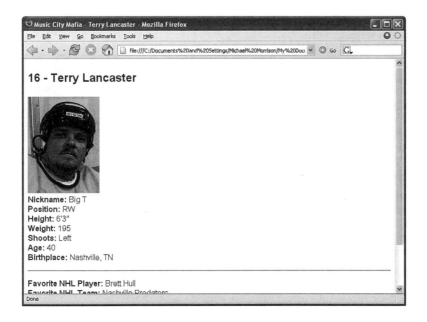

FIGURE 5.7
If you don't have the Verdana font installed, the text from Listing 5.6 appears in Arial or Times New Roman.

Because only fonts that each user has on his system show up, you have no real control over which fonts appear on your pages. Furthermore, the exact spelling of the font names is important, and many common fonts go by several slightly different names. This means that the only absolutely reliable choices beyond Times New Roman are Arial (on Windows machines) and Helvetica (on Macintosh machines). Don't be afraid to specify other fonts, but make sure that your pages look acceptable in Times New Roman as well.

To see a list of the most common fonts used on the Web, and to find out which of them are installed on your computer, visit *Sams Publishing* at http://www.samspublishing.com/.

By the Way

Working with Special Characters

Most fonts now include special characters for European languages, such as the accented *é* in *Café*. There are also a few mathematical symbols and special punctuation marks such as the circular • bullet.

You can insert these special characters at any point in an HTML document by looking up the appropriate codes in Table 5.2. You'll find an even more extensive list of codes for multiple character sets online at http://www.webstandards.org/learn/reference/named_entities.html.

For example, the word *café* would look like this:

```
caf&#233;
```

HTML/XHTML uses a special code known as a *character entity* to represent special characters such as © and ®. Character entities are always specified starting with a & and ending with a ;. Table 5.2 lists the most commonly used character entities, although HTML supports many more.

> Looking for the copyright © and registered trademark ® symbols? The codes you need are © and ® respectively.
>
> To create an unregistered trademark ™ symbol, use ^{tm}, or <small>^{tm}</small> for a smaller version.

Although you can specify character entities by number, each symbol also has a mnemonic name that is often easier to remember. Here is another way to write *café*:

```
caf&eacute;
```

Notice that there are also codes for the angle brackets, quotation, and ampersand in Table 5.2. You need to use the codes if you want these symbols to appear on your pages; otherwise, the web browser interprets them as HTML commands.

In Listing 5.7 and Figure 5.8, several of the symbols from Table 5.2 are shown in use.

LISTING 5.7   Special Character Codes

```
<?xml version="1.0" encoding="UTF-8"?>
<!DOCTYPE html PUBLIC "-//W3C//DTD XHTML 1.1//EN"
  "http://www.w3.org/TR/xhtml11/DTD/xhtml11.dtd">

<html xmlns="http://www.w3.org/1999/xhtml" xml:lang="en">
  <head>
    <title>Punctuation Lines</title>
  </head>
```

LISTING 5.7 Continued

```
<body>
  <p>
    Q: What should you do when a British banker picks a fight with you?<br />
    A: &pound; some &cent;&cent; into him.
    <hr />
    Q: What do you call it when a judge takes part of a law off the
    books?<br />
    A: &sect; violence.
    <hr />
    Q: What did the football coach get from the locker room vending machine
    in the middle of the game?<br />
    A: A &frac14; back at &frac12; time.
    <hr />
    Q: How hot did it get when the police detective interrogated the
    mathematician?<br />
    A: x&sup3;&deg;
    <hr />
    Q: What does a punctilious plagiarist do?<br />
    A: &copy;
    <hr />
  </p>
</body>
</html>
```

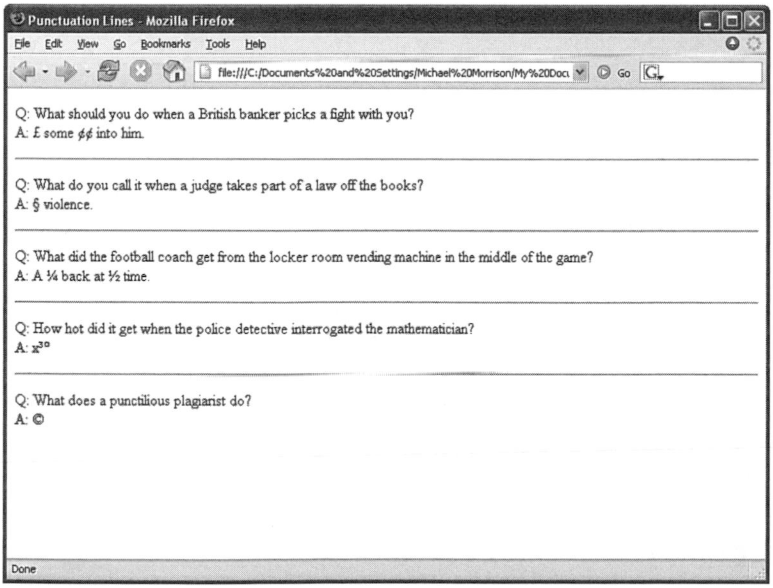

FIGURE 5.8
This is how the HTML page in Listing 5.7 will look in most web browsers.

TABLE 5.2   Commonly Used English Language Special Characters

Character	Numeric Code	Code Name	Description
"	&#34;	&quot;	Quotation mark
&	&#38;	&amp;	Ampersand
<	&#60;	&lt;	Less than
>	&#62;	&gt;	Greater than
¢	&#162;	&cent;	Cent sign
£	&#163;	&pound;	Pound sterling
¦	&#166;	¦ or &brkbar;	Broken vertical bar
§	&#167;	&sect;	Section sign
©	&#169;	&copy;	Copyright
®	&#174;	&reg;	Registered trademark
°	&#176;	&deg;	Degree sign
±	&#177;	&plusmn;	Plus or minus
^{2}	&#178;	&sup2;	Superscript two
^{3}	&#179;	&sup3;	Superscript three
·	&#183;	&middot;	Middle dot
^{1}	&#185;	&sup1;	Superscript one
¼	&#188;	&frac14;	Fraction one-fourth
½	&#189;	&frac12;	Fraction one-half
¾	&#190;	&frac34;	Fraction three-fourths
Æ	&#198;	&AElig;	Capital AE ligature
æ	&#230;	&aelig;	Small ae ligature
É	&#201;	&Eacute;	Accented capital E
é	&#233;	&eacute;	Accented small e
×	&#215;	&times;	Multiplication sign
÷	&#247;	&divide;	Division sign

Summary

In this hour you learned that attributes are used to specify options and special behavior of many HTML tags, and you also learned to use the style attribute with CSS style rules to center or right-justify text. You also found out how to create and combine three basic types of HTML list: ordered lists, unordered lists, and definition lists. Lists can be placed within other lists to create outlines and other complex arrangements of text.

This hour also showed you how to make text appear as boldface or italic, or with superscripts, subscripts, underlines, special symbols, and accented letters. You saw how to make everything line up properly in preformatted passages of monospaced text and how to control the size, color, and typeface of any section of text on a web page.

Table 5.3 summarizes the tags and attributes discussed in this hour. Don't feel like you have to memorize all these tags, by the way! That's why you have this book: You can look up the tags when you need them. Remember that all the HTML tags are listed in Appendix C, "Complete XHTML 1.1 and CSS 2 Quick Reference."

TABLE 5.3 HTML Tags and Attributes Covered in Hour 5

Tag/Attribute	Function
`<em>...</em>`	Emphasis (usually italic).
`<strong>...</strong>`	Stronger emphasis (usually bold).
`<b>...</b>`	Boldface text.
`<i>...</i>`	Italic text.
`<tt>...</tt>`	Typewriter (monospaced) font.
`<pre>...</pre>`	Preformatted text (exact line endings and spacing will be preserved—usually rendered in a monospaced font).
`<big>...</big>`	Text is slightly larger than normal.
`<small>...</small>`	Text is slightly smaller than normal.
`<sub>...</sub>`	Subscript.
`<sup>...</sup>`	Superscript.
`<div>...</div>`	A region of text to be formatted.
Attributes	
`style="text-align:alignment"`	Align text to center, left, or right. (Can also be used with `<p>`, `<h1>`, `<h2>`, `<h3>`, and so on.)
`style="font-family:typeface"`	The typeface (family) of the font, which is the name of a font, such as Arial. (Can also be used with `<p>`, `<h1>`, `<h2>`, `<h3>`, and so on.)
`style="font-size:size"`	The size of the font, which can be set to small, medium, or large, as well as x-small, x-large, and so on. Can also be set to a specific point size such as 12pt.

TABLE 5.3   Continued

Tag/Attribute	Function
style="color:*color*"	Changes the color of the text.
<ol>...</ol>	An ordered (numbered) list.
Attributes	
style="list-style-type: *numtype*"	The type of numerals used to label the list. Possible values are decimal, lower-roman, upper-roman, lower-alpha, upper-alpha, and none.
<ul>...</ul>	An unordered (bulleted) list.
Attributes	
style="list-style-type: *bullettype*"	The bullet dingbat used to mark list items. Possible values are disc, circle, square, and none.
<li>...</li>	A list item for use with <ol> or <ul>.
Attributes	
style="list-style-type:*type*"	The type of bullet or number used to label this item. Possible values are disc, circle, square, decimal, lower-roman, upper-roman, lower-alpha, upper-alpha, and none.
<dl>...</dl>	A definition list.
<dt>...</dt>	A definition term, as part of a definition list.
<dd>...</dd>	The corresponding definition to a definition term, as part of a definition list.

Q&A

Q *I've seen pages on the Internet that use three-dimensional little balls or other special graphics for bullets. How do they do that?*

A That trick is a little bit beyond what this hour covers. You'll find out how to do it yourself at the end of Hour 8.

Q *How do I "full justify" text so that both the left and the right margins are flush?*

A You don't, at least not with HTML/XHTML alone. HTML and XHTML do not support full-justified text by themselves. You can full-justify text using style sheets, which you'll learn about in Part III.

Q *How do I find out the exact name for a font I have on my computer?*

A On a Windows or Macintosh computer, open the Control Panel and click the Fonts folder—the fonts on your system are listed. Use the exact spelling of font names when specifying them in the font-family style rule; case doesn't matter, however.

Q *How do I put Kanji, Arabic, Chinese, and other non-European characters on my pages?*

A First of all, everyone you want to be able to read these characters on your pages must have the appropriate language fonts installed. They must also have selected that language character set and font in their web browser. You can use the Character Map program in Windows (or a similar program in other operating systems) to get the numerical codes for each character in any language font; click Start, All Programs, Accessories, and then System Tools to find Character Map. If the character you want has a code of 214, use Ö to place it on a web page.

The best way to include a short message in an Asian language (such as We Speak Tamil—Call Us!) is to include it as a graphics image. That way everyone will see it, even if they use English as their primary language for web browsing.

Workshop

The workshop contains quiz questions and activities to help you solidify your understanding of the material covered. Try to answer all questions before looking at the "Answers" section that follows.

Quiz

1. How would you center everything on an entire page?

2. How would you indent a single word and put a square bullet in front of it?

3. Use a definition list to show that the word "glunch" means "a look of disdain, anger, or displeasure" and that the word "glumpy" means "sullen, morose, or sulky."

4. How do you say "© 2004, Webwonks Inc." on a web page?

Answers

1. If you thought about putting a `<div style="text-align:center">` immediately after the `<body>` tag at the top of the page, and `</div>` just before the `</body>` tag at the end of the page, then you're correct. However, the `text-align` style is also supported directly in the `<body>` tag, which means you can forego the `<div>` tag and place the `style="text-align:center"` style directly in the `<body>` tag. Presto, the entire page is centered!

2. `<ul style="list-style-type:square">`

   ```
     <li>supercalifragilisticexpealidocious</li>
   </ul>
   ```

   (Putting the `style="list-style-type:square"` in the `<li>` tag would give the same result because there's only one item in this list.)

3. `<dl>`

   ```
   <dt>glunch</dt><dd>a look of disdain, anger, or displeasure</dd>
   <dt>glumpy</dt><dd>sullen, morose, or sulky</dd>
   </dl>
   ```

4. `&copy; 2004, Webwonks Inc.`

   The following produces the same result:

   ```
   &#169; 2004, Webwonks Inc.
   ```

Exercises

Try producing an ordered list outlining the information you'd like to put on your web pages. This will give you practice formatting HTML lists and also give you a head start on thinking about the issues covered in Part V, "Building a Web Site."

HOUR 6

Creating Text Links

In Hour 3, "Linking to Other Web Pages," you learned to use the <a> tag to create links between HTML pages. This hour takes linking a step or two forward by showing you how to use the same tag to enable viewers to jump between different parts of the same web page. This allows you to break a document into sections, and opens up opportunities for creating a table of contents with links or to put a link at the bottom of a page that returns you to the top. You'll find out how to link to a specific point within a separate page, too.

Links aren't just for connecting web pages with each other; this lesson also tells you how to embed a live link to your email address in a web page so that readers can instantly compose and send messages to you. I even show you a trick to help prevent spammers from ripping your email address from your web pages and sending you junk mail.

Linking Within a Page Using Anchors

If you recall from Hour 3, the <a> tag got its name from the word "anchor," which means a link serves as a designation for a spot in a web page. So far you've seen only how to use the <a> tag to link to somewhere else, but that's only half of its usefulness.

Identifying Locations in a Page with Anchors

The <a> tag is also used to mark a spot on a page as an anchor. This allows you to create a link that points to that exact spot. Listing 6.1, which is presented a bit later in the chapter, demonstrates a link to an anchor within a page. To see how such links are made, let's take a quick peek ahead at the first <a> tag in the listing:

```
<a id="top"></a>
```

An **anchor** is a named point on a web page. The same tag is used to create hypertext links and anchors (which explains why the tag is named <a>).

If you recall from earlier lessons, the <a> tag normally uses the href attribute to specify a hyperlinked target. In this example, the <a> tag is still specifying a target but no actual link is created. Instead, the <a> tag gives a name to the specific point on the page where the tag occurs. The </a> tag must be included, and a unique name assigned to the id attribute, but no text between <a> and </a> is necessary. The <a> tag creates an anchor that can then be linked to from this page or any other web page.

> Older versions of HTML used an attribute called `name` instead of `id`. Later versions of HTML and XHTML did away with the `name` attribute and instead use `id`.

Linking to Anchor Locations

To link to an anchor on a page, you use the `href` attribute of the `<a>` tag. Take a look at the last `<a>` tag in Listing 6.1 to see what I mean:

```
<a href="#top">Return to Index.</a>
```

The # symbol means that the word top refers to a named anchor point within the current document, rather than to a separate page. When a reader clicks "Return to Index," the web browser displays the part of the page starting with the `<a id="top">` tag.

LISTING 6.1 Setting Anchor Points by Using the `<a>` Tag with an `id` Attribute

```
<?xml version="1.0" encoding="UTF-8"?>
<!DOCTYPE html PUBLIC "-//W3C//DTD XHTML 1.1//EN"
  "http://www.w3.org/TR/xhtml11/DTD/xhtml11.dtd">

<html xmlns="http://www.w3.org/1999/xhtml" xml:lang="en">
  <head>
    <title>Alphabetical Shakespeare</title>
  </head>

  <body>
    <h2><a id="top"></a>First Lines of Every Shakespearean Sonnet</h2>
    <p>
      Don't ya just hate when you go a-courting, and there you are down on one
      knee about to rattle off a totally romantic Shakespearean sonnet, and
      zap! You space it. <i>"Um... It was, uh... I think it started with a
      B..."</i>
    </p>
    <p>
      Well, appearest thou no longer the dork. Simply pull this page up on your
      laptop computer, click on the first letter of the sonnet you want, and
      get an instant reminder of the first line to get you started. <i>"Beshrew
      that heart that makes my heart to groan..."</i> She's putty in your
      hands.
    </p>
    <h3 style="text-align:center">Alphabetical Index<br />
    (click on a letter)<br />
    <a href="#A">A</a> <a href="#B">B</a> <a href="#C">C</a>
    <a href="#D">D</a> <a href="#E">E</a> <a href="#F">F</a>
    <a href="#G">G</a> <a href="#H">H</a> <a href="#I">I</a>
    <a href="#J">J</a> <a href="#K">K</a> <a href="#L">L</a>
    <a href="#M">M</a> <a href="#N">N</a> <a href="#O">O</a>
    <a href="#P">P</a> <a href="#Q">Q</a> <a href="#R">R</a>
    <a href="#S">S</a> <a href="#T">T</a> <a href="#U">U</a>
    <a href="#V">V</a> <a href="#W">W</a> <a href="#X">X</a>
```

LISTING 6.1   Continued

```
<a href="#Y">Y</a> <a href="#Z">Z</a></h3>
<hr />
<h2><a id="A"></a>A</h2>
<p>
   A woman's face with nature's own hand painted,<br />
   Accuse me thus, that I have scanted all,<br />
   Against my love shall be as I am now<br />
   Against that time (if ever that time come)<br />
   Ah wherefore with infection should he live,<br />
   Alack what poverty my muse brings forth,<br />
   Alas 'tis true, I have gone here and there,<br />
   As a decrepit father takes delight,<br />
   As an unperfect actor on the stage,<br />
   As fast as thou shalt wane so fast thou grow'st,<br />
</p>
<p>
   <a href="#top"><i>Return to Index.</i></a>
</p>
<hr />
...
<h2><a id="X"></a>X</h2>
<p>
   (No sonnets start with X.)
</p>
<p>
   <a href="#top"><i>Return to Index.</i></a>
</p>
<hr />
<h2><a id="Y"></a>Y</h2>
<p>
   Your love and pity doth th' impression fill,<br />
</p>
<p>
   <a href="#top"><i>Return to Index.</i></a>
</p>
<hr />
<h2><a id="Z"></a>Z</h2>
<p>
   (No sonnets start with Z.)<br />
</p>
<p>
   <a href="#top">Return to Index.</a>
</p>
</body>
</html>
```

Here's an easy way to remember the difference between these two types of <a> tags:
<a href> is what you click, and <a id> is where you go when you click there.
Similarly, each of the <a href> links in Listing 6.1 makes an underlined link leading to a corresponding <a id> anchor. Clicking the letter B under Alphabetical Index in Figure 6.1, for instance, takes you to the part of the page shown in Figure 6.2.

Anchor names specified via the id attribute in the <a> tag must start with an alphanumeric character. So if you want to simply number the IDs of anchors, be sure to start them with text, as in photo1, photo2, and so on, instead of just 1, 2, and so on. Purely numeric anchor IDs will work in browsers but they don't qualify as valid XHTML code.

FIGURE 6.1
The <a id> tags in Listing 6.1 don't appear at all on the web page. The <a href> tags appear as underlined links.

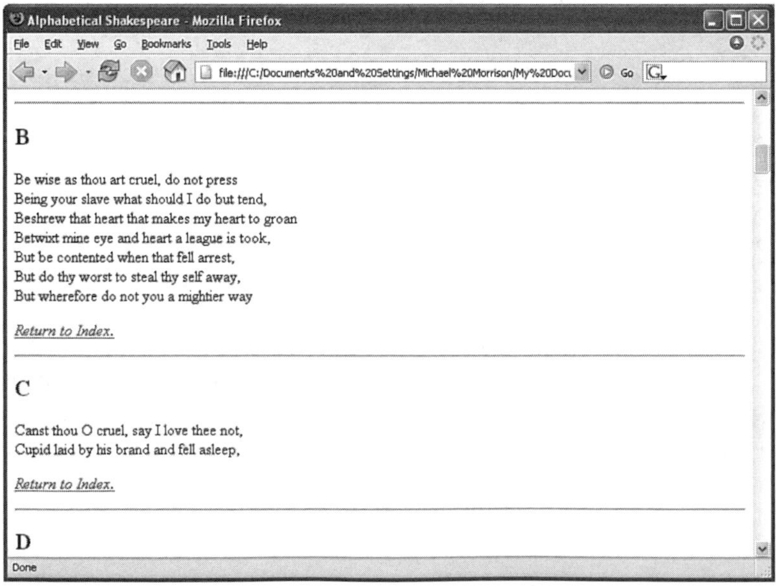

FIGURE 6.2
Clicking the letter B in the page shown in Figure 6.1 takes you to the appropriate section of the same page.

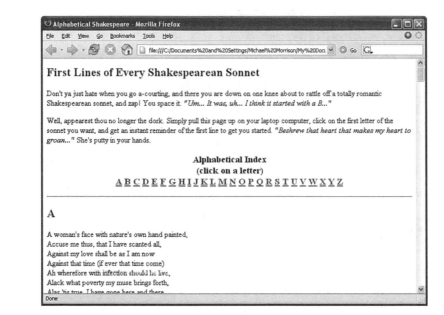

Hopefully you now have several pages of your own linked together. It's a good time to add an index at the top of your home page so that people can easily get an overview of what your pages have to offer:

▶ Place <a id> tags in front of each major topic on your home page or any longish page you make.

▶ Copy each of the major topic headings to a list at the top of the page, and enclose each heading in an <a href> linking to the corresponding <a id> tag.

One of the most common uses for the <a id> tag is creating an alphabetical index. The bad news for anyone with an alphabetical list that he wants to index is that typing out 26 links to 26 anchors is a rather tedious endeavor. The good news is that I've already done it for you and dropped off the indexed page at the *Sams Publishing* website at http://www.samspublishing.com/.

By the Way

▲

Linking to a Specific Part of Another Page

Linked anchors within pages aren't limited to the same page. You can link to a named anchor on another page by including the address or name of that page followed by # and the anchor name. Listing 6.2 shows several examples, such as the following:

```
<a href="sonnets.html#sonnet131">
You're bossy, ugly and smelly, but I still love you.</a>
```

Clicking "You're bossy, ugly and smelly, but I still love you," which is shown in Figure 6.3, brings up the page named sonnets.html and goes directly to the point where <a id="sonnet131"></a> occurs on that page (see Figure 6.4). (The HTML code for sonnets.html is not listed here because it is quite long. It's just a bunch of sappy old sonnets with <a id> tags in front of each one.) Note that anchor IDs can be a combination of letters and numbers provided that the ID begins with a letter. In this case, I used the sonnet number preceded by the word sonnet.

LISTING 6.2   Using the Page Address and Anchor Name in the
                  `<a href>` Tag

```
<?xml version="1.0" encoding="UTF-8"?>
<!DOCTYPE html PUBLIC "-//W3C//DTD XHTML 1.1//EN"
  "http://www.w3.org/TR/xhtml11/DTD/xhtml11.dtd">

<html xmlns="http://www.w3.org/1999/xhtml" xml:lang="en">
  <head>
    <title>Topical Shakespeare</title>
  </head>

  <body>
    <h2>Shakespearean Sonnets for Every Occasion</h2>
    <p>
      Choose your message for a genuine Shakespearean sonnet which expresses
      your feelings with tact and grace.
    </p>
    <p>
      <i><a href="sonnets.html#sonnet131">You're bossy, ugly and smelly, but I
      still love you.</a><br />
      <a href="sonnets.html#sonnet2">Life is short. Let's make babies.</a><br />
      <a href="sonnets.html#sonnet140">Say you love me or I'll tell lies about
      you.</a><br />
      <a href="sonnets.html#sonnet31">You remind me of all my old
      girlfriends.</a><br />
      <a href="sonnets.html#sonnet57">You abuse me, but you know I love
      it.</a><br />
      <a href="sonnets.html#sonnet141">I think you're hideous, but I'm
      desperate.</a><br />
      <a href="sonnets.html#sonnet150">You don't deserve me, but take me
      anyway.</a><br />
      <a href="sonnets.html#sonnet36">I feel bad about leaving, but see ya
      later.</a></i>
    </p>
  </body>
</html>
```

Coffee
Break

A popular technique for improving the visibility of a web site without spending a bunch of (if any) marketing money is to join a link exchange service such as Linkalizer (http://www.linkalizer.com/) or GoTop (http://www.gotop.com/). Such services allow you to include your site in a group of sites that willingly promote themselves to each other as part of a linked network. Link exchanging can be an affordable way to get some visibility for a new site.

Watch
Out!

Be sure to include the # symbol only in `<a href>` link tags. Don't put the # symbol in the `<a id>` tag; links to that name won't work in that case.

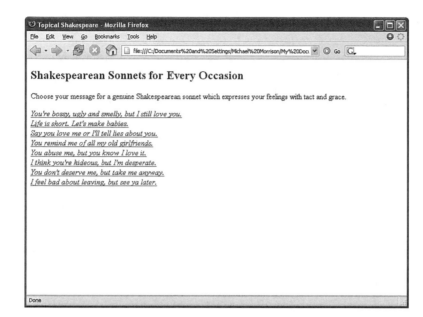

FIGURE 6.3
This page is list-ed in Listing 6.2. All the links on this page go to dif-ferent parts of a separate page named `sonnets.html`.

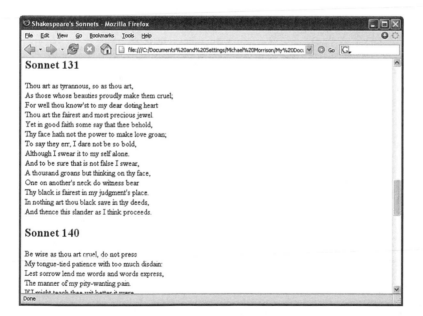

FIGURE 6.4
Clicking the "bossy" link in Figure 6.3 brings you directly to this part of the son-nets.html page. The HTML code for this page isn't shown, although it is available from the com-panion web site.

Linking Your Email Address into a Page

In addition to linking between pages and between parts of a single page, the <a> tag allows you to link to your email address. This is the simplest way to enable readers of your web pages to "talk back" to you. Of course, you could just tell readers your email address and trust them to type it into whatever email program they use if they want to say something to you, but that would be much more error prone. You can make it almost completely effortless for them to send you messages by providing a clickable link to your email address.

An HTML link to an email address looks like the following:

```
<a href="mailto:dicko@netletter.com">Send me an email message.</a>
```

The words "Send me an email message" will appear just like any other `<a>` link. In most web browsers, when someone clicks the link she gets a window in which to type a message that is immediately sent to you—whatever email program the person uses to send and receive email will automatically be used.

If you want people to see your actual email address (so that they can make note of it or send a message using a different email program), include it both in the `href` attribute and as part of the message between the `<a>` and `</a>` tags, like this:

```
<a href="mailto:dicko@netletter.com">dicko@netletter.com</a>
```

As I mentioned earlier, when someone clicks an email link her email program will open and a new message will be started with the email recipient already filled in. You can provide some additional information in the link so that the subject and body of the message also have default values. You do this by adding `subject` and `body` attributes to the `mailto` link. These attributes are a little different from typical HTML attributes, and therefore must be coded slightly differently. You separate the attributes from the email address with a question mark (?), and then separate each attribute with an ampersand (&). Following is an example of specifying a subject and body for the preceding email example:

```
<a href="mailto:dicko@netletter.com?subject=Book Question&amp;body=
When is the next edition coming out?">dicko@netletter.com</a>
```

When a user clicks this link, an email message is created with dicko@netletter.com as the recipient, `Book Question` as the subject of the message, and `When is the next edition coming out?` as the message body.

> If you want to specify only an email message subject and not the body, you can just leave off the ampersand and the body attribute in the link.

Before you run off and start plastering your email address all over your web pages, I have to give you a little warning and then let you in on a handy trick. You're no doubt familiar with spammers that build up databases of email addresses and then bombard them with junk mail advertisements. One way spammers "harvest" email addresses is by using programs that automatically search web pages for `mailto` links. I have personally seen the negative effects of publishing an email address on a web page and then promptly seeing a spike in junk mail. So I'm very careful about revealing email addresses now.

Fortunately, there is a little trick that will thwart the vast majority of spammers. This trick involves using character entities to encode your email address, which confuses "scraper" programs that are attempting to "harvest" your email address from your web pages. As an example, take the earlier sample email address, `dicko@netletter.com`. If you replace a few of the letters in the address with their character entity equivalents, most email harvesting programs will be thrown off. Lowercase ASCII character entities begin at `&#97;` for letter a and increase through the alphabet in order. So, for example, letter c is `&#99;`. Replacing both of the c's in the sample address yields the following code:

```
<a href="mailto:di&#99;ko@netletter.&#99;om">Send me an email message.</a>
```

The important thing to note is that a web browser ends up interpreting the `&#99;` character entity as a letter c, which means that the end result is the same from the browser's perspective. However, automated email harvesting programs search the raw HTML code for pages, which in this case is showing a fairly jumbled-looking email address.

Pulling all of what you've learned about email links into a practical example, check out Listing 6.3 and Figure 6.5, which show yet another version of a hockey player web page with a link to email my friend Terry.

Terry is far too dangerous for me to be printing his real email address in thousands of books, so please understand that the email address in the sample code isn't real.

By the Way

LISTING 6.3 Using the `<a>` Tag to Link to an Email Address

```
<?xml version="1.0" encoding="UTF-8"?>
<!DOCTYPE html PUBLIC "-//W3C//DTD XHTML 1.1//EN"
  "http://www.w3.org/TR/xhtml11/DTD/xhtml11.dtd">

<html xmlns="http://www.w3.org/1999/xhtml" xml:lang="en">
  <head>
    <title>Music City Mafia - Terry Lancaster</title>
  </head>

  <body>
    <p style="font-family:verdana, arial; font-size:18pt; font-weight:bold">16 -
    Terry Lancaster</p>
```

LISTING 6.3   Continued

```
  <p style="font-family:verdana, arial; font-size:12pt; color:navy">
    <img src="tlancaster.jpg" alt="Terry &quot;Big T&quot; Lancaster" /><br />
    <span style="font-weight:bold">Nickname:</span> Big T<br />
    <span style="font-weight:bold">Position:</span> RW<br />
    <span style="font-weight:bold">Height:</span> 6'3"<br />
    <span style="font-weight:bold">Weight:</span> 195<br />
    <span style="font-weight:bold">Shoots:</span> Left<br />
    <span style="font-weight:bold">Age:</span> 40<br />
    <span style="font-weight:bold">Birthplace:</span>
    <a href="http://en.wikipedia.org/wiki/Nashville%2C_Tennessee">Nashville,
    TN</a>
  </p>
  <hr />
  <p style="font-family:verdana, arial; font-size:12pt; color:navy">
    <span style="font-weight:bold">Favorite NHL Player:</span>
    <a href="http://www.nhl.com/players/8448091.html">Brett Hull</a><br />
    <span style="font-weight:bold">Favorite NHL Team:</span>
    <a href="http://www.nashvillepredators.com/">Nashville Predators</a><br />
    <span style="font-weight:bold">Favorite Southern Fixin:</span>
    <a href="http://southernfood.about.com/od/potatorecipes/r/blbb442.htm">
    Skillet Fried Potatoes</a><br />
    <span style="font-weight:bold">Favorite Meat and Three:</span>
    <a href="http://www.hollyeats.com/Swetts.htm">Swett's</a>
    (<a href="http://maps.google.com/maps?q=2725+clifton+ave,+nashville,+tn"
    rel="external">map</a>)
    <br />
    <span style="font-weight:bold">Favorite Country Star:</span>
    <a href="http://www.patsycline.com/">Patsy Cline</a><br />
    <span style="font-weight:bold">Favorite Mafia Moment:</span>
    "<a href="mcmplayer_chale.html">Chet</a> finishing the game with his
    eyelid completely slashed through."
  </p>
  <hr />
  <p style="font-family:verdana, arial; font-size:12pt">
    <a href="mailto:l&#97;ncastert@musiccitym&#97;fi&#97;.com?subject=
    Fan Question&amp;body=What's your secret?">Contact Terry.</a>
  </p>
  </body>
</html>
```

The email link in this code occurs near the bottom of the code when the text
Contact Terry. is used as linking text for a mailto link. What is important to note
is how the letter a's in the email address are replaced by their character entity equivalents (a), which helps hide the address from spammers. Pay attention to the
status bar in the figure and you'll see that the browser interprets the correct email
address. When someone clicks the email link shown in Figure 6.5, a separate window (see Figure 6.6) opens; the window has spaces for a subject line and an email
message. The email address from the link is automatically entered, and the user can
simply click the Send button to send the message.

FIGURE 6.5
The mailto:
link in Listing
6.3 looks a lot
like http://
links on the
page.

It is customary to put an email link to the web page author at the bottom of every web page. Not only does this make it easy for others to contact you, but it also gives them a way to tell you about any problems with the page that your testing may have missed. Just don't forget to use the email address character entity trick so that your address flies under the radar of spammers.

Did you Know?

FIGURE 6.6
Clicking the top
link shown in
Figure 6.5
brings up this
email window
(or the email
software set
up on your
computer).

If you paid extremely close attention to Figure 6.5, you may have noticed a new link in addition to the email link. I'm referring to the birthplace information field, which is now shown with the text "Nashville, TN" as a link. This text wasn't linked in the last version of this page in the previous hour. In this latest example, I used one of my favorite web sites to add another informative link to the page. I'm referring to Wikipedia, the free online encyclopedia. Read on to learn more!

Linking to Wikipedia

Back in Hour 3 I raved about the usefulness of Google Maps and how handy they can be for sharing location information with people via your web pages. Another site that I have nothing but good things to say about is Wikipedia, which is located at http://www.wikipedia.org/. Wikipedia is a free online encyclopedia, which may not sound all that special. What makes Wikipedia so unique is that anyone can edit it. That's right, you can go visit Wikipedia right now and edit any encyclopedia entry on there. Although you may think that this open-ended aspect of Wikipedia would turn it into an editorial three-ring circus, it has actually worked incredibly well. People who care about certain subjects will monitor those subjects and make sure that contributions are objective and accurate. I'm not saying Wikipedia is perfect, but it's one of the more successful online social "experiments" that has turned into a quite useful information tool.

So what does Wikipedia have to do with a book on HTML and CSS? Well, I think you'll find it useful to occasionally link information on your web pages to Wikipedia so that visitors to your site can learn more. In the hockey player web site you just saw, I included a link to Wikipedia for the player's birthplace, which allows visitors to learn more about the city. Here's the link code from the page:

```
<a href="http://en.wikipedia.org/wiki/Nashville%2C_Tennessee">Nashville, TN</a>
```

This code reveals another interesting thing about Wikipedia: Its links flow directly from the subject matter. More specifically, links on Wikipedia are created by the subject simply being added to the end of the Wikipedia web page address. In the example, the subject of the link is `Nashville, Tennessee`. The only trick is changing the comma to `%2C`, which is a special code used to represent a comma in a web address, as well as replacing spaces with underscore characters (_). This subject is then added to the end of the Wikipedia base URL, http://en.wikipedia.org/wiki/.

By the Way

In case you forgot, URL stands for Uniform Resource Locator, and is just the address of a resource on the Web, as in a web page.

The good news about Wikipedia addresses is that you can copy and paste them directly from a web browser into your web pages. As an example, let's say you wanted to link to the Wikipedia entry for the musician Tom Waits. Based on my brief explanation of how Wikipedia addresses are constructed, you could guess that the address of the page is http://en.wikipedia.org/wiki/Tom_Waits. But you don't have to guess. You could enter `Tom Waits` as the search text in Wikipedia and it would take you to the page shown in Figure 6.7.

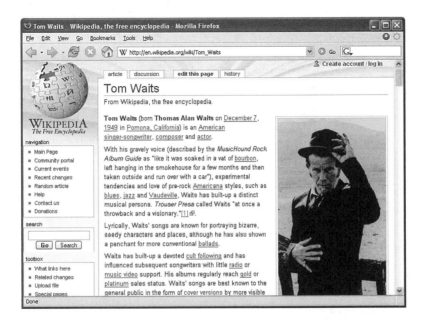

FIGURE 6.7
Wikipedia serves as an excellent resource for linking to interesting topics from your web pages.

Indeed, the figure reveals that your guess regarding the Tom Waits Wikipedia address is correct. Rather than guess, however, you can just copy the address from the address field of your web browser.

Wikipedia is directly related to this lesson in that you can use the table of contents of a Wikipedia page to construct links to specific parts of the page. For example, if you visit the Tom Waits page (http://en.wikipedia.org/wiki/Tom_Waits) and scroll down a bit, you'll find a table of contents with a list of headings such as "Early Career," "Discography," "Tours," etc. These headings correspond to anchor points on the page, which means you can create links to specific parts of the page by appending one of the table of contents headings onto the page address. Just don't forget to precede the heading with a # character, like this:

```
http://en.wikipedia.org/wiki/Tom_Waits#Discography
```

| If a heading contains spaces, be sure to replace those spaces with underscore characters (_) when creating a link to the anchor point.

This link takes you to the Discography section of the Tom Waits page, as shown in Figure 6.8.

FIGURE 6.8
Most Wikipedia pages include anchor points based on the table of contents of the page.

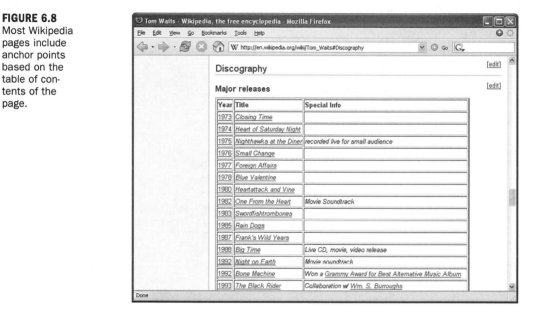

Summary

This hour has shown you two uses for the <a> tag not covered in Hour 3. You learned how to create named anchor points within a page and how to create links to a specific anchor. You also saw how to link to your email address so that readers can easily send you messages. You even learned how to protect your email address from spammers. The hour concluded by showing you how to link to Wikipedia encyclopedia topics from your own pages. Table 6.1 summarizes the two attributes of the <a> tag discussed in this hour.

TABLE 6.1   HTML Tags and Attributes Covered in Hour 6

Tag/Attribute	Function
`<a>...</a>`	With the `href` attribute, creates a link to another document or anchor; with the `name` attribute, creates an anchor that can be linked to.
Attributes	
`href="address"`	The address of the document or anchor point to which to link.
`id="name"`	The name for this anchor point in the document.

Q&A

Q *Can I put both* `href` *and* `id` *in the same* `<a>` *tag? Would I want to for any reason?*

A You can, and it might save you some typing if you have a named anchor point and a link right next to each other. It's generally better, however, to use `<a href>` and `<a id>` separately to avoid confusion because they play very different roles in an HTML document.

Q *What happens if I accidentally spell the name of an anchor wrong or forget to put the # in front of it?*

A If you link to an anchor name that doesn't exist within a page or misspell the anchor name, the link goes to the top of that page.

Q *What if I use a different company to handle my email than handles my web pages? Will my email links still work?*

A Yes. You can put any email address on the Internet into a link, and it will work fine. The only situation in which email links won't work is when the person who clicks the link doesn't have an email program set up on his computer, and therefore isn't capable of sending email.

Workshop

The workshop contains quiz questions and activities to help you solidify your understanding of the material covered. Try to answer all questions before looking at the "Answers" section that follows.

Quiz

1. Write the HTML to make it possible for someone clicking the words "About the authors" at the top of a page to skip down to a list of credits at the bottom of the page.

2. Suppose your company has three employees and you want to create a company directory page listing some information about each of them. Write the HTML for that page and the HTML to link to one of the employees from another page.

3. If your email address is bon@soir.com, how would you make the text "goodnight greeting" into a link that people can click to compose and send you an email message? How would you code the o's in the email address to help hide the address from spammers?

Answers

1. Type this at the top of the page:

```
<a href="#credits">About the Authors</a>
```

Type this at the beginning of the credits section:

```
<a id="credits"></a>
```

2. The company directory page would look like the following:

```
<?xml version="1.0" encoding="UTF-8"?>
<!DOCTYPE html PUBLIC "-//W3C//DTD XHTML 1.1//EN"
  "http://www.w3.org/TR/xhtml11/DTD/xhtml11.dtd">

<html>
  <head>
    <title>company directory</title>
  </head>

  <body>
    <h1>company directory</h1>
    <h2><a id="jones"></a>jane jones</h2>
    <p>
      ms. jones is our accountant... etc.
    </p>
    <h2><a id="smith"></a>sam smith</h2>
    <p>
      mr. smith is our salesman... etc.
    </p>
    <h2><a id="bharwaniji"></a>r.k. satjiv bharwahniji</h2>
    <p>
      mr. bharwahniji is our president... etc.
    </p>
  </body>
</html>
```

If the file were named `directory.html`, a link to one employee's information from another page would look like the following:

```
<a href="directory.html#bharwaniji">about our president</a>
```

3. Type the following on your web page:

```
send me a <a href="mailto:bon@soir.com">goodnight greeting</a>!
```

To help hide the email address from spammers, replace the o's in the address with `&#111;`, like this:

```
send me a <a href="mailto:b&#111;n@s&#111;ir.c&#111;m">goodnight
greeting</a>!
```

Exercises

▶ When you link back to your home page from other pages, you might want to skip some of the introductory information at the top of the home page. Using a link to a named anchor just below that introductory information will avoid presenting it to people who have already read it, making your pages seem less repetitive. Also, if any pages on your site are longer than two screens of information when displayed in a web browser, consider putting a link at the bottom of the page back up to the top.

▶ Look through your web pages and consider whether there are any places in the text where you'd like to make it easy for people to respond to what you're saying. Include a link right there to your email address. You can never provide too many opportunities for people to contact you and tell you what they need or think about your products, especially if you're running a business.

HOUR 7

Creating Your Own Web Page Graphics

You don't have to be an artist to put high-impact graphics and creative type on your web pages. You don't need to spend hundreds or thousands of dollars on software, either. This hour tells you how to create the images you need in order to make visually exciting web pages. Although the sample figures in this chapter use a popular Windows graphics program (Paint Shop Pro from Corel), you can easily follow along with any major Windows or Macintosh graphics application.

This hour is concerned only with creating the graphics files for web images, so it doesn't discuss HTML tags at all. In Hour 8, "Putting Graphics on a Web Page," you'll see how to integrate your graphics with your HTML pages.

Did you Know?

One of the best ways to save time creating the graphics and media files for web pages is, of course, to avoid creating them altogether. Grabbing a graphic from any web page is as simple as right-clicking it (or holding down the button, on a Macintosh mouse) and selecting Save Image As in Mozilla Firefox or Save Picture As in Microsoft Internet Explorer. Extracting a background image from a page is just as easy: Right-click it and select Save Background As.

You may also want to consider royalty-free clip art, which doesn't require you to get copyright permission. A good source of clip art online is Microsoft's Office Online Clip Art and Media web site, which is located at http://office.microsoft.com/clipart/. Barry's Clipart Server is another popular clip art destination, located at http://www.barrysclipart.com/.

Watch Out!

Any image or media clip you see on any web site is instantly reusable provided that the copyright holder grants (or sells) you the right to copy it. Be sure to ask before using any copyrighted media on your own pages. To learn more about copyrights as they apply to images on the Web, visit http://www.2learn.ca/copyright/images.html. Along with potentially getting you in a lot of legal trouble, taking images without permission is considered highly unprofessional, not to mention unethical.

Choosing Graphics Software

You can use almost any computer graphics program to create graphics images for your web pages, from the simple paint program that comes free with your computer's operating system to an expensive professional program such as Adobe Photoshop. If you have a digital camera or scanner attached to your computer, it probably came with some graphics software capable of creating web page graphics.

> Adobe Photoshop is without a doubt the cream of the crop when it comes to image-editing programs. However, it is expensive and quite complex if you don't have experience working with computer graphics. Adobe now offers a more affordable, easier to use version of Photoshop called Photoshop Elements, which you might want to take a look at. For more information on Adobe's products, visit the Adobe web site at http://www.adobe.com/.

If you already have software you think might be good for creating web graphics, try using it to do everything described in this hour. If it can't do some of the tasks covered here, it probably won't be a good tool for web graphics. In that case, you might want to consider downloading the evaluation version of Paint Shop Pro or Adobe Photoshop Elements if you're using a Windows computer, or Adobe Photoshop Elements if you're using a Macintosh. For Windows users, another new and very interesting image program is Google Picasa, which is available free at http://picasa.google.com/. Picasa is Google's entry into the image-editing market, and it offers some unusual features not found in other image editors. However, Picasa is better suited toward organizing and editing digital photographs, as opposed to creating web graphics from scratch. Even so, it's a powerful (and free) tool that is worth checking out.

▼ Try It Yourself

An excellent and inexpensive program that provides everything you're likely to need for web images is Paint Shop Pro from Corel. If you are using a Windows computer, you can download a fully functional evaluation copy of Paint Shop Pro before reading the rest of this lesson. (Macintosh users should download Adobe Photoshop Elements from http://www.adobe.com/ instead, because Paint Shop Pro is currently available for Windows only. There is also a version of Photoshop Elements for Windows if you're partial to Adobe products.) Here's how to get Paint Shop Pro:

1. Start your web browser and go to http://www.corel.com/. You are prompted to select your country of origin. Select it and you will see the main Corel web page.

▼

2. Click the Free Trials link, followed by the Download button next to the Paint Shop Pro trial version.

3. Click the Download button once more and the file will transfer to your hard drive. You are asked to Run or Save the file. Choose Save and confirm where you want to put the file on your hard drive—be sure to remember which folder it goes into!

4. After the download transfer is complete, use Windows Explorer to find the file you downloaded and double-click it to install Paint Shop Pro.

The Paint Shop Pro software you can get online is a fully functional shareware evaluation copy. If you find it useful for working with web page images, you'll want to register the program with Corel for a fee. The evaluation copy of Paint Shop Pro is good for only 30 days, so you'll have to make up your mind at some point about registering the software or finding an alternative.

By the Way

Almost all the graphics you see in this book were created with Paint Shop Pro, and this chapter uses Paint Shop Pro to illustrate several key web graphics techniques you'll need to know. Of course, there are so many ways to produce images with Paint Shop Pro that I can't even begin to explain them all. Fortunately, the latest version of Paint Shop Pro includes a Learning Center that guides you through common image-editing tasks—resizing, auto-correcting brightness and color, and so on.

The Least You Need to Know About Graphics

Two forces are always at odds when you post graphics and multimedia on the Internet. Your eyes and ears want everything to be as detailed and accurate as possible, but your clock and wallet want files to be as small as possible. Intricate, colorful graphics mean big file sizes, which increase the transfer time even over a fast connection. How do you maximize the quality of your presentation while minimizing file size? To make these choices, you need to understand how color and resolution work together to create a subjective sense of quality.

The resolution of an image is the number of individual dots, or pixels (the individual dots that make up a digital image), that make up an image. Large, high-resolution images generally take longer to transfer and display than small, low-resolution images. Resolution is usually specified as the width times the height of the image, in pixels; a 300×200 image, for example, is 300 pixels wide and 200 pixels high.

You might be surprised to find that resolution isn't the most significant factor determining an image file's storage size (and transfer time). This is because images used on web pages are always stored and transferred in compressed form. Image compression is the mathematical manipulation that images are put through to squeeze out repetitive patterns. The mathematics of image compression is complex, but the basic idea is that repeating patterns or large areas of the same color can be squeezed out when the image is stored on a disk. This makes the image file much smaller and allows it to be transferred faster over the Internet. The web browser then restores the original appearance of the image when the image is displayed.

In the rest of this hour, you'll learn exactly how to create graphics with big visual impact and small file sizes. The techniques you'll use to accomplish this depend on the contents and purpose of each image. There are as many uses for web page graphics as there are web pages, but four types of graphics are by far the most common:

▶ Photos of people, products, or places

▶ Graphical banners and logos

▶ Snazzy-looking buttons or icons to link between pages

▶ Background textures or wallpaper to go behind pages

The last of these is covered in Hour 9, "Custom Backgrounds and Colors," but you can learn to create the other three kinds of graphics right now.

Preparing Photographic Images

To put photos on your web pages, you need some kind of scanner or digital camera, even if it's a digital camera that is built into your mobile phone. You'll often need to use the custom software that comes with your scanner or camera to save pictures onto your hard drive. Note, however, that you can control just about any scanner directly from Paint Shop Pro and most other graphics programs—see the software documentation for details.

Did you Know?

If you don't have a scanner or digital camera, most film-developing stores can transfer photos from 35mm film to a CD-ROM for a modest fee. You can then use Paint Shop Pro to open and modify the image files directly from the CD-ROM; actually, you'll want to copy the files from the CD-ROM to your hard drive before modifying them because the CD-ROM is probably read-only.

After you have the pictures on your computer, you can use Paint Shop Pro (or another similar graphics program) to get them ready for the Web.

Cropping an Image

You want web page graphics to be as compact as possible, so you'll usually need to crop or reduce the size of your digital photos. In Paint Shop Pro, the Learning Center window on the left edge of the screen provides easy access to lots of common image-editing tasks, including image cropping. Follow these steps to crop a picture in Paint Shop Pro:

1. Click Adjust in the Learning Center window, followed by Crop. (The Learning Center is shown in the left in Figure 7.1.)

2. Click the upper-left corner of the portion of the image you want to keep, and hold down the left mouse button while you drag down to the lower-right corner.

> To retain the original aspect ratio while cropping an image, hold down the Shift key before clicking and dragging the mouse.

Did you Know?

3. Click the Apply button (green checkmark) on the tool palette near the top of the application window.

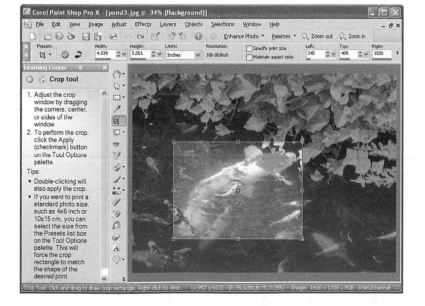

FIGURE 7.1
Use the rectangular selection tool to crop images as tightly as possible.

Even after your image has been cropped, it may be larger than it needs to be for a web page. Depending on the design of a specific web page, you may want to limit large images to no more than 800×600 or maybe even 640×480 pixels or smaller. And in some cases you may want to also provide a thumbnail version of the image that links to a larger version, in which case you'll probably stick closer to 100 pixels in the larger dimension for the thumbnail.

Notice that in Paint Shop Pro the resolution of the current image is shown in the lower-right corner of the window. The image may look larger or smaller than it really is because Paint Shop Pro automatically adjusts the image to fit in the window while you're working on it. (The current magnification ratio is shown above each image, in the title bar.) To see the image at the size it will appear on a web page, select View, Zoom to 100% on the main menu.

Resizing an Image

To change an image's resolution, and therefore its apparent size, use the Image, Resize command. You can also select Adjust again in the Learning Center window, followed by Resize. You'll get the Resize dialog box shown in Figure 7.2.

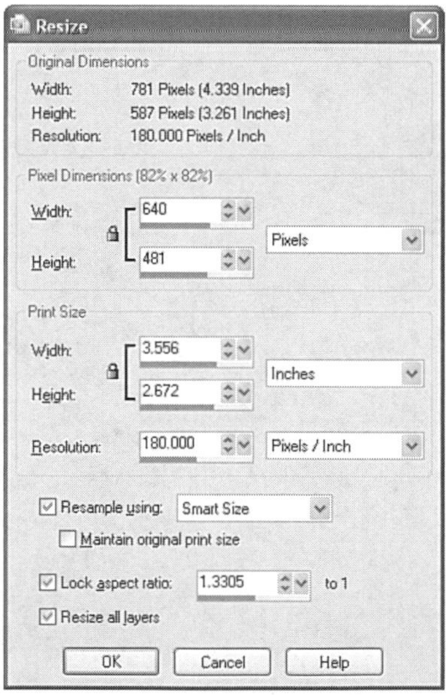

FIGURE 7.2
To change the size of an image, select Image, Resize to get this dialog box.

You'll almost always want Resample Using: Smart Size, Lock Aspect Ratio, and Resize All Layers selected (near the bottom of the dialog box). If you opt to maintain the aspect ratio, when you enter the width you'd like the image to be, the height will be calculated automatically to keep the image from squishing out of shape. It also works the same way if you specify the height and allow Paint Shop Pro to alter the width automatically. Also notice that I opted to change the image size based on pixel dimensions as opposed to percentages because I wanted the size of the resulting image to be close to 640×480.

Tweaking Image Colors

Many photographs will require some color correction to look their best on a computer screen. Like most photo-editing programs, Paint Shop Pro offers many options for adjusting an image's brightness, contrast, and color balance.

Most of these options are pretty intuitive, but the most important and powerful one is surprisingly the easiest one to use. Select Adjust, One Step Photo Fix from the main menu, or click One-Step Photo Fix in the Adjust section of the Learning Center. The brightness, contrast, and colors of the image are automatically adjusted, and in many cases the automatic results will work just fine.

Another option is to take a bit more control of the image correction process, which you do by selecting Adjust, Smart Photo Fix (also available in the Adjust section of the Learning Center). As shown in Figure 7.3, you can move the various sliders in the Smart Photo FixSmarS dialog box to adjust the brightness, saturation, and focus (sharpness) until the image looks about right; the default values are often sufficient, which you can restore by clicking the Suggest Settings button.

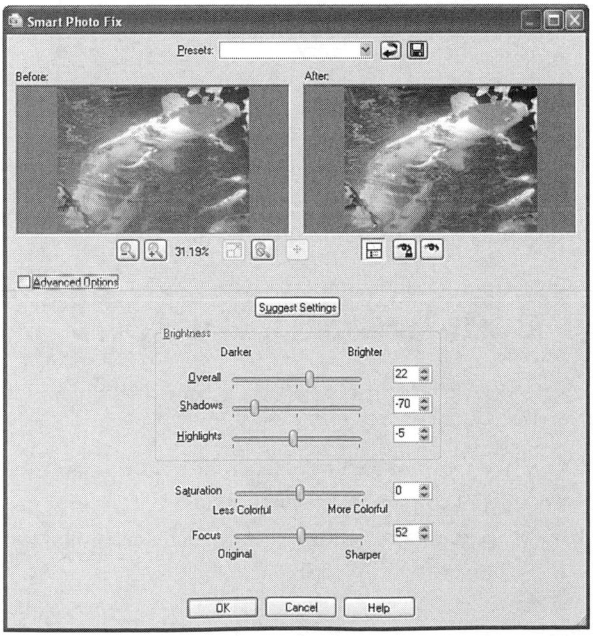

FIGURE 7.3
The Smart Photo Fix feature gives you an opportunity to fine-tune the photo-correction process based on suggested fixes.

Most of the other image-editing tools in Paint Shop Pro offer small preview windows like the one shown in Figure 7.3, so a little playful experimentation is the best way to find out what each of them does.

Controlling JPEG Compression

Photographic images look best when saved in the JPEG file format. When you're finished adjusting the size and appearance of your photo, select File, Save As and choose the JPG JPEG file type with Standard Encoding.

Figure 7.4 shows the Save Options dialog box you'll see when you click the Options button. You can control the compression ratio for saving JPEG files by adjusting the Compression Factor setting between 1% (high quality, large file size) and 99% (low quality, small file size).

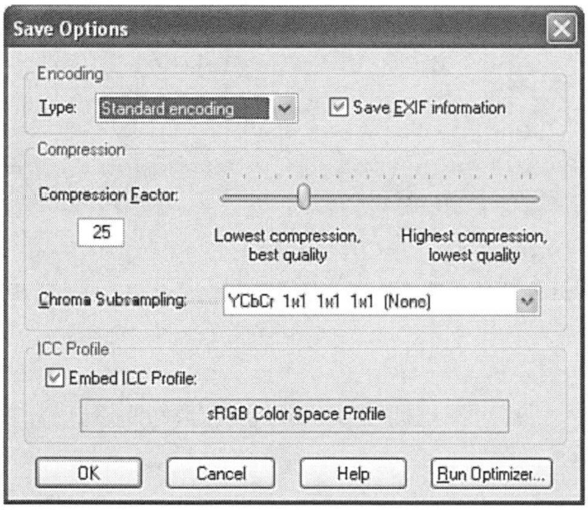

FIGURE 7.4
Paint Shop Pro allows you to trade reduced file size for image quality when saving JPEG images.

You may want to experiment a bit to see how various JPEG compression levels affect the quality of your images, but 25% compression is generally a good compromise between speed and quality for most photographic images.

Creating Banners and Buttons

Graphics that you create from scratch, such as banners and buttons, require you to make considerations uniquely different from photographs.

The first decision you need to make when you produce a banner or button is how big it should be. Most people accessing the web now have a computer with a screen that is at least 800×600 pixels in resolution, if not considerably larger; for example, my screen is currently set at 1,280×1,024 pixels. You should generally plan your graphics so that they will always fit within smaller screens (800×600), with room to spare for scrollbars and margins. The crucial size constraint is the horizontal width of your pages because scrolling a page horizontally is a huge hassle and source of confusion for web users. Vertically scrolling a page is much more acceptable, so it's okay if your pages are taller than the minimum screen sizes.

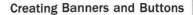

Screen resolution is something that is gradually increasing as time marches on. It's now safe to assume an 800×600 resolution for the vast majority of web users, and we may not be far from being able to ratchet that minimum up to 1,024×768.

Assuming that you target a minimum resolution of 800×600 pixels, this means that full-sized banners and title graphics should be no more than 770 pixels wide by 430 pixels tall, which is the maximum viewable area of the page after you've accounted for scrollbars, toolbars, and other parts of the browser window. Within a page, normal photos and artwork should be from 100 to 300 pixels in each dimension, and smaller buttons and icons should be 20 to 100 pixels tall and wide.

Figure 7.5 shows the dialog box you get when you select File, New to start a new image. Don't worry if you aren't sure exactly how big the image needs to be—just accept the default size if you aren't sure. Otherwise, enter the width and height of the new image. You can leave the Resolution field alone if you're entering the width and height in pixels. Also, the Raster Background setting is fine for most of your graphics creations. You should always begin with RGB - 8 Bits/Channel as the Color Depth because this results in a very high-quality image.

For the image's background color, you should usually choose white to match the background that most web browsers use for web pages. (You'll see how to change a page's background color in Hour 9.) When you know that you'll be making a page with a background other than white, you can choose a different background color. In fact, you may want to create an image with no background at all, in which case you'll click the Transparent check box. When an image's background is transparent, the web page underneath the image is allowed to show through those areas of the image.

When you enter the width and height of the image in pixels and click OK, you are faced with a blank canvas—an intimidating sight if you're as art-phobic as most of us! Fortunately, computer graphics programs such as Paint Shop Pro make it amazingly easy to produce professional-looking graphics for most web page applications.

By the Way

If the new image initially appears with a white-and-gray checkered pattern, it simply means that you've selected a transparent background. Transparent areas in Paint Shop Pro are always displayed in this checkered pattern.

Often, you will want to incorporate some fancy lettering into your web page graphics. For example, you might want to put a title banner at the top of your page that uses a decorative font with a drop-shadow or other special effects. To accomplish this task in Paint Shop Pro, perform the following steps:

1. Click Text and Graphics in the Learning Center window, and then click Add Text.

2. Click a spot on the image where you want the lower-left corner of the new text to appear. The Text Entry dialog box shown in Figure 7.6 appears.

FIGURE 7.6
Use Paint Shop Pro's text tool to create elegant lettering in a graphics image.

3. Type the text you want to add to the image and then click and drag the mouse to highlight the text.

4. Choose the color you want the lettering to be from the color palette that appears on the right edge of the Paint Shop Pro window. You'll likely want to select a color for both the outline and the fill area of the text, which appear as two overlapping boxes in the color palette.

> The Text Entry window in Paint Shop Pro continues to appear while you fine-tune the text in it via the main application toolbars. The window doesn't go away until you're completely finished editing the text.

By the Way

5. Choose a font and point size for the lettering, along with any font styles and other lettering settings on the tool palette (see Figure 7.7). Make sure that Anti-Alias is set to Smooth, which helps to ensure that the edges of the text are smoothed out. Click Apply in the Text Entry dialog box to accept the new text.

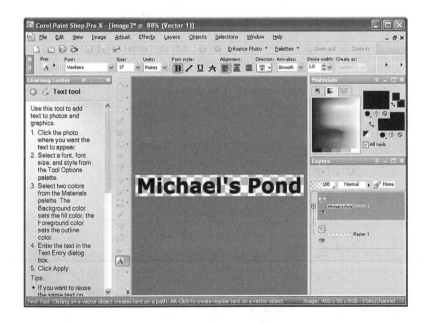

FIGURE 7.7
The font, point size, and other text settings are accessed from the tool palette in the main Paint Shop Pro application window.

6. Click to select the Pick tool (arrow), and then drag the text to fine-tune its position on the image (usually in the center of the image).

Did you
Know?

After the text is selected using the Pick tool, you can use the arrow keys on the keyboard to precisely position it within the image.

When you first put the text onto the image, it appears with a rectangle drawn around it. This means that it is selected and that any special effects you choose from the menu will apply to the shape of the letters you just made. For example, you might select Effects, 3D Effects, Drop Shadow from the main menu to add a drop shadow to the text. Figure 7.8 shows the dialog box that appears. You will be prompted to convert the text to a raster object before applying the drop shadow effect—just click OK to convert the text.

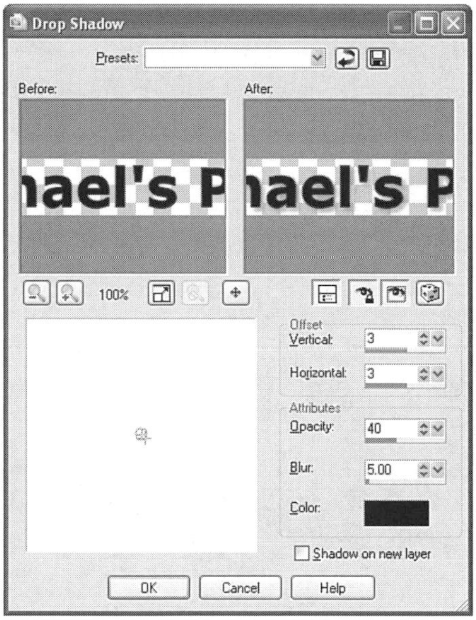

FIGURE 7.8
Like most menu choices in Paint Shop Pro, the Effects, 3D Effects, Drop Shadow command gives you an easy-to-use preview.

Notice that you can adjust the drop shadow effect and see the results in a small preview window before you actually apply the changes to the image. This makes it very easy to learn what various effects do simply by experimenting with them. Using only the text tool and the choices on the Effects, 3D Effects submenu (Buttonize, Chisel, Cutout, Drop Shadow, and Inner Bevel), you can create quite a variety of useful and attractive web graphics.

You may also want to deform, blur, sharpen, or otherwise play around with your text after you've applied an effect to it. To do so, simply select Effects, Effect Browser and select an effect to use. You see a dialog box like the one shown in Figure 7.9, which lets you pick from a list of effects and preview each one.

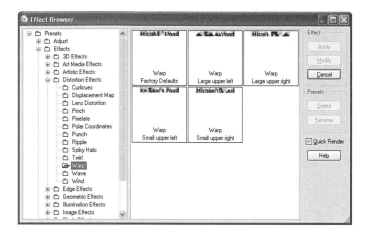

FIGURE 7.9
Select Effects, Effect Browser to play with all the image-altering special effects available, and then choose the one you want.

In the figure, the Warp effect from the Effect Browser is being used, which stretches and distorts the text in some strange ways. You can have a lot of fun playing around with all the different options in the effect browser!

If you're interested in creating interesting text effects and you don't want to fool around with an image editing tool such as Paint Shop Pro, then you might want to consider an online alternative. Cool Text is an online graphics generator that allows you to enter text along with a customized effect—Cool Text then generates an image for you. Take a moment to explore Cool Text at http://cooltext.com/.

Coffee Break

Reducing the Number of Colors in an Image

One of the most effective ways to reduce the size of, and therefore the download time for, an image is to reduce the number of colors used in the image. This can drastically reduce the visual quality of some photographic images, but it works great for most banners, buttons, and other icons.

In Paint Shop Pro, you can do this by selecting ImageIma, Decrease Color Depth, followed by one of the specific reduced color menu options (most other graphics programs have a similar option). Choose 16 Color Palette when your image has very few colors in it. If the image has lots of colors (or the image doesn't look good when you try 16 Colors), select Image, Decrease Color Depth, 256 Color Palette instead. The software will automatically find the best palette of 16 or 256 colors for approximating the full range of colors in the image.

> Even if you use only two or three colors in an image, you should still select Image, Decrease Color Depth, 16 Color Palette before you save it. If you don't, the image file will waste some space "leaving room for" lots of colors—even though very few are actually in use.

When you reduce the number of colors in an image, you will see a dialog box with several choices (see Figure 7.10). For web page images, you will almost always want to choose Optimized Octree and Nearest Color. Leave all the options on the right side of the dialog box unchecked; they will seldom improve the quality of an image noticeably.

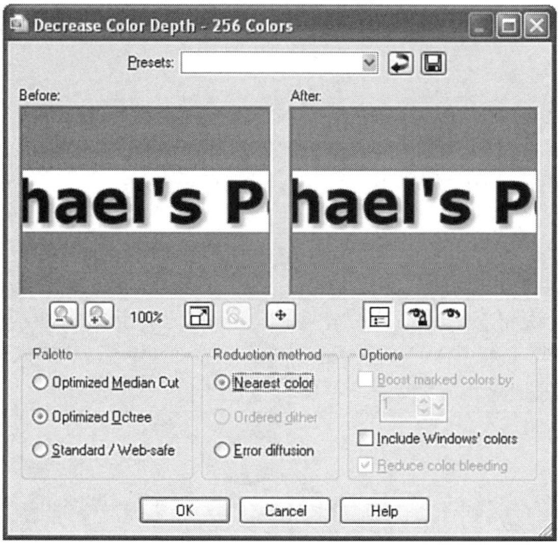

FIGURE 7.10
Reducing the number of colors in an image can dramatically decrease file size without noticeably changing the appearance of the image.

Did you Know?

> *Dithering* (also called *error diffusion* in Paint Shop Pro) is a technique used by image-editing programs to simulate a color that isn't in the color palette with alternating pixels of two similar colors. For example, a dithered pink color would consist of alternating pixels of red and white pixels, which would give the general impression of pink. Dithering can make images look better in some cases, but it should usually be avoided for web page graphics. Why? It substantially increases the information complexity of an image, and that usually results in much larger file sizes and slower downloads.

You'll be glad to know that there is a special file format for images with a limited number of colors; it's called the Graphics Interchange Format (GIF). To save a GIF image in Paint Shop Pro, select File, Save As and choose GIF CompuServe Graphics Interchange as the image type. The GIF image format is designed for images that contain areas of solid colors, such as web page titles and other illustrated graphics; the GIF format is not ideal for photographs.

Even better than the GIF image format is another format called PNG (pronounced "ping"), which is now supported in all major web browsers. The GIF image format allows you to specify a transparent color, which means that the background of the web page will show through those areas of an image. However, PNG takes things a step further by allowing you to specify varying degrees of transparency, as opposed to a single color. Select PNG Portable Network Graphics as the image type to save an image in Paint Shop Pro as a PNG image. I encourage you to experiment with both formats. Later, in Hour 9, I demonstrate how the PNG format's advanced transparency feature is superior to GIF transparency when you place transparent images on real web pages.

Interlaced GIFs and Progressive JPEGs

The JPEG, GIF, and PNG image file formats all offer a nifty feature that makes images appear faster than they otherwise could. An image can be stored in such a way that a "rough draft" of the image appears quickly, and the details are filled in as the download finishes. This has a profound psychological effect, because it gives people something to look at instead of drumming their fingers, waiting for a large image to pour slowly onto the screen.

A file stored with this feature is called an interlaced GIF, an interlaced PNG, or a progressive JPEG. Despite the different names, the visual results are similar with all the formats. An interlaced GIF or interlaced PNG file is an image that appears blocky at first, and then more and more detailed as it finishes downloading. Similarly, a progressive JPEG file appears blurry at first and then gradually comes into focus.

Most graphics programs that can handle GIF files enable you to choose whether to save them interlaced or noninterlaced. In Paint Shop Pro, for example, you can choose Version 89a (the latest GIF image version) and Interlaced by clicking the Options button in the Save As dialog box just before you save a GIF file (see Figure 7.11). PNG images offer a similar option in allowing you to choose between Interlaced and Noninterlaced in the Save Options dialog box.

To save a progressive JPEG file, select Save As (or Save Copy As), choose the JPG JPEG image type, click the Options button, and select Progressive Encoding instead of Standard Encoding. Many larger GIF and JPEG images used on the web these days take advantage of interlacing and progression to provide a better browsing experience for web surfers.

By the Way

Image files smaller than about 3KB will usually load so fast that nobody will ever see the interlacing or progressive display anyway. In fact, very small images may actually load more slowly when interlaced. Save these tricks for larger images.

Creating Animated Web Graphics

The GIF image format allows you to create animated images that can be used to add some motion and spice up any web page. Animated GIF images also transfer much faster than most video or multimedia files. The Paint Shop Pro image editor originally included a module called Animation Shop, which was designed especially for creating web page GIF animations. This module is now an entirely separate product also called Animation Shop that is offered by Corel, which acquired Paint Shop Pro from its previous manufacturer, Jasc. You can download a trial version of Animation Shop from the Corel web site at http://www.corel.com/. A few other GIF animation programs are available, including both freeware and advanced commercial software packages. Animation Shop offers a solid mix of great features, ease of use, and low price.

The first step in creating a GIF animation is to create a series of images to be displayed one after the other. Each of these images is called a *frame*. (By the way, this use of the word *frame* has nothing whatsoever to do with the *frames* you'll learn about in Hour 16, "Multipage Layout with Frames.") You can use any graphics software you like to make the images, though Paint Shop Pro is an obvious choice if you plan on using Animation Shop to put the animation together.

If you know how to use the Paint Shop Pro (or any other advanced graphics software) Layers feature, you'll find that creating animation frames is easier because you can easily turn parts of a picture on and off to make variations or move layers to simulate motion. Don't fret, however; layer manipulation is a bit beyond this discussion at the moment. You can easily make very effective animations by copying an ordinary one-layer image and painting on some variations, or moving some parts of it around to make the next frame.

When you have your animation's individual frames ready, use Colors, Decrease Color Depth to limit the frames to 256 or 16 colors, and then save each of them as a separate GIF file in your image editor.

Assembling Images into an Animation

After you have the individual GIF files saved, launch Animation Shop to start putting them together into a single animation file.

The fastest way to create a simple GIF animation with Animation Shop is to select File, Animation Wizard. This starts an "interview" that leads you through all the steps discussed next.

In this hour, however, I show you how to create animations by hand, without using the Animation Wizard. This will give you a head start when you want to use the advanced animation tricks discussed toward the end of the lesson.

Did you Know?

The basic idea here couldn't be simpler: You just need to tell Animation Shop which pictures to show and in what order. There are also a couple of other picky details you need to specify: how long to show each picture before moving on to the next one and how many times to repeat the whole sequence. Follow this step-by-step procedure to assemble an animation:

1. Select File, Open in Animation Shop. Select the image file that you want to be the first frame of the animation. It will appear as shown in Figure 7.12. Notice that the transparency is preserved, as indicated by the gray checkerboard pattern showing through. In this case, you're building an animation of a film projector.

2. Select Animation, Insert Frames, From File to get the dialog box shown in Figure 7.13. Click the Add File button and choose the image you want to appear second in the animation. Click Add File again to add the third frame, and so forth, until the list contains all the images you made for this animation. Change the Insert Before setting to 2 so that the new frames are inserted after the original frame. Click OK.

FIGURE 7.12
This is a single-frame GIF image as it first appears when opened in Animation Shop.

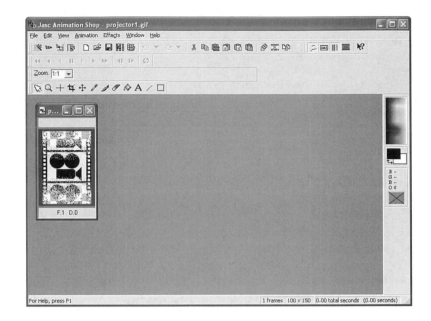

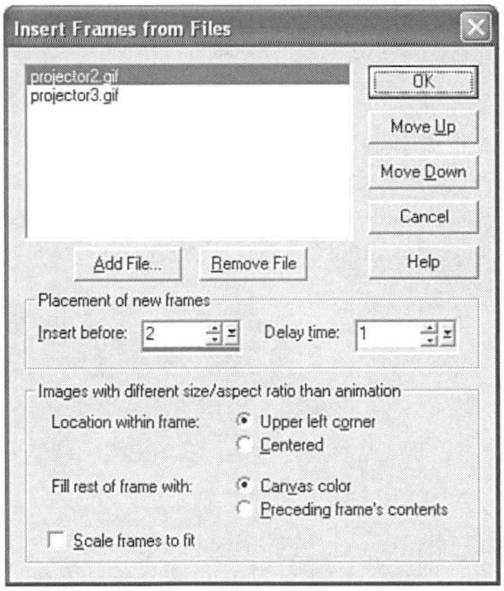

FIGURE 7.13
Selecting Animation, Insert Frames, From File gives you this dialog box. The Add File button lets you choose images to add to the animation.

3. You should now see all the frames laid out next to each other like a filmstrip (see Figure 7.14). You can resize the animation window and use the scrollbar to move forward and back through the filmstrip if all the frames aren't visible at once. If you'd like to see a preview of the animation, select View, Animation. If any frames are in the wrong order, simply grab and drag them into the proper positions with the mouse. Of course, the animation is likely moving so fast that you can't tell the order. This is because Animation Shop

defaults to putting a hundredth of a second between each frame of the animation. You will typically want to increase the length of time each individual
frame is displayed before the next one replaces it.

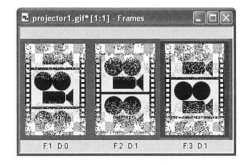

FIGURE 7.14
Animation Shop
displays all of
an animation's
frames side-by-
side, like a film-
strip.

4. To set the timing for a frame, click it; the border around it will turn blue and
red. Select Animation, Frame Properties. Alternatively, you can right-click the
frame and pick Frame Properties from the pop-up menu. You'll get a dialog
box that allows you to specify the display time in hundredths of a second. In
this example, 25 is a decent setting for the display time of each frame, which
results in each frame being shown for one-fourth of a second; a setting of 100
would result in 1 second.

> Animation Shop remembers the last setting you made for the frame display time
> and will automatically set the display time of newly added frames to this value. So
> if you initially set the display time of the first frame before adding new frames, the
> new frames will automatically take on the initial frame's setting.

Did you Know?

5. One final detail and your animation will be done! Select Animation,
Animation Properties (alternatively, right-click any of the animation frames
and pick Animation Properties from the pop-up menu) to get the Animation
Properties dialog box. You want the projector film animation to run as long as
someone is viewing it, so you should click the Looping tab and choose Repeat
the Animation Indefinitely. In some cases, however, you may want your animation sequence to play only once (or some other number of times) before
stopping to display the last frame as a still image. In that case, you'd select
the second choice and enter the number of repetitions.

6. Your animation is complete. Select File, Save As to save it. After specifying the
filename and clicking the Save button, you are presented with a slider control
that allows you to choose a balance between good image quality and small
file size. Animation Shop usually does an excellent job of choosing the most

appropriate optimizations for you based on the slider setting. Move the slider up for better image quality, down for smaller file size. Pick a setting and click Next.

After some chugging and crunching are done, you'll be prompted to click Next once more, after which you'll see a preview of the animation. Click Next one more time to see a report like the one shown in Figure 7.15. This makes it much easier for you to decide how big too big is and return to adjust the slider by clicking Back. When the file size seems acceptable, click Finish.

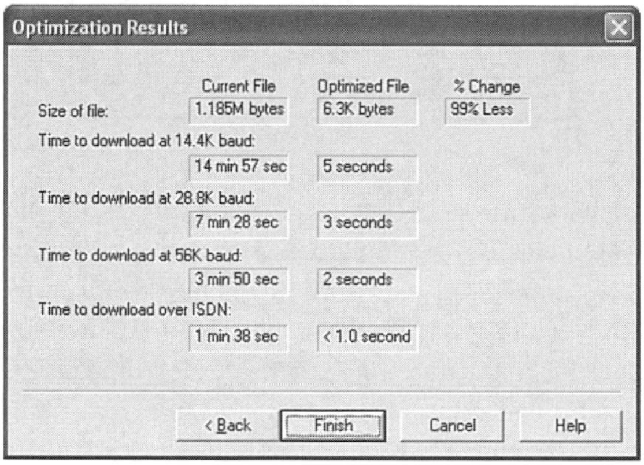

FIGURE 7.15
This report helps you decide whether you found the right balance of image quality and file size.

Optimization Results				
	Current File	Optimized File	% Change	
Size of file:	1.185M bytes	6.3K bytes	99% Less	
Time to download at 14.4K baud:				
	14 min 57 sec	5 seconds		
Time to download at 28.8K baud:				
	7 min 28 sec	3 seconds		
Time to download at 56K baud:				
	3 min 50 sec	2 seconds		
Time to download over ISDN:				
	1 min 38 sec	< 1.0 second		

< Back   Finish   Cancel   Help

Generating Transitions and Text Effects

Animation Shop (like some other GIF animation programs) can do much more than just collect multiple GIF images into a single animation file. It can also generate some impressive special effects and even create scrolling text banners all by itself. Unfortunately, there's just not room in this book to explain in detail how to use these features, but they're easy enough that you can probably pick them up on your own with a little help from the Animation Shop online help system.

Just to get you started, Figure 7.16 and Figure 7.17 show a transition and text effect being constructed. You use the image transition feature (Effects, Insert Image Transition) to smoothly fade between two banner ads. (You'll see these banner ads used in a JavaScript animation later in the book, in Hour 17, "Web Page Scripting for Nonprogrammers.") The other example uses text transitions (Effects, Insert Text Effect) to scroll the text Limited Online Offer! smoothly across a white background. This didn't require any images at all, because the text transition effects generate their own pictures of the text as they do their magic.

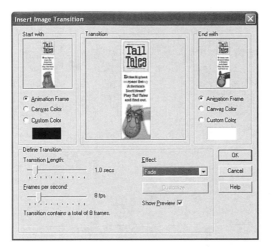

FIGURE 7.16
Use Effects, Insert Image Transition to generate fades, wipes, dissolves, and other automatic transitions between images.

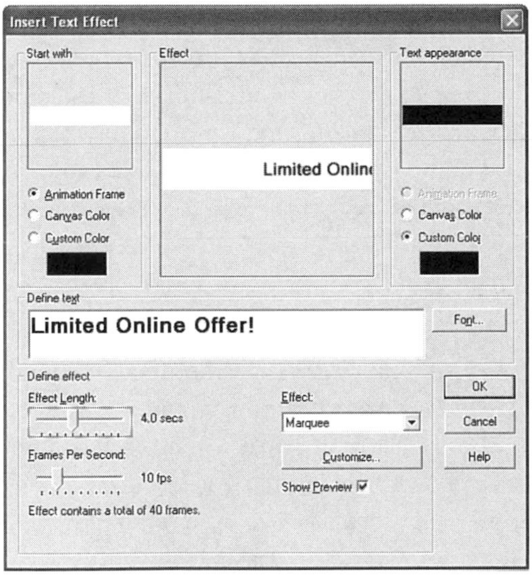

FIGURE 7.17
Use Effects, Insert Text Effect to generate moving text and special-effect text over a frame or a set of frames.

Summary

In this hour you learned the basics of preparing graphics for use on web pages. You saw how to download and use the popular graphics program Paint Shop Pro when working with photos, banners, buttons, and other web page images (though the techniques you learned will work with many other graphics programs as well). You also found out how to decide among the various graphics file formats used for web page graphics, and how to make images that appear in stages, for the illusion of speed.

Q&A

Q *Shouldn't I just hire a graphics artist to design my pages instead of learning all this stuff?*

A If you have plenty of money and need a visually impressive site—or if you think that ugly building with chartreuse trim that people are always complaining about actually looks pretty nice—hiring some professional help might not be a bad idea. Remember, however, that you probably know what you want better than anyone else does, which often counts more than artistic skills in producing a good web page.

Q *I've produced graphics for printing on paper. Is making web page graphics much different?*

A Yes. In fact, many of the rules for print graphics are reversed on the Web. Web page graphics have to be low-resolution, while print graphics should be as high-resolution as possible. White washes out black on computer screens, while black bleeds into white on paper. Also, someone may stop a web page when only half the graphics are done. Try to avoid falling into old habits if you've done a lot of print graphics design.

Q *I have a Windows AVI video clip. Can I turn it into a GIF animation?*

A Yes. Simply open the AVI file with Animation Shop to convert it to a GIF animation. (You are given the option to reduce the number of frames; it's usually a good idea to sample every third frame or so to keep the file size down to reasonable proportions.) You can also embed AVI files directly into web pages, as discussed in Hour 19, "Embedding Multimedia in Web Pages."

Workshop

The workshop contains quiz questions and activities to help you solidify your understanding of the material covered. Try to answer all questions before looking at the "Answers" section that follows.

Quiz

1. Suppose that you have a scanned picture of a horse that you need to put on a web page. How big should you make it, and in what file format should you save it?

2. Your company logo is a black letter Z with a red circle behind it. What size should you draw or scan it, and in what file format should you save it for use on your web page?

3. Should you save a 100×50 pixel button graphic as an interlaced GIF file?

4. How would you modify a GIF animation that repeats infinitely to instead play only three times before stopping?

Answers

1. Depending on how important the image is to your page, as small as 100×40 pixels or as large as 300×120 pixels. The JPEG format, with about 50% compression, would be best. Of course, you could also provide a thumbnail link to a larger image that is viewed by itself. You'll learn how to use images as links in the next lesson.

2. About 100×100 pixels is generally good for a logo, but a simple graphic like that will compress very well; you could make it up to 300×300 pixels if you want. Save it as a 16-color GIF file.

3. No. A small file like that will load just as fast or faster without interlacing.

4. Using Animation Shop, select Animation, Animation Properties. Click the Looping tab, choose Play It, and enter the number 3.

Exercises

▶ If you have an archive of company (or personal) photos, look through it to find a few that might enhance your web site. Scan them (or send them out to be scanned) so that you'll have a library of graphics all ready to draw from as you produce more pages in the future. If you have photos taken on a digital camera, you can obviously skip the scanning step and jump straight into prepping the images for your web pages.

▶ Before you start designing graphics for an important business site, try spicing up your own personal home page. This will give you a chance to learn Paint Shop Pro (or your other graphics software) so that you'll look like you know what you're doing when you tackle the task at work.

HOUR 8

Putting Graphics on a Web Page

In Hour 7, "Creating Your Own Web Page Graphics," you learned how to make digital images for your web pages, both still and animated. This hour shows you how easy it is to put those graphics on your pages with HTML. Fortunately, there is nothing special you have to do to place an animated image on a web page, as compared to a still image.

Try It Yourself ▼

You should get two or three images ready now so that you can try putting them on your own pages as you follow along with this hour. If you have some image files already saved in the GIF, PNG, or JPEG format (the filenames will end in .gif, .png, or .jpg), use those. It's also fine to use any graphics you created while reading the preceding lesson.

At the *Sams Publishing* website, you'll find live links to many graphics and multimedia hot lists and sites, where you can find ready-to-use graphics.

The familiar web search engines and directories, such as google.com, yahoo.com, and lycos.com, can become a gold mine of graphics images just by leading you to sites related to your own theme. They can also help you discover the oodles of sites specifically dedicated to providing free and cheap access to reusable media collections. Also, don't forget Microsoft's massive clip art library at the Office Online Clip Art and Media web site, located at http://office.microsoft.com/clipart/.

▲

Placing an Image on a Web Page

To put an image on a web page, first move the image file into the same folder as the HTML text file. Insert the following HTML tag at the point in the text where you want the image to appear. Use the name of your image file instead of *myimage.gif*:

```
<img src="myimage.gif" alt="My Image" />
```

Both the src and the alt attributes of the <img /> tag are required in XHTML web pages. The src attribute identifies the image file, and the alt attribute allows you to specify descriptive text about the image, the latter of which is intended to serve as an alternative to the image in the event that a user is unable to view the image. You'll read more on the alt attribute later, in the section "Describing an Image with Text."

The <img /> tag also supports a title attribute that is used to describe an image. Unlike the alt attribute, the title attribute is truly intended to provide an image description with the assumption that the image is visible. The alt attribute serves a more important purpose, and enters the picture primarily when an image cannot be displayed, such as when a blind user is "viewing" a page. The alt attribute is required but it's a good idea to provide both alt and title attributes if you want to ensure that your images are all well-described.

As an example of how to use the <img /> tag, Listing 8.1 inserts several images at the top and bottom of a page. Whenever a web browser displays the HTML file in Listing 8.1, it automatically retrieves and displays the image files as shown in Figure 8.1. Notice that these are some of the same images you saw created and edited in Paint Shop Pro in the preceding lesson.

LISTING 8.1   The <img /> **Tag Is Used to Place Images on a Web Page**

```
<?xml version="1.0" encoding="UTF-8"?>
<!DOCTYPE html PUBLIC "-//W3C//DTD XHTML 1.1//EN"
  "http://www.w3.org/TR/xhtml11/DTD/xhtml11.dtd">

<html xmlns="http://www.w3.org/1999/xhtml" xml:lang="en">
  <head>
    <title>Michael's Pond</title>
  </head>

  <body>
    <p>
      <img src="pondtitle.gif" alt="Michael's Pond" />
    </p>
    <p>
      My backyard pond is not only a fun hobby but also an ongoing home
      improvement project that is both creative and relaxing. I have numerous
      fish in the pond, all Koi from various places as far as Japan, Israel,
      and Australia. Although they don't bark, purr, or fetch anything other
      than food, these fish are my pets, and good ones at that. The pond was
      built in a matter of weeks but has evolved over several years through
      a few different improvements and redesigns. I still consider it a work in
      progress, as there are always things to improve upon as I continue to
      learn more about how the pond ecosystem works, how to minimize
      maintenance, and how to get a more aesthetically pleasing look.
    </p>
    <p>
```

LISTING 8.1   Continued

```
      <img src="pond1.jpg" alt="The Lotus, Floating Hyacinth, Japanese Lantern,
      and Waterfall All Add to the Drama of the Pond" /> <br />
      <img src="pond2.jpg" alt="Feeding Time is Always Full of
      Excitement" /> <br />
      <img src="pond3.jpg" alt="One of the Larger Fish Cruises for
      Dinner" /> <br />
      <img src="pond4.jpg" alt="A Dragonfly Hovers Over the Lotus for a Quick
      Drink" />
    </p>
  </body>
</html>
```

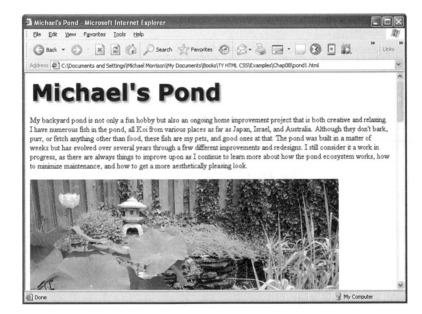

FIGURE 8.1
When a web browser displays the HTML page from Listing 8.1, it adds the images named pondtitle.gif, pond1.jpg, pond2.jpg, pond3.jpg, and pond4.jpg.

If you guessed that img stands for *image*, you're right; src stands for *source*, which is a reference to the location of the image file. (As discussed in Hour 1, "Understanding HTML and XHTML," a web page image is always stored in a file separate from the text, even though it appears to be part of the same page when viewed in a browser.)

Just as with the <a href> tag (covered in Hour 3, "Linking to Other Web Pages"), you can specify any complete Internet address in the src attribute of the <img /> tag. Alternatively, you can specify just the filename if an image is located in the same folder as the HTML file. You can also use relative addresses such as images/birdy.jpg or ../smiley.gif.

By the Way

Theoretically, you can include an image from any Internet web page within your own pages. For example, you could include a picture of my steely glare by putting the following on your web page:

```
<img src="http://www.michaelmorrison.com/mmintro1.jpg" />
```

The image would be retrieved from my web server whenever your page was displayed. You could do this, but you shouldn't! Not only is it bad manners (it often costs people money whenever you pull something from their server computer), but it also can make your pages display more slowly. You also have no way of controlling whether the image has been changed or deleted.

If someone gives you permission to republish an image from one of his pages, always transfer a copy of that image to your computer and use a local file reference such as `<img src="mmintro1.jpg" />`. In other words, you should host all images used on your pages.

Describing an Image with Text

Each `<img />` tag in Listing 8.1 includes a short text message, such as `alt="One of the Larger Fish Cruises for Dinner"`. The `alt` stands for *alternate text* because this message will appear in place of the image if a user turns off automatic image downloading in her web browser preferences. Everyone else will see the message you put in the `alt` attribute too—because graphics files sometimes take a while to transfer over the Internet, most web browsers show the text on a page first with the `alt` messages in place of the graphics (as shown in Figure 8.2).

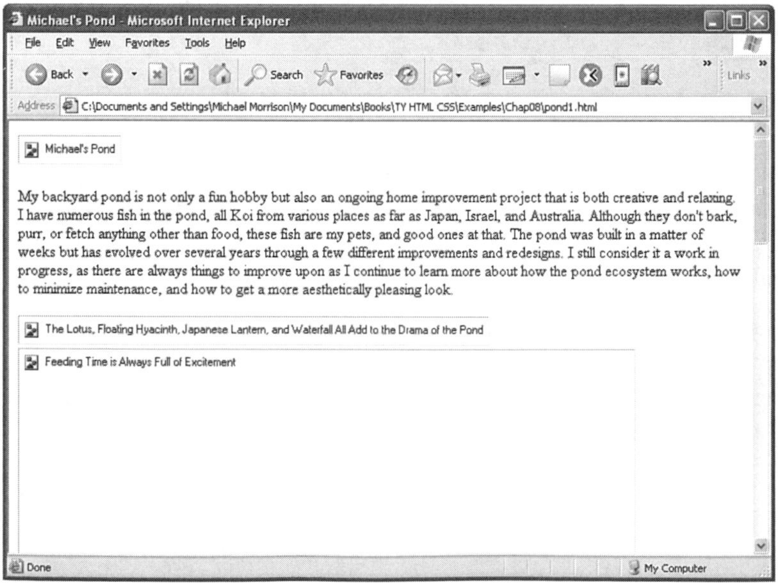

FIGURE 8.2
People will see the alt messages while waiting for the graphics to appear.

Even after the graphics replace the alt messages, the alt message typically appears in a little box (tool tip) whenever the mouse pointer passes over an image. The alt message also helps anyone who is visually impaired (or is using a voice-based interface to read the web page).

You must include a suitable alt attribute in every <img /> tag on your web pages, keeping in mind the variety of situations in which people might see that message. A very brief description of the image is usually best, but web page authors sometimes put short advertising messages or subtle humor in their alt messages. For small or unimportant images, it's tempting to omit the alt message altogether, but it is a required attribute of the <img /> tag. This doesn't mean your page won't display properly, but it does mean you'll be in violation of the latest XHTML standards. I recommend assigning an empty text message to alt if you absolutely don't need it (alt=""), which is sometimes the case with small or decorative images.

There is also a title attribute that is not required by the <img /> tag. The title attribute is similar to the alt attribute except that it does not enter the picture in regard to accessibility. However, the title attribute does supersede the alt attribute for tool tips if both attributes are present. Knowing this, the best approach for describing images via text is to use the alt attribute to store a brief text description of an image and then use the title attribute to provide any relevant notation or helpful hints about the image that you think might be useful when viewed as a tool tip.

Coffee Break

Speaking of text and images, you may not realize that you can search just for images on the Web using Google. Check out Google's Image Search service here: http://www.google.com/imghp?hl=en&tab=wi&q=. Strange URL aside, Google Image Search is a very powerful search tool that can come up with some interesting results. If nothing else, try searching for your name on there—you may be surprised at what you find!

Turning Images into Links

You probably noticed in Figure 8.1 that the images on the page are quite large, which isn't ideal when you're trying to present multiple images. It makes more sense in this case to create smaller image thumbnails that link to larger versions of each image. Then you can arrange the thumbnails on the page so that visitors can easily see all the content, even if they see only a sampling of what is to come. Thumbnails are one of many ways you can use image links to spice up your pages.

You can turn any image into a clickable link to another page or image using the same <a href> tag used to make text links. Listing 8.2 contains the code for a modified Pond sample page that takes advantage of image links and thumbnails to improve on the page layout. This page is shown in Figure 8.3.

LISTING 8.2   Thumbnail Images Serve as a Great Example of How to Effectively Use Image Links

```
<?xml version="1.0" encoding="UTF-8"?>
<!DOCTYPE html PUBLIC "-//W3C//DTD XHTML 1.1//EN"
  "http://www.w3.org/TR/xhtml11/DTD/xhtml11.dtd">

<html xmlns="http://www.w3.org/1999/xhtml" xml:lang="en">
  <head>
    <title>Michael's Pond</title>
  </head>

  <body>
    <p style="text-align:center">
      <img src="pondtitle.gif" alt="Michael's Pond" />
    </p>
    <p>
      My backyard pond is not only a fun hobby but also an ongoing home
      improvement project that is both creative and relaxing. I have numerous
      fish in the pond, all Koi from various places as far as Japan, Israel,
      and Australia. Although they don't bark, purr, or fetch anything other
      than food, these fish are my pets, and good ones at that. The pond was
      built in a matter of weeks but has evolved over several years through
      a few different improvements and redesigns. I still consider it a work in
      progress, as there are always things to improve upon as I continue to
      learn more about how the pond ecosystem works, how to minimize
      maintenance, and how to get a more aesthetically pleasing look.
    </p>
    <p style="text-align:center">
      <a href="pond1.jpg"><img src="pond1_sm.jpg"
      alt="The Lotus, Floating Hyacinth, Japanese Lantern, and Waterfall All
      Add to the Drama of the Pond" style="border-style:none" /></a>
      <a href="pond2.jpg"><img src="pond2_sm.jpg"
      alt="Feeding Time is Always Full of Excitement"
      style="border-style:none" /></a>
      <a href="pond3.jpg"><img src="pond3_sm.jpg"
      alt="One of the Larger Fish Cruises for Dinner"
      style="border-style:none" /></a>
      <a href="pond4.jpg"><img src="pond4_sm.jpg"
      alt="A Dragonfly Hovers Over the Lotus for a Quick Drink"
      style="border-style:none" /></a>
    </p>
  </body>
</html>
```

As the code reveals, not a whole lot has changed in this version of the page beyond the anchor tags that now wrap around each of the pond images. Also pay close attention to the fact that the images on this page are now thumbnail images, as is evident by their different file names (pond1_sm.jpg, pond2_sm.jpg, and so on). The _sm in the filenames simply means "small," as compared to the larger versions of the images that are referenced in the <a> tags.

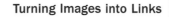

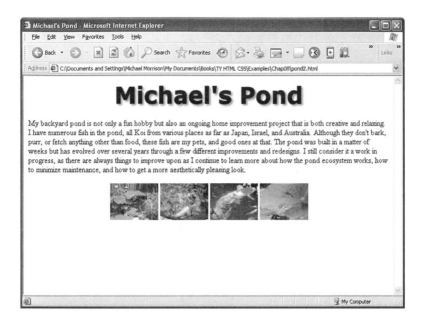

FIGURE 8.3
Using linked thumbnail images allows you to dramatically improve the layout of pages with large images.

Normally, web browsers draw a colored rectangle around the edge of each image link. Like text links, the rectangle usually appears blue to people who haven't visited the link recently, and purple to people who have. Because you seldom, if ever, want this unsightly line around your linked images, you should usually include `style="border-style:none"` in any `<img />` tag within a link. (You'll learn more about the `border` attribute in Hour 13, "Digging Deeper into Style Sheet Formatting.")

A practical example of an image link that you may want to eventually incorporate into your own web pages is a PayPal Buy Now button. Such a button allows visitors to purchase items from you via PayPal, which automatically handles collecting the money and notifying you of the purchase. PayPal's Buy Now buttons involve the use of forms, which are covered in Hour 18, "Gathering Information with HTML Forms." You'll also learn how to create and use a PayPal Buy Now button in Hour 18.

All the same linking rules and possibilities discussed in Hour 3 and Hour 6 apply to image links exactly as they do for text links. (You can link to another part of the same page with `<a href="#name">`, for example.)

When you click one of the thumbnail images on the Pond sample page, the full-size image is opened in the browser, as shown in Figure 8.4.

FIGURE 8.4
Clicking a linked
thumbnail
image opens
the large ver-
sion of the
image in the
web browser.

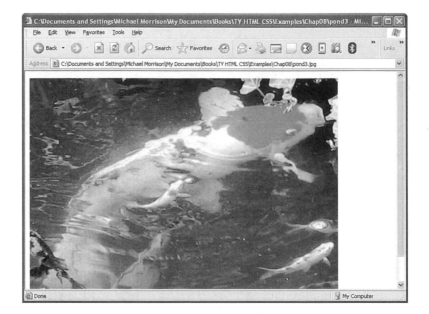

Aligning Images

Similarly to text, images can be aligned on the page using special attributes. Not only can you align images horizontally, but you also can align them vertically with respect to text and other images that surround them.

Horizontal Image Alignment

As discussed in Hour 5, "Basic Text Alignment and Formatting," you can use `<div style="text-align:center">`, `<div style="text-align:right">`, and `<div style="text-align:left">` to align an element to the center, right margin, or left margin. These style settings affect both text and images, and can be used within the `<p>` tag as well.

For example, the first `<img />` tag in Listing 8.2 occurs between the `<p style="text-align:center">` tag and the closing `</p>` tag. This causes the title image to be centered on the page. Like text, images are normally lined up with the left margin unless a `style="text-align:center"` or `style="text-align:right"` setting indicates that they should be centered or right-justified. In other words, `left` is the default value of the `text-align` style property.

As the final four images in Listing 8.2 and Figure 8.3 demonstrate, you can also use `style="text-align:center"` to center more than one image at a time. Because there are no `<br />` or `<p>` tags between them, the four thumbnail images all appear on one line and the entire line is centered horizontally in the browser window.

You can also make text wrap around images, in which case you use the `float` style property directly within the `<img />` tag. Following is an example of how you might do this:

```
<img src="fish.jpg" alt="A Fish" style="float:left" />
<img src="turtle.jpg" alt="A Turtle" style="float:right" />
```

`<img style="float:left" />` aligns the image to the left and causes text to wrap around the right side of it, as you might expect. Similarly, `<img style="float:right" />` aligns the image to the right and causes text to wrap around the left side of it. There is no concept of floating an image to the center because there would be no way to determine how to wrap text on each side of it.

> The `float` style property is actually more powerful than I've let on here, and in fact applies to more than just images. You can use the `float` style property creatively to arrive at some interesting page layouts, as you'll find out later in Hour 14, "Using Style Sheets for Page Layout."

By the Way

Vertical Image Alignment

Sometimes, you may want to insert a small image in the middle of a line of text; or you might like to put a single line of text next to an image as a caption. In either case, it would be handy to have some control over how the text and images line up vertically. Should the bottom of the image line up with the bottom of the letters, or should the text and images all be arranged so that their middles line up? You can choose between these and several other options:

▶ To line up the top of an image with the top of the tallest image or letter on the same line, use `<img style="vertical-align:text-top" />`.

▶ To line up the bottom of an image with the bottom of the text, use `<img style="vertical-align:text-bottom" />`.

▶ To line up the middle of an image with the overall vertical center of everything on the line, use `<img style="vertical-align:middle" />`.

▶ To line up the bottom of an image with the baseline of the text, use `<img style="vertical-align:baseline" />`.

> The vertical-align style property also supports values of top and bottom, which can be used to align images with the overall top or bottom of a line of elements regardless of any text on the line.

All four of these options are illustrated in Listing 8.3 and Figure 8.5. The four pond thumbnail images are now listed vertically down the page, along with descriptive text next to each of them. Various settings for the vertical-align style property are used to align each image and its relevant text.

> If you don't include any align attribute in an <img /> tag, the bottom of the image will line up with the baseline of any text next to it. That means you never actually have to type in style="vertical-align:baseline" because it is assumed by default. However, if you specify a margin for an image and intend for the alignment to be a bit more exacting with the text, you may want to explicitly set the vertical-align attribute to text-bottom. Take a look at the last image in Figure 8.5 to see what I'm talking about in regard to the text appearing slightly below the image due to the image margin—this is a result of the baseline setting for vertical-align.

LISTING 8.3   Horizontal Alignment, Vertical Alignment, and Text Wrapping All Enter the Picture in This Example

```
<?xml version="1.0" encoding="UTF-8"?>
<!DOCTYPE html PUBLIC "-//W3C//DTD XHTML 1.1//EN"
  "http://www.w3.org/TR/xhtml11/DTD/xhtml11.dtd">

<html xmlns="http://www.w3.org/1999/xhtml" xml:lang="en">
  <head>
    <title>Michael's Pond</title>
  </head>

  <body>
    <p style="text-align:center">
      <img src="pondtitle.gif" alt="Michael's Pond" />
    </p>
    <p>
      My backyard pond is not only a fun hobby but also an ongoing home
      improvement project that is both creative and relaxing. I have numerous
      fish in the pond, all Koi from various places as far as Japan, Israel,
      and Australia. Although they don't bark, purr, or fetch anything other
      than food, these fish are my pets, and good ones at that. The pond was
      built in a matter of weeks but has evolved over several years through
      a few different improvements and redesigns. I still consider it a work in
      progress, as there are always things to improve upon as I continue to
      learn more about how the pond ecosystem works, how to minimize
      maintenance, and how to get a more aesthetically pleasing look.
    </p>
    <p>
```

LISTING 8.3 Continued

```
        <a href="pond1.jpg"><img src="pond1_sm.jpg" alt="Pond Plants"
        title="Click to view larger picture." style="border-style:none;
        margin:2px; vertical-align:text-top"/></a>
        The Lotus, Floating Hyacinth, Japanese Lantern, and Waterfall All Add to
        the Drama of the Pond<br/>
        <a href="pond2.jpg"><img src="pond2_sm.jpg" alt="Fish Feeding Frenzy"
        title="Click to view larger picture." style="border-style:none;
        margin:2px; vertical-align:middle" /></a>
        Feeding Time is Always Full of Excitement<br/>
        <a href="pond3.jpg"><img src="pond3_sm.jpg" alt="Large Fish Having
        Dinner" title="Click to view larger picture." style="border-style:none;
        margin:2px; vertical-align:text-bottom" /></a>
        One of the Larger Fish Cruises for Dinner<br/>
        <a href="pond4.jpg"><img src="pond4_sm.jpg"
        alt="Hovering Dragonfly" title="Click to view larger picture."
        style="border-style:none; margin:2px; vertical-align:baseline" /></a>
        A Dragonfly Hovers Over the Lotus for a Quick Drink<br/>
    </p>
  </body>
</html>
```

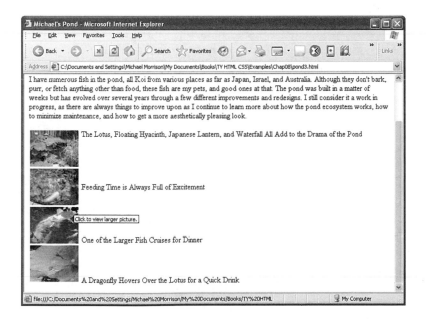

FIGURE 8.5
The newly modified Pond sample page listed in Listing 8.3, as it appears in a web browser.

Notice in the figure a subtle change that makes sense given that the text descriptions now appear alongside the images on the page. I'm referring to the new title attributes, which are now used to display the message Click to view larger picture for all the images. The required alt attributes now contain brief descriptions of each image.

This usage of the `title` attribute addresses the problem of some Web developers using the `alt` attribute simply to house tool tip text. The problem stems from the fact that some browsers display a pop-up (tool tip) containing the `alt` text. However, you can just as easily use the `title` attribute for this purpose, as is done in the example, and then use the `alt` attribute for its original intent of providing alternative text for the image. The bottom line is that it's a good idea to use both the `alt` and the `title` attributes with images whenever possible.

▼   **Try It Yourself**

Try adding some images to your web pages now, and experiment with different values of `text-align`, `vertical-align`, and `float`. To get you started, here's a quick review of how to add a hypothetical fish image (`fish.jpg`) to any web page.

- ▶ Copy the fish.jpg image file to the same directory folder as the HTML file.

- ▶ With a text editor, add `<img src="fish.jpg" alt="Fishy" />` where you want the image to appear in the text.

- ▶ If you want the image to be centered, put `<div style="text-align:center">` before the `<img />` tag and `</div>` after it. To wrap text around the image instead, add `style="float:right"` or `style="float:left"` to the `<img />` tag. And finally, use the `vertical-align` style property directly within the `<img />` tag to control the vertical alignment of the image with respect to other images and text next to it.

- ▶ If you have time for a little more experimentation, try combining multiple images of various sizes with various vertical alignment settings.

▲

Specifying Image Width and Height

Because text moves over the Internet much faster than do graphics, most web browsers will display the text on a page before the images. This gives people something to read while they're waiting to see the pictures, which makes the whole page seem faster.

You can make sure that everything on your page appears as quickly as possible and in the right places by explicitly stating each image's width and height. That way, a web browser can immediately and accurately make room for each image as it lays out the page and while it waits for the images to finish transferring.

Did you Know?

Although specifying the width and height of an image can help web browsers render a page a bit quicker, it can also be a pain if you're developing pages in which the image sizes still aren't set in concrete. You don't want to have to constantly be changing the width and height attributes as you're tweaking images on a page. For this reason, you can think of the width and height attributes of the <img /> tag as somewhat of an optimization that you apply when a page is ready to be published.

For each image on your page, use Paint Shop Pro or another graphics program to find out the exact width and height in pixels. (In Paint Shop Pro, this information appears in the lower-right corner of the main window when you move the mouse over any part of an image.) Then include those dimensions in the <img /> tag, like this:

```
<img src="myimage.gif" alt="" width="200" height="100" />
```

Did you Know?

The width and height specified for an image don't have to match the image's actual width and height. The web browser program will try to squish or stretch the image to whatever size you specify. However, this is generally a bad idea because browsers aren't particularly good at resizing images. If you want an image to appear smaller, you're definitely better off resizing it in an image editor.

Allowing a web browser to resize an image usually makes it look very ugly due to the squishing or stretching, but there is one excellent use for it: You can save a very small, totally transparent image and use it as any size spacer by specifying the width and height of the blank region you want to create on your page. This is a clever trick that some web designers use when they're in a pinch with a difficult page layout.

Summary

This hour has shown you how to use the <img /> tag to place graphics images on your web pages. You learned to include a short text message to appear in place of the image as it loads and to appear whenever someone moves the mouse pointer over the image. You also learned to control the horizontal and vertical alignment of each image and how to make text wrap around the left or right of an image.

Finally, you learned how to take advantage of thumbnail images that link to larger images as means of improving the layout of pages. This required using the same <a> tag introduced in Hour 3. What you didn't see is how to use images as custom page backgrounds, which is coming up next, in Hour 9, "Custom Backgrounds and Colors."

Table 8.1 summarizes the attributes of the `<img />` tag covered in this hour, along with relevant style properties.

TABLE 8.1   HTML Tags and Attributes Covered in Hour 8

Tag/Attribute	Function
`<img />`	Places an image file within the page.
Attributes	
`src="address"`	The address or filename of the image.
`alt="altdescription"`	An alternative description of the image that is displayed in place of the image, primarily for users who can't view the image itself.
`title="title"`	A text message that is displayed as an image title, typically in a small pop-up box (tool tip) over the image.
`width="width"`	The width of the image, in pixels.
`height="height"`	The height of the image, in pixels.
`style="border-style:none"`	Gets rid of the border around the image if it is serving as a link.
`style="vertical-align:alignment"`	Aligns the image vertically to `text-top`, `top`, `text-bottom`, `bottom`, `middle`, or `baseline`.
`style="float:float"`	Floats the image to one side so that text can wrap around the other. Possible values are `left`, `right`, and `none` (default).

Q&A

Q *I found a nice image on a web page on the Internet. Can I just use Save Image As to save a copy and then put the image on my web pages?*

A It's easy to do that, but unfortunately it's also illegal in most countries if you don't have permission to reuse the image; of course, this excludes images found on royalty-free clip art web sites. You should first get written permission from the original creator of the image. Most web pages include the author's email address, which makes it a simple matter to ask for permission—a lot simpler than going to court!

Q *How long can I make a message that I put after alt= in an* `<img />` *tag?*

A Theoretically, as long as you want. For practicality, you should keep the message short enough that it will fit in less space than the image itself. For big images, 10 words may be fine, and I've even seen people include a small paragraph of text in some cases. For small images, a single word is better.

Q *I used the* `<img />` *tag just as you said, but all I get is a little box with an ¥ or some shapes in it when I view the page. What's wrong?*

A The broken image icon you're seeing can mean one of two things: Either the web browser couldn't find the image file, or the image isn't saved in a format the browser can understand. To solve either one of these problems, open the image file by using Paint Shop Pro (or your favorite graphics software), select Save As, and be sure to save the file in either GIF or JPEG format. Also make sure that you save it in the same folder as the web page that contains the `<img />` tag referring to it and that the filename on the disk precisely matches the filename you put in the `<img />` tag (including capitalization). And make sure that the image file is in the same folder as the web page, or the exact relative folder if you've elected to place and reference images from their own folder.

Q *Why do the examples in this book put a slash at the end of every* `<img />` *tag? None of the web pages I see on the Internet do that.*

A As discussed in Hour 2, "Create a Web Page Right Now" (yes, I know that was a long time ago), the XTHML standards require any empty tag (a tag that doesn't have a closing tag) to include a slash at the end. Although it may be unlikely that anyone will ever write software that fails to accept the traditional `<img>` tag without the slash, you should use `<img />` so that your pages are ready for the future Web as it continues to unfold. (Remember, people once thought it was unlikely that four-digit year codes for dates would ever be necessary in the software they were writing....)

Workshop

The workshop contains quiz questions and activities to help you solidify your understanding of the material covered. Try to answer all questions before looking at the "Answers" section that follows.

Quiz

1. How would you insert an image file named `elephant.jpg` at the very top of a web page?

2. How would you make the word `Elephant` appear whenever the actual `elephant.jpg` image couldn't be displayed by a web browser?

3. Write the HTML code to make the `elephant.jpg` image appear on the right side of the page, with a big headline reading "Elephants of the World Unite!" on the left side of the page next to it.

4. Write the HTML code to make a tiny image of a mouse (named `mouse.gif`) appear between the words "Wee sleekit, cow'rin," and the words "tim'rous beastie."

Answers

1. Copy the image file into the same directory folder as the HTML text file, and type `<p><img src="elephant.jpg" alt="" /></p>` immediately after the `<body>` tag in the HTML text file.

2. Use the following HTML:

   ```
   <img src="elephant.jpg" alt="elephant" />
   ```

3. ```
   <img src="elephant.jpg" alt="Elephant" style="float:right" />
   <h1>Elephants of the World Unite!</h1>
   ```

4. ```
   Wee sleekit, cow'rin,<img src="mouse.gif" alt="" />tim'rous
   beastie
   ```

Exercises

Try using any small image as a "bullet" to make lists with more flair. If you also want the list to be indented, use the `<dl>` definition list and `<dd>` for each item (instead of `<ul>` and `<li>`, which would give the standard boring bullets). Here's a quick example, using a hypothetical `star.gif` image file:

```
<dl><dd><img src="star.gif" alt="" />A murder of crows</dd>
<dd><img src="star.gif" alt="" />A rafter of turkeys</dd>
<dd><img src="star.gif" alt="" />A muster of peacocks</dd></dl>
```

HOUR 9

Custom Backgrounds and Colors

Nearly every sample web page in Hours 1 through 8 has a white background and black text. In this hour, you'll find out how to make pages with background and text colors of your choosing. You'll also discover how to make your own custom background graphics and how to let the background show through parts of any image you put on your web pages.

Try It Yourself ▼

The black-and-white figures printed in this book obviously don't convey colors very accurately, so you may want to view the sample pages online. You can also try the colors on your own web pages as you read about how to make them.

To find all the examples from this hour online, go to http://www.samspublishing.com/.

Did you Know?

▲

Exploring Background and Text Colors

Specifying a background color other than white for a web page is easier than you probably realize. For example, to specify blue as the background color for a page, put style="background-color:blue" inside the <body> tag. Of course, you can use many colors other than blue. You can choose from a long list of standard color names, including such unusually descriptive choices as BurlyWood, LavenderBlush, and MistyRose. Admittedly, this sounds more like a box of designer crayons than it does a list of web color choices. Of course, the 16 standard Windows colors are also supported: Black, White, Red, Green, Blue, Yellow, Magenta, Cyan, Purple, Gray, Lime, Maroon, Navy, Olive, Silver, and Teal. (You can call Magenta by the name Fuchsia and Cyan by the name Aqua if you want to feel more artsy and less geeky.)

It's certainly worth pointing out that case doesn't matter when specifying color names. So, Black, black, and BLACK are all allowed, although most web designers stick with lowercase or mixed case. I happen to prefer lowercase because it helps make your code look a little cleaner.

You can also specify colors for text in the <body> tag. For example, in Listing 9.1 you'll notice the following <body> tag:

```
<body style="background-color:teal; color:fuchsia">
```

As you probably guessed, color:fuchsia makes the text color for the page fuchsia (which is the same as magenta). When placed in the <body> tag, the color style property impacts all the text on the page. However, you can set the color property for specific elements within the page to override the setting in the <body> tag.

For a detailed list of all the color names you can use when specifying colors in your HTML code, visit http://www.w3schools.com/css/css_colornames.asp. This page lists the name of each color, along with its hexadecimal representation (more on this in a moment) and what it looks like onscreen.

You can also change the color of text links, including various properties of links such as the color for when a user hovers over a link versus when the user clicks a link. Setting the colors for text links involves using an internal style sheet, which you won't learn about until Hour 12, "Formatting Web Pages with CSS Style Sheets." In that lesson you'll learn all the details of how to apply colors to text links via CSS styles.

Listing 9.1 and Figure 9.1 illustrate somewhat atrociously how to set the background color and text color of a web page. Because I used pure, beautiful teal as the background color in the graphics images, they blend right into the background of the web page. (I didn't need to use transparent images, which you'll learn about later in this hour.)

LISTING 9.1   Specifying the Background and Text Colors in the <body> Tag

```
<?xml version="1.0" encoding="UTF-8"?>
<!DOCTYPE html PUBLIC "-//W3C//DTD XHTML 1.1//EN"
  "http://www.w3.org/TR/xhtml11/DTD/xhtml11.dtd">

<html xmlns="http://www.w3.org/1999/xhtml" xml:lang="en">
  <head>
    <title>The Teal and the Fuchsia</title>
  </head>
```

LISTING 9.1   Continued

```
<body style="background-color:teal; color:fuchsia">
  <h1>CREDLEY HIGH SCHOOL</h1>
  <h2>"The Old Teal and Fuchsia"</h2>
  <div style="text-align:center">
    <p style="font-style:italic">
      <img src="c.gif" alt="Cheer!" style="float:right" />
      Oh, hail! Hail! Sing Credley!<br />
      Our colors jump and shout!<br />
      Deep teal like ocean's highest waves,<br />
      Fuchsia like blossoms bursting out!
    </p>
    <p style="font-style:italic">
      <img src="cheer.gif" alt="Cheer!" style="float:left" />
      As Credley conquers every team<br />
      So do our brilliant colors peal<br />
      From mountain tops &amp; florist shops<br />
      Sweet sacred fuchsia, holy teal!
    </p>
    <p style="font-style:italic">
      Our men are tough as vinyl siding<br />
      Our women, strong as plastic socks<br />
      Our colors tell our story truly<br />
      We may be ugly, but we rock!
    </p>
  </div>
</body>
</html>
```

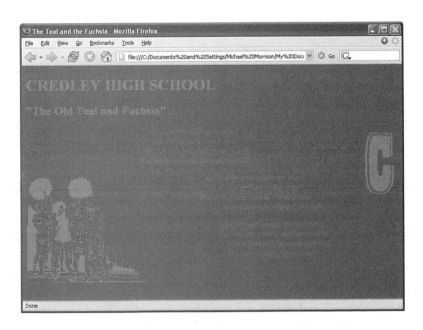

FIGURE 9.1
On a color screen, this ever-so-attractive page has a teal background and fuchsia body text, as specified in Listing 9.1.

Just in case you didn't catch on, this page is somewhat of a sarcastic example of web page color at its worst. Fortunately, you can change the entire look and feel of this page by altering the two colors that are specified in the <body> tag. In other words, a single line of code is all you have to change to make a dramatic change to the page's appearance.

Specifying Custom Colors

If none of the named colors imparts the exact hue you're after, you can mix your own custom colors by specifying how much red, green, and blue light should be mixed into each color. It works a little bit like Play-Doh—just mix in the amounts of red, blue, and green you want to get the appropriate color.

The format is *#rrggbb*, in which *rr*, *gg*, and *bb* are two-digit hexadecimal values for the red, green, and blue components of the color. If you're not familiar with hexadecimal numbers, don't sweat it. Just remember that FF is the maximum and 00 is the minimum, and use one of the following codes for each component:

- ▶ FF means full brightness.
- ▶ CC means 80 percent brightness.
- ▶ 99 means 60 percent brightness.
- ▶ 66 means 40 percent brightness.
- ▶ 33 means 20 percent brightness.
- ▶ 00 means none of this color component.

For example, bright red is #FF0000, dark green is #003300, bluish-purple is #660099, and medium-gray is #999999. To make a page with a red background and dark green text, the HTML code would look like the following:

```
<body style="background-color:#FF0000; color:#003300">
```

Although the colors you specify in the <body> tag apply to all text on the page, you can also use either color names or hexadecimal color codes to change the color of a particular word or section of text by using the color style property in conjunction with the <span> tag. This is discussed in Hour 12.

Did you Know?

For a very handy chart showing the 216 most commonly used hexadecimal color codes, along with the colors they create, go to http://www.samspublishing.com.

You should be aware that different computer monitors may display colors in very different hues. I recently designed a page with a beautiful blue background for a client, only to find out later that the president of the company saw it on his computer as a lovely purple background! Neutral, earth-tone colors such as medium gray, tan, and ivory can lead to even more unpredictable results on many computer monitors, and may even seem to change color on one monitor depending on lighting conditions in the room and the time of day.

The moral of the story: Consider sticking to the named colors unless you have precise control over your intended audience's computer displays or you're willing to test your page on various monitors. Of course, testing your pages on different computers is very important, and should be done anyway.

Using Background Image Tiles

Background tiles let you specify an image to be used as a wallpaper pattern behind all text and graphics in a document. You specify the background image filename using the background-image style property in the <body> tag at the beginning of your page:

```
<body style="background-image:url(backimage.jpg)">
```

Like other web graphics, background tiles must be in the GIF, PNG, or JPEG file format, and you can create them by using graphics software. For example, the water.jpg file referred to by the <body> tag in Listing 9.2 is an image of one small tile with a watery texture. As you can see in Figure 9.2, most web browsers will repeat the image behind any text and images on the page, like tiles on a floor.

> You might be wondering what happens if you set both a background color and a background image for a web page. The background image is displayed over the background color but the color is allowed to show through any transparent areas of the image. So you can certainly use both styles at once if you plan on taking advantage of transparent areas in the background image.

By the Way

LISTING 9.2   Tiling Background Images with the background-image Style Property in the <body> Tag

```
<?xml version="1.0" encoding="UTF-8"?>
<!DOCTYPE html PUBLIC "-//W3C//DTD XHTML 1.1//EN"
  "http://www.w3.org/TR/xhtml11/DTD/xhtml11.dtd">

<html xmlns="http://www.w3.org/1999/xhtml" xml:lang="en">
  <head>
    <title>Michael's Pond</title>
  </head>
```

LISTING 9.2   Continued

```
<body style="background-image:url(water.jpg)">
  <p style="text-align:center">
    <img src="pondtitle.gif" alt="Michael's Pond" />
  </p>
  <p>
    My backyard pond is not only a fun hobby but also an ongoing home
    improvement project that is both creative and relaxing. I have numerous
    fish in the pond, all Koi from various places as far as Japan, Israel,
    and Australia. Although they don't bark, purr, or fetch anything other
    than food, these fish are my pets, and good ones at that. The pond was
    built in a matter of weeks but has evolved over several years through
    a few different improvements and redesigns. I still consider it a work in
    progress, as there are always things to improve upon as I continue to
    learn more about how the pond ecosystem works, how to minimize
    maintenance, and how to get a more aesthetically pleasing look.
  </p>
  <p style="text-align:center">
    <a href="pond1.jpg"><img src="pond1_sm.jpg"
    alt="The Lotus, Floating Hyacinth, Japanese Lantern, and Waterfall All
    Add to the Drama of the Pond" style="border-style:none" /></a>
    <a href="pond2.jpg"><img src="pond2_sm.jpg"
    alt="Feeding Time is Always Full of Excitement"
    style="border-style:none" /></a>
    <a href="pond3.jpg"><img src="pond3_sm.jpg"
    alt="One of the Larger Fish Cruises for Dinner"
    style="border-style:none" /></a>
    <a href="pond4.jpg"><img src="pond4_sm.jpg"
    alt="A Dragonfly Hovers Over the Lotus for a Quick Drink"
    style="border-style:none" /></a>
  </p>
</body>
</html>
```

FIGURE 9.2
The water.jpg
file (specified in
Listing 9.2 and
shown separate-
ly in Figure 9.3)
is automatically
repeated to
cover the entire
page.

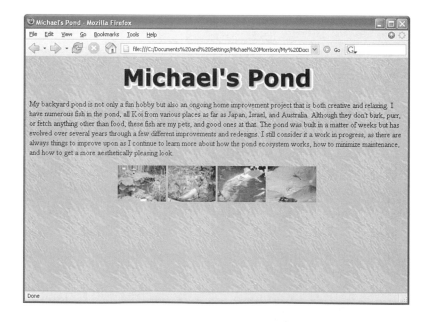

FIGURE 9.3
The water.jpg background tile is surprisingly small, but when it's tiled repeatedly (see Figure 9.2), the effect is relatively seamless.

Watch Out!

Tiled background images should be implemented with great care to avoid distracting from the main content of the page itself. Many pages on the Web are almost impossible to read due to overdone backgrounds.

Before you include your company logo or baby pictures as wallpaper behind your web pages, stop and think. If you had an important message to send someone on a piece of paper, would you write it over the top of the letterhead logo or on the blank part of the page? Backgrounds should be like fine papers: attractive, yet unobtrusive.

As Figure 9.2 reveals, the pond sample page is made considerably more interesting with the addition of the water background image. However, the title image now has a funny-looking white edge around it, which certainly looks out of place. The problem has to do with the fact that the GIF image format supports only a single transparent color, which can't accommodate for the various levels of shading in the drop shadow of the text. This is where the PNG image you saw back in Hour 7, "Creating Your Own Web Page Graphics," enters the picture, as you'll see in the next section.

There is a style property I haven't mentioned that impacts tiled background images. I'm referring to the background-repeat property, which determines exactly how a background image is tiled on the page. Possible values for this style include repeat, repeat-x, repeat-y, and no-repeat. The default setting is repeat, which results in the image being repeated in both the X and the Y directions; this explains why I didn't have to use this style property in the example. The repeat-x and repeat-y settings allow you to repeat an image only across or down the page, but not both. And finally, the no-repeat setting causes the background image to be displayed only once, in the upper-left corner of the page.

Following is an example of tiling a background image across a page:

```
<body style="background-image:url(backimage.jpg); background-repeat:repeat-x">
```

You might initially think that the no-repeat setting for the background-repeat style property makes no sense. However, you may come up with an unusual page design that requires a very large background image that doesn't need to tile. This is where the no-repeat setting could come in handy.

Working with Transparent Images

You will see how to make your own background tiles later in this hour, but first a word about how to let the background show through parts of your foreground graphics.

Web page images are always rectangular. However, the astute observer of Figure 9.2 (that's you) will notice that the background tiles show through portions of the title image, and therefore the title picture doesn't look rectangular at all. This works because portions of the image are transparent, which allows the background to show through. You'll often want to use partially transparent images to make graphics look good over any background color or background image tile.

To make part of an image transparent, the image must be saved in the GIF or PNG file format. (JPEG images can't be made transparent.) Most graphics programs that support the GIF format allow you to specify one color to be transparent, whereas PNG images allow for a range of transparency. Largely because of this transparency range, the PNG format is superior to GIF. All the latest web browsers already support PNG images. For more information on the PNG image format, visit http://www.libpng.org/pub/png/pngintro.html.

In the pond sample page in the preceding section, the title image was specified as a GIF with transparency. However, because GIF images allow only a single transparency color, the drop shadow doesn't quite work as desired. You'll quickly realize that GIF images with transparency often look good only with one type of background image or color. In this case, the pond title looked great on a white background but doesn't work so well on a tiled image background.

The solution is to use a PNG image for the tiled background, which can support varying degrees of transparency, as opposed to a single color. Figure 9.4 shows the same web page with a PNG version of the same title image.

The figure reveals how the drop shadow now allows some of the background image to filter through, which is the intended effect. This difference between GIF and PNG transparency may seem subtle but it can have a huge impact on the visual appeal of your pages.

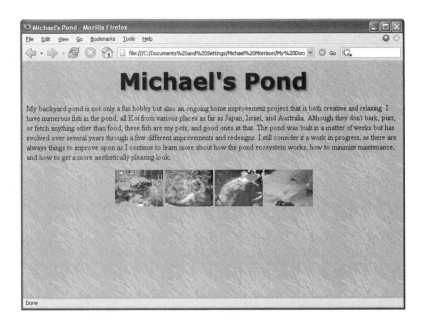

FIGURE 9.4
The PNG version of the pond title image with improved transparency provides the desired drop-shadow effect regardless of the background.

To see a practical example of a PNG image with transparency at work, visit the Google Maps online mapping tool at http://maps.google.com/. Zoom in on your hometown and then enter a search for anything you want, such as "pizza." Several markers will appear on the screen that show locations on the map that match your search request. Click one of the markers to open a pop-up that provides additional information. See the really slick shadow made by the pop-up? That's a transparent PNG image! The effect in this case is dramatic because all the underlying map details are allowed to show through the shadow.

Try It Yourself ▼

Follow these steps to save a transparent GIF in Paint Shop Pro:

1. Choose the eyedropper tool and right-click the color you want to make transparent.

2. Select ImageImage, Palette, Set Palette Transparency. If the image has more than 256 colors, you will be prompted to reduce the colors to 256—just click OK.

3. You should see the dialog box shown in Figure 9.5. Choose Set the Transparency Value to the Current Background Color, and then click OK.

▼

4. Now select Image, Palette, View Palette Transparency, and the transparent parts of the image will turn to a gray checkerboard pattern.

5. You can use any of the painting tools to touch up parts of the image where there is too little or too much of the transparent background color.

6. When everything looks right, select File, Save As (or File, Save Copy As) and choose CompuServe Graphics Interchange (*.gif) as the file type.

If you select Colors, View Palette Transparency (or when you click the Proof button shown in Figure 9.5), Paint Shop Pro shows transparent regions of an image with a gray checkerboard pattern. You can change the grid size and colors used under File, Preferences, General Program Preferences, Transparency.

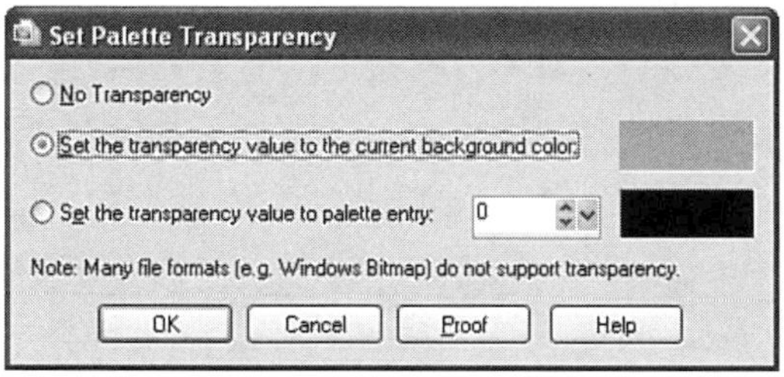

FIGURE 9.5
This dialog box appears when you select Image, Palette, Set Palette Transparency. You will usually want the middle option.

Transparency in PNG images is a slightly more complex issue because it doesn't involve a single transparency color. The trick with PNG images is to make sure that the background itself has no color in it when you create the image. For example, when you first create the image in Paint Shop Pro, be sure to specify the background as being transparent. Then any effects you use that have varying degrees of transparency, like a drop shadow, will automatically take into consideration the transparency of the background.

Creating Your Own Tiled Backgrounds

Any GIF or JPEG image can be used as a background tile. Pages look best, however, when the top edge of a background tile matches seamlessly with the bottom edge, and the left edge matches with the right.

If you're clever and have some time to spend on it, you can turn any image into a seamless tile by meticulously cutting and pasting, while touching up the edges. Paint Shop Pro provides a much easier way to automatically make any texture into a seamless tile: Simply crop out the rectangular area you want to make into a tile, and then choose EffectsEffEfE, Image Effects, Seamless Tiling. Paint Shop Pro crops the image and uses a sophisticated automatic procedure to overlay and blur together opposite sides of the image.

Figure 9.6 shows the Seamless Tiling dialog box in Paint Shop Pro as I turn a photograph of a piece of travertine stone into a seamless tile. The resulting tile—shown as the background of a web page in Figure 9.7—tiles seamlessly but has the tone and texture of a piece of natural travertine stone.

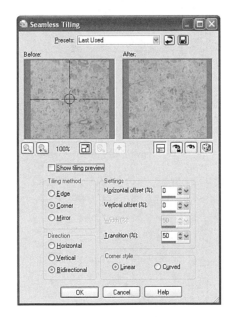

FIGURE 9.6
Paint Shop Pro can automatically take any region of an image and turn it into a background pattern that can be easily made into tiles.

You'll find similar features in other graphics programs, including Photoshop (use Filter, Other, Offset with Wrap Turned On), Kai's Power Tools, and the Macintosh programs Mordant and Tilery.

FIGURE 9.7
These are the results of using the seamless tile created in Figure 9.6 as a background image for a web page.

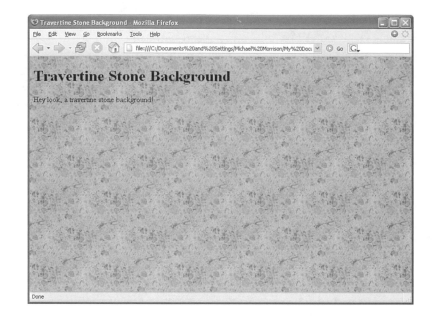

Try It Yourself

Here are some tips for making your own background tiles with Paint Shop Pro:

▶ If you have a scanner or digital camera, try using some textures from around the house or office, such as the top of a wooden desk, leaves of houseplants, or clothing.

▶ Using the AdjustAdju, Blur, Blur More filter on an image before you turn it into a seamless tile will help it look better as a background. Using Adjust, Brightness and Contrast usually is also necessary to keep the background subtle in color variation.

▶ When you select an area to be turned into a tile, try to choose part of the image that is fairly uniform in brightness from side to side. Otherwise, the tile may not look seamless even after you use Convert to Seamless Pattern.

▶ You can also make some almost-automatic textures with the paper texture feature in the paintbrush style palette in Paint Shop Pro. You can also make great paper textures by selecting AdjustAdju, Add/Remove Noise, Add Noise followed by AdjustAdjust, Blur, Blur.

If you just cannot seem to get the pattern you want, you can check out some of the hundreds of sites on the Internet offering public-domain background images that are free or inexpensive and professionally designed.

Summary

In this hour you learned how to set the background and text colors for a web page. You also found out how to make a tiled background image appear behind a web page, how to make foreground images partially transparent so that the background shows through, and how to create seamless image tiles for use as backgrounds.

Table 9.1 summarizes the attributes of the <body> tag discussed in this hour, along with the style properties covered.

TABLE 9.1   Attributes and Styles of the <body> Tag Covered in Hour 9

Tag/Attribute/Style	Function
<body>...</body>	Encloses the body (text and tags) of the HTML document.
style="background-color:*color*"	Sets the background color of the page; can be overridden in child elements.
style="color:*color*"	Sets the color of all text on the page; can be overridden in child elements.
style="background-image:url(*imageurl*)"	Sets the background image of the page, which is typically a tiled image.
style="background-repeat:*repeat*"	Determines how the background image repeats. Possible values include repeat, repeat-x, repeat-y, and no-repeat.

Q&A

Q *Don't web browsers let people choose their own background and text color preferences?*

A Yes, web browsers allow users to override the colors that you, as a web page author, specify. Some may see your white-on-blue page as green-on-white or their own favorite colors instead, but very few people actually use this option. The colors specified in the <body> tag will usually be seen.

Q *I've heard that there are 231 "browser-safe colors" that I should use on web pages, and that I shouldn't use any other colors. Is that true?*

A Here's the real story: There are 231 colors that will appear less "fuzzy" to people who operate their computers in a 256-color (8-bit) video mode. (The other 25 colors are used for menus and stuff like that.) Some web page authors try to stick to those colors. However, true-color or high-color computer displays are all but standard these days, and they show all colors with equal clarity. So if your graphics program can display color values in hexadecimal format, feel free to plug those codes straight into your pages for custom colors. In other words, we're pretty much past the era of having to worry about "browser-safe colors."

Q *My background image looks okay in my graphics editing program, but has weird white or colored gaps or dots in it when it comes up behind a web page. Why?*

A There are two possibilities: If the background image you're using is a GIF file, it probably has transparency turned on, which makes one of the colors in the image turn white (or whatever color you specified in the background-color style property). The solution is to open the file with your graphics program and turn off the transparency. (In Paint Shop Pro, select Image, Palette, Set Palette Transparency, and pick No Transparency.) Resave the file.

If a JPEG or nontransparent GIF or PNG image looks spotty when you put it on a web page, it may just be the web browser's dithering. That's the method the software uses to try to show more colors than your system is set up to display at once by mixing colored dots together side-by-side. There's not much you can do about it, though you'll find hints for minimizing the problem back in Hour 7.

Workshop

The workshop contains quiz questions and activities to help you solidify your understanding of the material covered. Try to answer all questions before looking at the "Answers" section that follows.

Quiz

1. How would you give a web page a black background and make all text bright green?

2. How would you make an image file named `texture.jpg` appear as a repeating tile behind the text and images on a web page with white text?

3. If `elephant.jpg` is a JPEG image of an elephant standing in front of a solid white backdrop, how do you make the backdrop transparent so only the elephant shows on a web page?

Answers

1. Put the following at the beginning of the web page:

   ```
   <body style="background-color:black; color:lime">
   ```

   The following would do exactly the same thing:

   ```
   <body style="background-color:#000000; color:#00FF00">
   ```

2. `<body style="background-image:url(texture.jpg);color:white">`

3. Open the image in Paint Shop Pro; right-click the white area; select Image, Palette, Set Palette Transparency; accept the reduction in colors if necessary; and elect to make the background color transparent. Touch up any off-white spots that didn't become transparent and then use File, Save As to save the image in the GIF 89a format. Optionally, you could crop out the elephant and paste it onto a new image with a transparent background, and then save it as a PNG image.

Exercises

▶ Take a shot at creating some of your own tiled background images out of unusual or unexpected images. If you go through your own collection of digital photographs, you may run across a patch of grass or some other texture in an area of a picture that could be turned into a cool background image.

▶ If you have some photos of objects for a web-based catalog, consider taking the time to paint a transparent color carefully around the edges of them. (Sometimes the magic wand tool in your image editor can help automate this process.) You can also use Paint Shop Pro's Effects, 3D Effects, Drop Shadow feature to add a slight shadow behind or beneath each object so that it appears to stand out from the background.

HOUR 10

Graphical Links and Imagemaps

If you haven't been skipping around too much and you've read Hour 8, "Putting Graphics on a Web Page," you know how to make an image link to another document. (If you don't quite recall how to do it right now, it looks like this: `<a href="gohere.htm"><img src="image.gif" alt="My image" /></a>`.)

You can also divide an image into regions that link to different documents, depending on where someone clicks. This is called an **imagemap**, and any image can be made into an imagemap. A web site with medical information might show an image of the human body and bring up different pages of advice for each body part. A map of the world could allow people to click any country for regional information. Many people use imagemaps to create a "navigation bar" that integrates icons for each page on their web site into one cohesive imagemap.

Modern browsers such as Mozilla Firefox and Microsoft Internet Explorer allow you to choose between two methods for implementing imagemaps. Nowadays, all your imagemaps should be done using the latest method, which is called a client-side imagemap. There really is no longer any reason to make them work the old-fashioned server-side way because web browsers have been supporting client-side imagemaps for years.

Why Imagemaps Aren't Always Necessary

The first thing I must say about imagemaps is that you probably won't need to use them except in very special cases! It's almost always easier and more efficient to use several ordinary images, placed right next to one another, with a separate link for each image.

As an example, consider a graphic that can be described by separate rectangular regions. One good example involves an illustration of an ice hockey rink, which could be used to highlight the rule changes introduced by the National Hockey League (NHL) for the 2005 season. Figure 10.1 shows an example of such an image. The obvious approach for using this rink graphic on a web page is to use a single imagemap for the image and then link specific regions of it to more detailed information.

FIGURE 10.1
An ice rink
image makes
for a good
example of how
to map regions
of an image to
different web
pages.

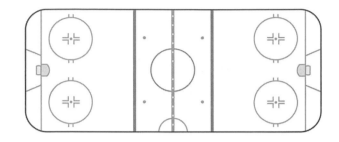

However, the better solution in this case is to cut the graphic into vertical strips
using an image editor such as Photoshop or Paint Shop Pro, and then make each
piece a separate image on the web page. The images can be arranged close together
so that they appear as one complete graphic. The advantages are that the page is
backward compatible with ancient web browsers and the code is a little simpler
because you aren't mathematically describing regions within a single image.
Figure 10.2 shows how to cut up the ice rink graphic so that each link area is a
separate image; the figure actually shows the images for the left side of the rink.

FIGURE 10.2
To avoid using
imagemaps, you
need to cut the
image shown in
Figure 10.1 into
these six
images for the
left side of the
rink. (Cut and
paste using the
rectangular
selection tool.)

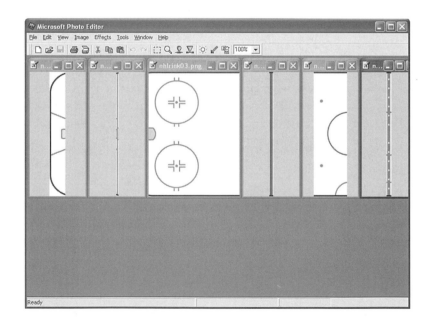

The image editor used in Figure 10.2 is Microsoft Photo Editor, which ships with
Microsoft Office. It's a very minimal photo editor but it works fine for slicing and
dicing images, as in this example.

Listing 10.1 shows the HTML code that creates a web page using the sliced ice rink images shown in Figure 10.2. The figure actually shows only the images for the left side of the rink—there are additional images for the right side of the rink that look very similar.

LISTING 10.1 Using Sliced Images to Implement a Simulated Imagemap

```
<?xml version="1.0" encoding="UTF-8"?>
<!DOCTYPE html PUBLIC "-//W3C//DTD XHTML 1.1//EN"
  "http://www.w3.org/TR/xhtml11/DTD/xhtml11.dtd">

<html xmlns="http://www.w3.org/1999/xhtml" xml:lang="en">
  <head>
    <title>NHL Rule Changes</title>
  </head>

  <body>
    <h1>NHL Rule Changes</h1>
    <p>
      Following is a graphical representation of some of the new NHL rule
      changes, and how they will affect the ice in 2005 and beyond.
    </p>
    <p style="text-align:center">
      <a href="nhltrapzone.html"><img src="nhlrink01.png" alt="Goalie Trap
      Zone" title="Goalie Trap Zone (click to learn more)" style="border:none"
      /></a>
      <a href="nhlgoallines.html"><img src="nhlrink02.png" alt="Goal Line"
      title="Goal Line (click to learn more)" style="border:none" /></a>
      <a href="nhloffensivezone.html"><img src="nhlrink03.png" alt="Offensive
      Zone" title="Offensive Zone (click to learn more)" style="border:none"
      /></a>
      <a href="nhlbluelines.html"><img src="nhlrink04.png" alt="Blue Line"
      title="Blue Line (click to learn more)" style="border:none" /></a>
      <a href="nhlneutralzone.html"><img src="nhlrink05.png" alt="Neutral Zone"
      title="Neutral Zone (click to learn more)" style="border:none" /></a>
      <a href="nhlcenterline.html"><img src="nhlrink06.png" alt="Center Red
      Line" title="Center Red Line (click to learn more)" style="border:none"
      /></a>
      <a href="nhlneutralzone.html"><img src="nhlrink07.png" alt="Neutral Zone"
      title="Neutral Zone (click to learn more)" style="border:none" /></a>
      <a href="nhlbluelines.html"><img src="nhlrink08.png" alt="Blue Line"
      title="Blue Line (click to learn more)" style="border:none" /></a>
      <a href="nhloffensivezone.html"><img src="nhlrink09.png" alt="Offensive
      Zone" title="Offensive Zone (click to learn more)" style="border:none"
      /></a>
      <a href="nhlgoallines.html"><img src="nhlrink10.png" alt="Goal Line"
      title="Goal Line (click to learn more)" style="border:none" /></a>
      <a href="nhltrapzone.html"><img src="nhlrink11.png" alt="Goalie Trap
      Zone" title="Goalie Trap Zone (click to learn more)" style="border:none"
      /></a>
    </p>
  </body>
</html>
```

Figure 10.3 shows the results of this code, which may not be quite what you were expecting.

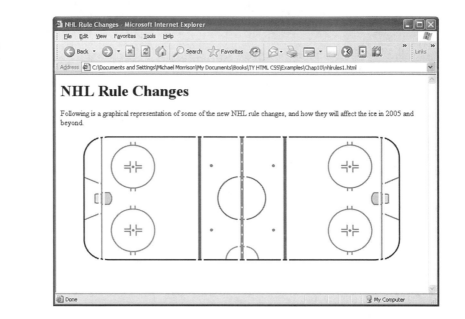

The problem with this code has to do with the fact that the code includes line breaks between the <a> tags, which effectively means that there are line breaks between the images. Such line breaks result in small spaces being placed on the page between the images. The solution is to modify the code so that the line breaks fall in the middle of each tag, as opposed to in between adjacent tags. Listing 10.2 shows a slightly different version of this code with the line break problem resolved.

LISTING 10.2   Rearranging the Line Breaks in the Code Solves the Spacing Problem on the Page

```
<?xml version="1.0" encoding="UTF-8"?>
<!DOCTYPE html PUBLIC "-//W3C//DTD XHTML 1.1//EN"
  "http://www.w3.org/TR/xhtml11/DTD/xhtml11.dtd">

<html xmlns="http://www.w3.org/1999/xhtml" xml:lang="en">
  <head>
    <title>NHL Rule Changes</title>
  </head>

  <body>
    <h1>NHL Rule Changes</h1>
    <p>
      Following is a graphical representation of some of the new NHL rule
      changes, and how they will affect the ice in 2005 and beyond.
    </p>
```

LISTING 10.2 Continued

```
  <p style="text-align:center">
    <a href="nhltrapzone.html"><img src="nhlrink01.png" alt="Goalie Trap
    Zone" title="Goalie Trap Zone (click to learn more)" style="border:none"
    /></a><a
    href="nhlgoallines.html"><img src="nhlrink02.png" alt="Goal Line"
    title="Goal Line (click to learn more)" style="border:none" /></a><a
    href="nhloffensivezone.html"><img src="nhlrink03.png" alt="Offensive
    Zone" title="Offensive Zone (click to learn more)" style="border:none"
    /></a><a
    href="nhlbluelines.html"><img src="nhlrink04.png" alt="Blue Line"
    title="Blue Line (click to learn more)" style="border:none" /></a><a
    href="nhlneutralzone.html"><img src="nhlrink05.png" alt="Neutral Zone"
    title="Neutral Zone (click to learn more)" style="border:none" /></a><a
    href="nhlcenterline.html"><img src="nhlrink06.png" alt="Center Line"
    title="Center Line (click to learn more)" style="border:none" /></a><a
    href="nhlneutralzone.html"><img src="nhlrink07.png" alt="Neutral Zone"
    title="Neutral Zone (click to learn more)" style="border:none" /></a><a
    href="nhlbluelines.html"><img src="nhlrink08.png" alt="Blue Line"
    title="Blue Line (click to learn more)" style="border:none" /></a><a
    href="nhloffensivezone.html"><img src="nhlrink09.png" alt="Offensive
    Zone" title="Offensive Zone (click to learn more)" style="border:none"
    /></a><a
    href="nhlgoallines.html"><img src="nhlrink10.png" alt="Goal Line"
    title="Goal Line (click to learn more)" style="border:none" /></a><a
    href="nhltrapzone.html"><img src="nhlrink11.png" alt="Goalie Trap Zone"
    title="Goalie Trap Zone (click to learn more)" style="border:none" /></a>
  </p>
 </body>
</html>
```

Notice that this time around I was very careful not to put any spaces or line breaks in between any of the <a> or <img /> tags. Again, a space or line break between these tags creates a small space between the images on the page, and the illusion of everything fitting together into one big image is totally destroyed. Figure 10.4 shows the results of the fixed code, in which the ice rink finally appears as you intended it to look.

Hovering over the ice rink shows the alt text for each sliced image, which helps to provide a clue regarding the image's meaning. Clicking any part of the rink displays a web page with details about the NHL rule changes that affect that particular portion of the rink. Figure 10.5 shows the rule changes that impact the blue lines, which delineate the offensive zones in hockey.

So I've proven that it's possible to get the illusion of an imagemap without actually using an imagemap. This begs the question, when *would* you want to use an imagemap, then? Only when the parts of an image you want to link are so numerous or oddly arranged that it would be a big hassle to chop the image into smaller images.

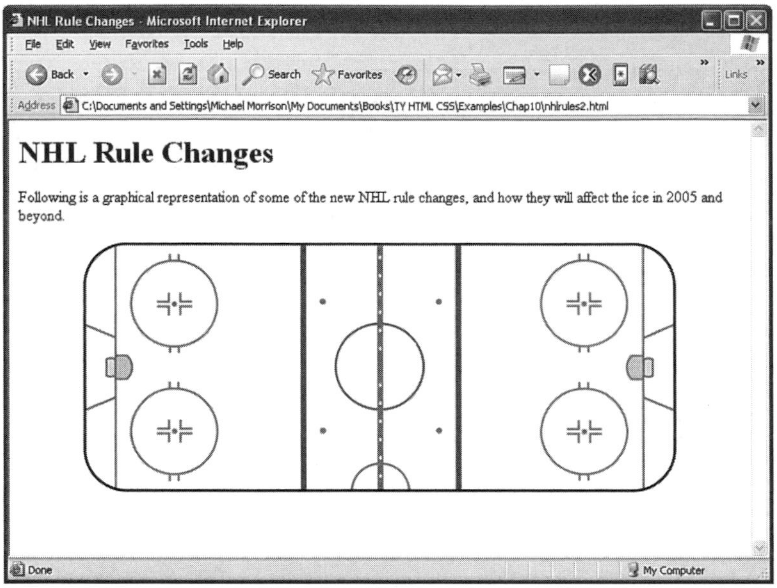

FIGURE 10.4
You can create this page using ordinary <img /> tags and <a href> links; imagemaps aren't always necessary.

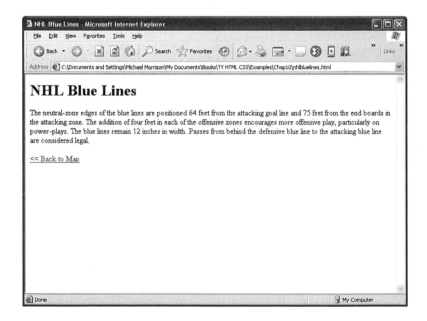

FIGURE 10.4
You can create this page using ordinary <img /> tags and <a href> links; imagemaps aren't always necessary.

FIGURE 10.5
Each region of the ice rink imagemap links to a page with more detailed information about that specific region.

That does happen from time to time, so it's a good idea to know how to create imagemaps when you truly need to. The rest of this hour shows you how.

Mapping Regions Within an Image

To make any type of imagemap, you need to figure out the numerical pixel coordinates of each region within the image that you want to turn into a clickable link. These clickable links are also known as **areas**. An easy way to do this is to open the image in an image editor and watch the coordinates at the bottom of the screen as you use the rectangle selection tool to select a rectangular region of the image (see Figure 10.6). When the mouse button is down, the coordinates at the bottom of the screen show both the upper-left and lower-right corners of the rectangle. When the mouse button isn't down, only the x,y position of the mouse is shown.

FIGURE 10.6
You can use an image editor to select regions within an image and determine the coordinates.

You could use the whole image in Figure 10.6 as an imagemap, linking to several images that provide somewhat of a virtual tour of a skateboard park. To do so, you would first need to decide which region of the image should be linked to each target image. You can use rectangles, circles, and irregular polygons as regions. Figure 10.7 shows an example of how you might divide the image into these shapes.

Graphical web page editors such as Microsoft FrontPage, Macromedia Dreamweaver, and Adobe GoLive allow you to paint *hotspots* onto an imagemap (see Figure 10.7) interactively and then generate the necessary HTML for you. This is one situation in which a graphical editor is very handy to have around.

Did you Know?

There are also programs available that let you highlight a rectangle with your mouse and automatically spew out imagemap coordinates into a file for you to cut-and-paste into your HTML, but they are rather cumbersome to use. If you don't have access to FrontPage or another good graphical web page editor, you can easily locate the pixel coordinates in your favorite general-purpose graphics program or image editor.

FIGURE 10.7
Microsoft
FrontPage lets
you draw click-
able hotspot
links onto your
imagemaps with
your mouse.

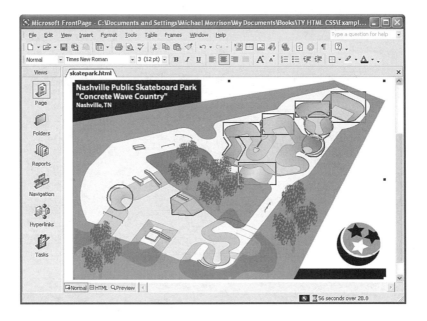

By the Way

FrontPage will gladly spit out imagemap code for you, but the goal in this lesson is to teach you how to code imagemaps from the ground up. So I'm just using FrontPage as an example of how to figure out the coordinates for each area within a map. You could just as easily use some other graphics tool.

To create the imagemap, first jot down the pixel coordinates of the upper-left and lower-right corners of each rectangular region shown in Figure 10.7. You also need to locate and record the center point and radius of the three circles, as well as the coordinates of each corner of the two irregularly shaped regions. (If you want to follow along with this by using an image of your own, just write the coordinates on a piece of paper for now. You'll see exactly how to put them into an HTML file momentarily.

These are the coordinates for the skatepark imagemap areas:

▶ Spike Pipe (region 1): A rectangle from 536,24 to 610,89.

▶ Coach's Corner (region 2): A rectangle from 461,43 to 535,78.

▶ Barnstormer (region 3): A rectangle from 342,170 to 422,218.

▶ Mitchell's Meadow (region 4): A rectangle from 392,69 to 460,114.

▶ MIA Bowl (region 5): A rectangle from 311,87 to 391,118.

▶ Bubba Bowl (region 6): A circle at 510,94 with a radius of 30.

▶ Flume Zoom (region 7): A circle at 499,135 with a radius of 25.

▶ Orange Peel (region 8): A circle at 98,243 with a radius of 28.

▶ Horsey Hip (region 9): An irregular polygon with corners at the following six points: (323,134), (309,154), (343,166), (358,139), (345,119), and (311,116).

▶ Devan's Divide (region 10): An irregular polygon with corners at the following six points: (227,229), (254,243), (273,267), (247,281), (206,278), and (203,244).

Try It Yourself ▼

You'll better remember how to make imagemaps if you get an image of your own and turn it into an imagemap as you continue on throughout the lesson:

▶ For starters, it's easiest to choose a fairly large image that is visually divided into roughly rectangular regions.

▶ If you don't have a suitable image handy, use your favorite graphics program to make one. One easy and useful idea is to put a word or an icon for each of your important pages together into a button bar or signpost. Or take a photograph containing multiple people and use each person as an area of the imagemap. ▲

Creating Client-Side Imagemaps

After you have the coordinates written down, you're ready to create an HTML imagemap. The following HTML code is required to start any imagemap:

```
<map id="skatepark">
```

By the Way

Prior to XHTML, the id and name attributes played the same role in the <map> tag, so you could have also entered the previous code as this:

<map name="skatepark">

However, XHTML standards require the use of id instead of name, which is why I've stuck with it throughout this lesson (and the rest of the book, for that matter).

Keep in mind that you can use whatever name you want for the id of the <map> tag, although it helps if you make it as descriptive as possible. If skateparkmap doesn't describe the image you're using very well, feel free to change it.

Next on the agenda is an <area /> tag for each region of the image. Following is an example of a single <area> tag that is used in the skatepark imagemap example:

```
<area shape="rect" coords="536, 24, 610, 89" href="skatepark_spikepipe.jpg"
alt="Spike Pipe" />
```

This <area /> tag has four attributes, which you will use with every area you describe in an imagemap:

- ▶ shape indicates whether the region is a rectangle (shape="rect"), a circle (shape="circle"), or an irregular polygon (shape="poly").

- ▶ coords gives the exact pixel coordinates for the region. For rectangles, give the x,y coordinates of the upper-left corner followed by the x,y coordinates of the lower-right corner. For circles, give the x,y center point followed by the radius in pixels. For polygons, list the x,y coordinates of all the corners, in connect-the-dots order.

- ▶ href specifies the page to which the region links. You can use any address or filename that you would use in an ordinary <a href> link tag.

- ▶ alt allows you to provide a piece of text that is associated with the shape. Most browsers (not Firefox) display this text in a small box when the user pauses with the mouse over the shape. This text adds a subtle but important visual cue to users who might not otherwise realize that they are looking at an imagemap. Firefox correctly uses the title attribute instead of the alt attribute to provide a visual cue, which is why you should strongly consider providing both attributes for images.

Every distinct clickable region in an imagemap must be described as a single area, which means a typical imagemap consists of a list of areas. After coding the <area /> tags, you are done defining the imagemap, so wrap things up with a closing </map> tag.

The last step in creating an imagemap is wiring it to the actual map image. The map image is placed on the page using an ordinary <img /> tag. However, there is an extra usemap attribute that is coded like this:

```
<img src="skatepark.png" alt="Nashville Public Skatepark"
title="Nashville Public Skatepark" usemap="#skateparkmap"
style="border:none" />
```

When specifying the value of the usemap attribute, use the name you put in the id of the <map> tag (and don't forget the # symbol). In the listing I also included the style attribute to turn off the border around the imagemap, which you may or may not elect to keep in imagemaps of your own.

By the Way

It is also possible to put the map definition in a separate file by including that file's name in the usemap attribute, like this:

```
<img src="thisthat.gif" usemap="maps.htm#thisthat">
```

For instance, if you used an imagemap on every page in your web site, you could just put the <map> and <area> tags for it on one page instead of repeating them on every page on which the imagemap appears.

Listing 10.3 shows the complete code for the skatepark imagemap sample web page, including the imagemap and all of its areas.

LISTING 10.3   The <map> and <area /> Tags Define the Regions of an Imagemap

```
<?xml version="1.0" encoding="UTF-8"?>
<!DOCTYPE html PUBLIC "-//W3C//DTD XHTML 1.0 Strict//EN"
  "http://www.w3.org/TR/xhtml1/DTD/xhtml1-strict.dtd">

<html xmlns="http://www.w3.org/1999/xhtml" xml:lang="en">
  <head>
    <title>Nashville Public Skatepark (Concrete Wave Country)</title>
  </head>

  <body>
    <h1>Nashville Public Skatepark (Concrete Wave Country)</h1>
    <p>
      Below is a map of Nashville's public skatepark, also known as
      Concrete Wave Country. Drag the mouse over the map and click to
      learn more about each area and obstacle.
    </p>
    <p style="text-align:center">
      <map id="skateparkmap">
        <area shape="rect" coords="536, 24, 610, 89"
        href="skatepark_spikepipe.jpg" alt="Spike Pipe" />
        <area shape="rect" coords="461, 43, 535, 78"
        href="skatepark_coachscorner.jpg" alt="Coach's Corner" />
        <area shape="rect" coords="342, 170, 422, 218"
        href="skatepark_barnstormer.jpg" alt="Barnstormer" />
```

LISTING 10.3   Continued

```
            <area shape="rect" coords="392, 69, 460, 114"
            href="skatepark_mitchellsmeadow.jpg" alt="Mitchell's Meadow" />
            <area shape="rect" coords="311, 87, 391, 118"
            href="skatepark_miabowl.jpg" alt="MIA Bowl" />
            <area shape="circle" coords="510, 94, 30"
            href="skatepark_bubbabowl.jpg" alt="Bubba Bowl" />
            <area shape="circle" coords="499, 135, 25"
            href="skatepark_flumezoom.jpg" alt="Flume Zoom" />
            <area shape="circle" coords="98, 243, 28"
            href="skatepark_orangepeel.jpg" alt="Orange Peel" />
            <area shape="poly" coords="323, 134, 309, 154, 343, 166, 358, 139,
            345, 119, 311, 116" href="skatepark_horseyhip.jpg"
            alt="Horsey Hip" />
            <area shape="poly" coords="227, 229, 254, 243, 273, 267, 247, 281,
            206, 278, 203, 244" href="skatepark_devansdivide.jpg"
            alt="Devan's Divide" />
          </map>
          <img src="skatepark.png" alt="Nashville Public Skatepark" alt="Nashville
          Public Skatepark" usemap="#skateparkmap" style="border:none" />
        </p>
      </body>
</html>
```

By the Way

> If you're a stickler for details, you might have noticed that this web page is coded as an XHTML 1.0 document, as opposed to XHTML 1.1 like most of the other examples in the book (check out the first few lines of code). The reason for this has to do with the fact that some browsers, Internet Explorer for one, are lagging in their support for one small XHTML 1.1 change in how imagemaps are used. I'm referring to the usemap attribute, which in XHTML 1.1 doesn't require the # symbol in front of the map name. In fact, it's not allowed in XHTML 1.1, which is why I designated this document as XHTML 1.0. The # symbol is allowed in XHTML 1.0, so to satisfy current web browsers and still provide you with a valid web page, I opted to go with XHTML 1.0 for this particular example.

Figure 10.8 shows the imagemap in action. Notice that Microsoft Internet Explorer displays the link address for whatever area the mouse is moving over at the bottom of the window, just as it does for "normal" links. Additionally, the alt text for an area is displayed on the imagemap if you pause with the mouse over the area.

Did you Know?

> You may want to include text links at the bottom of your imagemap that lead to the same pages the map itself links to. This allows people who have older web browsers—or who don't want to wait for the image to finish loading—to access those pages.

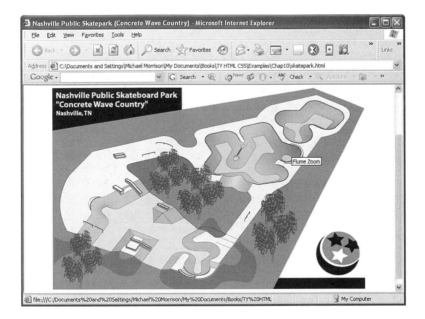

FIGURE 10.8
The imagemap
defined in
Listing 10.3 as
it appears on
the web page.

If you click where the `alt` text is shown in Figure 10.8, the image named
`skatepark_flumezoom.jpg` opens in the browser. In fact, Figure 10.9 shows an
image of my friend Paul Sexton riding the Flume Zoom that appears after the Flume
Zoom obstacle is clicked on the imagemap.

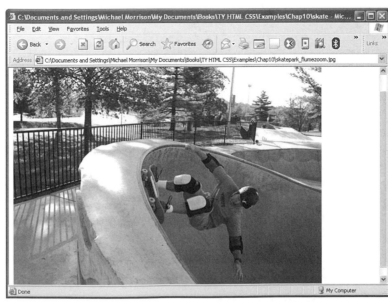

FIGURE 10.9
Each area on
the skatepark
imagemap links
to a photo of
that particular
skateboard
obstacle.

Summary

This hour explained how to create imagemaps—links that lead to more than one place, depending on where you click an image—as well as why and how to avoid using them in some circumstances. You saw how to define rectangular and circular link regions within an image, as well as irregularly shaped polygonal regions. You saw how imagemaps, although highly specialized in function, can nonetheless be very useful in some situations. When used selectively, imagemaps can be an important part of a web page's user interface.

Table 10.1 is a summary of the tags and attributes covered in this hour.

TABLE 10.1   HTML Tags and Attributes Covered in Hour 10

Tag/Attribute	Function
`<img />`	Inserts an image into the document.
Attributes	
`src="imageurl"`	The image's URL.
`alt="description"`	A text description of the map image, intended to be used as an image replacement for situations where the image cannot be viewed.
`title="description"`	A text description of the area that may appear as a visual cue alongside the image.
`usemap="name"`	The name of an imagemap specification for client-side image mapping. Used with `<map>` and `<area />`.
`<map>...</map>`	A client-side imagemap, referenced by `<img usemap="..." />`. Includes one or more `<area />` tags.
`<area />`	Defines a clickable link within a client-side imagemap.
Attributes	
`shape="value"`	The shape of the clickable area. Valid options for this attribute are `rect`, `poly`, and `circle`.
`coords="values"`	The coordinates of the clickable region within an image; its meaning and setting vary according to the type of area.
`href="linkurl"`	The URL that should be loaded when the area is clicked.
`alt="decription"`	A text description of the area, intended to be used as an image replacement for situations in which the image cannot be viewed.

Q&A

Q *I don't have Paint Shop Pro and my graphics software doesn't tell me x,y coordinates. How do I figure out the coordinates for my imagemaps?*

A Here's a sneaky way to do it using your web browser. Put the image on a page with the `ismap` attribute and an `<a>` tag around it, like the following:

```
<a href="nowhere"><img src="myimage.gif" ismap="ismap" /></a>
```

When you view that page with a web browser, move the mouse over the image. You will see the coordinates in the status bar along the bottom of the window. This works because the `ismap` attribute is intended for use with older server-side imagemaps, which had to relay the mouse coordinates back to a web server to determine what part of the map was clicked.

Q *What happens if I overlap areas on an imagemap?*

A You are allowed to overlap areas on an imagemap; just keep in mind that one area will have precedence over the other one when it comes to determining which link to follow. Precedence is assigned according to which areas are listed first in the imagemap. For example, the first area in the map has precedence over the second area if they overlap, which means that a click in the overlapping portion of the areas will link to the first area. If you have an area within an imagemap that you don't want to link to anything, you can use this overlap trick to deliberately keep it from linking to anything—just place the "dead" area before other areas so that it will overlap them, and then set its `href` attribute to `""`.

Workshop

The workshop contains quiz questions and activities to help you solidify your understanding of the material covered. Try to answer all questions before looking at the "Answers" section that follows.

Quiz

1. You have a 200×200-pixel image named `quarters.gif` for your web page. When viewers click the upper-left quarter of the image, you want them to get a page named `topleft.html`. When they click the upper-right quarter, they should get `topright.html`. Clicking the lower left should bring up `bottomleft.html`, and the lower right should lead to `bottomright.html`. Write the HTML to implement this as an imagemap.

2. How could you implement the effect described in question 1 without using imagemaps at all?

Answers

1.
```
<map id="quartersmap">

    <area shape="rect" coords="0,0,99,99" href="topleft.html" alt="" />
    <area shape="rect" coords="100,0,199,99" href="topright.html" alt="" />
    <area shape="rect" coords="0,100,99,199" href="bottomleft.html" alt="" />
    <area shape="rect" coords="100,100,199,199" href="bottomright.html"
    alt="" />
</map>
<img src="quarters.gif" width="200" height="200" usemap="#quartersmap"
alt="" title="" />
```

2. Use a graphics program to chop the image into four quarters and save them as separate images named `topleft.gif`, `topright.gif`, `bottomleft.gif`, and `bottomright.gif`. Then write this:

```
<a href="topleft.html"><img src="topleft.gif"
width="100" height="100" border="0" /></a>
<a href="topright.html"><img src="topright.gif"
width="100" height="100" border="0" /></a> <br />
<a href="bottomleft.html"><img src="bottomleft.gif"
width="100" height="100" border="0" /></a>
<a href="bottomright.html"><img src="bottomright.gif"
width="100" height="100" border="0" /></a>
```

Be careful to break the lines of the HTML *inside* the tags as shown in this code, to avoid introducing any spaces between the images. Also, keep in mind that the `width` and `height` attributes are optional, and are specified only to help web browsers lay out the page a bit quicker.

Exercises

▶ If you have some pages containing short lists of links, see whether you can cook up an interesting imagemap to use instead.

▶ Imagemaps are usually more engaging and attractive than a row of repetitive-looking icons or buttons. Can you come up with a visual metaphor related to your site that would make it easier—and maybe more fun—for people to navigate through your pages? (Thinking along these lines is a good preparation for the issues you'll be tackling in Part III, "Creative Web Page Design," by the way.)

PART III

Creative Web Page Design

Using Tables to Organize and Lay Out Your Pages

One of the most powerful tools for creative web page design is the table, which allows you to arrange text and graphics into multiple columns and rows. This hour shows you how to build HTML tables you can use to control the spacing, layout, and appearance of tabular data in web pages you create. You'll find that tables are not only useful for arranging information into rows and columns, but also useful for laying out images and text on your pages. I also explain how using tables for page layout isn't always the best idea, along with clueing you in on an alternative approach. A **table** is an orderly arrangement of text and/or graphics into vertical *columns* and horizontal *rows*.

Try It Yourself ▼

As you read this hour, think about how arranging text into tables could benefit your web pages. The following are some specific ideas to keep in mind:

▶ Of course, the most obvious application of tables is to organize tabular information, such as a multicolumn list of names and numbers.

▶ If you want more complex relationships between text and graphics than <img align="left" /> or <img align="right" /> can provide, tables can do it.

▶ Tables can be used to draw borders around text or around several graphics images.

▶ Whenever you need multiple columns of text, tables are the answer.

For each of your pages that meets one of these criteria, try adding a table modeled after the examples in this hour. The "Exercises" section at the end of this hour offers a couple of detailed suggestions along these lines as well. ▲

Creating a Simple Table

A table consists of rows of information with individual cells inside. To make tables, you have to start with a <table> tag. Of course, you end your tables with the </table> tag. If you want the table to have a border, use a border attribute to specify the width of the border in pixels. A border size of 0 or none (or leaving the border attribute out entirely) will make the border invisible, which is often handy when you are using a table as a page layout tool.

> There are some style properties that allow you to take much more control over table borders. For example, you can set the border width (border-width), style (border-style), and color (border-color). These properties work fine but you have to apply them to each table element, which can be cumbersome.

With the <table> tag in place, the next thing you need is the <tr> tag. The <tr> tag creates a table row, which contains one or more cells of information before the closing </tr>. To create these individual cells, you use the <td> tag (<td> stands for table data). You place the table information between the <td> and </td> tags. A **cell** is a rectangular region that can contain any text, images, and HTML tags. Each row in a table is made up of at least one cell. Multiple cells within a row form columns in a table.

There is one more basic tag involved in building tables: The <th> tag works exactly like a <td> tag, except <th> indicates that the cell is part of the heading of the table. Most web browsers render the text in <th> cells as centered and boldface.

You can create as many cells as you want, but each row in a table should have the same number of columns as the other rows. The HTML code in Listing 11.1 creates a simple table using only the four table tags I've mentioned thus far. Figure 11.1 shows the resulting page as viewed in a web browser.

LISTING 11.1   Creating Tables with the <table>, <tr>, <td>, and <th> Tags

```
<?xml version="1.0" encoding="UTF-8"?>
<!DOCTYPE html PUBLIC "-//W3C//DTD XHTML 1.1//EN"
  "http://www.w3.org/TR/xhtml11/DTD/xhtml11.dtd">

<html xmlns="http://www.w3.org/1999/xhtml" xml:lang="en">
  <head>
    <title>Hockey Stats</title>
  </head>

  <body>
    <table>
      <tr>
        <th>Season</th>
        <th>GP</th>
        <th>G</th>
        <th>A</th>
        <th>P</th>
        <th>PIM</th>
      </tr>
```

LISTING 11.1   Continued

```
    <tr>
      <td>Summer 2005</td>
      <td>8</td>
      <td>4</td>
      <td>4</td>
      <td>8</td>
      <td>0</td>
    </tr>
    <tr>
      <td>Winter 2004</td>
      <td>24</td>
      <td>14</td>
      <td>14</td>
      <td>28</td>
      <td>2</td>
    </tr>
    <tr>
      <td>Summer 2004</td>
      <td>18</td>
      <td>9</td>
      <td>9</td>
      <td>18</td>
      <td>2</td>
    </tr>
    <tr>
      <td>Spring 2004</td>
      <td>19</td>
      <td>7</td>
      <td>17</td>
      <td>24</td>
      <td>0</td>
    </tr>
  </table>
 </body>
</html>
```

> **Did you Know?**
>
> As you know, HTML ignores extra spaces between words and tags. However, you might find your HTML tables easier to read (and less prone to time-wasting errors) if you use spaces to indent <tr> and <td> tags, as I did in Listing 11.1.

The table in the example contains hockey statistics, which are perfect for arranging in rows and columns. The headings in the table stand for Games Played (GP), Goals (G), Assists (A), Points (P), and Penalties In Minutes (PIM).

You can place virtually any HTML element into a table cell. However, tags used in one cell don't carry over to other cells, and tags from outside the table don't apply within the table. For example, consider the following table:

```
<div style="font-weight:bold">
  <table>
```

```
    <tr>
      <td style="font-style:italic">hello</td>
      <td>there</td>
    </tr>
  </table>
</div>
```

FIGURE 11.1
The HTML code in Listing 11.1 creates a table with five rows and six columns.

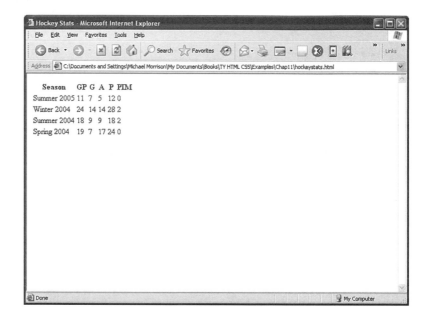

If you recall from Hour 5, "Basic Text Alignment and Formatting," the <div> tag is used to enclose regions of information on a page so that you can align it and apply styles. In this example, the <div> tag is used around a table to demonstrate how tables are immune to outside tags. The word there would be neither boldface nor italic because neither the font-weight:bold style outside the table nor the font-style:italic style from the previous cell affects it. The word hello in this example is in italics, however.

To make the words hello and there both boldface, you would need to change the table code to this:

```
<table style="font-weight:bold">
  <tr>
    <td style="font-style:italic">hello</td>
    <td>there</td>
  </tr>
</table
```

In this example, both words are in bold and the word hello is also in italics. Of course, you don't have to apply styles at the table level if you don't want. The font-weight:bold style could just as easily be applied to each cell individually if you want.

Controlling the Size of Tables

Ordinarily, the size of a table and its individual cells automatically expand to fit the data you place into it. However, you can choose to control the exact size of the entire table by putting width and/or height styles in the <table> tag. You can also control the size of each cell by putting width and height styles in the individual <td> tags. The width and height styles can be specified as either pixels or percentages. For example, the following code creates a table 500 pixels wide and 400 pixels high:

```
<table style="width:500px; height:400px">
```

By the Way

There are actually width and height attributes that were deprecated in the move to XHTML. They still work in web browsers but you should focus on using the width and height style properties instead, because they represent the appropriate approach to use in XHTML.

To make the first cell of the table 20% of the total table width and the second cell 80% of the table width, you would type the following:

```
<table style="width:100%">
  <tr>
    <td style="width:20%">skinny cell</td>
    <td style="width:80%">fat cell</td>
  </tr>
</table>
```

Notice that the table is sized to 100%, which makes sure that the table fills the entire width of the browser window. When you use percentages instead of fixed pixel sizes, the table will resize automatically to fit any size browser window, while maintaining the aesthetic balance you're after. In this case, the two cells within the table are automatically resized to 20% and 80% of the total table width, respectively.

Alignment and Spanning Within Tables

By default, anything you place inside a table cell is aligned to the left and vertically centered. You can align the contents of table cells both horizontally and vertically with the text-align and vertical-align style properties.

You can apply these attributes to any <tr>, <td>, or <th> tag. Alignment attributes assigned to a <tr> tag apply to all cells in that row. Depending on the size of your table, you can save yourself a considerable amount of time and effort by applying these attributes at the <tr> level and not in each individual <td> or <th> tag. The HTML code in Listing 11.2 uses style="vertical-align:top" to bring the text to the top of each cell. Figure 11.2 shows the result.

> Following are some of the more commonly used `vertical-align` style property values: top, middle, bottom, text-top, text-bottom, and baseline (for text). These property values give you plenty of flexibility in aligning table data vertically.

LISTING 11.2   Alignment, Cell Spacing, Borders, and Background Colors in Tables

```
<?xml version="1.0" encoding="UTF-8"?>
<!DOCTYPE html PUBLIC "-//W3C//DTD XHTML 1.1//EN"
  "http://www.w3.org/TR/xhtml11/DTD/xhtml11.dtd">

<html xmlns="http://www.w3.org/1999/xhtml" xml:lang="en">
  <head>
    <title>Things to Fear</title>
  </head>

  <body>
    <table border="2" cellpadding="4" cellspacing="2">
      <tr style="background-color:silver">
        <th colspan="2">Description</th>
        <th>Size</th>
        <th>Weight</th>
        <th>Speed</th>
      </tr>
      <tr style="vertical-align:top">
        <td><img src="handgun.gif" alt=".38 Special"/></td>
        <td><h2>.38 Special</h2></td>
        <td>Five-inch barrel.</td>
        <td>Twenty ounces.</td>
        <td>Six rounds in four seconds.</td>
      </tr>
      <tr style="vertical-align:top">
        <td><img src="rhino.gif" alt="Rhinoceros" /></td>
        <td><h2>Rhinoceros</h2></td>
        <td>Twelve feet, horn to tail.</td>
        <td>Up to two tons.</td>
        <td>Thirty-five miles per hour in bursts.</td>
      </tr>
      <tr style="vertical-align:top">
        <td><img src="axeman.gif" alt="Broad Axe " /></td>
        <td><h2>Broad Axe</h2></td>
        <td>Thirty-inch blade.</td>
        <td>Twelve pounds.</td>
        <td>Sixty miles per hour on impact.</td>
      </tr>
    </table>
  </body>
</html>
```

At the top of Figure 11.2, a single cell (Description) spans two columns. This is accomplished with the `colspan="2"` attribute in the `<th>` tag for that cell. As you might guess, you can also use the rowspan attribute to create a cell that spans more than one row.

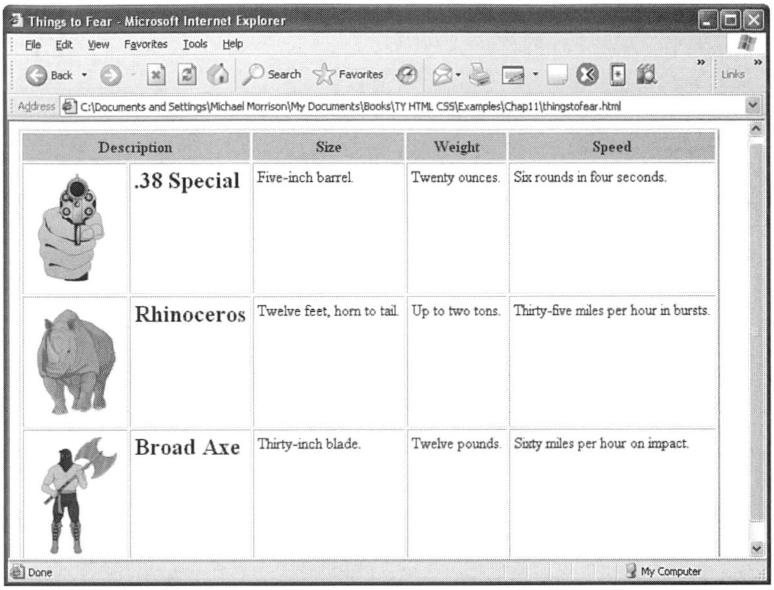

FIGURE 11.2
The colspan attribute in Listing 11.2 allows the upper-left cell to span multiple columns.

Spanning is the process of forcing a cell to stretch across more than one row or column of a table. The colspan attribute causes a cell to span across multiple columns; rowspan has the same effect on rows.

Keeping the structure of rows and columns organized in your mind can be the most difficult part of creating tables with cells that span multiple columns or rows. The tiniest error can often throw the whole thing into disarray. You'll save yourself time and frustration by sketching your tables on paper before you start writing the HTML to implement them.

You can also use visual web design software to arrange the rows and columns in your table. This can make table design much easier, as long as you choose a program (such as Microsoft FrontPage or Macromedia Dreamweaver) that creates well-formatted HTML that you can edit by hand when you choose.

Did you Know?

Table Backgrounds and Spacing

There are a few tricks in Listing 11.2 that I haven't explained yet. You can give an entire table—and each individual row or cell in a table—its own background, distinct from any background you might use on the web page itself. You do this by placing the background-color or background-image style in the <table>, <tr>, <td>, or <th> tag exactly as you would in the <body> tag (see Hour 9, "Custom

Backgrounds and Colors"). To give an entire table a yellow background, for example, you would use `<table style="background-color:yellow">` or the equivalent `<table style="background-color:#FFFF00">`.

Similar to the `background-color` style property is the `background-image` property, which is used to set an image for a table background. If you wanted to set the image `leaves.gif` as the background for a table, you would use `<table style="background-image:url(leaves.gif)"`. Notice that the image file is placed within parentheses and preceded by the word `url`, which indicates that you are describing where the image file is located.

Tweaking tables goes beyond just using style properties. For example, you can control the space around the borders of a table with the `cellpadding` and `cellspacing` attributes. The `cellspacing` attribute sets the amount of space (in pixels) between table borders and between table cells themselves. The `cellpadding` attribute sets the amount of space around the edges of information in the cells, also in pixels. Setting the `cellpadding` value to `0` causes all the information in the table to align as closely as possible to the table borders, possibly even touching the borders. `cellpadding` and `cellspacing` give you good overall control of the table's appearance.

By the Way

> Although the `cellpadding` and `cellspacing` attributes are still allowed in XHTML, a CSS equivalent for them exists in the form of the padding and border-spacing style properties. However, these style properties still aren't supported consistently across current web browsers, so I encourage you to stick with `cellpadding` and `cellspacing` to fine-tune your table spacing for the time being.

You saw the effect of background color and spacing attributes in Figure 11.2, which used a silver background color for the table heading and gave the text and images a little room to breathe within each table cell.

Did you Know?

> You can place an entire table within a cell of a different table, and the inner table will possess the qualities of the "parent" table. In other words, you can *nest* tables inside one another.
>
> Nested tables open a vast universe of possibilities for creative web page layout. For example, if you want a column of text to appear to the left of a table, you could create a two-column table with the text in one column and the subtable in the other column, like the following:
>
> ```
> <table>
>   <tr>
>     <td>To the right, you see all our telephone numbers.</td>
>     <td>
>       <table border="1">
>         <tr>
> ```

```
          <td>voice</td>
          <td>802-888-2828</td>
        </tr>
        <tr>
          <td>fax</td>
          <td>802-888-6634</td>
        </tr>
        <tr>
          <td>data</td>
          <td>802-888-3009</td>
        </tr>
      </td>
    </tr>
  </table>
</table>
```

Notice that the inner table has borders, but the outer table does not.

A drawback to nested tables is that if you get carried away and nest them too deeply, this can slow down the rendering of the page in a browser. You definitely shouldn't go deeper than three levels without a very good reason, and two levels is really a more realistic limit if you can help it.

Creative Page Layout with Tables

The proper and conventional way to use tables is for tabular arrangements of text and numbers. Web designers realized that tables could go beyond that usage and serve as a means of laying out entire pages. For example, a table with invisible borders can be used as a guide for arranging graphics and columns of text any way you please. Take a look at Listing 11.3, which contains the table layout for a familiar page that now relies on tables for a much more efficient layout. The resulting page is displayed in Figure 11.3.

By the Way

Although laying out pages with invisible tables is a highly popular and useful technique, it is technically discouraged by the World Wide Web Consortium (W3C), the standards body that oversees the future of the Web. The W3C promotes style sheets as the proper way to lay out pages, as opposed to using tables. Although I agree with the W3C in principle, tables are simply too useful for page layout to completely ignore them. Don't worry, I teach you the style sheet approach to page layout in Hour 14, "Using Style Sheets for Page Layout." Style sheets are ultimately much more powerful than tables, so you definitely should lean toward using them for pages with more complex designs. However, tables aren't entirely wrong for simple layouts and some pesky layouts that are tricky to arrange using style sheets. As an example, a three-column page is notoriously difficult to code properly using style sheets.

LISTING 11.3   Using Tables for a More Efficient Multicolumn Page
Layout

```
<table cellspacing="5">
  <tr>
    <td colspan="3">
      <div style="font-family:verdana, arial; font-size:18pt; font-weight:bold">
      16 - Terry Lancaster</div>
    </td>
  </tr>
  <tr style="height:10px">
    <td>
      <img src="tlancaster.jpg" alt="Terry &quot;Big T&quot; Lancaster" />
    </td>
    <td style="vertical-align:top">
      <div style="font-family:verdana, arial; font-size:12pt; color:navy">
        <span style="font-weight:bold">Nickname:</span> Big T<br />
        <span style="font-weight:bold">Position:</span> RW<br />
        <span style="font-weight:bold">Height:</span> 6'3"<br />
        <span style="font-weight:bold">Weight:</span> 195<br />
        <span style="font-weight:bold">Shoots:</span> Left<br />
        <span style="font-weight:bold">Age:</span> 40<br />
        <span style="font-weight:bold">Birthplace:</span>
        <a href="http://en.wikipedia.org/wiki/Nashville%2C_Tennessee">
        Nashville, TN</a>
      </div>
    </td>
    <td style="vertical-align:top">
      <div style="font-family:verdana, arial; font-size:12pt; color:navy">
        <span style="font-weight:bold">Favorite NHL Player:</span>
        <a href="http://www.nhl.com/players/8448091.html">Brett Hull</a><br />
        <span style="font-weight:bold">Favorite NHL Team:</span>
        <a href="http://www.nashvillepredators.com/">Nashville Predators</a>
        <br /><span style="font-weight:bold">Favorite Southern Fixin:</span>
        <a href="http://southernfood.about.com/od/potatorecipes/r/blbb442.htm">
        Skillet Fried Potatoes</a><br />
        <span style="font-weight:bold">Favorite Meat and Three:</span>
        <a href="http://www.hollyeats.com/Swetts.htm">Swett's</a>
        (<a href="http://maps.google.com/maps?q=2725+clifton+ave,+nashville,+tn"
        rel="external">map</a>)
        <br />
        <span style="font-weight:bold">Favorite Country Star:</span>
        <a href="http://www.patsycline.com/">Patsy Cline</a><br />
        <span style="font-weight:bold">Favorite Mafia Moment:</span>
        "<a href="mcmplayer_chale.html">Chet</a> finishing the game with his
        eyelid completely slashed through."
      </div>
    </td>
  </tr>
  <tr>
    <td colspan="3">
      <table style="width:100%; text-align:right; font-family:verdana, arial;
      font-size:11pt; color:navy" border="1" >
        <tr style="background-color:navy; color:white">
          <th style="text-align:left">Season</th>
          <th>GP</th>
          <th>G</th>
          <th>A</th>
          <th>P</th>
          <th>PIM</th>
          <th>PPG</th>
```

LISTING 11.3   Continued

```
        <th>SHG</th>
        <th>GWG</th>
      </tr>
      <tr style="background-color:white">
        <td style="text-align:left">Summer 2005</td>
        <td>11</td>
        <td style="width:75px">7</td>
        <td>5</td>
        <td>12</td>
        <td>0</td>
        <td>0</td>
        <td>0</td>
        <td>0</td>
      </tr>
      <tr style="background-color:#EEEEEE">
        <td style="text-align:left">Winter 2004</td>
        <td>24</td>
        <td>14</td>
        <td>14</td>
        <td>28</td>
        <td>2</td>
        <td>0</td>
        <td>0</td>
        <td>5</td>
      </tr>
      <tr style="background-color:white">
        <td style="text-align:left">Summer 2004</td>
        <td>18</td>
        <td>9</td>
        <td>9</td>
        <td>18</td>
        <td>2</td>
        <td>0</td>
        <td>0</td>
        <td>2</td>
      </tr>
      <tr style="background-color:#EEEEEE">
        <td style="text-align:left">Spring 2004</td>
        <td>19</td>
        <td>7</td>
        <td>17</td>
        <td>24</td>
        <td>0</td>
        <td>0</td>
        <td>0</td>
        <td>1</td>
      </tr>
    </table>
  </td>
</tr>
<tr>
  <td colspan="3">
    <div style="font-family:verdana, arial; font-size:12pt">
      <a href="mailto:l&#97;ncastert@musiccitym&#97;fi&#97;.com?subject=
      Fan Question&amp;body=What's your secret?">Contact Terry.</a>
    </div>
  </td>
</tr>
</table>
```

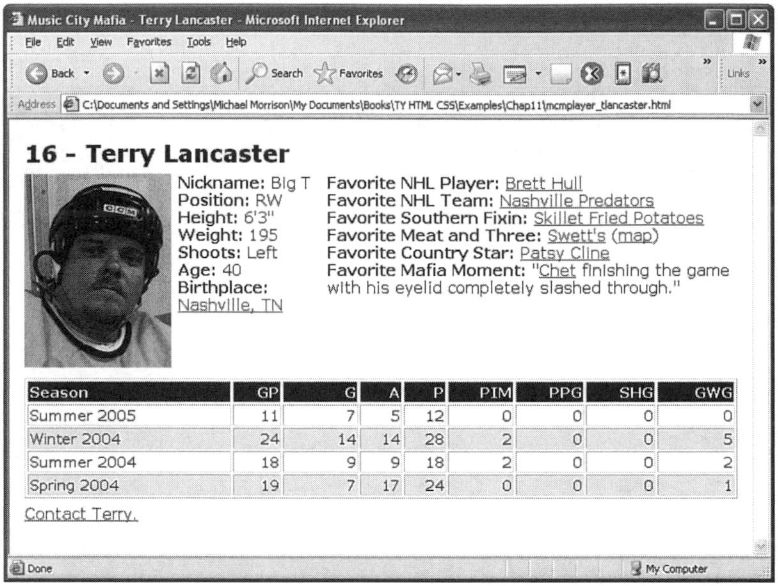

FIGURE 11.3
HTML tables give you greater flexibility and control when you're laying out your web pages.

I realize that this is a lot of code but most of it you've already seen. It's the code for one of the hockey player pages except it has been reworked to use tables to achieve a more efficient page layout. While I worked on building this table, I left the borders visible so that I could make sure everything was placed the way I wanted. Then, before incorporating this table into the final web page, I removed the border="1" attribute from the outer <table> tag to make the lines invisible.

There are actually three different tables in Listing 11.3 and Figure 11.3. The first table is used to arrange the images and text into four rows. The second table takes up the second row, and takes care of providing three columns of information within the subtable. The final table is the hockey stats table, which is simply placed on a row of its own in the main table.

If you're having trouble visualizing the layout of the hockey player tables, check out Figure 11.4, which shows how the tables relate to each other on the page.

Did you Know?

For an example of how you can use tables for creative layout, check out "The Site of the '90s" at http://www.samspublishing.com/.

Your real-world site will probably be a bit tamer than the LOOK site—but some of you will start getting even crazier ideas....

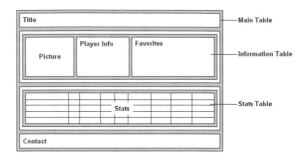

FIGURE 11.4
Visualizing the arrangement of tables without the actual content can help greatly in figuring out a table layout design.

Summary

In this hour you learned to arrange text and images into organized arrangements of rows and columns called tables. You learned the three basic tags for creating tables and many optional attributes and styles for controlling the alignment, spacing, and appearance of tables. You also saw that tables can be used together and nested within one another for an even wider variety of layout options.

Table 11.1 summarizes the tags and attributes covered in this hour.

TABLE 11.1   HTML Tags and Attributes Covered in Hour 11

Tag/Attribute	Function
`<table>...</table>`	Creates a table that can contain any number of rows (`<tr>` tags).
Attributes	
`border="width"`	Indicates the width in pixels of the table borders. Using `border="0"` or omitting the border attribute makes borders invisible.
`cellspacing="spacing"`	The amount of space between the cells in the table, in pixels.
`cellpadding="padding"`	The amount of space between the edges of the cell and its contents, in pixels.
`style="width:width"`	The width of the table on the page, either in exact pixel values or as a percentage of the page width.
`style="height:height"`	The height of the table on the page, either in exact pixel values or as a percentage of the page height.

TABLE 11.1 Continued

Tag/Attribute	Function
style="background-color:*color*"	Background color of the table and individual table cells that don't already have a background color.
style="backgroundimage: url(*imageurl*)"	A background image to display within the table and individual table cells that don't already have a background image (if a background color is also specified, the color will show through transparent areas of the image).
<tr>...</tr>	Defines a table row containing one or more cells (<td> tags).
Attributes	
style="text-align:*alignment*"	The horizontal alignment of the contents of the cells within this row. Possible values are left, right, and center.
style="vertical-align:*alignment*"	The vertical alignment of the contents of the cells within this row. Common used values include top, middle, and bottom.
style="background-color:*color*"	Background color of all cells in the row that do not already have a background color.
style="backgroundimage: url(*imageurl*)"	Background image to display within all cells in the row that do not already have their own background image.
<td>...</td>	Defines a table data cell.
Attributes	
style="text-align:*alignment*"	The horizontal alignment of the contents of the cell. Possible values are left, right, and center.
style="vertical-align:*alignment*"	The vertical alignment of the contents of the cell. Commonly used values are top, middle, and bottom.
rowspan="*numrows*"	The number of rows this cell will span.
colspan="*numcols*"	The number of columns this cell will span.
style="width:*width*"	The width of this column of cells, in exact pixel values or as a percentage of the table width.
style="height:*height*"	The height of this row of cells, in exact pixel values or as a percentage of the table height.

TABLE 11.1 Continued

Tag/Attribute	Function
style="background-color:*color*"	Background color of the cell.
style="backgroundimage: url(*imageurl*)"	Background image to display within the cell.
<th>...</th>	Defines a table heading cell. (Accepts all the same attributes and styles as <td>.)

Q&A

Q *I made a big table and when I load the page, nothing appears for a long time. Why the wait?*

A Because the web browser has to figure out the size of everything in the table before it can display any part of it, complex tables can take a while to appear on the screen. You can speed things up a bit by always including width and height tags for every graphics image within a table. Using width attributes in the <table> and <td> tags also helps.

Q *I've noticed that a lot of pages on the Web have tables in which one cell changes while others stay the same. How do they do that?*

A Those sites are using *frames*, not tables. Frames are similar to tables except that each frame contains a separate HTML page and can be updated independently of the others. The newer *floating frames*, or *iframes*, can actually be put inside a table, so they can look just like a regular table even though the HTML that creates them is quite different. You'll find out how to create and use frames in Hour 16, "Multipage Layout with Frames."

Q *Aren't there some new table tags in XHTML? Why aren't those mentioned?*

A The latest XHTML standard indeed introduces several new table tags not discussed in this book. The primary practical uses of these extensions are to prepare for some advanced features that web browsers aren't fully supporting just yet, such as tables with their own scrollbars and more reliable reading of tables for visually impaired users. If either of these things is of direct concern to you, you can find out about the new tags at the W3C web site (http://www.w3.org/). The new tags do not directly affect how tables are displayed in any existing web browser.

Don't worry—the new tags do not and will not make any of the table tags covered in this hour obsolete. They will all continue to work just as they do now.

Workshop

The workshop contains quiz questions and activities to help you solidify your understanding of the material covered. Try to answer all questions before looking at the "Answers" section that follows.

Quiz

1. You want a web page with two columns of text side by side. How do you create it?

2. You think the columns you created for question 1 look too close together. How do you add 30 pixels of space between them?

3. Write the HTML to create the table shown in the following figure:

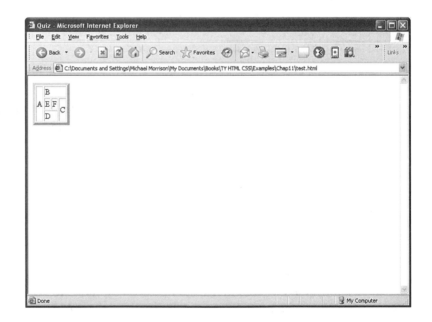

Answers

1. With the following table:

```
<table>
  <tr>
    <td style="vertical-align:top">
    First column of text goes here...
    </td>
    <td style="vertical-align:top">
    Second column of text goes here...
    </td>
  </tr>
</table>
```

2. Add `cellspacing="30"` to the `<table>` tag. (Alternatively, you could use `cellpadding="15"` to add 15 pixels of space inside the edge of each column.)

3. `<table border="5">`

```
  <tr>
    <td rowspan="3">A</td>
    <td colspan="3">B</td>
  </tr>
  <tr>
    <td>E</td>
    <td>F</td>
    <td rowspan="2">C</td>
  </tr>
  <tr>
    <td colspan="2">D</td>
  </tr>
</table>
```

Exercises

▶ You can use a simple one-celled table with a border to draw a rectangle around any section of text on a web page. By nesting that single-cell table in another two-column table, you can put a sidebar of text to the left or right side of your web page. Outlined sections of text and sidebars are very common on printed paper pages, so you'll probably find uses for them on your web pages too. Try adding one to a page of your own.

▶ Do you have any pages where different visitors might be interested in different information? Use a table to present two or three columns of text, each with its own heading (and perhaps its own graphic). That way, something of interest to everyone will be visible at the top of the page when it first appears.

Formatting Web Pages with CSS Style Sheets

In the preceding hour you learned how to use tables to lay out information in rows and columns. Tables have been used heavily across the Web as a page layout tool, but they're now being phased out for that particular purpose thanks to style sheets. Tables are still fine to use but you should focus on using them for their true intent, which is arranging tabular information into rows and columns. In addition to replacing tables as the page layout mechanism of choice, style sheets also are the preferred way to apply fonts, control margins, specify borders, and tweak just about every other visible aspect of web pages.

The concept behind style sheets is simple: You create a single style sheet document that specifies the fonts, colors, backgrounds, and other characteristics that establish a unique look for a web site. You then link every page that should have that look to the style sheet, instead of specifying all those styles repeatedly in each separate document. When you decide to change your official corporate typeface or color scheme, you can modify all your web pages at once just by changing one or two style sheets. So a *style sheet* is a grouping of formatting instructions that can control the appearance of many HTML pages at once.

Style sheets go far beyond simply separating the content of web pages from how they are formatted. CSS style sheets enable you to set a great number of formatting characteristics that were never possible before with any amount of effort. These include exacting typeface controls, letter and line spacing, margins and page borders, and expanded support for non-European languages and characters. They also enable sizes and other measurements to be specified in familiar units such as inches, millimeters, points, and picas. You can also use style sheets to precisely position graphics and text anywhere on a web page.

In short, style sheets bring the sophistication level of paper-oriented publishing to the Web. And they do so—you'll pardon the expression—with style.

> **By the Way**
>
> If you have three or more web pages that share (or should share) similar formatting and fonts, you may want to create a style sheet for them as you read this hour. Even if you choose not to create a complete style sheet, you'll find it helpful to apply styles to individual HTML elements directly within a web page.

Understanding CSS

The technology behind style sheets is called CSS, which stands for Cascading Style Sheets. CSS is a language that defines style constructs such as fonts, colors, and positioning, which are used to describe how information on a web page is formatted and displayed. CSS styles can be stored directly in an HTML web page or in a separate style sheet file. Either way, style sheets contain style rules that apply styles to elements of a given type. When used externally, style sheet rules are placed in an external style sheet document with the file extension `.css`.

A *style rule* is a formatting instruction that can be applied to an element on a web page, such as a paragraph of text or a link. Style rules consist of one or more *style properties* and their associated values. An *internal style sheet* is placed directly within a web page, whereas an *external style sheet* exists in a separate document and is simply linked to a web page via a special tag—more on this tag in a moment.

The "cascading" part of the name CSS refers to the manner in which style sheet rules are applied to elements in an HTML document. More specifically, styles in a CSS style sheet form a hierarchy in which more specific styles override more general styles. It is the responsibility of CSS to determine the precedence of style rules according to this hierarchy, which establishes a cascading effect. If that sounds a bit confusing, just think of the cascading mechanism in CSS as being similar to genetic inheritance, in which general traits are passed on from a parent to a child, but more specific traits are entirely unique to the child; base style rules are applied throughout a style sheet but can be overridden by more specific style rules.

A quick example should clear things up. Take a look at the following code, and see whether you can tell what's going on with the color of the text:

```
<div style="color:green">
  This text is green.
  <p style="color:blue">
    This text is blue.
  </p>
  <p>
    This text is still green.
  </p>
</div>
```

In this example, the color green is applied to the `<div>` tag via the `color` style property. So the text in the `<div>` tag is colored green. Because both `<p>` tags are children of the `<div>` tag, the green text style cascades down to them. However, the first `<p>` tag overrides the color style and changes it to blue. The end result is that the first paragraph is blue, and the second paragraph retains the cascaded green color.

By the Way

You may notice that I use the term *element* a fair amount in this hour, and the next few hours, for that matter. An *element* is simply a piece of information (content) in a web page, such as an image, a paragraph, or a link. Tags are used to code elements, and you can think of an element as a tag complete with descriptive information (attributes, text, images, and so on) within the tag.

Like many web technologies, CSS has evolved over the years. The original version of CSS, known as *Cascading Style Sheets Level 1*, or *CSS1*, was created back in 1996. The later CSS2 standard was created in 1998, and although that still seems like a long time ago, only recently has CSS2 fully caught on with web browsers. With all the power and promise of CSS, browser support has always been an issue. Fortunately, browsers have finally caught up for the most part, and you can now safely use CSS2 style sheets without too much concern. So when I talk about CSS throughout the book, I'm referring to CSS2.

Watch Out!

Even with the latest web browsers, there are still a few CSS2 features that aren't properly supported. I point out these features, along with workarounds, as I present CSS in the next few lessons of the book.

You'll find a complete reference guide to both the CSS1 and the CSS2 style sheet languages at http://www.w3.org/Style/CSS/, which is also where you can go to find out which styles are part of which CSS version. The rest of this hour explains how to put the information from those reference documents to use in a way that is compatible with the current generation of web browsers.

A Basic Style Sheet

Despite their intimidating power, style sheets can be simple to create. Consider the web pages shown in Figure 12.1 and Figure 12.2. These pages share several visual properties that could be put into a common style sheet:

- ▶ They use the Book Antiqua font for body text and Prose Antique for headings.
- ▶ They use an image named parchment.jpg as a tiled background image.
- ▶ All text is maroon colored (on a color screen, not in this book!).
- ▶ They have wide margins and indented body text.
- ▶ There is lots of vertical space between lines of text.
- ▶ The footnotes are centered and in small print (not visible in the figures).

FIGURE 12.1
This page uses a style sheet to fine-tune the appearance and spacing of the text and background.

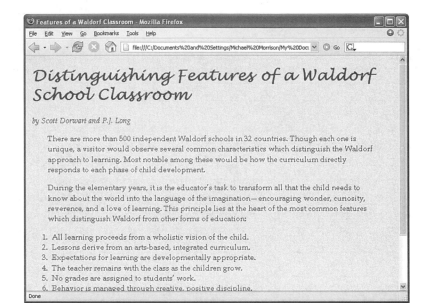

FIGURE 12.2
This page uses the same style sheet as the one shown in Figure 12.1, and therefore maintains a consistent look and feel.

Some of these properties, such as text color, background image, and centered small print, are possible to achieve with ordinary (deprecated) HTML tags. Others, such as line spacing and wide margins, are beyond the scope of standard HTML/XHTML. All of them can now be achieved easily with style sheets.

Listing 12.1 shows how a style sheet that specified these properties would look.

LISTING 12.1   A Single External Style Sheet Can Specify the Properties of Any Number of Pages

```
body {
  font-size:12pt;
  font-family:Book Antiqua;
  color:maroon;
  line-height:16pt;
  margin-left:10pt;
  margin-right:10pt;
  background:url(parchment.gif);
}

p {
  margin-left:24pt;
  margin-right:24pt;
}

h1 {
  font:24pt Prose Antique, Lucida Handwriting;
  font-weight:bold;
  line-height:30pt;
}

h2 {
  font:18pt Prose Antique, Lucida Handwriting;
  font-weight:bold;
  line-height:22pt;
}

a {
  text-decoration:none;
}

a:link {
  color:red;
}

a:visited {
  color:red;
}

a:active {
  color:black;
}

div.byline {
  font-style:italic;
}

div.footnote {
  font-size:9pt;
  line-height:12pt;
  text-align:center
}
```

This may initially appear to be a lot of code, but if you pay close attention you'll see that there isn't a lot of information on each line of code. It's fairly standard to place individual style rules on their own line to help make style sheets more readable. Speaking of code readability, perhaps the first thing you noticed about this style sheet code is that it doesn't look anything like normal HTML code. CSS uses a language all its own to specify style sheets.

Of course, there are some familiar HTML tags in there. As you might guess, body, p, h1, h2, a, and div in the style sheet refer to the corresponding tags in the HTML documents to which the style sheet will be applied. In curly braces after each tag name are the specifications for how all content within that tag should appear.

In this case, all body text should be rendered at a size of 12 points, in the Book Antiqua font if possible, and with the color maroon and 16 points between lines. The page should have 10-point margins, and the background should be the image found at the relative URL parchment.jpg.

> The sample style sheet uses the background style property to set a background image. There are also background-color, background-image, background-repeat, and background-position properties that allow you to set each facet of the background individually. When it comes to simply setting a tiled background image or solid-colored background, you can use background or the more specific background-image or background-color styles.

Any paragraph starting with a <p> tag will be indented an additional 24 points on both sides (the margins). Any text within <h1> or <h2> tags should be rendered in boldface Prose Antique at a size of 30 points and 22 points, respectively. If a user doesn't have a font named Prose Antique installed, the Lucida Handwriting font is used instead.

The pt after each measurement in Listing 12.1 means *points* (there are 72 points in an inch). If you prefer, you can specify any style sheet measurement in inches (in), centimeters (cm), pixels (px), or widths-of-a-letter-m, which are called ems (em).

You might have noticed that each style rule in the listing ends with a semicolon (;). Semicolons are used to separate style rules from each other. It is therefore customary to end each style rule with a semicolon so that you can easily add another style rule after it.

> You can specify font sizes as large as you like with style sheets, although some display devices and printers will not correctly handle fonts over 200 points.

To link this style sheet to HTML documents, you include a `<link />` tag in the `<head>` section of each document. Listing 12.2 is the HTML code for the page shown in Figure 12.1. It contains the following `<link />` tag:

```
<link rel="stylesheet" type="text/css" href="styles.css" />
```

This assumes that the style sheet is stored under the name `styles.css` in the same folder as the HTML document. As long as the web browser supports style sheets, and all modern browsers do, the properties specified in the style sheet will apply to the content in the page without the need for any special HTML formatting code. This confirms the ultimate goal of XHTML, which is to provide a separation between the content in a web page and the specific formatting required to display that content.

LISTING 12.2   The Page Shown in Figure 12.1 Contains Virtually No Formatting Code Because All of That Is Left to the External Style Sheet

```
<?xml version="1.0" encoding="UTF-8"?>
<!DOCTYPE html PUBLIC "-//W3C//DTD XHTML 1.1//EN"
  "http://www.w3.org/TR/xhtml11/DTD/xhtml11.dtd">

<html xmlns="http://www.w3.org/1999/xhtml" xml:lang="en">
  <head>
    <title>Features of a Waldorf Classroom</title>
    <link rel="stylesheet" type="text/css" href="styles.css" />
  </head>

  <body>
    <h1>Distinguishing Features of a Waldorf School Classroom</h1>
    <div class="byline">
      by Scott Dorwart and P.J. Long
    </div>
    <p>
      There are more than 500 independent Waldorf schools in 32 countries.
      Though each one is unique, a visitor would observe several common
      characteristics which distinguish the Waldorf approach to learning.
      Most notable among these would be how the curriculum directly responds
      to each phase of child development.
    </p>
    <p>During the elementary years, it is the educator&rsquo;s task to
    transform all that the child needs to know about the world into the
    language of the imagination&mdash;encouraging wonder, curiosity,
    reverence, and a love of learning. This principle lies at the heart of
    the most common features which distinguish Waldorf from other forms of
    education:</p>
    <ol>
      <li>All learning proceeds from a wholistic vision of the child.</li>
      <li>Lessons derive from an arts-based, integrated curriculum.</li>
      <li>Expectations for learning are developmentally appropriate.</li>
      <li>The teacher remains with the class as the children grow.</li>
      <li>No grades are assigned to students&rsquo; work.</li>
      <li>Behavior is managed through creative, positive discipline.</li>
      <li>The classroom provides a cooperative social environment.</li>
    </ol>
```

LISTING 12.2   Continued

```
    <div class="footnote">
      <hr />
      <span style="font-style:italic">Scott Dorwart is a carpenter and father
      of two children who attend the Green Mountain Waldorf School. P.J. Long
      is a psychotherapist and mother of two.</span>
      <hr />
      <a href="http://netletter.com/GMWS/HHH.htm">Head, Heart, Hands: A
      Waldorf Family Newsletter</a><br />
      Published by <a href="http://netletter.com/GMWS/GMWS.htm">The Green
      Mountain Waldorf School</a>
      <hr />
    </div>
  </body>
</html>
```

By the Way

In most web browsers, you can view the style rules in a style sheet by opening the `.css` file and choosing Notepad or another text editor as the helper application to view the file. (To determine the name of the `.css` file, look at the HTML source of any web page that links to it.) To edit your own style sheets, just use a text editor.

Although CSS is widely supported in all modern web browsers, it hasn't always enjoyed such wide support. Additionally, not every browser's support of CSS is flawless. To find out about how major browsers compare to each other in terms of CSS support, take a look at this web site: http://www.westciv.com/style_master/academy/browser_support/.

The code in Listing 12.2 is interesting because it contains no formatting of any kind. In other words, there is nothing in the HTML code that dictates how the text and images are to be displayed—no colors, no fonts, nothing. Yet the page is carefully formatted and rendered to the screen thanks to the link to the external style sheet, `styles.css`. The real benefit to this approach is that you can easily create a site with multiple pages that maintain a consistent look and feel. And you have the benefit of isolating the visual style of the page to a single document (the style sheet) so that one change impacts all pages.

A CSS Style Primer

You now have a basic knowledge of CSS style sheets and how they are based on style rules that describe the appearance of information in web pages. The next few sections of this lesson provide a quick overview of some of the most important style properties, and allow you to get started using CSS in your own style sheets.

CSS includes various style properties that are used to control fonts, colors, alignment, and margins, to name just a few facets of web page styling. The style properties in CSS can be generally grouped into two major categories:

▶ Layout properties

▶ Formatting properties

Layout properties consist of properties that impact the positioning of elements on a web page. For example, layout properties allow you to control the width, height, margin, padding, and alignment of content, and even go so far as to allow you to place content at exact positions on a page. This is something impossible to carry out in HTML code alone!

Layout Properties

CSS layout properties are used to determine how content is placed on a web page. One of the most important layout properties is the `display` property, which describes how an element is displayed with respect to other elements. There are four possible values for the `display` property:

▶ `block`—The element is displayed on a new line, as in a new paragraph.

▶ `list-item`—The element is displayed on a new line with a list-item mark (bullet) next to it.

▶ `inline`—The element is displayed inline with the current paragraph.

▶ `none`—The element is not displayed; it is hidden.

It's easier to understand the `display` property if you visualize each element on a web page occupying a rectangular area when displayed—the `display` property controls the manner in which this rectangular area is displayed. For example, the `block` value results in the element being placed on a new line by itself, whereas the `inline` value places the element next to the content just before it. The `display` property is one of the few style properties that can be applied in most style rules. Following is an example of how to set the `display` property:

```
display:block;
```

The `display` property relies on a concept known as *relative positioning*, which means that elements are positioned relative to the location of other elements on a page. CSS also supports *absolute positioning*, which allows you to place an element at an exact location on a page independent of other elements. You'll learn more about both of these types of positioning in Hour 14, "Using Style Sheets for Page Layout."

By the Way

You control the size of the rectangular area for an element with the `width` and `height` properties. Like many size-related CSS properties, `width` and `height` property values can be specified in several different units of measurement:

- ▶ in—Inches.
- ▶ px—Pixels.
- ▶ cm—Centimeters.
- ▶ pt—Points.
- ▶ mm—Millimeters.

You can mix and match units however you choose within a style sheet, but it's generally a good idea to be consistent across a set of similar style properties. For example, you might want to stick with points for font properties or pixels for dimensions. Following is an example of setting the width of an element using pixel units:

```
width:200px;
```

Formatting Properties

CSS formatting properties are used to control the appearance of content on a web page, as opposed to controlling the physical positioning of the content. One of the most popular formatting properties is the `border` property, which is used to establish a visible boundary around an element with a box or partial box. The following border properties provide a means of describing the borders of an element:

- ▶ border-width—The width of the border edge.
- ▶ border-color—The color of the border edge.
- ▶ border-style—The style of the border edge.
- ▶ border-left—The left side of the border.
- ▶ border-right—The right side of the border.
- ▶ border-top—The top of the border.
- ▶ border-bottom—The bottom of the border.
- ▶ border—All the border sides.

The `border-width` property is used to establish the width of the border edge. It is often expressed in pixels, as the following code demonstrates:

```
border-width:5px;
```

Not surprisingly, the `border-color` and `border-style` properties are used to set the border color and style. Following is an example of how these two properties are set:

```
border-color:blue;
border-style:dotted;
```

The border-style property can be set to any of the following values:

- solid—A single-line border.

- double—A double-line border.

- dashed—A dashed border.

- dotted—A dotted border.

- groove—A border with a groove appearance.

- ridge—A border with a ridge appearance.

- inset—A border with an inset appearance.

- outset—A border with an outset appearance.

- none—No border.

The default value of the border-style property is none, which is why elements don't have a border unless you set the border property to a different style. The most common border styles are the solid and double styles.

> The exception to the default border-style of none is when an image is placed within an <a> tag so that it serves as a linked image. In that case, a solid border is automatically set by default. That's why you often see linked images with the style border-style:none, which turns off the automatic border.

By the Way

The border-left, border-right, border-top, and border-bottom properties allow you to set the border for each side of an element individually. If you want a border to appear the same on all four sides, you can use the single border property by itself, which expects the following styles separated by a space: border-width, border-style, and border-color. Following is an example of using the border property to set a border that consists of two (double) red lines that are a total of 10 pixels in width:

```
border:10px double red;
```

Whereas the color of an element's border is set with the border-color property, the color of the inner region of an element is set using the color and background-color properties. The color property sets the color of text in an element (foreground), and the background-color property sets the color of the background

behind the text. Following is an example of setting both color properties to predefined colors:

```
color:black;
background-color:orange;
```

You can also assign custom colors to these properties by specifying the colors in
hexadecimal or as RGB (Red Green Blue) decimal values, just as you do in HTML:

```
background-color:#999999;
color:rgb(0,0,255);
```

You can also control the alignment and indentation of web page content without
too much trouble. This is accomplished with the text-align and text-indent
properties, as the following code demonstrates:

```
text-align:center;
text-indent:12px;
```

After you have an element properly aligned and indented, you might be interested
in setting its font. The following font properties are used to set the various parameters associated with fonts:

- font-family—The family of the font.

- font-size—The size of the font.

- font-style—The style of the font (normal or italic).

- font-weight—The weight of the font (light, medium, bold, and so on).

The font-family property specifies a prioritized list of font family names. A prioritized list is used instead of a single value to provide alternatives in case a font isn't
available on a given system. The font-size property specifies the size of the font
using a unit of measurement, usually points. Finally, the font-style property sets
the style of the font, and the font-weight property sets the weight of the font.
Following is an example of setting these font properties:

```
font-family: Arial, sans-serif;
font-size: 36pt;
font-style: italic;
font-weight: medium;
```

Now that you know a whole lot more about style properties and how they work,
take a look back at Listing 12.1 and see whether it makes a bit more sense.

Here's a recap of the style properties used in that style sheet, which you can use as a guide for understanding how it works:

▶ font—Lets you set many font properties at once. You can specify a list of font names separated by commas; if the first is not available, the next is tried, and so on. You can also include the words bold and/or italic and a font size. Each of these font properties can be specified separately with font-family:, font-size:, font-weight:bold, and font-style:italic if you prefer.

▶ line-height—Also known in the publishing world as *leading*. This sets the height of each line of text, usually in points.

▶ color—Sets the text color, using the standard color names or hexadecimal color codes (see Hour 9 for more details).

▶ text-decoration—Useful for turning link underlining off—simply set it to none. The values of underline, italic, and line-through are also supported. The application of styles to links is covered in more detail in the next hour, "Digging Deeper into Style Sheet Formatting."

▶ text-align—Aligns text to the left, right, or center, along with justifying the text with a value of justify.

▶ text-indent—Indents beyond the left margin by a specified amount. You can say how far to indent in units (px, in, cm, mm, pt, pc), or you can specify a percentage of the page width (such as 20%).

▶ margin—Sets the left and right margins to the same value, which can be in measurement units or a percentage of the page width. Use margin-left and margin-right if you want to set the left and right margins independently, and margin-top to set the top margin. You'll learn more about these style properties in the Hour 14.

▶ background—Places a solid color or image behind text, with either a color or url(*address*), where *address* points to a background image tile. Note that this can be assigned not only to the <body> tag, but also to any tag or span of text to highlight an area on a page. The background-color and background-image style properties can be used to achieve the same effect.

Using Style Classes

This is a "teach yourself" book, so you don't have to go to a single class to learn how to give your pages great style, although you do need to learn what a style class is. Whenever you want some of the text on your pages to look different from the other text, you can create what amounts to a custom-built HTML tag. Each type of specially formatted text you define is called a *style class*. A *style class* is a custom set of formatting specifications that can be applied to any element in a web page.

Before showing you a style class, I need to take a quick step back and clarify some CSS terminology. First off, a CSS *style property* is a specific style that can be assigned a value, such as `color` or `font-size`. You associate a style property and its respective value with elements on a web page by using a selector. A *selector* is used to identify tags on a page to which you apply styles. Following is an example of a selector, a property, and a value all included in a basic style rule:

```
h1 { font:36pt Courier; }
```

In this code, `h1` is the selector, `font`, is the style property, and `36pt Courier` is the value. The selector is important because it means that the font setting will be applied to all `h1` elements in the web page. But maybe you want to differentiate between some of the `h1` elements—what then? The answer lies in style classes.

Suppose you want two different kinds of `<h1>` headings in your documents. You would create a style class for each one by putting the following CSS code in a style sheet:

```
h1.silly { font:36pt Comic Sans; }
h1.serious { font:36pt Arial; }
```

Notice that these selectors include a period (.) after `h1`, followed by a descriptive class name. To choose between the two style classes in an HTML page, you would use the `class` attribute, like this:

```
<h1 class="silly">Marvin's Munchies Inc.</h1>
<p>
  Text about Marvin's Munchies goes here.
</p>
<h1 class="serious">MMI Investor Information</h1>
<p>
  Text for business investors goes here.
</p>
```

When referencing a style class in HTML code, you simply specify the class name in the `class` attribute of an element. In this example, the words `Marvin's Munchies Inc.` would appear in a 36-point Comic Sans font, assuming that you included a `<link />` to the style sheet at the top of the web page and assuming that the user has the Comic Sans font installed). The words `MMI Investor Information` would appear in the 36-point Arial font instead.

What if you want to create a style class that could be applied to any element, rather than just headings or some other particular tag? You can associate a style class with the <div> tag (which, as you may recall from Hour 5, "Basic Text Alignment and Formatting," is used to enclose any text in a block that is somewhat similar to a paragraph of text).

You can essentially create your own custom HTML tag by using the div selector followed by a period (.) followed by any style class name you make up and any style specifications you choose. That tag can control any number of font, spacing, and margin settings all at once. Wherever you want to apply your custom tag in a page, use a <div> tag with the class= attribute followed by the class name you created.

For example, the style sheet in Listing 12.1 includes the following style class specification:

```
div.footnote {
  font-size:9pt;
  line-height:12pt;
  text-align:center;
}
```

Did you Know?

You may have noticed a change in the coding style when multiple properties are included in a style rule. For style rules with a single style, you'll commonly see the property placed on the same line as the rule, like this:

```
div.footnote { font-size:9pt; }
```

However, when a style rule contains multiple style properties, it's much easier to read and understand the code if you list the properties one-per-line, like this:

```
div.footnote {
  font-size:9pt;
  line-height:12pt;
  text-align:center;
}
```

This style class is applied in Listing 12.2 with the following tag:

```
<div class="footnote">
```

Everything between that tag and the closing </div> tag in Listing 12.2 appears in 9-point centered text with 12-point vertical line spacing.

What makes style classes so valuable is how they isolate style code from web pages, effectively allowing you to focus your HTML code on the actual content in a page, not how it is going to appear on the screen. Then you can focus on how the content is rendered to the screen by fine-tuning the style sheet. You may be surprised by how a relatively small amount of code in a style sheet can have significant effects across an entire web site. This makes your pages much easier to maintain and manipulate.

Internal Style Sheets and Inline Styles

In some situations, you might want to specify styles that will be used in only one web page, in which case you can enclose a style sheet between `<style>` and `</style>` tags and include it directly in an HTML document. Style sheets used in this manner must appear in the head of an HTML document. No `<link />` tag is needed, and you cannot refer to that style sheet from any other page (unless you copy it into the beginning of that document too). This kind of style sheet is known as an internal style sheet, as you learned earlier in the lesson.

Listing 12.3 contains an example of how you might specify an internal style sheet.

LISTING 12.3   A Minimal Web Page That Demonstrates How to Use an Internal Style Sheet

```
<?xml version="1.0" encoding="UTF-8"?>
<!DOCTYPE html PUBLIC "-//W3C//DTD XHTML 1.1//EN"
  "http://www.w3.org/TR/xhtml11/DTD/xhtml11.dtd">

<html xmlns="http://www.w3.org/1999/xhtml" xml:lang="en">
  <head>
    <title>Some Page</title>

    <style type="text/css">
      div.footnote {
        font-size:9pt;
        line-height:12pt;
        text-align:center;}
    </style>
  </head>

  <body>
  ...
  <div class="footnote">
  Copyright 2006 Acme Products, Inc.
  </div>
  </body>
</html>
```

In the listing code, the `div.footnote` style class is specified in an internal style sheet that appears in the head of the page. The style class is now available for use within the body of this page. And, in fact, it is used in the body of the page to style the copyright notice.

Internal style sheets are handy if you want to create a style rule that is used multiple times within a single page. However, in some instances you may need to apply a unique style to one particular element. This calls for an inline style rule, which allows you to specify a style for only a small part of a page, such as an individual element. For example, you can create and apply a style rule within a `<p>`, `<div>`, or

`<span>` tag via the `style` attribute. This type of style is known as an *inline style* because it is specified right there in the middle of the HTML code.

> `<span>` and `</span>` are *dummy* tags that do nothing in and of themselves except specify a range of content to apply any `style` attributes that you add. The only difference between `<div>` and `<span>` is that `<div>` is a block element and therefore forces a line break, whereas `<span>` doesn't. Therefore, you should use `<span>` to modify the style of any portion of text that is to appear in the middle of a sentence or paragraph without any line break.

Here's how a sample `style` attribute might look:

```
<p style="color:green">
  This text is green, but <span style="color:red">this text is red.</span>
  Back to green again, but...
</p>
<p>
  ...now the green is over, and we're back to the default color for this page.
</p>
```

This code makes use of the `<span>` tag to show how to apply the color style property in an inline style rule. In fact, both the `<p>` tag and the `<span>` tag in this example use the color property as an inline style. What's important to understand is that the `color:red` style property overrides the `color:green` style property for the text appearing between the `<span>` and `</span>` tags. Then in the second paragraph, neither of the `color` styles applies because it is a completely new paragraph that adheres to the default color of the entire page.

> To give the pages at the *Sams Publishing* website a consistent look and feel, I created a style sheet that is linked to every page in the site. For your edification and convenience, I copied that style sheet text into an HTML page, which you can access from the same zip file.

A Quick Style Sheet Recap

Just so you understand your options in regard to applying CSS styles to your web pages, following are the three main approaches you have at your disposal:

▶ *External style sheet*—A collection of CSS style rules that is placed in a document of its own with a `.css` file extension, and then linked to web pages via the `<link />` tag in the head of each page.

▶ *Internal style sheet*—A collection of CSS style rules that is placed in the head of a document via the `<style>` tag. These style rules apply only to the page in which they are placed.

▶ *Inline style rules*—One or more CSS style rules that are placed directly within a tag via the `style` attribute. These style rules apply only to the specific tag in which they are placed.

As you can see, there is plenty of flexibility when it comes to how you apply CSS style rules. I highly recommend using an external style sheet if you're building a site with multiple pages that need to maintain a similar look. An internal style sheet isn't a bad option for a single page where you want to organize and possibly reuse some common styles. And finally, inline style rules are handy anytime you need to quickly apply a unique style to an element on a page.

Summary

In this hour you learned that a style sheet can control the appearance of many HTML pages at once. It can also give you extremely precise control over typography, spacing, and the positioning of HTML elements. You also learned that by adding a `style` attribute to almost any HTML tag, you can control the style of any part of an HTML page without referring to a separate style sheet document.

Table 12.1 summarizes the tags discussed in this hour. Refer to the CSS1 and CSS2 style sheet standards at www.w3c.org for details on what options can be included after the `<style>` tag or the `style` attribute.

TABLE 12.1   HTML Tags and Attributes Covered in Hour 12

Tag/Attributes	Function
`<style>...</style>`	Allows an internal style sheet to be included within a document. Used between `<head>` and `</head>`.
Attribute	
`type="contenttype"`	The Internet content type. (Always `"text/css"` for a CSS style sheet.)
`<link />`	Links to an external style sheet (or other document type). Used in the `<head>` section of the document.
Attribute	
`href="url"`	The address of the style sheet.
`type="contenttype"`	The Internet content type. (Always `"text/css"` for a CSS style sheet.)

TABLE 12.1 Continued

Tag/Attributes	Function
`rel="stylesheet"`	The link type. (Always `"stylesheet"` for style sheets.)
`<span>...</span>`	Does nothing at all except provide a place to put `style` or other attributes. (Similar to `<div>...</div>` but does not cause a line break.)
Attribute	
`style="style"`	Includes inline style specifications. (Can be used in `<span>`, `<div>`, `<body>`, and most other HTML tags.)

Q&A

Q *Say I link a style sheet to my page that says all text should be blue, but there's a* `<span style="font-color:red">` *tag in the page somewhere. Will that text come out blue or red?*

A Red. Local inline styles always take precedence over external style sheets. Any style specifications you put between `<style>` and `</style>` tags at the top of a page will also take precedence over external style sheets (but not over inline styles later in the same page). This is the cascading effect of style sheets that I mentioned earlier in the hour. So you can think of cascading style effects as starting with an external style sheet, which is overridden by an internal style sheet, which is overridden by inline styles.

Q *Can I link more than one style sheet to a single page?*

A Sure. For example, you might have a sheet for font stuff and another one for margins and spacing—just include a `<link />` for both. Technically speaking, the CSS standard requires web browsers to give the user the option to choose between style sheets when multiple sheets are presented via multiple `<link />` tags. However, in practice all major web browsers simply include every style sheet. The preferred technique for linking in multiple style sheets involves using the special `@import` command. Following is an example of importing multiple style sheets with `@import`:

```
@import url(styles1.css);
@import url(styles2.css);
```

Similar to the `<link />` tag, the `@import` command must be placed in the head of a web page. You learn more about this handy little command in Hour 15, "Creating Print-Friendly Web Pages," when you find out how to create a style sheet specifically for printing web pages.

Workshop

The workshop contains quiz questions and activities to help you solidify your understanding of the material covered. Try to answer all questions before looking at the "Answers" section that follows.

Quiz

1. Create a style sheet to specify 30-point blue Arial headings, and all other text in double-spaced 10-point blue Times Roman (or the default browser font).

2. If you saved the style sheet you made for question 1 as `corporate.css`, how would you apply it to a web page named `intro.html`?

Answers

1. `h1 { font:30pt blue Arial; }`
   `body { font: 10pt blue; }`

2. Put the following tag between the `<head>` and `</head>` tags of the `intro.html` document:
   `<link rel="stylesheet" type="text/css" href="corporate.css" />`

Exercises

▶ Develop a standard style sheet for your web site and link it into all your pages. (Use internal style sheets and/or inline styles for pages that need to deviate from it.) If you work for a corporation, chances are it has already developed font and style specifications for printed materials. Get a copy of those specifications and follow them for company web pages too.

▶ Be sure to explore the official style sheet specs at http://www.w3.org/Style/CSS/ and try some of the more esoteric style properties I didn't mention in this hour.

Digging Deeper into Style Sheet Formatting

The preceding hour covered the basics of style sheets and showed you how to do some pretty neat things with them. This hour picks up where that lesson left off by digging into some more advanced CSS topics that you will no doubt find useful as you embark on your own web creations. CSS is an extremely powerful technology that can make your life much easier when it comes to creating visually appealing web pages with minimal effort. The techniques you'll learn in this hour will not only add to your CSS knowledge but also improve your understanding of how style sheets fit into practical web pages.

Advanced Text Formatting with CSS

You've already learned how to use several CSS style properties that allow you to carefully control the formatting of text on your web pages. In addition to the common text-formatting properties that you've already seen, there are several other lesser-used properties worth filing away in your CSS knowledge bank.

First off is the font-variant style property, which can be used to apply a small-caps effect to text. If you aren't familiar with this text effect, it causes all the text in a paragraph to use uppercase characters; capitalized characters are simply displayed larger than other characters when the small-caps effect is applied.

Following is an example of using the font-variant style property:

```
<p style="font-variant:small-caps">
  This paragraph is in small caps.
</p>
```

The possible values for the font-variant property include none (default) and small-caps. Figure 13.1 shows how this small-caps text appears in a web page.

Two other interesting text-formatting properties are letter-spacing and word-spacing, which allow you to alter the spacing between individual letters and words. Both of these style properties are specified using standard CSS size units, such as pixels (px).

Following is an example of how to use the letter-spacing style property to add five pixels between each letter in the paragraph:

```
<p style="letter-spacing:5px">
  This paragraph has its letters spaced apart by 5 pixels.
</p>
```

If you want to control the spacing between words instead of between letters, here's an example of how to use the word-spacing property to add 10 pixels of space between each word:

```
<p style="word-spacing:10px">
  This paragraph has its words spaced apart by 10 pixels.
</p>
```

Both of the last two examples are shown in Figure 13.1.

The last text-formatting style property of interest here is not quite as commonly used as the others you just saw. However, it is fairly powerful in its own right. I'm referring to the text-transform property, which can be used to automatically transform the case of a paragraph of text. Allowed values for the property include none (default), uppercase, lowercase, and capitalize. The uppercase and lowercase values render text entirely in uppercase or lowercase, respectively, and capitalize capitalizes every word.

Following is an example of how to use the text-transform property to transform a paragraph of text so that every word is capitalized:

```
<p style="text-transform:capitalize">
  This paragraph has its text transformed so that every word is capitalized.
</p>
```

Figure 13.1 shows the results of this code as well.

Listing 13.1 contains the complete code for the advanced text-formatting page shown in Figure 13.1.

LISTING 13.1   CSS Gives You a Surprising Amount of Control over the Formatting of Text

```
<?xml version="1.0" encoding="UTF-8"?>
<!DOCTYPE html PUBLIC "-//W3C//DTD XHTML 1.1//EN"
  "http://www.w3.org/TR/xhtml11/DTD/xhtml11.dtd">

<html xmlns="http://www.w3.org/1999/xhtml" xml:lang="en">
  <head>
    <title>Textual Styles</title>
  </head>

  <body>
    <p style="font-variant:small-caps">
      This paragraph is in small caps.
    </p>
    <p style="letter-spacing:5px">
```

LISTING 13.1   Continued

```
      This paragraph has its letters spaced apart by 5 pixels.
    </p>
    <p style="word-spacing:10px">
      This paragraph has its words spaced apart by 10 pixels.
    </p>
    <p style="text-transform:capitalize">
      This paragraph has its text transformed so that every word is capitalized.
    </p>
  </body>
</html>
```

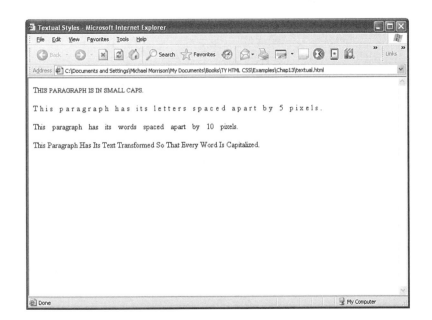

FIGURE 13.1
Advanced CSS style properties allow you to alter the capitalization and spacing of text.

Keep in mind that you can mix-and-match any of these style properties, as well as all the other font- and text-related properties you've seen throughout the book. In fact, later in the lesson, in the section "Revisiting the Hockey Player Example," you'll see how to use many of the text-formatting properties in conjunction with each other to get interesting text effects.

> The CSS standard defines more style properties than what you can currently use today. For example, the font-stretch and text-shadow properties are technically part of the standard but have yet to see support in a major web browser. The font-stretch property will eventually allow you to stretch text in a single direction, and the text-shadow property will allow you to apply a drop shadow simply by applying a style—no tricky image editing required!

By the Way

Changing the Appearance of Links

You've no doubt seen web pages that contain links that respond differently than the default behavior, which is to simply appear as underlined blue text (in most web browsers). Most browsers also change the color of a link to purple after the linked page or resource has been opened. This helps to indicate whether you've followed a link before.

CSS includes a mechanism that allows you to change the appearance of links based on the state of the link. For the purposes of applying styles, you can think of a link as having four distinct states:

▶ *Link*—A link that has not yet been visited.

▶ *Hover*—A link that has the mouse pointer hovering over it.

▶ *Active*—A link that is being activated, such as with a mouse click.

▶ *Visited*—A link that has already been visited.

Each of these link states corresponds with a CSS *pseudoclass*, which is a special type of style class that applies to the state of an element. Pseudoclasses are unique in that you specify them using a colon (:) instead of a period (.). The pseudoclasses that apply to links are `link`, `hover`, `active`, and `visited`. To apply these pseudoclass styles, you attach them to the a element like this: `a:link`, `a:hover`, `a:active`, and `a:visited`.

Following is an example of how to set styles for the `a:link` pseudoclass, which determines what a normal link looks like:

```
a:link {
  color:#19619A;
  font-weight:bold;
  text-decoration:none;
}
```

Notice that underlining is removed from the link via the `text-decoration:none` setting, but the link is bolded via the `font-weight:bold` setting. The color #19619A is a light blue color. This style rule appears later in the lesson in a new version of the hockey player style sheet that you saw earlier in the book.

Coffee
Break

For a practical example of how link styles can be used to get a different effect for links, check out the Wired News web site at http://www.wired.com/. The Wired News site displays links underlined, which is to be expected, but it also changes the color of links from blue to red when you hover over them with the mouse. Visited links are then displayed in purple.

Following is how you would alter the previous link style so that it appears in a different color when the user hovers over it with the mouse:

```
a:hover {
  background-color:gold;
  font-weight:bold;
  text-decoration:none;
}
```

Keep in mind that you can also change the appearance of a link when the link is active and after it has been visited. However, if you want a link to change its appearance only in response to a mouse hover, just set the a:active and a:visited style classes to match the a:link class.

Did you Know?

Here's a neat trick: If you make the color of a:visited the same as the background color of a page, links to pages that a visitor has already seen will become invisible. This can make your pages seem "smart"—offering people only links to places they haven't been. On the other hand, some users may think quite the opposite of your page because they may wonder where the links went. So use this trick with caution.

Commenting CSS Code

Similar to HTML code, CSS code allows you to include comments that describe or otherwise include notations about the style sheet. Unlike HTML, however, comments in CSS use a different approach to specifying comments. More specifically, you enclose CSS comments inside /* and */. So a simple CSS comment looks like this:

```
/* This is a CSS comment. */
```

It is very important to always start a CSS comment with /* and then end it with */. Also, CSS comments can appear only in style sheets (internal or external), not inline styles.

By the Way

If you've done any programming in the C, C++, or Java programming languages, the /* */ format of CSS comments will be very familiar—CSS borrowed its commenting syntax from those languages.

Listing 13.2 contains modified style sheet code from the Waldorf School sample pages shown in the preceding hour. This version of the style sheet is just like the previous version except for the new comments that help to explain the meaning of the styles.

LISTING 13.2   CSS Comments Can Be Helpful in Explaining the Meaning of Style Rules

```css
/* Make all body text maroon-colored 12-point Book Antiqua
   with 16-point vertical spacing between lines of text
   and 10-point margins. Use parchment.gif as the background. */
body {
  font-size:12pt;
  font-family:Book Antiqua;
  color:maroon;
  line-height:16pt;
  margin-left:10pt;
  margin-right:10pt;
  background:url(parchment.gif);
}

/* Indent paragraphs */
p {
  margin-left:24pt;
  margin-right:24pt;
}

/* Make headings Prose Antique bold with generous line spacing.
   If user doesn't have Prose Antique, use Lucida Handwriting. */
h1 {
  font:24pt Prose Antique, Lucida Handwriting;
  font-weight:bold;
  line-height:30pt;
}

h2 {
  font:18pt Prose Antique, Lucida Handwriting;
  font-weight:bold;
  line-height:22pt;
}

/* Don't underline links, and make all links red.
   Make links flash black when activated. */
a {
  text-decoration:none;
}

a:link {
  color:red;
}

a:visited {
  color:red;
}

a:active {
  color:black;
}

/* Format footnotes as 9-point Book Antiqua, and center them. */
div.footnote {
  font-size:9pt;
  line-height:12pt;
  text-align:center
}
```

This code demonstrates the usefulness of comments in CSS style sheets, and how they can be used to help paint a more detailed picture of what is going on with each style rule.

CSS Tips and Tricks

Although you've covered some interesting new style sheet territory in this hour already, there are still a few unique CSS features you've yet to uncover. The next few sections tie up some CSS loose ends by introducing you to some very handy CSS techniques.

Using Generic Classes

Every CSS style rule you've seen thus far in the book relies on a base tag when you put together the selector portion of the rule. For example, if you wanted to create a paragraph of text that is shown in bold, you would use the following style rule:

```
p.bold { font-weight:bold; }
```

Notice in this example that the p element is provided on the left side of the period in the rule. If you want to create a style rule that can be applied to any element, you can leave off the left side of the selector and create a generic style class. A *generic style class* can be applied to any element that supports the properties within the style rule. Following is an example of creating a generic bold style class:

```
.bold { font-weight:bold; }
```

This generic style class is like the one you just saw except that the p part of the selector has been removed. This means you can now use the class with any element that supports the font-weight property. Following is an example:

```
<p class="bold">
  This paragraph is bold.
</p>
<p>
  This <span class="bold">word</span> is bold.
</p>
```

In this example, the first paragraph is bold due to the bold setting in the class attribute. However, the second paragraph is normal except for the <span> tag, which also uses the bold setting in the class attribute. Because the bold style class is a generic style class, it can be used with both the <p> and the <span> tags, among others.

Specifying Multiple Selectors

Another neat trick you can perform when creating style rules is to specify multiple selectors for a single rule. This effectively allows you to tighten up your style sheet code and eliminate unnecessary repeated code. Check out the following example:

```
a:link, a:visited, a:active {
  color:#19619A;
  font-weight:bold;
  text-decoration:none;
}
```

In this example, the a:link, a:visited, and a:active style classes are all set to the same rule. Without the multiple selector trick, you'd have to repeat the rule three times, which is an unnecessary hassle.

Here's one more example just to make sure that you understand how to use multiple selectors:

```
h1, h2 { text-align:center; font-style:italic; }
```

In this code, both the h1 and the h2 elements are styled so that text within them is center aligned and italicized. By using a multiple selector, you simplify the style sheet code and make it easier to maintain it. In other words, should you ever need to change the style rule for the h1 and h2 elements, all you have to do is edit a single rule.

Mixing Style Classes

One final style sheet trick that certainly ranks up there in terms of craftiness involves the use of mixed style classes. More specifically, you can create a custom style class for a particular element that also applies to pseudoclasses. If you recall, pseudoclasses are built-in classes that relate to the state of an element, such as a:link and a:hover. Maybe you want to create several types of links in your web pages, in which case it may make sense to create multiple link style classes.

To understand how you might use mixed style classes, check out the following code:

```
a:link, a:visited, a:active {
  color:#19619A;
  font-weight:bold;
  text-decoration:none;
}

a:hover {
  background-color:gold;
  font-weight:bold;
  text-decoration:none;
}
```

This code should look somewhat familiar, because it combines some of the link styles you've already learned about. If you pay close attention, you'll notice that these style classes result in a link being displayed in a bold font with no underline. What if you wanted a link that was similar but that used italicized text instead of bold text? Here's the code:

```
a.emphasis:link, a.emphasis:visited, a.emphasis:active {
  color:#19619A;
  font-style:italic;
  text-decoration:none;
}

a.emphasis:hover {
  background-color:gold;
  font-style:italic;
  text-decoration:none;
}
```

A hyperlink set to the emphasis class will be displayed in italicized text instead of bold text.

Revisiting the Hockey Player Example

This lesson has covered some interesting new territory with respect to CSS style sheets, and it's time to put some of this new knowledge to work in a practical example. Listing 13.3 contains the HTML code for the familiar hockey player web page, which now relies on an external style sheet to format and display all of its content.

LISTING 13.3   The Hockey Player Web Page Now Takes Advantage of Using an External Style Sheet

```
<?xml version="1.0" encoding="UTF-8"?>
<!DOCTYPE html PUBLIC "-//W3C//DTD XHTML 1.1//EN"
  "http://www.w3.org/TR/xhtml11/DTD/xhtml11.dtd">

<html xmlns="http://www.w3.org/1999/xhtml" xml:lang="en">
  <head>
    <title>Music City Mafia - Terry Lancaster</title>
    <link rel="stylesheet" type="text/css" href="player.css" />
    <script type="text/javascript" src="external.js"></script>
  </head>

  <body>
    <div class="title">16 - Terry Lancaster</div>
    <div>
      <div class="image">
        <img src="tlancaster.jpg" alt="Terry &quot;Big T&quot; Lancaster" />
      </div>
      <div class="info">
        <div>
          <span class="label">Nickname:</span> Big T<br />
```

LISTING 13.3   Continued

```
          <span class="label">Position:</span> RW<br />
          <span class="label">Height:</span> 6'3"<br />
          <span class="label">Weight:</span> 195<br />
          <span class="label">Shoots:</span> Left<br />
          <span class="label">Age:</span> 40<br />
          <span class="label">Birthplace:</span>
          <a
href="http://en.wikipedia.org/wiki/Nashville%2C_Tennessee">Nashville,
          TN</a>
        </div>
      </div>
      <div class="favorites">
        <div>
          <span class="label">Favorite NHL Player:</span>
          <a href="http://www.nhl.com/players/8448091.html">Brett Hull</a><br />
          <span class="label">Favorite NHL Team:</span>
          <a href="http://www.nashvillepredators.com/">Nashville Predators</a>
          <br />
          <span class="label">Favorite Southern Fixin:</span>
          <a
href="http://southernfood.about.com/od/potatorecipes/r/blbb442.htm">
          Skillet Fried Potatoes</a><br />
          <span class="label">Favorite Meat and Three:</span>
          <a href="http://www.hollyeats.com/Swetts.htm">Swett's</a>
          (<a
href="http://maps.google.com/maps?q=2725+clifton+ave,+nashville,+tn"
          rel="external">map</a>)
          <br />
          <span class="label">Favorite Country Star:</span>
          <a href="http://www.patsycline.com/">Patsy Cline</a><br />
          <span class="label">Favorite Mafia Moment:</span>
          "<a href="mcmplayer_chale.html">Chet</a> finishing the game with his
          eyelid completely slashed through."
        </div>
      </div>
    </div>
    <div>
      <table class="stats" border="1">
        <tr class="heading">
          <th class="season">Season</th>
          <th>GP</th>
          <th>G</th>
          <th>A</th>
          <th>P</th>
          <th>PIM</th>
          <th>PPG</th>
          <th>SHG</th>
          <th>GWG</th>
        </tr>
        <tr class="light">
          <td class="season">Summer 2005</td>
          <td>11</td>
          <td>7</td>
          <td>5</td>
          <td>12</td>
          <td>0</td>
          <td>0</td>
```

LISTING 13.3 Continued

```
          <td>0</td>
          <td>0</td>
        </tr>
        <tr class="dark">
          <td class="season">Winter 2004</td>
          <td>24</td>
          <td>14</td>
          <td>14</td>
          <td>28</td>
          <td>2</td>
          <td>0</td>
          <td>0</td>
          <td>5</td>
        </tr>
        <tr class="light">
          <td class="season">Summer 2004</td>
          <td>18</td>
          <td>9</td>
          <td>9</td>
          <td>18</td>
          <td>2</td>
          <td>0</td>
          <td>0</td>
          <td>2</td>
        </tr>
        <tr class="dark">
          <td class="season">Spring 2004</td>
          <td>19</td>
          <td>7</td>
          <td>17</td>
          <td>24</td>
          <td>0</td>
          <td>0</td>
          <td>0</td>
          <td>1</td>
        </tr>
      </table>
    </div>
    <div class="contact">
      <a href="mailto:l&#97;ncastert@musiccitym&#97;fi&#97;.com?subject=
      Fan Question&amp;body=What's your secret?">Contact Terry.</a>
    </div>
  </body>
</html>
```

> **By the Way**
>
> The `external.js` JavaScript file that is referenced in Listing 13.3 was covered back in Hour 3, "Linking to Other Web Pages," when you learned how to use JavaScript as a workaround for targeting links that open a new browser window. The JavaScript code is required in order to allow Web pages to validate under XHTML—XHTML doesn't support the `target="_blank"` approach to opening links in a new window.

Most of this code should be somewhat familiar because it is similar to code you've seen a few times in the book thus far. If anything, this code is simpler than earlier versions of hockey player pages because it has all the CSS inline styles removed. This is because the page now takes advantage of style classes, which are defined in an external style sheet.

The external style sheet used in the hockey player sample page is titled `player.css`, and its code is shown in Listing 13.4.

LISTING 13.4   The `player.css` External Style Sheet Includes Several Style Classes for Carefully Formatting Content in Hockey Player Pages

```css
body {
  font-family:Verdana, Arial;
  font-size:12pt;
  color:navy;
}

div {
  padding:3px;
}

div.title {
  font-size:18pt;
  font-weight:bold;
  font-variant:small-caps;
  letter-spacing:2px;
  color:black;
}

div.image {
  float:left;
}

div.info, div.favorites {
  float:left;
  vertical-align:top;
}

table.stats {
  width:100%;
  clear:both;
  text-align:right;
  font-size:11pt;
}

.label {
  font-weight:bold;
  font-variant:small-caps;
}
```

LISTING 13.4 Continued

```
tr.heading {
  font-variant:small-caps;
  background-color:navy;
  color:white;
}

tr.light {
  background-color:white;
}

tr.dark {
  background-color:#EEEEEE;
}

th.season, td.season {
  text-align:left;
}

a:link, a:visited, a:active {
  color:#19619A;
  font-weight:bold;
  text-decoration:none;
}

a:hover {
  background-color:gold;
  font-weight:bold;
  text-decoration:none;
}
```

The goal behind this style sheet is to isolate and style each unique piece of information in the hockey player web page. Additionally, it is important for the styles to be consistently applicable to multiple player pages while providing a consistent look. Figure 13.2 shows the player page for Terry Lancaster, which is styled solely through the player.css external style sheet.

The true power of external style sheets isn't revealed until you apply player.css to another hockey player page, and then view the results. Figure 13.3 shows another player page styled with the same sheet.

This example demonstrates how powerful an external style sheet can be when applied consistently to multiple pages. Not only that, but if you explore the player.css style sheet carefully, you'll find that it uses many of the advanced CSS tips and tricks that were covered throughout this lesson.

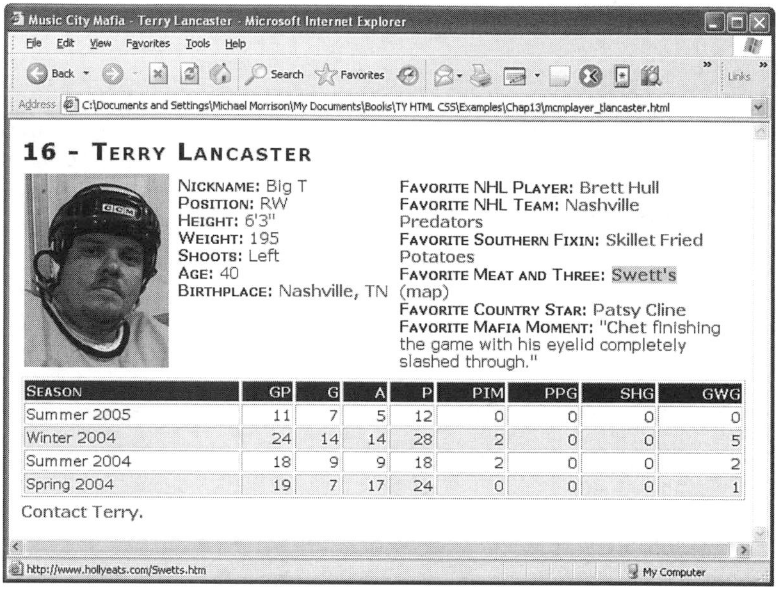

FIGURE 13.2
This hockey
player web page
is styled entirely
through an
external style
sheet.

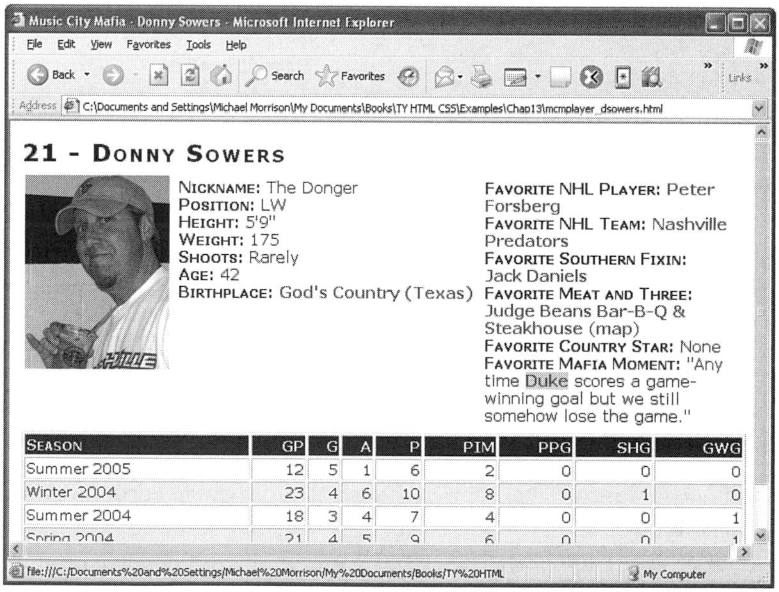

FIGURE 13.3
This player page
retains the
same look as
the page in
Figure 13.2
thanks to the
player.css
external style
sheet.

Summary

This lesson picked up where the preceding lesson left off by continuing to explore the power of style sheets. The hour began by unveiling some new text-formatting style properties that you had yet to see. You then found out how to use CSS pseudo-classes to change the look and feel of links. CSS comments were next on the agenda, as you saw how to place notes and explanations amidst your CSS code. Several CSS tips and tricks were then introduced, most of which you will find useful in just about all of your own style sheets. The lesson concluded by pulling most of what you've learned about CSS into a practical sample page.

Q&A

Q *I've seen style sheets that define style rules that begin with #. What are those, and can I use them in my style sheets?*

A Style rules that begin with # are called *ID classes*, and they allow you to create a style rule that is applied to elements via the id attribute. Although you can certainly create and use ID classes if you want, they are discouraged because they tempt you to set the id attribute of multiple elements to the same value, which isn't allowed in XHTML. XHTML requires every id attribute in a page to be unique, which means you can never use an ID class with more than one element. Knowing this, it's a better idea to use a normal style class and then have the option of using it with multiple elements via the class attribute if you so choose.

Q *Sometimes when I set the* a:hover *pseudoclass, I notice that the page flickers and shakes in the browser as I drag the mouse over a link. What's going on?*

A It is possible, in fact easy, to set an a:hover pseudoclass that requires the browser to constantly redraw the page in response to a mouse hover. This typically happens if the link changes font size, although it can sometimes happen even if you're just changing the text from normal to bold. This is because the link's overall size changes in response to a hover event, which means that the browser must recalculate the location of everything on the page below the link, and then redraw the results. The solution is to try to not change a link in response to a hover event such that its size changes.

Workshop

The workshop contains quiz questions and activities to help you solidify your understanding of the material covered. Try to answer all questions before looking at the "Answers" section that follows.

Quiz

1. How do you create a heading that is displayed in small caps?

2. How do you create style rules that display every link on a page in the color red unless it is in hover mode, in which case it should change to green?

3. How do you go about inserting a comment in CSS code?

4. What is the significance of a generic style class?

Answers

1. `<h1 style="font-variant:small-caps">My Heading</h1>`

2.
```
a:link, a:visited, a:active {
   color:red;
}

a:hover {
   color:green;
}
```

3. Just place the text of the comment between `/*` and `*/`.

4. A generic style class allows you to establish a style class that can be applied to any elements, not just an element of a specific type. Elements that apply a generic style class must still support the style rules within the class, but otherwise there are no limitations on generic style classes. You can easily spot a generic style class in a style sheet because it will start with nothing more than a period (.).

Exercises

▶ Try modifying some of the style rules in the `player.css` hockey player style sheet, paying particular attention to how the changes translate into a different look for each of the different player pages.

▶ Create your own style sheet (internal or external) that takes advantage of some of the CSS style techniques covered in this lesson. For example, try your hand at creating some interesting link pseudoclasses that add some spark to the links on your pages.

Using Style Sheets for Page Layout

In the preceding two lessons you learned a little bit about how to position HTML content using the default approach to CSS positioning, which is known as *relative positioning*. In relative positioning, elements on a page are displayed according to the flow of the page, with each element physically appearing after the element preceding it on the page. This is the way elements have been positioned in every HTML document you've seen throughout the book thus far. Although relative positioning has its merits, style sheets offer another approach that gives you much more control over how to position elements on a page.

This hour explores HTML positioning as controlled by style sheets. You'll find out how to carry out both relative and absolute positioning, as well as how to deliberately overlap elements and control how they stack on top of each other. You'll also find out how to tweak the margins and spacing between elements on a page. By the end of this hour, you'll realize why tables are now passé as a page layout mechanism—you'll realize that style sheets are just too powerful not to use.

The Whole Scoop on Positioning

I already mentioned that relative positioning is the default type of positioning used by HTML. You can think of relative positioning as being akin to laying out checkers on a checkerboard: The checkers are arranged from left to right, and when you get to the edge of the board you move on to the next row. Elements that are styled with the block value for the display style property are automatically placed on a new row, whereas inline elements are placed on the same row immediately next to the element preceding them. As an example, <p> and <div> tags are considered block elements, whereas the <span> tag is considered an inline element.

> Relative positioning is the default positioning approach used by CSS, so if you don't specify the positioning of a style rule, it will default to relative positioning.
>
> **By the Way**

The other type of positioning supported by CSS is known as *absolute positioning* because it allows you to set the exact position of HTML content on a page. Although absolute positioning gives you the freedom to spell out exactly where an element is to appear, the position is still relative to any parent elements that appear on the page. In other words, absolute positioning allows you to specify the exact location of an element's rectangular area with respect to its parent's area, which is very different from relative positioning.

As with most things in life, with freedom comes responsibility. And with the freedom of placing elements anywhere you want on a page, you can run into the problem of overlap, which is when an element takes up space used by another element. There is nothing stopping you from specifying the absolute locations of elements such that they overlap. In this case, CSS relies on the z-index of each element to determine which element is on the top and which is on the bottom. You'll learn more about the z-index of elements later in the hour. For now, let's take a look at exactly how you control whether a style rule uses relative or absolute positioning.

The type of positioning (relative or absolute) used by a particular style rule is determined by the `position` property, which is capable of having one of the following two values: `relative` or `absolute`. After specifying the type of positioning, you then provide the specific position using the following properties:

- ▶ `left`—The left position offset.
- ▶ `right`—The right position offset.
- ▶ `top`—The top position offset.
- ▶ `bottom`—The bottom position offset.

You might think that these position properties make sense only for absolute positioning, but they actually apply to both types of positioning. Under relative positioning, the position of an element is specified as an offset relative to the original position of the element. So if you set the `left` property of an element to 25px, the left side of the element will be shifted over 25 pixels from its original (relative) position. An absolute position, on the other hand, is specified relative to the parent of the element to which the style is applied. So if you set the `left` property of an element to 25px under absolute positioning, the left side of the element will appear 25 pixels to the right of the parent element's left edge. On the other hand, using the `right` property with the same value would position the element so that its *right* side is 25 pixels to the right of the parent's *right* edge.

You might understand this positioning stuff better by looking at an example. Check out the code in Listing 14.1 for a very simple web page.

LISTING 14.1 A Very Simple Web Page That Relies on an External Style Sheet for Its Content Layout

```
<?xml version="1.0" encoding="UTF-8"?>
<!DOCTYPE html PUBLIC "-//W3C//DTD XHTML 1.1//EN"
  "http://www.w3.org/TR/xhtml11/DTD/xhtml11.dtd">

<html xmlns="http://www.w3.org/1999/xhtml" xml:lang="en">
  <head>
    <title>Color Blocks</title>
    <link rel="stylesheet" type="text/css" href="colors_rel.css" />
  </head>

  <body>
    <div class="one">One</div>
    <div class="two">Two</div>
    <div class="three">Three</div>
    <div class="four">Four</div>
  </body>
</html>
```

Admittedly, this page isn't all that interesting, but it's a good way to demonstrate the difference between relative and absolute positioning. Notice in the code that there are several div elements, each with a different style class, and therefore a different style rule. Before applying a style sheet to this page, take a look at it in Figure 14.1.

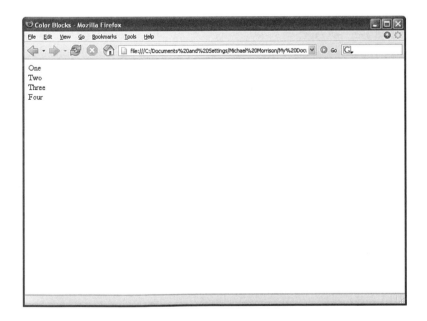

FIGURE 14.1
The Color Blocks web page is far beyond boring without the help of any style sheets.

I know, this is an extremely unimpressive page. In fact, it demonstrates perfectly how much style sheets impact otherwise-boring content, as you're about to see. Listing 14.2 contains a style sheet for this page that uses relative positioning to arrange the content as colored squares.

LISTING 14.2   Using Relative Positioning in the `colors_rel.css` Style Sheet

```
div {
  position:relative;
  width:250px;
  height:100px;
  border:10px single black;
  color:black;
  text-align:center;
}

div.one {
  background-color:red;
}

div.two {
  background-color:green;
}

div.three {
  background-color:blue;
}

div.four {
  background-color:yellow;
}
```

This code first sets the `position` style property for the `div` element to `relative`. Because the remaining style rules are inherited from the `div` style rule, they inherit its relative positioning. In fact, the only difference between the other style rules is that they have different background colors. Figure 14.2 shows the Color Blocks page as it is displayed in Firefox using this relative positioning style sheet.

Notice in the figure that the `div` elements are displayed one after the next, which is what you would expect with relative positioning. To make things more interesting, you can change the positioning to absolute and explicitly specify the placement of the colors. Listing 14.3 contains a modified style sheet for the Color Blocks page that uses absolute positioning to arrange the colors.

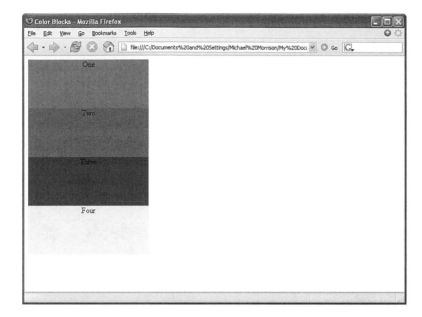

FIGURE 14.2
The Color
Blocks web
page is dis-
played using
a style sheet
with relative
positioning.

LISTING 14.3 Using Absolute Positioning in the `colors_abs.css` Style Sheet

```
div {
  position:absolute;
  width:250px;
  height:100px;
  border:10px single black;
  color:black;
  text-align:center;
}

div.one {
  background-color:red;
  left:0px;
  top:0px;
}

div.two {
  background-color:green;
  left:75px;
  top:25px;
}

div.three {
  background-color:blue;
  left:150px;
  top:50px;
}
```

LISTING 14.3   Continued

```
div.four {
  background-color:yellow;
  left:225px;
  top:75px;
}
```

This style sheet sets the `position` property to `absolute`, which is necessary in order for the style sheet to use absolute positioning. Additionally, the `left` and `top` properties are set for each of the inherited `div` style rules. However, the position of each of these rules is set so that the elements are displayed overlapping each other, as shown in Figure 14.3.

FIGURE 14.3
The Color Blocks web page is displayed using a style sheet with absolute positioning.

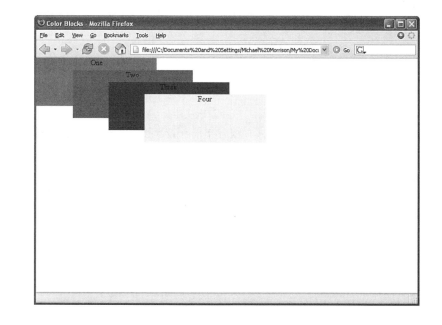

This figure shows how absolute positioning allows you to place elements exactly where you want them. It also reveals how easy it is to arrange elements so that they overlap each other. You might be curious as to how a web browser knows which elements to draw on top when they overlap. Read on to find out!

Controlling the Way Things Stack Up

There are no doubt situations in which you'd like to be able to carefully control the manner in which elements overlap each other on a web page. The `z-index` style property allows you to set the order of elements with respect to how they stack on top of each other. Although the name *z-index* might sound a little strange, it refers to the notion of a third dimension (Z) that points into the computer screen, in addition to the two dimensions (X and Y) that go across and down the screen. Another way to think of the z-index is the relative position of a single magazine within a stack of magazines. A magazine nearer the top of the stack has a higher z-index than a magazine lower in the stack. Similarly, an overlapped element with a higher z-index is displayed on top of an element with a lower z-index.

The z-index property is used to set a numeric value that indicates the relative z-index of a style rule. The number assigned to z-index has meaning only with respect to other style rules in a style sheet, which means that setting the z-index property for a single rule doesn't mean much. On the other hand, if you set z-index for several style rules that apply to overlapped elements, the elements with higher z-index values will appear on top of elements with lower z-index values.

Regardless of the z-index value you set for a style rule, an element displayed with the rule will always appear on top of its parent.

By the Way

Listing 14.4 contains another version of a style sheet for the Color Blocks sample page that has z-index settings to alter the natural overlap of elements.

LISTING 14.4   The `colors_z.css` Style Sheet Alters the Z-index of Elements in the Color Blocks Sample Page

```
div {
  position:absolute;
  width:250px;
  height:100px;
  border:10px single black;
  color:black;
  text-align:center;
}

div.one {
  background-color:red;
  z-index:0;
  left:0px;
  top:0px;
}

div.two {
  background-color:green;
  z-index:3;
  left:75px;
  top:25px;
}

div.three {
  background-color:blue;
  z-index:2;
```

LISTING 14.4   Continued

```
   left:150px;
   top:50px;
}

div.four {
  background-color:yellow;
  z-index:1;
  left:225px;
  top:75px;
}
```

The only change in this code from what you saw in Listing 14.3 is the addition of the z-index property in each of the numbered div style classes. Notice that the first numbered div has a setting of 0, which should make it the lowest element in terms of the z-index, whereas the second div has the highest z-index. Figure 14.4 shows the Color Blocks page as displayed with this style sheet, which clearly shows how the z-index affects the displayed content.

FIGURE 14.4
The Color Blocks sample page is displayed using a style sheet that alters the z-index of the colors.

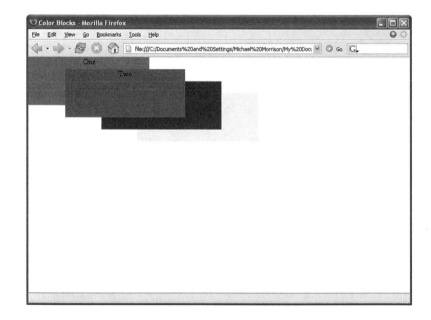

The figure reveals how the z-index style property makes it possible to carefully control the overlap of elements.

Just to show how the z-index style property can impact any HTML content, check out Figure 14.5, which shows a page with images that overlap thanks to absolute positioning and the z-index property.

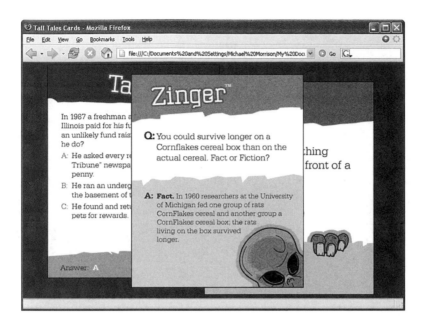

FIGURE 14.5
You can use absolute positioning and set the z-index for any block content, including images.

This figure reveals how it's possible to overlap just about any content on a page if you so choose.

Working with Margins

If you look at the left and right sides of the pages in this book, you'll notice that there is whitespace that appears between the paragraphs of text and the edge of the pages; you probably know this space as the margin of the book. Style sheet *margins* allow you to add empty space around the outside of the rectangular area for an element on a web page. Following are the style properties for setting margins:

▶ margin-top—Sets the top margin.

▶ margin-right—Sets the right margin.

▶ margin-bottom—Sets the bottom margin.

▶ margin-left—Sets the left margin.

▶ margin—Sets the top, right, bottom, and left margins as a single property.

You can specify margins using any of the individual margin properties, or with the single margin property. If you decide to set a margin as a percentage, keep in mind that the percentage is calculated based on the size of the entire page, not the size of the element. So if you set the `margin-left` property to 25%, the left margin of the element will end up being 25% of the width of the entire page. The following code shows how to set the top and bottom margins for one of the colors in the Color Blocks sample page that you've been working with throughout this lesson:

```
div.two {
  background-color:green;
  margin-top:5px;
  margin-bottom:20px;
}
```

In this example, the top margin is set to 5 pixels, and the bottom margin is set to 20 pixels. The results of this code are shown in Figure 14.6.

FIGURE 14.6
The Color Blocks sample page is displayed using a style sheet that sets top and bottom margins for one of the colors.

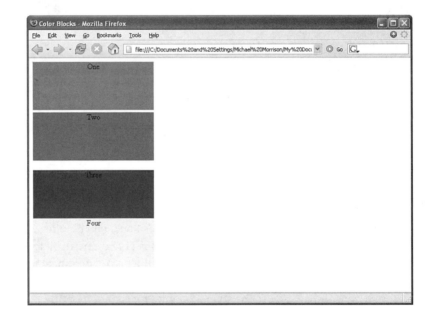

This figure shows how the top and bottom margins appear above and below the second `div` element. Keep in mind that these margins don't encroach on the content area of any of the colors—they all maintain their original size. In other words, the margins appear around the elements.

If you want to set all the margins for a style rule, you'll probably want to simplify the code and use the `margin` property. This property is somewhat flexible in that it offers three different approaches to specifying the margins for a style rule. These approaches vary based on how many values you use when setting the property:

- One value—The size of all the margins.

- Two values—The size of the top/bottom margins and the left/right margins (in that order).

- Four values—The size of the top, right, bottom, and left margins (in that order).

Following is an example of how you would set the vertical margins (top/bottom) to 5 pixels and the horizontal margins (left/right) to 10% for a style rule:

```
margin:5px 10%;
```

In this code, the top and bottom margins are both set to 5 pixels, and the left and right margins are both set to 10%. Of course, if you wanted to be a little clearer, you could achieve the same effect with the following setting:

```
margin:5px 10% 5px 10%;
```

A Little Padding for Safety

Similar to margins, padding is used to add extra space to elements. However, padding differs from margins in that padding adds space inside the rectangular area of an element, as opposed to around it. As an example, if you create a style rule for an element that establishes a width of 50 pixels and a height of 30 pixels, and then sets the padding of the rule to 5 pixels, the remaining content area will be 40 pixels by 20 pixels. Also, because the padding of an element appears within the element's content area, it will assume the same style as the content of the element, including the background color.

You specify the padding of a style rule using one of the padding properties, which work very much like the margin properties. The following padding properties are available for use in setting the padding of style rules:

- `padding-top`—Sets the top padding.

- `padding-right`—Sets the right padding.

- `padding-bottom`—Sets the bottom padding.

- `padding-left`—Sets the left padding.

- `padding`—Sets the top, right, bottom, and left padding as a single property.

As with margins, you can set the padding of style rules using individual padding properties or the single `padding` property. Padding can also be expressed using either a unit of measurement or a percentage. Following is an example of how you might set the left and right padding for a style rule so that there are 10 pixels of padding on each side of an element's content:

```
padding-left:10px;
padding-right:10px;
```

Also as with margins, you can set all the padding for an element with a single property, the padding property. You can use the same three approaches available for the margin property to set the padding property. Following is an example of how you would set the vertical padding (top/bottom) to 12 pixels and the horizontal padding (left/right) to 8 pixels for a style rule:

```
padding:12px 8px;
```

Following is more explicit code that performs the same task by specifying all the padding values:

```
padding:12px 8px 12px 8px;
```

Keeping Everything Aligned

Knowing that content on a web page doesn't always fill the entire width of the rectangular area in which it is displayed, it is often helpful to control the alignment of the content. Even if text within a rectangular area extends to multiple lines, alignment still enters the picture because you may want the text justified left or right, or centered. There are a couple of style properties that allow you to control the alignment of web page content: text-align and vertical-align. I touched on these properties in Hour 5, "Basic Text Alignment and Formatting," but it doesn't hurt to mention them again here in a bit more detail while we're deep into CSS layout styles.

The text-align property aligns an element horizontally within its bounding area, and it can be set to left, right, center, or justify. The justify value performs a full justification on an element. Following is an example of using the text-align property to center a hypothetical web page advertisement:

```
div.ad {
  width:275px;
  margin-bottom:10px;
  border:5px double black;
  color:black;
  background-color:yellow;
  text-align:center
}
```

The last style property defined in this style rule involves setting the text-align style to center, which results in the div.ad element being centered within its parent. If the parent of this element is the web page itself, the element will be centered on the page.

The vertical-align property is similar to text-align except that it is used to align elements vertically. The vertical-align property specifies how an element is aligned with its parent, or in some cases the current line of elements on the page. When I say "current line," I'm really referring to the vertical placement of elements that appear within the same parent element. In other words, I'm talking about inline elements. If several inline elements appear on the same line, you can set their vertical alignments the same to align them vertically. A good example would be a row of images that appear one after the next—the vertical-align property allows you to align them vertically.

Following are the acceptable values for use with the vertical-align property:

- ▶ top—Aligns the top of an element with the current line.

- ▶ middle—Aligns the middle of an element with the middle of its parent.

- ▶ bottom—Aligns the bottom of an element with the current line.

- ▶ text-top—Aligns the top of an element with the top of its parent.

- ▶ baseline—Aligns the baseline of an element with the baseline of its parent.

- ▶ text-bottom—Aligns the bottom of an element with the bottom of its parent.

- ▶ sub—Aligns an element as a subscript of its parent.

- ▶ super—Aligns an element as a superscript of its parent.

Following is an example of how the vertical-align property is used to center text vertically:

```
div.ad {
  width:275px;
  margin-bottom:10px;
  border:5px double black;
  color:black;
  background-color:yellow;
  text-align:center;
  vertical-align:middle
}
```

This code shows how simple it is to modify a style rule so that the element is aligned vertically. In this case, the div.ad element is vertically aligned with the middle of its parent.

Managing the Flow of Text

A moment ago I discussed the concept of the "current line," which is an invisible line used to place elements on a page. This line has to do with the flow of elements on a page; it comes into play as elements are arranged next to each other across and down the page. Part of the flow of elements is the flow of text on a page. When you mix text with other elements such as images, it's important to control how the text flows around the other elements.

Following are some style properties that provide you with control over text flow:

- ▶ float—Determines how text flows around an element.

- ▶ clear—Stops the flow of text around an element.

- ▶ overflow—Controls the overflow of text when an element is too small to contain all the text.

The float property is used to control how text flows around an element. It can be set to either left or right. These values determine where to position an element with respect to flowing text. So setting the float property to left for an image would result in the image being positioned to the left of flowing text.

You can prevent text from flowing next to an element by using the clear property, which can be set to none, left, right, or both. The default value for the clear property is none, indicating that text is to flow with no special considerations for the element. The left value causes text to stop flowing around an element until the left side of the page is free of the element. Likewise, the right value means that text is not to flow around the right side of the element. The both value indicates that text isn't to flow around either side of the element.

The overflow property handles overflow text, which is text that doesn't fit within its rectangular area; this can happen if you set the width and height of an element too small. The overflow property can be set to visible, hidden, or scroll. The visible setting automatically enlarges the element so that the overflow text will fit within it; this is the default setting for the property. The hidden value leaves the element the same size, allowing the overflow text to remain hidden from view. Perhaps the most interesting value is scroll, which adds scrollbars to the element so that you can move around and see the text.

Taking Advantage of a Style Sheet Template

I've mentioned a couple of times how style sheets allow you to cleanly separate the content (text, images, and links) on a web page from the manner in which is displayed. This means that your HTML code can focus solely on information, which is then rendered to the screen according to the rules you establish in a style sheet. Knowing this, it stands to reason that with the right style sheet, you could effectively create interesting web pages with very little effort.

A *style sheet template* is a reusable style sheet that solves a particular problem, such as allowing you to create a newsletter or a blog. Although Hour 21, "Create Your Own Blog," shows you how to use an online blog service to create a blog, I thought it would be neat to show you how to create a simplified blog yourself using nothing more than a style sheet template and some HTML code.

By the Way

If you're new to the world of blogging, allow me to clarify that the term "blog" stands for web log, and it just refers to a specialized web page that contains a sequence of articles by a certain person or on a certain topic. Political blogs have become quite popular, although there are blogs out there for practically every topic imaginable.

First off, it's important to understand that a blog in its simplest terms is just a series of short articles, kind of like mini news stories. Each blog entry typically consists of a title, a date and time, and the actual text of the entry. Blog entries are displayed in reverse chronological order, meaning that the latest (most recent) blog entry is displayed first on the page.

Figure 14.7 shows an example of a relatively simple blog page that is driven entirely by an external style sheet. You're about to see the style sheet behind this blog.

Coffee Break

If you want to get a feel for what other blogs actually look like, take some time to explore http://www.blogwise.com/. This site serves as a global directory for blogs, and it can be browsed by location or topic.

The HTML code for the blog shown in the figure is listed in Listing 14.5. It's important to note that the HTML code is entirely focused on the content of the blog and has virtually no concern with how it is rendered in a web browser.

FIGURE 14.7
It is possible to
create a simple
blog using noth-
ing more than
some HTML
code and an
external CSS
style sheet.

LISTING 14.5   This Web Page Relies Entirely on the `blog.css` Style
Sheet for Its Layout and Formatting

```
<?xml version="1.0" encoding="UTF-8"?>
<!DOCTYPE html PUBLIC "-//W3C//DTD XHTML 1.1//EN"
  "http://www.w3.org/TR/xhtml11/DTD/xhtml11.dtd">

<html xmlns="http://www.w3.org/1999/xhtml" xml:lang="en">
  <head>
    <title>Big T's Hockey Blog</title>
    <link rel="stylesheet" type="text/css" href="blog.css" />
  </head>

  <body>
    <div class="pagetitle" id="top">Big T's Hockey Blog</div>
    <div class="author">Terry &quot;Big T&quot; Lancaster</div>

    <div class="entry">
      <div class="title">Predators Win Pre-Season Opener</div>
      <div class="datetime">September 23, 2005 - 10:17PM CST</div>
      <div class="text">My home team, the Nashville Predators, outplayed the
      Columbus Blue Jackets to win their pre-season home opener 3-2. Predators
      up and comer Alexander Radulov also scored a shoot-out goal to give the
      Preds a 1-0 win in the simulated overtime shoot-out. Things are looking
      bright for the young team under the new NHL collective bargaining
      agreement.</div>
      <div class="link">
        <a href="#top">&lt;&lt; Back To Top</a>
      </div>
    </div>
```

LISTING 14.5   Continued

```
    <div class="entry">
      <div class="title">Music City Mafia Wins with Authority</div>
      <div class="datetime">September 21, 2005 - 11:09PM CST</div>
      <div class="text">My main recreational hockey team, Music City Mafia, won
      handily in one of the few blow-out games of the season thus far,
      dominating Gober's Goobers 7-2. The Mafia record improves to 2-3-2. Let's
      hope we have a few more wins in us to close out the season strong.</div>
      <div class="link">
        <a href="#top">&lt;&lt; Back To Top</a>
      </div>
    </div>

    <div class="entry">
      <div class="title">Music City Mafia Attacked By Monkeys</div>
      <div class="datetime">September 18, 2005 - 10:43PM CST</div>
      <div class="text">The Mafia boys were attacked by a rogue pack of wild Ice
      Monkeys tonight, and the result wasn't pretty. The 5-1 loss saw few bright
      moments, with one of them being a goal by Chet that was set up by Duke
      early in the game. It was downhill from then on, as the Monkeys proceeded
      to frustrate and aggravate the Mafia. Retribution plans are already
      underway!</div>
      <div class="link">
        <a href="#top">&lt;&lt; Back To Top</a>
      </div>
    </div>
  </body>
</html>
```

This code reveals that the blog makes use of seven style classes to organize its content:

- ▶ pagetitle—The title of the blog, centered at the top of the page in a large font.

- ▶ author—The author of the blog, centered at the top of the page just below the title.

- ▶ entry—A block-level element that is used to hold a single blog entry.

- ▶ title—The title of an individual blog entry.

- ▶ datetime—The date and time of an individual blog entry.

- ▶ text—The body text of an individual blog entry.

- ▶ link—A link within an individual blog entry that returns the user to the top of the blog page.

If you take a closer look at Listing 14.5 and Figure 14.7, you may see how each of these style classes maps to content on the blog page. If you're having trouble making the connection, maybe Listing 14.6 will help clear things up.

LISTING 14.6 The `blog.css` Style Sheet Serves as a Reusable
Template for Blog Web Pages

```css
body {
  background-color:#FFFFCA;
}

div {
  font-family:Verdana;
}

div.pagetitle {
  text-align:center;
  font-size:24pt;
  font-weight:bold;
  color:#19619A;
}

div.author {
  text-align:center;
  font-size:16pt;
  font-weight:bold;
  font-style:italic;
  color:#19619A;
}

div.entry {
  background:#EEEEEE;
  border:3px solid #19619A;
  margin:20px;
  padding:10px;
}

div.title {
  text-align:left;
  font-size:12pt;
  font-weight:bold;
  color:#19619A;
}

div.datetime {
  text-align:left;
  font-size:10pt;
  font-style:italic;
}

div.text {
  text-align:left;
  font-size:11pt;
}

div.link {
  text-align:right;
  font-size:10pt;
  margin-top:10px;
}

a { font-weight:bold }
```

LISTING 14.6   Continued

```
a:link {
  color:#19619A;
  text-decoration:none;
}

a:visited {
  color:#19619A;
  text-decoration:none;
}

a:hover {
  color:#3D9DE9;
  text-decoration:none;
}

a:active {
  color:#19619A;
  text-decoration:none;
}
```

This style sheet contains all the gory details for the previously mentioned style class-es, along with a few extra style rules to help complete the blog effect. First off, the body selector is used to specify a background color for the entire page. A font (Verdana) is then established for all `div` elements, which means that the same font is applied throughout the page.

The specific style classes are then specified, beginning with `div.pagetitle` and `div.author`. The `div.entry` style class is interesting in that it sets a border and a lighter background color so that each blog entry stands out on the page. The remaining blog style classes all utilize various font settings to help improve the lay-out and readability of the blog.

The last few style rules in the `blog.css` style sheet pertain to links and how they change with mouse hovers and clicks. The `text-decoration` style property is used to prevent links from being underlined, and the `color` property is used to highlight a link when you drag the mouse over it.

You can easily make small tweaks to the `blog.css` style sheet and reuse it to create your own simple blogs. Of course, if you want a fancier, more professional blog then you may want to check out Hour 21.

Summary

This lesson continued along in the exploration of CSS style sheets, and primarily tackled the use of style sheets to lay out web pages. You started the lesson by learn-ing the difference between relative and absolute positioning, and how each is used to position elements. You then learned about other CSS positioning features such as z-index, margins, padding, and content alignment. You then found out about a few nifty little style properties that allow you to control the flow of text on a page. And finally, the lesson concluded by showing you how create a reusable style sheet template for a simplified blog.

Q&A

Q *How do you know when to use relative versus absolute positioning?*

A Although there are no set guidelines regarding the usage of relative versus absolute positioning, the general idea is that absolute positioning is required only when you want to exert a fine degree of control over how content is positioned. This has to do with the fact that absolute positioning allows you to position content down to the exact pixel, whereas relative positioning is much less predictable in terms of how it positions content. This isn't to say that relative positioning can't do a good job of positioning elements on a page; it just means that absolute positioning is more exact. Of course, this also makes absolute positioning potentially more susceptible to changes in screen size, which you can't really control.

Q *If you don't specify the z-index of two elements that overlap each other, how do you know which element will appear on top?*

A If the z-index property isn't set for overlapping elements, the element appearing later in the web page will appear on top. The easy way to remember this is to think of a web browser drawing each element on a page as it reads it from the HTML document; elements read later in the document are drawn on top of those read earlier.

Workshop

The workshop contains quiz questions and activities to help you solidify your understanding of the material covered. Try to answer all questions before looking at the "Answers" section that follows.

Quiz

1. What's the difference between relative and absolute positioning?

2. Which CSS style property do you use to control the manner in which elements overlap each other?

3. Write the HTML code to display the words `What would you like to`, starting exactly at the upper-left corner of the browser window, and THROW TODAY? in large type exactly 80 pixels down and 20 pixels to the left of the corner.

Answers

1. In relative positioning, content is displayed according to the flow of a page, with each element physically appearing after the element preceding it in the HTML code. Absolute positioning, on the other hand, allows you to set the exact position of content on a page.

2. The z-index style property is used to control the manner in which elements overlap each other.

3. `<span style="position:absolute; left:0px; top:0px">`

```
What would you like to</span>
<h1 style="position:absolute; left:80px; top:20px">
THROW TODAY?</H1>
```

Exercises

▶ Modify the hockey player style sheet from the preceding hour to use absolute positioning. Try placing each element in an exact location on the page.

▶ Further enhance the blog style sheet from this hour by adding a background image and altering the colors, as well as tweaking the font for a different look.

Creating Print-Friendly Web Pages

If you've ever used an online mapping tool such as MapQuest or Google Maps, you've no doubt experienced the need to print a web page. It's true, web pages aren't designed entirely for viewing on the screen. You may not realize this, but it's possible to specifically design and offer print-friendly versions of your pages for visitors who want to print a copy for offline reading. In fact, CSS makes it very straightforward to create web pages that can change appearance based on how they are viewed. This lesson shows you how to create such pages.

Try It Yourself ▼

As you work your way through this lesson, consider any of your own web pages that might look good in print. Then think about what you would want to change about them to make them look even better on the printed page. Here are some ideas to consider:

1. Do you have pages that use a background image or an unusual background color with contrasting text? This kind of page can be difficult to print because of the background, so you might consider a print version of the page with no background and black text.

2. Do your pages include lots of links? If so, you might consider changing the appearance of links for printing so that they don't stand out. Remember, you can't click a piece of paper!

3. Finally, is every image on your pages absolutely essential? Colorful images cost valuable ink to print on most printers, so you might consider leaving some, if not all, images out of print-friendly pages. ▲

What Makes a Page Print-Friendly?

I already touched on this topic a bit in the preceding Try It Yourself, but it's worth a more thorough exploration of what constitutes a print-friendly web page. First off, it's important to point out that some web pages are print-friendly already. If your pages use a white background with dark contrasting text and few images, you may not even need to concern yourself with a special print-friendly version. On the other hand, a page with a dark background, dynamic links, and loads of images may prove to be unwieldy for the average printer.

The main things to keep in mind as you consider what it takes to make your pages more print-friendly are the limitations imposed by the medium. In other words, what is it about a printed page that makes it uniquely different from a computer screen? The obvious difference is size—a printed page is at a fixed size, typically 8 1/2 by 11 inches, whereas the size of screens can vary greatly. In addition to size, printed pages also have color limitations, even on color printers. Very few users want to waste the ink required to print a full-color background when all they are likely interested in is the text on the page.

Most users also aren't interested in printing more than the text that serves as the focus on the page. For example, take a look at Figure 15.1, which shows an entry from the blog on my personal web site as viewed as a normal web page.

FIGURE 15.1
This page isn't very print-friendly due to the various menus and other content surrounding the main article.

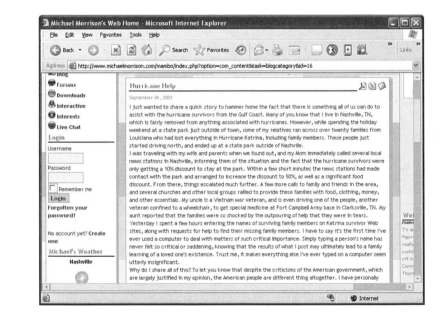

If you notice in the upper-right corner of the page in the figure, there is a print icon that allows you to view a print-friendly version of the page. Figure 15.2 shows this version of the blog article, which is much better suited to printing.

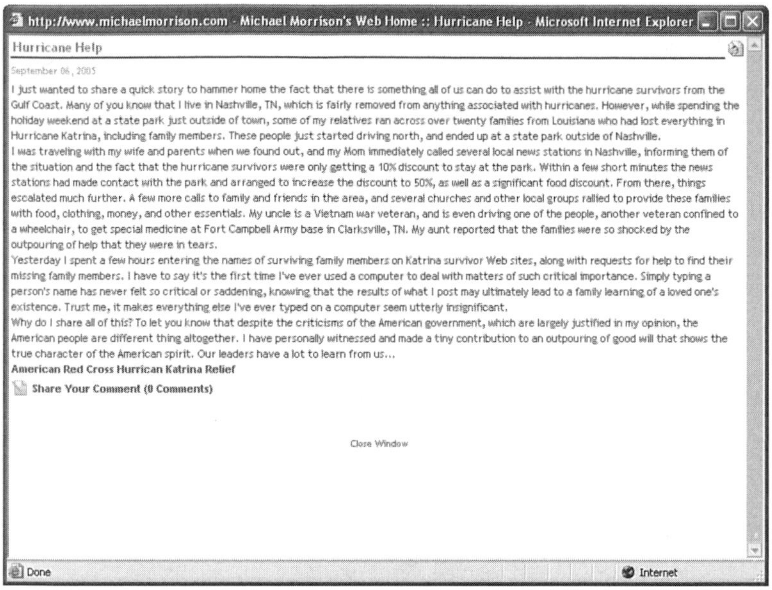

FIGURE 15.2
The print-friendly version of the page isolates the text in the article so that it can be printed by itself.

As the figure reveals, the print-friendly version of my blog represents a significant improvement over the original page, at least from the perspective of a printer. All the navigation and other decorative items surrounding the page were removed, along with the background image that surrounded the original blog article.

In the spirit of giving you a better grasp on what specifically to consider as you move toward creating print-friendly pages, following is a list of changes you should at least consider:

▶ Remove the background of the page, which effectively gives the printed page a white background.

▶ Change text colors to black; it's okay to have some color in the text but black is preferred.

▶ Make sure that the font size is large enough that the page can be easily read when printed—you may have to test some different sizes.

Some web designers even recommend changing the font of printer-specific pages to Serif, which is considered easier to read in print. I can go either way on this one, because I'm often fond of maintaining the core look of a page in print, which means keeping the same font used in the screen version of the page.

By the Way

▶ Remove link formatting or simply revert to a basic underlined link. I don't really see the significance of retaining any special link appearance in a printed page, but some designers like to retain an underline just so a visitor knows that a link exists in the original page.

▶ Remove any and all nonessential images. This typically includes any images that aren't critical to conveying the content in the page, such as navigation buttons, most ads, and animated images.

In addition to these suggestions, you may find it useful to add a byline with information about the author of the page, along with a URL for the page and copyright information. This is all information that could potentially get lost after the user leaves your web site and has only the printed version of the page in hand.

Coffee
Break

> Forgive me if this web site clashes with your political views, but it is a great example of how to execute a print-specific web page. I'm referring to AlterNet (http://www.alternet.org/), which is a news and opinion site that provides a print icon for every article that links to a print-friendly version of each article. The print-friendly articles on AlterNet are perfect examples of how to cleanly format web page content for printing.

Keep in mind that I'm not suggesting you run out and make these changes to your pages just yet. The idea is to plant the seed of what constitutes a print-friendly page so that you can do a better job of creating a printer-specific style sheet. That's right, it's possible to create a style sheet that is applied to pages only when they are printed. The next section tells you how.

Applying a Media-Specific Style Sheet

Earlier, in Figure 15.1, you saw how a little printer icon allows you to view a special print-friendly version of a page. This type of icon is popular on many news sites, and it's an important feature because you otherwise might not want to hassle with printing a page and wasting paper and ink on the graphics and ads surrounding an article. Although the printer-icon approach is intuitive and works great, there is a more automatic option.

The option I'm talking about involves using a print-specific style sheet that is automatically applied to a page if the user elects to print the page. CSS supports the concept of *media-specific style sheets*, which are style sheets that target a particular medium, such as the screen or printer. CSS doesn't stop with those two media, however. Check out the following list of media that CSS allows you to support with a unique style sheet:

- ► Computer screen
- ► Printer
- ► Television
- ► Projection screen
- ► Handheld

- ► Braille
- ► Embossed
- ► Text-only
- ► Aural

Perhaps the most interesting of these media is the last one, which allows for web pages that can be read aloud or otherwise listened to. Clearly, the architects of CSS envision a Web with a much broader reach than we currently think of as we design pages primarily for computer screens. Although I'm not suggesting that you worry too much about aural web page design just yet, it serves as a good heads-up as to what may be on the horizon.

The good news about style sheets as applied to other media is that they don't require you to learn anything new. Okay, maybe in the case of aural web pages you'll need to learn a few new tricks, but for now you can use the exact same style properties you've already learned to create print-specific style sheets. The trick is knowing how to apply a style sheet for a particular medium.

If you recall, the <link /> tag is used to link an external style sheet to a web page. This tag supports an attribute named media that you haven't seen yet. This attribute is where you specify the name of the medium to which the style sheet applies. By default, this attribute is set to all, which means that an external style sheet will be used for all media if you don't specify otherwise. Following are the other accepted values for this attribute: screen, print, tv, projection, handheld, braille, embossed, and aural. Not surprisingly, these attribute values correspond to the list of media you just saw.

Establishing a print-specific style sheet for a web page involves using two <link /> tags, one for the printer and one for every remaining medium. Following is code that handles this task:

```
<link rel="stylesheet" type="text/css" href="player.css" media="all" />
<link rel="stylesheet" type="text/css" href="player_print.css" media="print" />
```

In this example, two style sheets are linked into a web page. The first sheet targets all media by setting the media attribute to all. If you did nothing else, the player.css style sheet would apply to all media. However, the presence of the second style sheet results in the player_print.css style sheet being used to print the page.

By the Way

> It is also possible to use the @import command to link media-specific style sheets. For example, the following code works just like the previous <link /> code:
>
> ```
> @import url(player.css) all;
> @import url(player_print.css) print;
> ```

Watch Out!

> You might have been tempted to specify media="screen" in the first linked style sheet in the previous code. Although this would work for viewing the page in a normal web browser, it would cause problems if someone viewed the page using a handheld browser or any of the other types of media. In other words, a style sheet applies only to the specific media types mentioned in the media attribute, and nothing more.

You can specify multiple media types in a single <link /> tag by separating the types with a comma, like this:

```
<link rel="stylesheet" type="text/css" href="player_pp.css" media="print,
projector" />
```

This code results in the player_pp.css style sheet applying solely to the print and projector media types, and nothing else.

Designing a Style Sheet for Print Pages

Using the punch list of modifications required for a print-friendly web page that you saw earlier in the hour, it's time to take a stab at creating a print-friendly style sheet. Let's first take a look at a page that is displayed using a normal (screen) style sheet—take a look at Figure 15.3.

This figure reveals how the page looks in a normal web browser. Although you can't quite make out the different colors on the printed page, you can open the page yourself in the files available at http://www.samspublishing.com/ to view the full-color page in your own browser. In reality, this page isn't really too terribly designed for printing already, but it could still stand some improvements.

The following changes can help make this web page print better:

▶ Change the color of all text to black.

▶ Remove link formatting (bold and color).

▶ Stack the two player information sections vertically because they are unlikely to fit horizontally on the printed page.

▶ Remove the contact link entirely.

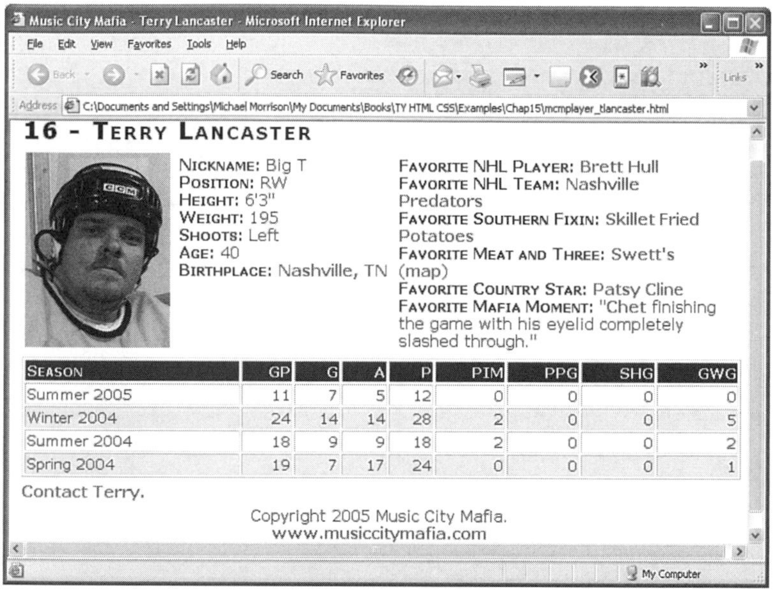

FIGURE 15.3
The CSS-styled hockey player page as viewed in a normal web browser.

The first two changes to the normal style sheet are fairly straightforward, and primarily involve changing or undoing existing styles. The third, however, requires a bit of thought. Because you know that printed pages are a fixed size, it makes sense to use absolute positioning for all the elements on the printed page. This makes it much easier to place the content sections exactly where you want them. Finally, the last item on the list is very easy to accommodate by simply setting the display style property of the contact element to none.

> Although absolute positioning works for the hockey player sample page, it's not always a good idea for styling print-specific pages. More specifically, if you have a page that contains more than a printed page worth of content, you're better off using relative positioning and letting content flow onto multiple pages.

Watch Out!

Listing 15.1 contains the CSS code for the player_print.css style sheet, which incorporates these changes into a style sheet that is perfectly suited for printing hockey player pages.

LISTING 15.1   CSS Code for the Print-Specific Hockey Player Style Sheet

```
body {
  font-family:Verdana, Arial;
  font-size:12pt;
  color:black;
}
```

LISTING 15.1   Continued

```
div {
  padding:3px;
}

div.title {
  font-size:18pt;
  font-weight:bold;
  font-variant:small-caps;
  letter-spacing:2px;
  position:absolute;
  left:0in;
  top:0in;
}

div.image {
  position:absolute;
  left:0in;
  top:0.5in;
}

div.info {
  position:absolute;
  left:1.75in;
  top:0.5in;
}

div.favorites {
  position:absolute;
  left:1.75in;
  top:2in;
}

div.footer {
  position:absolute;
  text-align:left;
  left:0in;
  top:9in;
}

table.stats {
  width:100%;
  text-align:right;
  font-size:11pt;
  position:absolute;
  left:0in;
  top:3.75in;
}

div.contact {
  display:none;
}

.label {
  font-weight:bold;
  font-variant:small-caps;
}
```

LISTING 15.1   Continued

```
tr.heading {
  font-variant:small-caps;
  background-color:black;
  color:white;
}

tr.light {
  background-color:white;
}

tr.dark {
  background-color:#EEEEEE;
}

th.season, td.season {
  text-align:left;
}

a, a:link, a:visited {
  color:black;
  font-weight:normal;
  text-decoration:none;
}
```

Probably the neatest thing about this code is how it uses inches (in) as the unit of measure for all the absolute positioning code. This makes sense when you consider that we think of printed pages in terms of inches, not pixels. If you study the code carefully, you'll notice that the text is all black, links have had all special style formatting removed, and content sections are now absolutely positioned so that they appear exactly where you want them.

Viewing a Web Page in Print

Figure 15.4 shows the print-friendly version of a hockey player page as it appears in Internet Explorer's print preview window.

The figure reveals another subtle change in the print-friendly version of the page—the footer now appears at the very bottom of the page.

Just to show you how print-friendly pages can be used in a practical situation, check out Figure 15.5. This figure shows the same hockey player page as a PDF document that can be viewed in Adobe Acrobat Reader.

I used Adobe's PDFWriter virtual printer to "print" the hockey player web page to a PDF document. This effectively creates a version of the print-friendly web page in a format that can be easily shared electronically for printing.

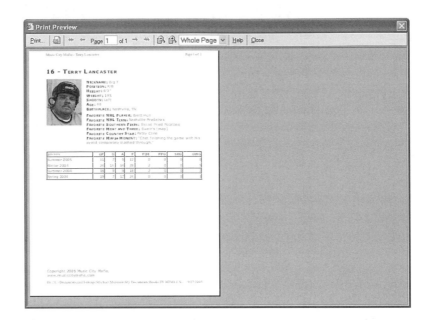

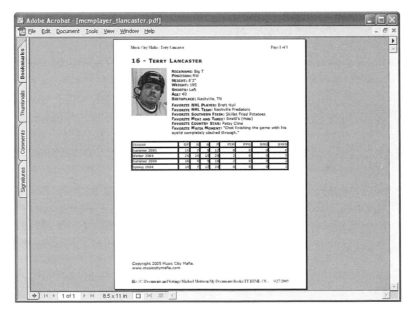

By the Way

Adobe Acrobat PDFWriter ships as part of the Adobe Acrobat line of products. To learn more about Acrobat, visit http://www.adobe.com/products/acrobat/.

Summary

This hour took a break from showing you another laundry list of CSS style properties, and instead focused on a practical application of CSS that solves a common problem: printed web pages. You began the lesson by learning what exactly constitutes a print-friendly web page. From there, you found out about the mechanism built into CSS that allows a page to distinguish between the media in which it is being rendered, and then selecting a style sheet accordingly. And finally, you created a print-specific style sheet that was used to style a page just for printing. Although most users prefer viewing a page on a large computer screen over reading it on paper, there are times when a printed web page is a necessity. Be sure to give your web page visitors the utmost in flexibility by offering print-friendly pages.

Q&A

Q *Can I use the* `media` *attribute of the* `<link />` *tag to create a style sheet specifically for viewing a web page on a handheld device?*

A Yes you can. By setting the media attribute of the `<link />` tag to `handheld`, you specifically target handheld devices with a style sheet. You will likely see all mobile web sites eventually shift toward this approach to serving mobile pages, as opposed to using specialized markup languages such as WML (wireless markup language).

Q *Do I still need to provide a printer icon on my pages so that they can be printed?*

A No. The linked style sheet technique you learned about in this hour allows you to support print-friendly web pages without any special links on the page. However, if you want to enable the user to view a print-friendly version of a page in a browser, you can link to another version of the page that uses the print-specific style sheet as its main (browser) style sheet. Or you can provide some "fine print" on the page that instructs the user to use the browser's print preview feature to view the print-friendly version of the page.

Workshop

The workshop contains quiz questions and activities to help you solidify your understanding of the material covered. Try to answer all questions before looking at the "Answers" section that follows.

Quiz

1. What is an aural web page?

2. What happens to an external style sheet that is linked to a page without any `media` attribute being specified?

3. How would you link a style sheet named `freestyle.css` to a page so that it applies only when the page is viewed on a television?

Answers

1. An aural web page is a page designed to be listened to. Right now, true aural web pages via CSS are a future consideration for web developers. However, they do provide a clue as to the direction the web is headed in, which is a heavier reliance on style sheets for more than just applying fonts, colors, and positioning.

2. The `media` attribute assumes its default value of `all`, which causes the style sheet to target all media types.

3. `<link rel="stylesheet" type="text/css" href="freestyle.css" media="tv" />`

Exercises

▶ Choose one of your pages that has a fair number of colors and images, and create a print-friendly style sheet for it. Be sure to add an extra `<link />` tag to the page that links in the print-specific style sheet.

▶ If you're feeling really ambitious, try using the `handheld` value of the `<link />` tag's `media` attribute to create a handheld-specific version of one of your web pages. The concept is the same as creating a print-friendly page, except in this case you're dealing with an extremely constrained screen size instead of a printed page. You can test the page by publishing it and then opening it using a mobile phone or handheld computer browser.

Multipage Layout with Frames

You've probably come into contact with web sites in which the browser window seemingly allowed you to move around between several different pages. The truth is that the browser really was allowing you to view several pages at once. An HTML feature known as frames allows you to divide the browser window into regions that contain separate web pages; each of these regions is known as a frame. Of course, from the user's perspective, everything comes together to form a single window of web content, but there are separate pages at work.

Frames are roughly similar to tables (covered in Hour 11, "Using Tables to Organize and Lay Out Your Pages") in that they allow you to arrange text and graphics into rows and columns. Unlike a table cell, however, any frame can contain links that change the contents of other frames (or itself). For example, one frame could display a table of contents page that changes the page displayed in another frame based on which links the user clicks.

Try It Yourself ▼

Frames are basically a way of arranging and presenting several web pages at once. You'll be able to work through this hour faster and get more out of it if you have a few related web pages ready before you continue:

▶ If you have an index page or table of contents for your web site, copy it to a separate directory folder so that you can experiment with it without changing the original. Copy a few of the pages that the index links to as well.

▶ As you read this hour, try modifying the sample frames I present to incorporate your own web pages. ▲

What Are Frames?

At first glance, Figure 16.1 may look like an ordinary web page, but it is actually two separate HTML pages, both displayed in the same web browser window. Each of these pages is displayed in its own frame, arranged horizontally and separated by the horizontal bar.

A **frame** is a rectangular region within the browser window that displays a web page alongside other pages in other frames.

FIGURE 16.1
Frames allow
more than one
web page to be
displayed at
once.

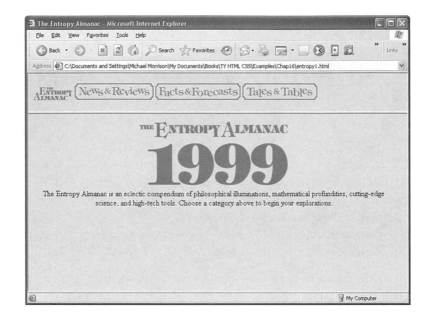

The main advantage of using frames becomes apparent when you click one of the navigational links in the top frame of Figure 16.1. The top frame will not change at all in this example, but a new page will be loaded and displayed in the bottom frame, as shown in Figure 16.2.

FIGURE 16.2
Clicking News &
Reviews in the
screen shown in
Figure 16.1
brings up a new
bottom page,
but leaves the
top frame the
same.

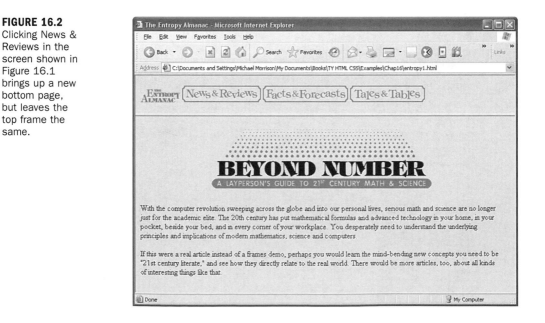

Although frames can certainly be useful, I must admit that I'm not a huge fan of them. The reason is simply because they can sometimes be confusing for users if you overdo it and create too many frames with too many cross links. When they're implemented properly with only two or three frames, the effect can be helpful, but more than that and you'll likely just cause confusion and frustration among your visitors.

Building a Frameset

You might be surprised to find out that frames aren't too difficult to work with in HTML code. So how did I make the pages shown in Figure 16.1 and Figure 16.2? First, I created the contents of each frame as an ordinary HTML page. These pages don't contain any tags you haven't already seen in other hours. To put them all together, I used a special kind of page called a frameset document.

Creating a Frameset Document

A frameset document actually has no content. It only tells the browser which other pages to load and how to arrange them in the browser window. Listing 16.1 shows the frameset document for the Entropy Almanac site shown in Figure 16.1 and Figure 16.2. The pages in this example serve as somewhat of a throwback to the 1990s, when the words *entropy* and *Internet* were practically synonymous.

A **frameset document** is an HTML page that instructs the web browser to split its window into multiple frames, and specifies which web page should be displayed in each frame.

LISTING 16.1   Frameset Document for the Site Shown in Figure 16.1

```
<?xml version="1.0" encoding="UTF-8"?>
<!DOCTYPE html PUBLIC "-//W3C//DTD XHTML 1.0 Frameset//EN"
  "http://www.w3.org/TR/xhtml1/DTD/xhtml1-frameset.dtd">

<html xmlns="http://www.w3.org/1999/xhtml" xml:lang="en">
  <head>
    <title>The Entropy Almanac</title>
  </head>

  <frameset rows="80,*">
    <frame src="banner.html" name="top" />
    <frame src="greeting.html" name="main" />
    <noframes>
     <body>
       <h1>The Entropy Almanac</h1>
       Your browser does not support frames. Please <a
href="noframes.html">click
       here</a> for the frameless version of this web site.
```

LISTING 16.1   Continued

```
      </body>
    </noframes>
  </frameset>
</html>
```

In the listing there is a <frameset> tag instead of a <body> tag. No tags that would normally be contained in a <body> tag can be within the <frameset> tag. The <frameset> tag in this example includes a rows attribute, meaning that the frames should be arranged on top of each other like the horizontal rows of a table. If you want your frames to be side by side, use a cols attribute instead of rows.

By the Way

It's important to notice that the DTD used in this sample page is not the familiar XHTML 1.1 DTD that you've been using throughout the book. This is because frames are not supported in the standard XHTML 1.1 DTD. Therefore, to validate a page with frames you must instead use the XHTML 1.0 Frameset DTD, which is a special DTD designed just for pages that use frames.

You must specify the sizes of the rows or cols, either as precise pixel values or as percentages of the total size of the browser window. You can also use an asterisk (*) to indicate that a frame should fill whatever space is available in the window. If more than one frame has an * value, the remaining space will be divided equally between them.

In Listing 16.1, <frameset rows="80,*"> means to split the window vertically into two frames. The top frame will be exactly 80 pixels tall, and the bottom frame will take up all the remaining space in the window. The top frame contains the document banner.html (see Listing 16.2), and the bottom frame contains greeting.html (see Listing 16.3).

Did you Know?

After the framesets in Listing 16.1, I included a complete web page between the <body> and </body> tags. Notice that this doesn't appear at all in Figure 16.1 or Figure 16.2. All web browsers that support frames will ignore anything between the <noframes> and </noframes> tags.

All major browsers these days support frames, so the issue of frames compatibility is much less significant now than in years past. Even so, it's easy enough to include the <noframes> tag and cover the few users who may still have an ancient browser.

LISTING 16.2   The `banner.html` Document Serves as a Navigation Bar
                    for the Entropy Almanac Web Page

```
<?xml version="1.0" encoding="UTF-8"?>
<!DOCTYPE html PUBLIC "-//W3C//DTD XHTML 1.0 Transitional//EN"
  "http://www.w3.org/TR/xhtml1/DTD/xhtml1-transitional.dtd">

<html xmlns="http://www.w3.org/1999/xhtml" xml:lang="en">
  <head>
    <title>The Entropy Almanac</title>
  </head>

  <body style="background-image:url(back.gif)">
    <div>
      <a href="greeting.html" target="main"><img
      src="eatiny.gif" alt="" style="border-style:none" /></a>
      <a href="news.html" target="main"><img
      src="news.gif" alt="" style="border-style:none" /></a>
      <a href="facts.html" target="main"><img
      src="facts.gif" alt="" style="border-style:none" /></a>
      <a href="tales.html" target="main"><img
      src="tales.gif" alt="" style="border-style:none" /></a>
    </div>
  </body>
</html>
```

LISTING 16.3   The `greeting.html` Document Acts as a Single Content
                    Frame Within the Entropy Almanac Web Page

```
<?xml version="1.0" encoding="UTF-8"?>
<!DOCTYPE html PUBLIC "-//W3C//DTD XHTML 1.0 Transitional//EN"
  "http://www.w3.org/TR/xhtml1/DTD/xhtml1-transitional.dtd">

<html xmlns="http://www.w3.org/1999/xhtml" xml:lang="en">
  <head>
    <title>The Entropy Almanac</title>
  </head>

  <body style="background-image:url(back.gif)">
    <div style="text-align:center">
      <img src="easmall.gif" alt="" /><br />
      <img src="1999.gif" alt="" /><br />
      The Entropy Almanac is an eclectic compendium of philosophical
      illuminations, mathematical profundities, cutting-edge science, and
      high-tech tools. Choose a category above to begin your explorations.
    </div>
  </body>
</html>
```

> *By the*
> *Way*
>
> The pages in Listing 16.2 and Listing 16.3 use the XHTML 1.0 Transitional DTD, which is in fact the most commonly used XHTML DTD. Although the XHTML 1.1 DTD is newer and much stricter, because frames require you to stick with XHTML 1.0 for validation purposes, it made sense to also use XHTML 1.0 for the pages that appear within the frames.

Because you can't predict the size of the window in which someone will view your web page, it is often convenient to use percentages rather than exact pixel values to dictate the size of the rows and columns. For example, to make a left frame 20% of the width of the browser window with a right frame taking up the remaining 80%, you would type the following :

```
<frameset cols="20%,80%">
```

An exception to this rule is when you want a frame to contain graphics of a certain size; then you would specify that size in pixels and add a few pixels for the margins and frame borders. This is the case in Listing 16.1, in which the images in the top frame are each 42 pixels tall. I allowed 38 extra pixels for margins and borders, making the entire frame 80 pixels tall.

Whenever you specify any frame size in pixels, it's a good idea to include at least one frame in the same frameset with a variable (*) width so that the document can grow to fill a window of any size.

Adding the Individual Frames

Within the `<frameset>` and `</frameset>` tags, you should have a `<frame />` tag indicating which HTML document to display in each frame. (If you have fewer `<frame />` tags than the number of frames defined in the `<frameset>` tag, any remaining frames will be left blank.)

Include a `src` attribute in each `<frame>` tag with the address of the web page to load in that frame. (You can put the address of an image file instead of a web page if you just want a frame with a single image in it.)

You can include any HTML/XHTML web page you want in a frame. For smaller frames, however, it's a good idea to create documents specifically for the frames with the reduced display area for each frame in mind. The top frame in Figure 16.1, for instance, is listed in Listing 16.2, and is much shorter than most web pages because it was designed specifically to fit in a frame under 80 pixels tall.

You may notice that the `<a>` and `<img />` tags in the `banner.html` document in Listing 16.2 are arranged a bit strangely. Because I didn't want any space between the graphics, I had to make sure that there were no spaces or line breaks between any of the tags. Therefore, I had to put all the line breaks inside the tags. This makes the HTML a bit harder to read, but keeps the images right next to each other on the page.

Linking Between Frames and Windows

The real power of frames begins to emerge when you give a frame a unique name with the name attribute in the <frame /> tag. You can then make any link on the page change the contents of that frame by using the target attribute in an <a> tag. For example, Listing 16.1 includes the following tag:

```
<frame src="greeting.html" name="main" />
```

> Technically speaking, the name tag is outdated and has been replaced by the id tag. However, current web browsers still rely on name instead of id when it comes to identifying frames as targets. So, for now, you need to stick with the name attribute when identifying frames. Of course, it wouldn't hurt to use both attributes.

This code displays the greeting.html page in that frame when the page loads and names the frame "main".

In the code for the top frame, which is shown in Listing 16.2, you will see the following link:

```
<a href="news.html" target="main"><img
src="news.gif" alt="" style="border-style:none" /></a>
```

When the user clicks this link, news.html is displayed in the frame named main (the lower frame). To accomplish this sort of interactivity before the invention of frames, you would have had to use complex programming or scripting languages. Now you can do it with a simple link!

If the target="main" attribute had been left out, the news.html page would be displayed in the current (top) frame instead.

To save space, I haven't provided a listing of the news.html page; it's just a regular web page with no special frame-related features. You can see what it looks like in Figure 16.2, and you can see this whole frameset in the files located at http://www.samspublishing.com/.

> Want to open a page in a new window without using frames? Just use one of the following special names with the target attribute of the <a> tag (for example, <a href="popup.html" target="_blank">Click here to open the popup.html document in a new window.</a>):

▶ _blank loads the link into a new, unnamed window.

▶ _top loads the link into the entire browser window. Use this when you want to get rid of all frames or replace the entire window with a whole new set of frames.

▶ _parent loads the link over the parent frame if the current frame is nested within other frames. (This name does the same thing as top unless the frames are nested more than one level deep.)

▶ _self loads the link into the current frame, replacing the document now being displayed in this frame. (You'll probably never use this because you can achieve the same thing by simply leaving out the target attribute altogether.)

In Hour 3, "Linking to Other Web Pages," you learned that XHTML 1.1 did away with the target attribute for opening a page in a new browser window. In that hour you also found out how to use a JavaScript trick to work around the limitation. This workaround isn't necessary in the news.html page because it uses the XHTML 1.0 Transitional DTD, which still supports target.

Nesting Frames Within Frames

By nesting one frameset within another, you can create rather complex frame layouts. For example, the document shown in Figure 16.3 and listed in Listing 16.4 has a total of nine frames. A cols frameset is used to split each row of the rows frameset into three pieces. Before you get to thinking that I'm contradicting myself when it comes to the complexities of frames, please understand that the purpose of this example is to demonstrate how nested frames work, not to encourage a particular technique.

LISTING 16.4   **Creating the Page Shown in Figure 16.3 Using Three Horizontal <frameset>s Within a Vertical <frameset>**

```
<?xml version="1.0" encoding="UTF-8"?>
<!DOCTYPE html PUBLIC "-//W3C//DTD XHTML 1.0 Frameset//EN"
  "http://www.w3.org/TR/xhtml1/DTD/xhtml1-frameset.dtd">

<html xmlns="http://www.w3.org/1999/xhtml" xml:lang="en">
  <head>
    <title>The Entropy Almanac</title>
  </head>

  <frameset rows="43,*,43">
    <frameset cols="43,*,43">
      <frame src="ctoplft.html" name="toplft" />
      <frame src="bordtop.html" name="top" />
      <frame src="ctoprgt.html" name="toprgt" />
    </frameset>
```

LISTING 16.4   Continued

```
  <frameset cols="43,*,43">
    <frame src="bordlft.html" name="left" />
    <frame src="main.html" name="main" />
    <frame src="bordrgt.html" name="right" />
  </frameset>
  <frameset cols="43,*,43">
    <frame src="cbtmlft.html" name="btmlft" />
    <frame src="bordbtm.html" name="btm" />
    <frame src="cbtmrgt.html" name="btmrgt" />
  </frameset>
  </frameset>
</html>
```

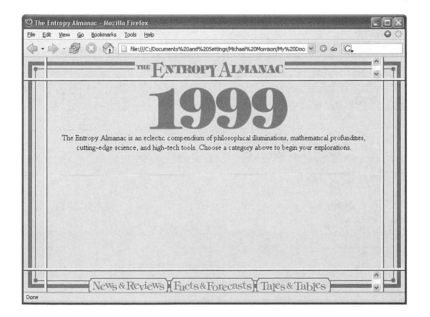

FIGURE 16.3
This window contains nine frames, some of which are nothing more than blank pages with custom background tiles.

Figure 16.3 consists of nine separate web pages laid out in different frames, many of which consist solely of a background image for decorative purposes. The corners and side frames contain blank HTML documents, showing nothing more than specially designed background tiles. The top frame is a permanent title graphic, and the bottom frame is a navigation bar similar to the one shown in the previous example. The net effect is to surround the middle frame within a sort of "picture frame" border. Figure 16.4 shows thumbnails of all the background tiles and other graphics incorporated into the pages.

FIGURE 16.4
To create the
border effect
shown in Figure
16.3, I designed
several custom
background tiles
and matching
title graphics.

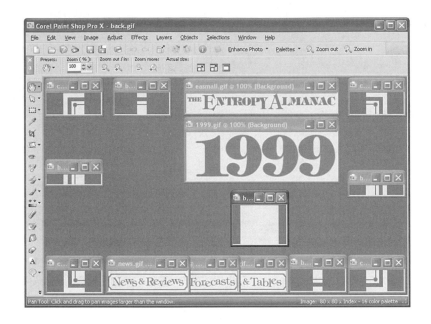

Controlling Frame Margins, Borders, and Scrolling

The problem with the nine-frame arrangement in Figure 16.3 is that it looks ugly and serves no practical purpose with all those annoying scrollbars. We can fix that.

The ugly parts are the gray dividers between the frames, which completely ruin the effect of surrounding the center frame with nicely designed graphics. There also isn't enough room in the top and bottom frames to display the graphics without scrollbars. Fortunately, there are HTML commands to get rid of the frame dividers, make more space in small frames by reducing the size of the margins, and force frames not to have scrollbars.

To see scrollbars in action on a real-world web page that takes advantage of frames, visit the Clint Eastwood web site at http://www.clinteastwood.net/. This site uses frames heavily to allow you to navigate and scroll through content within limited regions of the page.

Before you read about these HTML magic tricks, take a look at the dramatic results they can achieve. Figure 16.5 is another version of the nine-frame window displaying the same web pages shown in Figure 16.3. Obviously, Figure 16.5 looks much nicer! In Listing 16.5, you can see the anti-ugliness medication I gave to the frameset you saw in Figure 16.3.

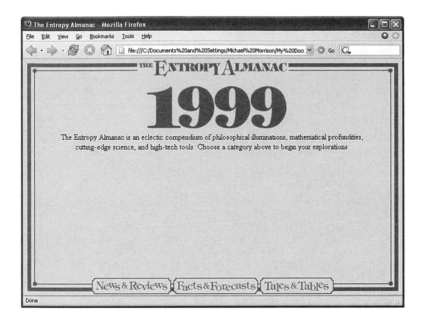

FIGURE 16.5
This is the page whose code is shown in Listing 16.5. By adding some attributes to the `<frame />` tags, I was able to make the frames look much nicer.

LISTING 16.5 Nine Separate Web Pages Displayed in Nine Frames

```
<?xml version="1.0" encoding="UTF-8"?>
<!DOCTYPE html PUBLIC "-//W3C//DTD XHTML 1.0 Frameset//EN"
  "http://www.w3.org/TR/xhtml1/DTD/xhtml1-frameset.dtd">

<html xmlns="http://www.w3.org/1999/xhtml" xml:lang="en">
  <head>
    <title>The Entropy Almanac</title>
  </head>

  <frameset rows="43,*,43" border="0">
    <frameset cols="43,*,43">
      <frame src="ctoplft.html" name="toplft" scrolling="no" frameborder="0" />
      <frame src="bordtop.html" name="top" scrolling="no" frameborder="0"
      marginheight="1" />
      <frame src="ctoprgt.html" name="toprgt" scrolling="no" frameborder="0" />
    </frameset>
    <frameset cols="43,*,43">
      <frame src="bordlft.html" name="left" scrolling="no" frameborder="0" />
      <frame src="main.html" name="main" frameborder="0" />
      <frame src="bordrgt.html" name="right" scrolling="no" frameborder="0" />
    </frameset>
    <frameset cols="43,*,43">
      <frame src="cbtmlft.html" name="btmlft" scrolling="no" frameborder="0" />
      <frame src="bordbtm.html" name="btm" scrolling="no" frameborder="0"
      marginheight="1" />
      <frame src="cbtmrgt.html" name="btmrgt" scrolling="no" frameborder="0" />
    </frameset>
  </frameset>
</html>
```

One problem with this code is the border attribute of the `<frameset>` tag, which technically isn't supported in XHTML. In other words, the document in Listing 16.5 will not validate even with the XHTML 1.0 Transitional DTD because of the border attribute. If you recall, you typically replace the border attribute with CSS styles to achieve the same results and conform to XHTML. The problem is that no current web browsers allow you to achieve the same results as the `border="0"` setting via CSS. So if you get rid of the border attribute, you'll see a nasty-looking gray border between the frames. Because I always err on the side of practicality, I opted to have the page look good and forego validation, knowing that eventually browsers will mend their ways.

In addition to the id and name attributes, the `<frame />` tag can take the following special frame-related attributes:

- `marginwidth`—Left and right margins of the frame (in pixels).

- `marginheight`—Top and bottom margins of the frame (in pixels).

- `scrolling`—Display scrollbar for the frame? ("yes" or "no")

- `frameborder`—Display dividers between this frame and adjacent frames? (1 means yes, 0 means no)

- `noresize`—Don't allow this frame to be resized by the user.

`marginwidth` and `marginheight` are pretty self-explanatory, but it's worth taking a close look at each of the other attributes.

Normally, any frame that isn't big enough to hold all of its contents will have its own scrollbar(s). The top and bottom frames you saw earlier in Figure 16.3 are examples. If you don't want a particular frame to ever display scrollbars, you can put `scrolling="no"` in the `<frame>` tag. Conversely, `scrolling="yes"` forces both horizontal and vertical scrollbars to appear, whether or not they are needed.

When graphics barely fit within a small frame, web browsers often display scrollbars that scroll only a few pixels down and have no real purpose. Rather than making the frame bigger (and taking up valuable window real estate with empty margin space), you will often want to just turn off the scrollbars with `scrolling="no"`.

The only situation I can think of in which you might want to use `scrolling="yes"` is if some graphics won't line up right unless you can count on the scrollbars always being there. Chances are that you'll never need `scrolling="yes"`.

People viewing your frames can ordinarily resize them by grabbing the frame borders with the mouse and dragging them around. If you don't want anyone messing with the size of a frame, put `noresize="noresize"` in the `<frame />` tag.

Frames are flexible enough to allow you to control the size of frame borders or eliminate borders altogether. This makes a frame document look just like a regular web page, with no ugly lines breaking it up. Just put a `frameborder="0"` attribute in every single `<frame />` tag—not just in the `<frameset>` tags.

When used together with custom graphics, borderless frames can allow you to create sites that are easier to navigate and more pleasant to visit. For example, when someone visits the site shown in Figure 16.5 and clicks one of the navigation choices in the bottom frame, the page he chose comes up in the middle frame quickly because the title graphic, navigation buttons, and border graphics all remain in place. The frames also automatically adapt to changes in the size of the browser window, so the nice "picture frame" effect looks just as good at 1,024×768 resolution and higher resolutions as it does at 800×600.

Coffee Break

I haven't made too big of a deal out of the fact that many web designers and users don't like frames. And unfortunately, it's beyond the scope of this lesson to detour into a philosophical debate about whether frames are good or evil. However, if you'd like to learn more about the pros and cons of using frames in your own pages, here's a great site you can visit to learn more: http://www.yourhtmlsource.com/frames/goodorbad.html.

Figure 16.6 shows the result of clicking the Facts & Forecasts link in the screen shown in Figure 16.5. Note that the middle frame gets its own scrollbar whenever the contents are too big to fit in the frame.

By the Way

If you'd like to get more advanced with frames, you might want to look into *inline frames*, which are frames you can place directly within a section of text in a page. Inline frames are created using the `<iframe>` tag, as the following code demonstrates:

```
<html>
  <head>
    <title>bios</title>
  </head>

  <body>
    <h1>Short Bios</h1>
    <p>
      <iframe name="bioframe" src="mybio.html" width="200" height="200">
      </iframe>
    </p>
    <p>
      <a href="yourbio.html" target="bioframe">Your Bio</a>
    </p>
    <p>
      <a href="mybio.html" target="bioframe">My Bio</a>
    </p>
```

```
    </body>
</html>
```

This code displays the page mybio.html in a 200×200-pixel region, under the heading Short Bios. If the document mybio.html doesn't fit in that small region, it would have its own little scrollbar(s) next to it. Clicking the Your Bio link would replace the contents of the 200×200-pixel region with yourbio.html. Clicking My Bio would put mybio.html back into that region.

You can view an <iframe> example online at http://www.samspublishing.com/.

FIGURE 16.6
Clicking a link at the top of the screen shown in Figure 16.5 brings up a new page in the middle frame, without redrawing any of the other frames.

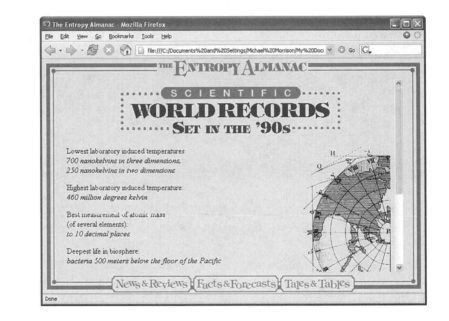

Summary

In this hour you learned how to display more than one page at a time by splitting the web browser window into frames. You learned to use a frameset document to define the size and arrangement of the frames, as well as which web page or image will be loaded into each frame. You saw how to create links that change the contents of any frame you choose, while leaving the other frames unchanged. You also discovered several optional settings that control the appearance of resizable borders and scrollbars in frames. Finally, you saw how to nest framesets to create complex frame layouts.

Table 16.1 summarizes the tags and attributes covered in this hour.

TABLE 16.1 HTML Tags and Attributes Covered in Hour 16

Tag/Attribute	Function
`<frameset>...` `</frameset>`	Divides the main window into a set of frames that can each display a separate document.
Attributes	
`rows="numrows"`	Splits the window or frameset vertically into a number of rows specified by a number (such as 7), a percentage of the total window width (such as 25%), or an asterisk (*) indicating that a frame should take up all the remaining space or divide the space evenly between frames (if multiple * frames are specified).
`cols="numcols"`	Works similar to `rows`, except that the window or frameset is split horizontally into columns.
`frameborder="yes/no"`	Specifies whether to display a border for a frame. Options are 1 (yes) and 0 (no).
`<frame />`	Defines a single frame within a `<frameset>`.
Attributes	
`src="url"`	The URL of the document to be displayed in this frame.
`id="name"`	A name to be used for targeting this frame with the `target` attribute in `<a href>` links; compliant with XHTML but not quite supported for frames in current web browsers.
`name="name"`	A name to be used for targeting this frame with the `target` attribute in `<a href>` links; will eventually be replaced by `id` but for the time being is still useful because it works in current web browsers.
`<marginwidth>`	The amount of space (in pixels) to leave to the left and right side of a document within a frame.
`<marginheight>`	The amount of space (in pixels) to leave above and below a document within a frame.
`scrolling="yes/no/auto"`	Determines whether a frame has scrollbars. Possible values are yes, no, and auto.
`noresize="noresize"`	Prevents the user from resizing this frame (and possibly adjacent frames) with the mouse.
`<noframes>...` `</noframes>`	Provides an alternative document body in `<frameset>` documents for browsers that do not support frames (usually encloses `<body>...</body>`).
`<iframe>...</iframe>`	Creates an inline frame. (`<iframe>` accepts all the same attributes as does `<frame />`.)

Q&A

Q *Can I display other people's web pages from the Internet in one frame, and my own pages in another frame at the same time? What if those sites use frames, too?*

A You can load any document from anywhere on the Internet (or an intranet) into a frame. If the document is a frameset, its frames are sized to fit within the existing frame into which you load it.

For example, you could put a hotlist of your favorite links in one frame and have the pages that those links refer to appear in a separate frame. This makes it easy to provide links to other sites without risking that someone will get lost and never come back to your own site. Note, however, that if any link within that site has `target="_top"`, it will replace all your frames.

You should also be aware that framing somebody else's pages so that they appear to be part of your own site may get you in legal trouble. Several major lawsuits are pending on this exact issue, so be sure to get explicit written permission from anyone whose pages you plan to put within one of your frames (just as you would if you were putting images or text from their site on your own pages).

Q *Do I need to put a `<title>` in all my frames? If I do, which title will be displayed at the top of the window?*

A The title of the frameset document is the only one that will be displayed. `<head>` and `<title>` tags are not required in framed documents, but it's a good idea to give all your pages titles just in case somebody opens one by itself outside any frame.

Workshop

The workshop contains quiz questions and activities to help you solidify your understanding of the material covered. Try to answer all questions before looking at the "Answers" section that follows.

Quiz

1. Write the HTML code to list the names Mickey, Minnie, and Donald in a frame taking up the left 25% of the browser window. Make it so that clicking each name brings up a corresponding web page in the right 75% of the browser window.

2. Write a frameset document to make the frame layout pictured here:

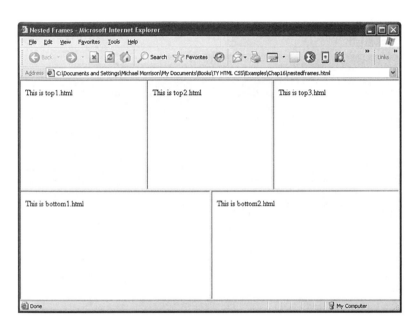

Answers

1. You need five separate HTML documents. The first document is the frameset:

```
<html>
  <head>
    <title>Our Friends</title>
  </head>

  <frameset cols="25%,75%">
    <frame src="index.html" />
    <frame src="mickey.html" name="mainframe" />
  </frameset>
</html>
```

Next, you need the index.html document for the left frame:

```
<html>
  <head>
    <title>Our Friends Index</title>
  </head>

  <body>
    <p>
      Pick a friend:
    </p>
    <p>
      <a href="mickey.html" target="mainframe">Mickey</a><br />
```

```
      <a href="minnie.html" target="mainframe">Minnie</a><br />
      <a href="donald.html" target="mainframe">Donald</a>
    </p>
  </body>
</html>
```

Finally, you need the three HTML pages named `mickey.html`, `minnie.html`, and `donald.html`. They contain the information about each friend.

2.
```
<html>
  <head>
    <title>Nested Frames</title>
  </head>

  <frameset rows="*,*">
    <frameset cols="*,*,*">
      <frame src="top1.html" />
      <frame src="top2.html" />
      <frame src="top3.html" />
    </frameset>
    <frameset cols="*,*">
      <frame src="bottom1.html" />
      <frame src="bottom2.html" />
    </frameset>
  </frameset>
</html>
```

Exercises

In Hour 23, "Helping People Find Your Web Pages," you'll discover how to make a page that loads another page automatically after a specified time interval. When you combine that trick with frames, you can create all sorts of interesting animated layout effects. Consider what kind of information you might display in this manner.

PART IV

Dynamic Web Pages

Web Page Scripting for Nonprogrammers

Scripting is a polite word for *computer programming*, and that's obviously an enormous topic you're not going to learn much about in a one-hour lesson. Still, there are some awfully handy things you can do in a snap with scripting—and many things you can't do any other way. So with a spirit of bold optimism, this hour aims to help you teach yourself just enough web page scripting to make your pages stand out from the "non-de-script" crowd.

Specifically, you'll learn in this hour how to make the images (or multimedia objects) on your web pages change in response to mouse movements or mouse clicks, as well as how to jump into the advertising business by adding animated banner ads to your web pages that cycle between different ad images. You'll also find out how to display a random quote, create a virtual fish tank, and make money off of Google ads. Yes, this lesson is a lot like an entire book packed into a single hour! And best of all, using the JavaScript language, you can do these tasks in a way that is compatible with all major web browsers.

> **By the Way**
>
> If the ease and power of the few JavaScript commands you learn in this hour whets your appetite for more (as I think it will), I encourage you to turn to books such as *Sams Teach Yourself JavaScript in 21 Days* or *JavaScript Bible*.

The Least You Need to Know About Scripting

Web page scripting allows you to access styles and content of elements in a web page. To develop your own custom scripts, you'll need to use a scripting language such as JavaScript or VBScript. Instead of teaching you a scripting language, which definitely would be beyond the scope of this lesson, I'll present you with some short scripts you can use in your own web pages. Script programming isn't terribly hard to learn, but it's best that you wait to tackle it until you've gotten really comfortable with HTML and CSS.

The primary scripting language in use on the Web is JavaScript. All the scripts in this hour were developed in JavaScript, but you don't need to worry too much about the details of each script; I'll point out the important parts to give you a feel for how they work. You may be surprised at how simple some scripts can be. If you happen to have any experience with the Java or C++ programming languages, you'll find JavaScript somewhat familiar. Even if you don't have any programming experience, you shouldn't have trouble incorporating an existing script into your own pages by copying and pasting code.

As you might guess, a special HTML tag is used to add scripts to web pages. The `<script>` tag encapsulates scripting code. Some older web browsers don't support scripts, so to be extra cautious you can use a little trick when placing script code in the `<script>` tag. Just enclose the script code inside an HTML comment, as the following example demonstrates:

```
<script type="text/javascript">
  <!-- Hide the script from old browsers
  alert("Hello!");
  // Stop hiding the script -->
</script>
```

In this brief script, the `<!--` code that signifies the start of a comment is used just before the single line of script code. Following the script code is the `-->` code that ends the comment. The script code displays an alert message of `Hello!`, as shown in Figure 17.1.

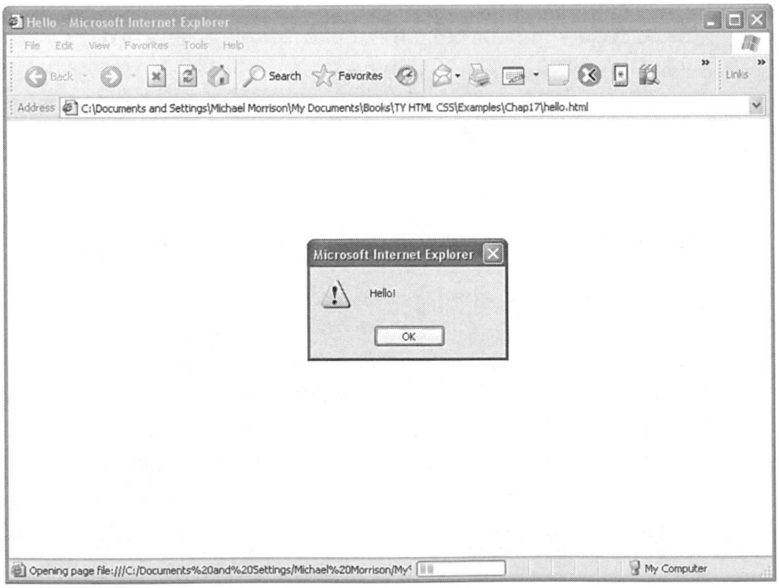

FIGURE 17.1
The Hello script simply displays a hello message in a dialog box.

The Hello sample web page simply shows how to create a minimal script that displays an alert message.

The primary way that scripts provide interactivity is by responding to actions taken by the user. For example, if the user clicks the mouse button or presses a key on the keyboard, the script might respond by changing the appearance of text or an image on the page. A user interaction such as a mouse click or key press is known as an *event*, and the process of a script taking action based on an event is known as *event handling*. You associate event-handling script code with elements on a web page using special attributes.

Following are some of the commonly used event attributes that come in handy in JavaScript, along with a description of when they occur with respect to a web page element:

- ▶ onload—Browser loads the element.
- ▶ onkeydown—User presses a key.
- ▶ onkeyup—User releases a key.
- ▶ onclick—User clicks the element with the left mouse button.
- ▶ ondblclick—User double-clicks the element with the left mouse button.
- ▶ onmousedown—User presses either mouse button while the mouse pointer is over the element.
- ▶ onmouseup—User releases either mouse button while the mouse pointer is over the element.
- ▶ onmouseover—User moves the mouse pointer into the boundaries of the element.
- ▶ onmousemove—User moves the mouse pointer while the pointer is over the element.
- ▶ onmouseout—User moves the mouse pointer out of the boundaries of the element.

As you can see, event attributes are used to respond to common user input events such as mouse clicks and key presses. You associate script code with an event by assigning the script code to the event attribute, like this:

```
<h1 onclick="this.style.color = 'red';">I turn red when clicked.</h1>
```

In this example, script code is assigned to the onclick event attribute of an <h1> tag, which means that the code runs in response to the user clicking the left mouse button on the text. The script code responds by setting the color of the text to red. So interactivity is added to normally bland text by changing the color of the text in response to a mouse click. This is the basis for how many interactive scripts work.

Jazzing Things Up with Interactive Highlighting

If you've used any graphical CD-ROM software application or if you've navigated a DVD menu, you have probably seen buttons that light up or change when your mouse pointer passes over them. This looks cool and gives you some visual feedback before you click something, which research shows can reduce confusion and errors— it makes for more intuitive user interfaces.

You can add the same sort of visual feedback to the links on your web pages, too. The first step toward achieving that effect is to create the graphics for both the static (dim) and the hover (highlighted) icons. Figure 17.2 shows some icons I created while developing the web site for my company, Stalefish Labs. I made two copies of each icon: one darkened and one illuminated as if it has a green shadow around it, along with highlighted colors throughout the icon.

FIGURE 17.2
Five graphics images, each with a highlighted version to replace it when the mouse hovers over it.

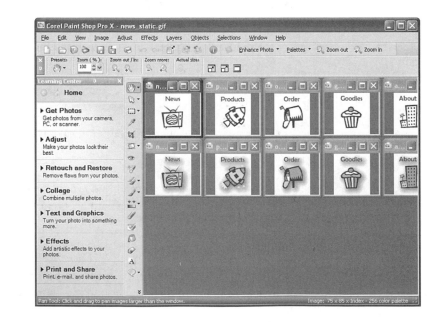

Try It Yourself ▼

Do you have any pages that would look flashier or be easier to understand if the navigation icons or other images changed when the mouse passed over them? If so, try creating some highlighted versions of the images, and try modifying your own page as you read the following few paragraphs. Here are a few ideas to get you started:

▶ Use Paint Shop Pro's text tool to make graphical titles that change color when the mouse points to them.

▶ Use the Effects, 3D Effects, Buttonize command in Paint Shop Pro with various background colors to make buttons that light up just before they're pressed.

▶ Use the techniques you learned in Hour 7, "Creating Your Own Web Page Graphics," to make icons that rotate, wiggle, or blink when the mouse passes over them. (You can use a regular, unanimated GIF for the image to present when the mouse isn't pointing to the icon.)

▶ If you have a list of choices, put a blank (totally transparent) image in front of each choice and make an arrow or bullet icon appear in front of the item to which the mouse is pointing. ▲

Here's how the HTML for a graphical link would look before any scripting is added:

```
<a href="http://www.stalefishlabs.com/news.html">
<img src="news_static.gif" alt="News" style="border-style:none" /></a>
```

This should all look familiar to you. (If it doesn't, review Hour 8, "Putting Graphics on a Web Page."

You can add interactive hovering functionality to any link on a web page by including two special attributes called onmouseover and onmouseout. With onmouseover, you tell the web browser what to do when the mouse passes over any text or images within that link. With onmouseout, you indicate what to do when the mouse moves out of the link area.

In this case, you want the image to change to news_hover.gif when the mouse passes over the corresponding link, and then change back to news_static.gif when the mouse moves away. Here's what that looks like in HTML and JavaScript:

```
<a href="http://www.stalefishlabs.com/news.html"><img
src="news_static.gif" alt="News" style="border-style:none"
onmouseover="this.src = 'news_hover.gif';"
onmouseout="this.src = 'news_static.gif';" /></a>
```

Notice that you need to enclose the name of the image file in single quotation marks (apostrophes), and enclose the entire piece of JavaScript code assigned to an event attribute in double quotation marks. This is because the JavaScript code is provided as an attribute, and attributes in HTML must be enclosed within double quotation marks. When you enter JavaScript code like this in your own pages, just follow my example closely, substituting your own image names and graphics files.

Listing 17.1 contains the complete HTML code for a web page using the navigation icons from Figure 17.2 as links. You can see how the icons highlight when the mouse passes over them in Figure 17.3 and Figure 17.4, or in the files located at http://www.samspublishing.com/.

LISTING 17.1   The JavaScript-Enhanced HTML Code for a Page with
                    Interactive Hover Buttons

```
<?xml version="1.0" encoding="UTF-8"?>
<!DOCTYPE html PUBLIC "-//W3C//DTD XHTML 1.1//EN"
  "http://www.w3.org/TR/xhtml11/DTD/xhtml11.dtd">

<html xmlns="http://www.w3.org/1999/xhtml" xml:lang="en">
  <head>
    <title>Hover Buttons</title>
  </head>

  <body>
    <h1>Hover Buttons</h1>
    <p>
      Try out these hover "buttons" to see how JavaScript makes hovering just a
      bit more fun.
    </p>
    <hr />
    <p>
      <a href="http://www.stalefishlabs.com/news.html"><img
      src="news_static.gif" alt="News" style="border-style:none"
      onmouseover="this.src = 'news_hover.gif';"
      onmouseout="this.src = 'news_static.gif';" /></a>
      <a href="http://www.stalefishlabs.com/products.html"><img
      src="products_static.gif" alt="Products" style="border-style:none"
      onmouseover="this.src = 'products_hover.gif';"
      onmouseout="this.src = 'products_static.gif';" /></a>
      <a href="http://www.stalefishlabs.com/order.html"><img
      src="order_static.gif" alt="Order" style="border-style:none"
      onmouseover="this.src = 'order_hover.gif';"
      onmouseout="this.src = 'order_static.gif';" /></a>
      <a href="http://www.stalefishlabs.com/goodies.html"><img
      src="goodies_static.gif" alt="Goodies" style="border-style:none"
      onmouseover="this.src = 'goodies_hover.gif';"
      onmouseout="this.src = 'goodies_static.gif';" /></a>
      <a href="http://www.stalefishlabs.com/about.html"><img
      src="about_static.gif" alt="About Us" style="border-style:none"
      onmouseover="this.src = 'about_hover.gif';"
      onmouseout="this.src = 'about_static.gif';" /></a>
    </p>
  </body>
</html>
```

FIGURE 17.3
When the mouse passes over the News icon, the television icon lights up and the alternate text appears.

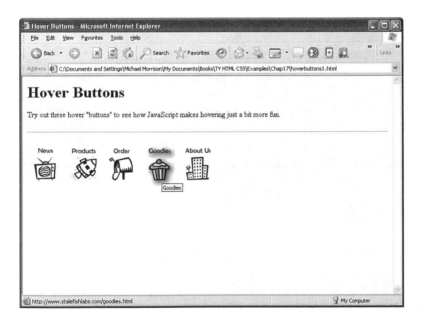

FIGURE 17.4
When you move the mouse to the Goodles icon, the cupcake is highlighted instead of the television.

You can also use the onmouseover and onmouseout attributes with imagemaps (which were covered in Hour 10, "Graphical Links and Imagemaps"). For an example of a large interactive imagemap, move your mouse cursor around the

Did you Know?

navigational clock in the files located at the *Sams Publishing* site at http://www.samspublishing.com/. Peeking at the source code shows you exactly how to incorporate JavaScript commands into an imagemap. Also, don't forget that you can use animated GIFs with scripts too!

You aren't limited to carrying out a single action in the JavaScript code for an event attribute. For example, you could modify multiple images by separating each image assignment with a semicolon (;).

Preloading Images for Speed

The code in Listing 17.1 works flawlessly in all major web browsers, but there is one minor problem: The lit images won't be downloaded from your web site until someone actually moves the mouse over the image. This can sometimes cause a noticeable delay before the highlighted image appears, primarily if the person is viewing your page over a slow Internet connection. The end result is a possible lowering of the all-important Gee Whiz Factor (GWF).

You can avoid this annoyance by including some JavaScript code telling the browser to preload the images as soon as possible when the page is displayed. That way, by the time the slow human reader gets around to passing his or her mouse over the link, those images will usually be ready to pop onto the screen. This makes the animations seem to appear without any download delay, giving the page a snappy feel and pumping the GWF back up to truly nerdy levels. Listing 17.2 shows the script code that makes this happen.

LISTING 17.2   The Script Code to Preload the Images from Figure 17.2

```
<script type="text/javascript">
  <!-- Hide the script from old browsers
  var image1 = new Image();
  image1.src = "news_static.gif";
  var image2 = new Image();
  image2.src = "news_hover.gif";
  var image3 = new Image();
  image3.src = "products_static.gif";
  var image4 = new Image();
  image4.src = "products_hover.gif";
  var image5 = new Image();
  image5.src = "order_static.gif";
  var image6 = new Image();
  image6.src = "order_hover.gif";
  var image7 = new Image();
  image7.src = "goodies_static.gif";
```

LISTING 17.2   Continued

```
  var image8 = new Image();
  image8.src = "goodies_hover.gif";
  var image9 = new Image();
  image9.src = "about_static.gif";
  var image10 = new Image();
  image10.src = "about_hover.gif";
  // Stop hiding the script -->
</script>
```

There are a couple of things worthy of note in this listing. The most important is the <script> tag, which can be placed in the <head> or <body> section of a document. However, if a script is intended to be run when a page is first loaded, as is the case here, most web developers would place the <script> tag in the head of the page.

As you learned earlier in the hour, the <!-- and //--> tags just inside the <script> and </script> tags are actually comment tags, which have the effect of hiding the script from older browsers that otherwise might become confused and try to display the code as text on the page.

I won't go too deep into an explanation of the JavaScript code in the listing because that would get us into a course on computer programming. You don't need to understand exactly how this works in order to copy it into your own pages, using your own image names and graphics files. The main thing to take note of is that it takes two lines of code to preload each image. The first line creates a blank image, and the second line sets it to an image file so that it is loaded. You can use this one-two JavaScript punch to preload as many of your own images as you want.

Creating an Animated Banner Ad

One of the most common uses of scripting is animating images, as you learned earlier in the hour. Although hover buttons and other forms of user interface improvements are certainly helpful, there is a more lucrative approach to animated images that you should consider when it comes to scripting. I'm referring to animated banner ads, which display a succession of advertisements over time. You've no doubt seen these kinds of ads around the Web because ads are now commonplace on virtually all large web sites.

The first step in putting together an animated banner ad is creating the individual ad images. Banner ads come in all shapes and sizes, but I personally like vertical banner ads that occupy space down the side of a web page. Figure 17.5 shows a series of three banner ad images that are oriented vertically.

FIGURE 17.5
An animated
banner ad con-
sists of several
images all cre-
ated the exact
same size.

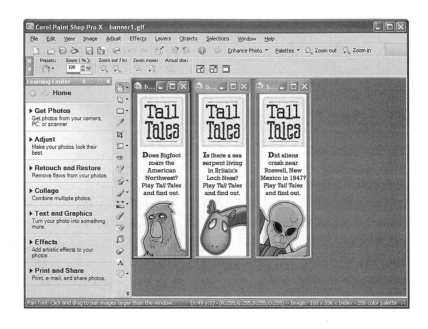

FIGURE 17.5
An animated banner ad consists of several images all created the exact same size.

The three images in the figure are displayed one after another to form an animated banner ad. The key to the ad working properly is establishing a timing mechanism so that each ad image is displayed for a few seconds before the next one is shown. This can be easily accomplished with JavaScript code, as shown in Listing 17.3.

LISTING 17.3   A Web Page That Displays a Carefully Timed Series of Ad Banner Images

```
<?xml version="1.0" encoding="UTF-8"?>
<!DOCTYPE html PUBLIC "-//W3C//DTD XHTML 1.1//EN"
  "http://www.w3.org/TR/xhtml11/DTD/xhtml11.dtd">

<html xmlns="http://www.w3.org/1999/xhtml" xml:lang="en">
  <head>
    <title>Tall Tales Banner Ad</title>

    <script type="text/javascript">
      <!--
      var bannerNum = 1;

      function rotateBanner() {
        if (++bannerNum > 3)
          bannerNum = 1;
        document.getElementById("ttbanner").src = "banner" + bannerNum +
          ".gif";
        window.setTimeout('rotateBanner();', 3000);
      }
      //-->
    </script>
  </head>
```

LISTING 17.3 Continued

```
<body onload="window.setTimeout('rotateBanner();', 3000);">
  <h1 style="text-align:center">Game Lovers Anonymous</h1>
  <p>
    <a href="http://www.talltalesgame.com/">
    <img src="banner1.gif" alt="Tall Tales" id="ttbanner" style="border:none;
    float:right" />
    </a>
    Welcome to Game Lovers Anonymous. We love to play
    games, and invite you to support us by visiting our
    sponsors as you enjoy our site.
  </p>
</body>
</html>
```

This code is another example of JavaScript code that you don't necessarily have to understand inside and out in order to use effectively in your own web pages. There are a few things worth pointing out so that you'll understand how to tweak the code to suit your own needs, but beyond that I'm suggesting that you don't worry too much about how it works. The idea is to add some sizzle to your web pages, not to become a programmer overnight.

Figure 17.6 shows the ad banner sample page in action. Okay, maybe the printed page is not the best way to show something in action, but you get the idea that you're seeing one of the ad banners as the page is flipping through all of them.

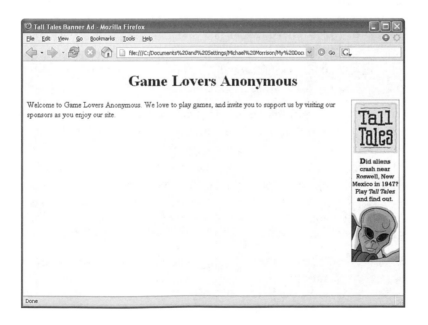

FIGURE 17.6
The JavaScript code in Listing 17.3 produces this vertical banner ad that cycles through three different ad images.

> Hour 7 showed you how to create a similar animated banner ad effect by creating an animated GIF image that cycled between the three individual ad images. Although that approach certainly worked, and in fact provided a smoother animation due to the fade effect, the resulting animated GIF is much larger than the three individual GIF images used in the JavaScript version. Furthermore, the JavaScript version of the animated banner ad is much easier to modify to accommodate additional ads or change out the existing ads.

There are several lines of code in Listing 17.3 worth taking a closer look at in order for you to be able to create your own banner ads. Let's start with the JavaScript function that actually changes (rotates) the ad image:

```
function rotateBanner() {
  if (++bannerNum > 3)
    bannerNum = 1;
  document.getElementById("ttbanner").src = "banner" + bannerNum + ".gif";
  window.setTimeout('rotateBanner();', 3000);
}
```

The `rotateBanner()` function is used to change the banner ad image once every 3 seconds. A *function* is a chunk of JavaScript code grouped together to carry out a specific task such as performing a calculation or, in this case, changing an image on the page.

You're probably wondering how the code can possibly know how long to wait before changing an image. This is accomplished in the next-to-last line of code. See the number `3000`? This `3000` is the *wait period* for the banner ad, which determines how long the ad is displayed before the next image is shown. The wait period is specified in milliseconds—3,000 milliseconds equals 3 seconds. To slow down or speed up how fast the images change, just change this number.

The other important piece of information in the `rotateBanner()` function is the number of banner ads, which in this code is set to 3 (look at the second line). If you want to provide more banner ad images and have the page cycle through all of them, just change this number to however many images you have. Also, I forgot to mention that this code assumes that your banner images are named `banner1.gif`, `banner2.gif`, `banner3.gif`, and so on. If you want to use JPEG images instead of GIFs, just change the fourth line of the code so that the `.jpg` file extension is used instead of `.gif`.

The other critical line of code in the ad banner example that you absolutely must not leave out is this one:

```
<body onload="window.setTimeout('rotateBanner();', 3000);">
```

This code is what gets everything started because it tells the `rotateBanner()` function to get started showing and changing the images. Notice that the `onload` attribute is used, which if you recall from earlier in the hour is a scripting attribute that results in script code being run whenever a page is first loaded. You may also notice that the number 3000 appears again in this code. This is because you must set an initial wait period for the banner ad to make sure that the first image is displayed for a moment before changing to the second one.

Displaying a Random Quote

I'm a sucker for a good quote. If you're the same way, you may find it fun to incorporate an ever-changing quote into your web pages. If quotes aren't your thing, maybe you have some other collection of text that you find interesting enough to include in your pages. The point is that you can use JavaScript to display a different piece of text each time a page is loaded.

To create a page with a quote that changes each time the page is loaded, you must first gather all the quotes together, along with their respective sources. You'll then place these quotes into a JavaScript *array*, which is a special script storage unit that is handy for holding lists of items. After the quotes are loaded into an array, the script code to pluck out a quote at random is fairly simple.

Listing 17.4 contains the complete HTML and JavaScript code for a web page that displays a random quote each time it is loaded.

LISTING 17.4   A Random-Quote Web Page

```
<?xml version="1.0" encoding="UTF-8"?>
<!DOCTYPE html PUBLIC "-//W3C//DTD XHTML 1.1//EN"
  "http://www.w3.org/TR/xhtml11/DTD/xhtml11.dtd">

<html xmlns="http://www.w3.org/1999/xhtml" xml:lang="en">
  <head>
    <title>Quotable Quotes</title>

  <script type="text/javascript">
    <!-- Hide the script from old browsers
    function getQuote() {
      // Create the arrays
      quotes = new Array(4);
      sources = new Array(4);

      // Initialize the arrays with quotes
      quotes[0] = "When I was a boy of 14, my father was so ignorant..." +
      "but when I got to be 21, I was astonished at how much he had learned " +
      "in 7 years.";
      sources[0] = "Mark Twain";
      quotes[1] = "Everybody is ignorant. Only on different subjects.";
```

LISTING 17.4   Continued

```
      sources[1] = "Will Rogers";
      quotes[2] = "They say such nice things about people at their funerals " +
      "that it makes me sad that I'm going to miss mine by just a few days.";
      sources[2] = "Garrison Keilor";
      quotes[3] = "What's another word for thesaurus?";
      sources[3] = "Steven Wright";

      // Get a random index into the arrays
      i = Math.floor(Math.random() * quotes.length);

      // Write out the quote as HTML
      document.write("<dl style='background-color:#EEEEEE'>\n");
      document.write("<dt>" + "\"<i>" + quotes[i] + "</i>\"\n");
      document.write("<dd>" + "- " + sources[i] + "\n");
      document.write("<dl>\n");
   }
   // Stop hiding the script -->
</script>
</head>

<body>
  <h1>Quotable Quotes</h1>
  <p>
    Following is a random quotable quote. To see a new quote just reload this
    page.
  </p>
  <script type="text/javascript">
    <!-- Hide the script from old browsers
    getQuote();
    // Stop hiding the script -->
  </script>
</body>
</html>
```

Although this code looks kind of long, if you look carefully you'll see that a lot of it consists of the four quotes available for display on the page. After you get past the shock of the code size, the script code for the page isn't too terribly complex.

After creating an array, or list, of quotes and their sources, the getQuote() script function picks a random number and uses it to select a quote to be displayed. The quote is formatted on the page by the HTML code that is generated by the getQuote() function. The standard JavaScript document.write() function is used to generate the HTML code that formats the quote. This script function is powerful because by using it, you can dynamically generate HTML code at any point in a web page.

Figure 17.7 shows the Quotable Quotes sample web page as it appears in Opera. To view a different quote, just click the Refresh button in your web browser, and the page reloads.

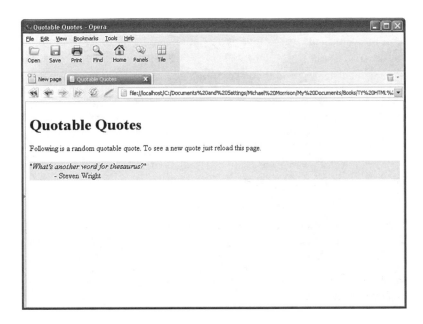

FIGURE 17.7
The Quotable
Quotes web
page displays a
random quote
each time it is
loaded.

Keep in mind that you can easily modify this page to include your own quotes or
other text that you want to display randomly. You can also increase the number of
quotes available for display by adding more entries in the quotes and sources
arrays in the code. I realize that some of this script code might be intimidating. Just
understand that the best way to learn how to use JavaScript is to take something
that works and experiment with making modifications to it.

If you use the Quotable Quotes page as a starting point, I guarantee you will be
able to alter the script and create your own interesting variation on the idea without
much trouble. And if you make mistakes along the way, so be it. The trick to getting
past mistakes in script code is to be patient and carefully analyze the code you've
entered. You can always remove code to simplify a script until you get it working,
and then add new code one piece at a time to make sure that each piece works.

Creating a Virtual Fish Tank

To really illustrate how powerful scripts can be, I'm now going to show you how to
dynamically move an image around on a page. One fun way to demonstrate how
moving an image can be useful is to create a virtual fish tank web page in which a
fish appears to swim across the page. This is made possible by using script code and
CSS style properties to change the position of a fish image so that it moves around
on the page.

You can use CSS styles to position images and text so that they appear in an exact location on the page. This type of positioning is known as absolute positioning, which you learned about in Hour 14, "Using Style Sheets for Page Layout." If you position an element using absolute positioning, you can easily alter its position on the page using script code. Here is an example of an image that's positioned using absolute positioning:

```
<img src="fish.gif" alt="Fish" id="fish" style="position:absolute; top:70px" />
```

Absolute positioning allows you to position HTML content at precise locations on a web page. Dynamic positioning involves using script code to alter the position of content after a page has already been loaded.

The fish image uses absolute positioning and will be displayed at a position 70 pixels down from its parent element; the parent element is the tag in which the <img> tag resides, such as a <p> tag or <div> tag. Notice that the image has its id attribute set to "fish". The id attribute is necessary so that script code can access the image and alter its position.

Listing 17.5 contains a sample web page that uses script code to animate the fish image by making it appear to swim across the page.

LISTING 17.5   JavaScript Code Is Used to Move a Fish Image in This Virtual Fish Tank Web Page

```
<?xml version="1.0" encoding="UTF-8"?>
<!DOCTYPE html PUBLIC "-//W3C//DTD XHTML 1.1//EN"
  "http://www.w3.org/TR/xhtml11/DTD/xhtml11.dtd">

<html xmlns="http://www.w3.org/1999/xhtml" xml:lang="en">
  <head>
    <title>Virtual Fish Tank</title>

    <script type="text/javascript">
      <!-- Hide the script from old browsers
      var fishStyle;
      function StartSwimming() {
        fishStyle = document.getElementById("fish").style;
        fishStyle.left = document.body.offsetWidth + "px";
        window.setInterval("Swim()", 75);
      }

      function Swim() {
        var left = parseInt(fishStyle.left) - 5;
        fishStyle.left = left + "px";
        if (left < -118)
          fishStyle.left = document.body.offsetWidth + "px";
      }
      // Stop hiding the script -->
    </script>
  </head>
```

LISTING 17.5   Continued

```
<body style="background-image:url(water.jpg)" onload="StartSwimming()">
  <h1 style="text-align:center">Virtual Fish Tank</h1>
  <p style="text-align:center">
    Welcome to the virtual fish tank, where you never have to worry about
    remembering to feed the fish.
    <img src="fish.gif" alt="Fish" id="fish"
    style="position:absolute; top:70px" />
  </p>
</body>
</html>
```

The script code in this page sets up a timer that runs a script function again and again on a regular interval, in this case every 75 milliseconds. The script function, Swim(), decreases the left property of the image, causing it to move across the page from right to left. The left property is also checked to see whether the image has moved off the left edge of the screen, in which case it is "wrapped" back around to the right edge.

> Depending on your specific browser and browser security settings, some web pages with JavaScript may set off a security alert. Such alerts are intended to help prevent rogue scripts from causing harm to your system. As a web page developer, you can't do a whole lot about them other than maybe including a small note on your pages that lets visitors know that your pages are safe.

By the Way

Figure 17.8 catches a glimpse of the fish during its swim across the page.

FIGURE 17.8
The Virtual Fish Tank web page shows how to dynamically change the position of an image using script code.

I didn't even mention that the fish image itself is an animated GIF, which adds considerably to the realism of the swimming effect.

I have glossed over some details in the Virtual Fish Tank sample web page, but it's another example of script code you can use in pages of your own without having to become a JavaScript expert.

Cashing In with Google Ads on Your Site

You probably didn't realize it but you can make money using JavaScript. And I'm not talking about your becoming a contract JavaScript programmer and hiring out your services. I'm talking about using your web pages to attract visitors, and then making money off of their responding to ads placed on your pages. Don't worry, I'm not going to show you how to create annoying pop-ups or anything like that.

Google, the popular search engine, offers a free service called AdSense that allows you to place content-driven Google ads on your pages. You then earn commissions on these ads when people click them. Yes, it really is as easy as that. The difficult part of making money off of ads is getting enough traffic to your site so that people will respond to ads.

Although Google can't do a whole lot to help increase your web site traffic, AdSense does go a long way toward improving ad response rates by intelligently placing ads on your pages based on the content in the pages. In other words, you're really giving Google space on your page to insert whatever ad they best see fit. In my experience, Google does a surprisingly good job of matching up content with page content.

Coffee
Break

> Not only is Google a powerful search engine and a great way to make a few extra bucks off your Web pages via ad placement but it also is capable of reading your mind! If you don't believe me, just try Google's MentalPlex feature at http://www.google.com/intl/en/mentalplex/.

If you're curious to see Google AdSense in action, check out Figure 17.9, which shows ads on my personal web page that are driven entirely by the subject of the page (BlackBerry devices).

The page in the figure is about a BlackBerry book that I wrote, and not surprisingly, the resulting ads displayed by Google all relate to BlackBerry devices. By the way, the American Red Cross ad is not an AdSense ad—I created it myself to help encourage people to contribute to the Red Cross's disaster relief efforts.

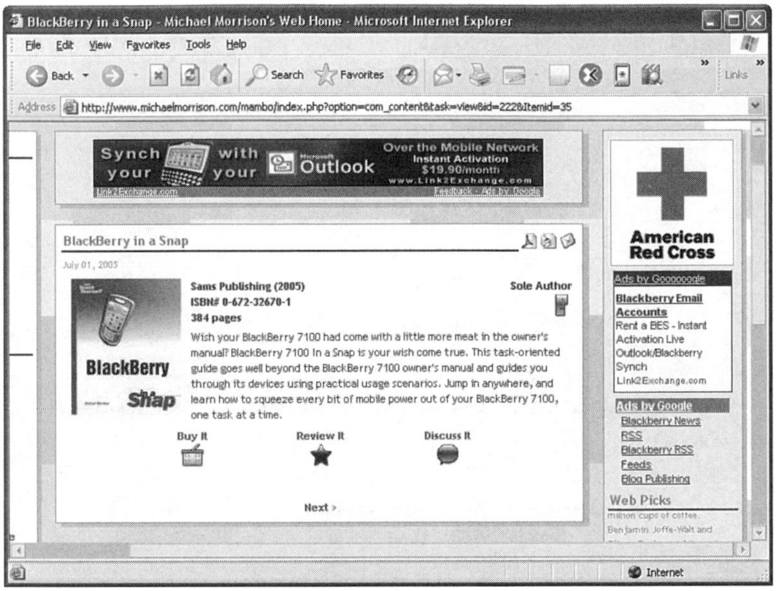

FIGURE 17.9
My personal web page uses Google AdSense to display content-driven ads.

To get started using Google AdSense, you'll first need to create a Google account. This is entirely free, and mainly just requires you to provide an email address and agree to Google's usage terms. To sign up for a Google account and start using AdSense, visit https://www.google.com/adsense/, and click the Click Here to Apply button. You'll receive a unique client ID that is used to connect your pages to AdSense so that you can earn commissions.

After creating an account and logging in, you can immediately start creating ads. What makes AdSense so easy to use is that Google automatically generates JavaScript code that you can paste directly into your web pages. The main AdSense code-generation tool is called AdSense for Content, and it is accessible online at https://www.google.com/adsense/code.

AdSense supports several kinds of ads, including text ads, image ads, and ads that can use either text or images. There are also various ad sizes from which you can choose. Figure 17.10 shows a partial sampling of some of the ad sizes and layouts you can use. You can view this page from within the Google AdSense for Content page by clicking the View Samples link.

In addition to selecting the ad type and size, you can also choose from one of several palettes. After specifying all the ad details, you'll eventually arrive at the bottom of the AdSense for Content page, which takes all of your selections and generates JavaScript code for the ad. This code will automatically include your Google client ID, so you don't have to worry about entering it. If you click in the edit box containing the JavaScript code, it will automatically highlight so that you can copy it (see Figure 17.11). Right-click the code and select Copy, or select Edit, Copy from the main browser menu.

The Google AdSense example shown in the figure relies on a hypothetical client id in the `google_ad_client` attribute of the `<script>` tag, as does the code in the `googlead.html` sample web page. Be sure to use your own Google client ID when placing ads on your own pages. If you use the script code generated by Google, this shouldn't be a problem.

Watch Out!

You now have some JavaScript code ready to place in your own web pages. Just paste the code into the body of a page, as shown in Listing 17.6. Be sure to copy and paste the code without modifying any of it.

LISTING 17.6   Google AdSense JavaScript Code Should Be Copied into the Body of a Web Page

```
<?xml version="1.0" encoding="UTF-8"?>
<!DOCTYPE html PUBLIC "-//W3C//DTD XHTML 1.1//EN"
  "http://www.w3.org/TR/xhtml11/DTD/xhtml11.dtd">

<html xmlns="http://www.w3.org/1999/xhtml" xml:lang="en">
  <head>
    <title>Google Ads</title>
  </head>

  <body>
    <h1>Oodles of Google Ads</h1>
    <p>
      Google AdSense uses the content of your Web page to determine what ads to
      place on the page. If it can't find a suitable ad to match your content,
      it will display a public service ad.
    </p>
    <script type="text/javascript"><!--
    google_ad_client = "pub-239211407";
    google_ad_width = 728;
    google_ad_height = 90;
    google_ad_format = "728x90_as";
    google_ad_type = "text_image";
    google_ad_channel ="";
    google_color_border = "000000";
    google_color_bg = "F0F0F0";
    google_color_link = "0000FF";
    google_color_url = "008000";
    google_color_text = "000000";
    //--></script>
    <script type="text/javascript"
      src="http://pagead2.googlesyndication.com/pagead/show_ads.js">
    </script>
  </body>
</html>
```

The page in Listing 17.6 is shown in Figure 17.12, complete with a public service Google AdSense ad.

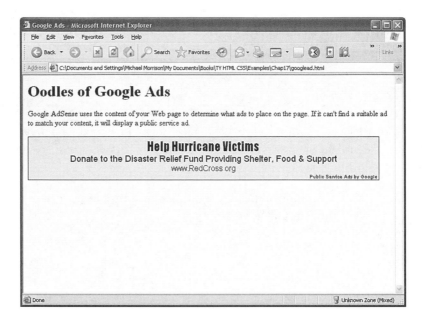

In this example, there isn't enough content on the page for AdSense to match up with an ad, so it opted to show a public service ad. This can happen if a page is light on content or if the content is very obscure and no ads exist for that particular content.

It's hard to imagine a better use of a coffee break than kicking back and counting the money you've earned for doing nothing. Visit https://www.google.com/ adsense/report/overview to view the latest commission report on your AdSense ads. Even if you haven't generated many click-throughs that convert to cash, you can at least see how many times people have viewed ads.

The Wide World of JavaScript

You've learned enough in this hour to have a head start on JavaScript and to add some snazzy interaction to your web pages. You've probably also gotten the idea that there's a lot more you can do, and it isn't as hard as you may have thought.

You may also find some scripts online that can be incorporated into a web page of your own with little or no modification. (Check out the JavaScript-related links in the files located at http://www.samspublishing.com/ for good places to find scripts.)

When you find scripts you'd like to reuse or experiment with, pay attention to the placement of the JavaScript code; generally, functions go in the `<head>` area, preceded by `<script type="text/javascript">` and followed by `</script>`. The parts of the script that actually carry out the actions when the page is loaded go in the `<body>` part of the page, but still need to be set aside with the `<script>` tag. Sections of script that respond to specific events such as mouse moves go in the `<a>` or `<input>` tags, with special event attributes such as `onmouseover`.

You can also put JavaScript code into a separate file (usually with a `.js` file extension) by putting the name of the file in a `src` attribute within the `<script />` tag, like the following:

```
<script type="text/javascript" src="bingo.js" />
```

This is especially handy when you are using a script that someone else wrote and you don't want it cluttering up your HTML.

Summary

In this hour you've seen how to use scripting to make the images on your web pages respond to mouse movements. You've also seen how similar JavaScript commands can be used to change multiple images at once and to create practical web page features such as animated ad banners. You even found out how to display random quotes, move images around dynamically, and place Google ads that can earn you money. None of these tasks requires much in the way of programming skills, though they may inspire you to learn the JavaScript language to give your pages more complex interactive features.

Q&A

Q *Doesn't Microsoft promote the usage of a different scripting language for Internet Explorer?*

A Yes. Microsoft definitely would prefer that you use its own scripting language based on Visual Basic called VBScript, but Internet Explorer also fully supports JavaScript. Some commands work slightly differently in the Microsoft implementation of JavaScript than they do in Mozilla Firefox, but because the JavaScript code covered in this hour works exactly the same in all major browsers, you can reuse it with confidence.

Q *I want to display ad banner images that each link to different web pages. How difficult is this?*

A It's not terribly difficult, but it does require a level of JavaScript programming knowledge that is outside the realm of this hour. If you'd like to build on the examples in this hour and tweak them to do more interesting things, I highly recommend that you spend some time to learn JavaScript. Otherwise, you should probably stick to using the examples without major modification.

Workshop

The workshop contains quiz questions and activities to help you solidify your understanding of the material covered. Try to answer all questions before looking at the "Answers" section that follows.

Quiz

1. Say you've made a picture of a button and named it `button.gif`. You've also made a simple GIF animation of the button flashing green and white and named it `flashing.gif`. Write the HTML and JavaScript code to make the button flash whenever someone moves the mouse pointer over it, and link to a page named `gohere.html` when someone clicks the button.

2. How would you modify what you wrote for question 1 so that the button starts flashing when someone moves the mouse over it, and keeps flashing even if he or she moves the mouse away?

3. Write the HTML code for a JavaScript function that displays five banner ads with a four-second delay between each one. The ID of the banner `<img>` tag is `mybanner`, and the banner images themselves are named `banthis1.jpg`, `banthis2.jpg`, and so on.

Answers

1. ```
   <a href="gohere.html"
   onmouseover="flasher.src='flashing.gif';
   onmouseout="flasher.src='button.gif'">
   <img src="button.gif" alt="" id="flasher" style="border-style:none" /></a>
   ```

2. ```
   <a href="gohere.html"
   onmouseover="flasher.src='flashing.gif'">
   <img src="button.gif" alt="" id="flasher" style="border-style:none" /></a>
   ```

```
3. function rotateBanner() {
     if (++bannerNum > 5)
       bannerNum = 1;
     document.getElementById("mybanner").src = "banthis" + bannerNum + ".jpg";
     window.setTimeout('rotateBanner();', 4000);
   }
```

Exercises

Hey, what are you waiting for? Now that you're an HTML expert, get yourself a copy of *Sams Teach Yourself JavaScript in 21 Days* or *JavaScript Bible* and take the next quantum leap in web publishing!

Gathering Information with HTML Forms

Up to this point, pretty much everything in this book has focused on getting information out to others. (Email links, introduced in Hour 6, "Creating Text Links," are a notable exception.) But HTML is a two-way street; you can use your web pages to gather information from the people who read them as well.

Web forms allow you to receive feedback, orders, or other information from the people who visit and read your web pages. If you've ever used a web search engine such as Google, Lycos, or Yahoo!, you're familiar with HTML forms. Product order forms are also an extremely popular use of forms. This lesson shows you how to create your own forms and the basics of how to handle form submissions.

An HTML **form** is part of a web page that includes areas where readers can enter information to be sent back to you, the publisher of the page.

How HTML Forms Work

Before you learn the HTML tags that are used to make your own forms, you should understand how the information that someone fills out on a form makes its way back to you. You also probably need to have the person who runs your web server computer set it up to process your forms.

Every form must include a button for the user to submit the form. When someone clicks that button, all the information he filled in is sent (in a standard format) to an Internet address that you specify in the form itself. You have to put a special forms-processing program at that address in order for that information to get to you, or you can choose to receive the formatted information via email.

Almost all ISP companies that offer web page hosting also provide preprogrammed scripts to their customers for processing forms. You don't need to use a script if you only want to have form information sent to your email address. Scripts allow you to take things a step further by somehow processing form information and possibly saving it to a database or routing it to a web service such as a secure payment service. A form-processing script usually generates some sort of reply page and sends it back to be displayed for the user.

It's possible to set things up so that much of the information from a form is interpreted and processed automatically. For example, server software exists to authorize a credit-card transaction automatically over the Internet, confirm an order to the customer's email address, and enter the order directly into your company's in-house database for shipment. Obviously, setting up that sort of thing can get quite complex, and it's beyond the scope of this book to explain all the things you can do with form data after it has been submitted.

Most ISPs that host web pages already have a "generic" form-processing script set up and will happily tell you the exact HTML code required to use it. If your ISP can't do this, or charges you an extra fee for it, frankly you are probably not using a very good ISP! In that case, you have the following choices:

- ▶ Switch to a more helpful web hosting service.
- ▶ Learn advanced server programming.
- ▶ Use a form-creation service such as freedback.com to create and process your forms. (Although such services are free and work great, they will display other companies' advertising to everyone who uses your forms.)

Try It Yourself

Before you put a form online, you should do the following:

- ▶ Ask your ISP what it offers in the way of form-processing scripts, along with the exact address to which your forms should send their information. Later in this hour, you'll see where and how to put that address into your forms.

- ▶ If you run your own web server computer, the server software probably came with some basic form-processing scripts. Consult your documentation to set them up properly and find the address on your server where each is located.

- ▶ If you're not sure what scripts are available and you want to start with the simplest form-processing approach, configure your forms to simply send the raw form data to your email address. The examples in this hour use such a technique. You can experiment with fancy scripts later.

Creating a Form

Every form must begin with a `<form>` tag, which can be located anywhere in the body of the HTML document. The form tag normally has two attributes, method and action:

```
<form method="post" action="mailto:me@mysite.com">
```

Nowadays, the method is almost always post, which means to send the form entry results as a document. (In some special situations, you may need to use method="get", which submits the results as part of the URL header instead. For example, get is sometimes used when submitting queries to search engines from a web form. Because you're not yet an expert on forms, just use post unless your web server administrator tells you to do otherwise.)

The action attribute specifies the address to which to send the form data. You have two options here:

▶ You can type the location of a form-processing program or script on a web server, and the form data will then be sent to that program.

▶ You can type mailto: followed by your email address, and the form data will be sent directly to you whenever someone fills out the form. However, this approach is completely dependent on the user's computer being properly configured with an email client. People accessing your site from a public computer without an email client will be left out in the cold.

Many ISPs offer free scripts you can use to process forms. Be sure to check with your ISP or web server administrator to find out whether any such scripts are available. If so, you'll simply reference the appropriate script in the action attribute of the <form> tag. Otherwise, you'll need to stick with receiving form data via email.

By the Way

The form given in Listing 18.1 and shown in Figure 18.1 includes just about every type of user input component you can currently use on HTML forms. Figure 18.2 shows how the form in Figure 18.1 might look after someone has filled it out. Refer to these figures as you read the following explanations of each type of input element.

LISTING 18.1   All Parts of a Form Must Fall Between the <form> and </form> Tags

```
<?xml version="1.0" encoding="UTF-8"?>
<!DOCTYPE html PUBLIC "-//W3C//DTD XHTML 1.1//EN"
  "http://www.w3.org/TR/xhtml11/DTD/xhtml11.dtd">

<html xmlns="http://www.w3.org/1999/xhtml" xml:lang="en">
  <head>
    <title>Guest Book</title>
  </head>

  <body>
    <h1>My Guest Book</h1>
    <p>
      Please let me know what you think of my web pages. Thanks!
    </p>
```

LISTING 18.1   Continued

```
<form method="post" action="mailto:you@youremail.com"
enctype="text/plain">
<p>
  What is your name? <input type="text" name="fullname" size="25" /><br />
  Your e-mail address: <input type="text" name="e-address" size="25" />
</p>
<p>
  Please check all that apply:<br />
  <input type="checkbox" name="likeit" checked="checked" />I really like
  your Web site.<br />
  <input type="checkbox" name="best" />One of the best sites I've
  seen.<br />
  <input type="checkbox" name="envy" />I sure wish my pages looked as good
  as yours.<br />
  <input type="checkbox" name="love" />I think I'm in love with you.<br />
  <input type="checkbox" name="idiot" />I have no taste and I'm pretty
  dense, so your site didn't do much for me.
</p>
<p>
  Choose the one thing you love best about my web pages:<br />
  <input type="radio" name="lovebest" value="me" checked="checked" />That
  gorgeous picture of you and your cats.<br />
  <input type="radio" name="lovebest" value="cats" />All those moving poems
  about your cats.<br />
  <input type="radio" name="lovebest" value="burbs" />The inspiring recap of
  your suburban childhood.<br />
  <input type="radio" name="lovebest" value="treasures" />The detailed list
  of all your Elvis memorabilia.
</p>
<p>
  Imagine my site as a book, video, or album. Select the number of copies
  you think it would sell:<br />
  <select size="3" name="potential">
    <option selected="selected">Million copy bestseller for sure!</option>
    <option>100,000+ (would be Oprah's favorite)</option>
    <option>Thousands (an under-appreciated classic)</option>
    <option>Very few: not banal enough for today's public</option>
  </select>
</p>
<p>
  How do you think I could improve my site?
  <select name="suggestion">
    <option selected="selected">Couldn't be better</option>
    <option>More about the cats</option>
    <option>More Elvis stuff</option>
    <option>More family pictures</option>
  </select>
</p>
<p>
  Feel free to type more praise, gift offers, etc. below:<br />
  <textarea name="comments" rows="4" cols="55">I just want to thank you so
  much for touching my life.</textarea><br />
  <input type="submit" value="Click Here to Submit" />
  <input type="reset" value="Erase and Start Over" />
</p>
</form>
</body>
</html>
```

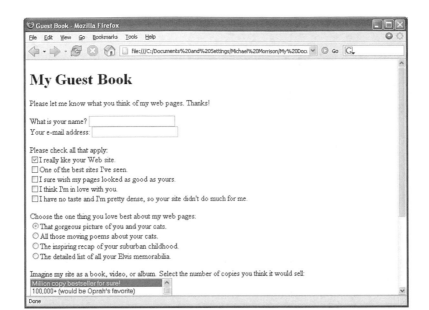

FIGURE 18.1
The form code shown in Listing 18.1 uses nearly every type of HTML form input element.

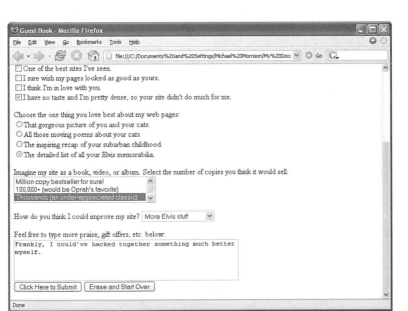

FIGURE 18.2
Visitors to your web site fill out the form and then click the Click Here to Submit button.

The code for this page (Listing 18.1) uses a <form> tag that contains quite a few <input /> tags. Each <input /> tag corresponds to a specific user input component, such as a check box or radio button. The next few sections dig into the <input /> tag in detail.

Accepting Text Input

To ask the user for a specific piece of information within a form, use the `<input />` tag. This tag must fall between the `<form>` and `</form>` tags, but it can be anywhere on the page in relation to text, images, and other HTML tags. For example, to ask for someone's name you could type the following:

```
What's your first name? <input type="text" size="20" maxlength="30"
name="firstname" />
What's your last name? <input type="text" size="20" maxlength="30"
name="lastname" />
```

The `type` attribute indicates what type of form element to display—a simple one-line text entry box in this case. (Each element type is discussed individually in the following sections.)

The `size` attribute indicates approximately how many characters wide the text input box should be. If you are using a proportionally spaced font, the width of the input will vary depending on what the user enters. If the input is too long to fit in the box, most web browsers will automatically scroll the text to the left.

`maxlength` determines the number of characters the user is allowed to type into the text box. If someone tries to type beyond the specified length, the extra characters won't appear. You can specify a length that is longer, shorter, or the same as the physical size of the text box. `size` and `maxlength` are used only for `type="text"` because other input types (check boxes, radio buttons, and so on) have a fixed size.

Did you Know?

> If you want the user to enter text without it being displayed on the screen, you can use `<input type="password" />` instead of `<input type="text" />`. Asterisks (***) are then displayed in place of the text the user types. The `size`, `maxlength`, and `name` attributes work exactly the same for `type="password"` as for `type="text"`. Keep in mind that this technique of hiding a password provides only visual protection—there is no encryption or other protection associated with the password being transmitted.

Identifying Each Piece of Form Data

No matter what type an input element is, you must give a name to the data it gathers. You can use any name you like for each input item, as long as each one on the form is different. When the form is sent to you (or to your form-processing script), each data item is identified by name.

For example, if someone entered Jane and Doe in the text box defined previously, you would see something like the following two lines in the email message you get when the form is submitted:

```
firstname=Jane
lastname=Doe
```

The following code is a sample email message generated by the form-processing script specified in the form in Listing 18.1. Notice that each data element is identified by the name given to it in Listing 18.1:

```
fullname=Frank Rizzo
e-address=frank@rizzoratchets.com
idiot=on
lovebest=treasures
potential=Thousands (an under-appreciated classic)
suggestion=More Elvis stuff
comments=Frankly, I could've hacked together something much better myself.
```

Depending on the specific manner in which your web server processes email forms, you might see the data in a different format than that shown here.

By the Way

Including Hidden Data in Forms

Want to send certain data items to the server script that processes a form but don't want the user to see them? Use the input type="hidden" attribute. This attribute has no effect on the display at all; it just adds any name and value you specify to the form results when they are submitted.

You might use this attribute to tell a script where to email the form results. For example, the following might indicate that the results should be mailed to me@mysite.com:

```
<input type="hidden" name="mail_to" value="me@mysite.com" />
```

For this attribute to have any effect, someone must create a script or program to read this line and do something about it. My ISP's form script uses this hidden value to determine where to email the form data.

Most scripts require at least one or two hidden input elements. Consult the person who wrote or provided you with the script for details.

Exploring Form Input Controls

Various input controls are available for retrieving information from the user. You've already learned about some text entry options for forms. The next few sections introduce you to most of the remaining form input options you can use to design forms.

Check Boxes

The simplest input type is a *check box*, which appears as a small square the user can select or deselect by clicking; a check box functions as an on/off switch. You must give each check box a name via the name attribute. If you want a check box to be checked by default when the form comes up, include the checked attribute. For example, the following code creates two check boxes:

```
<input type="checkbox" name="baby" checked="checked" />Baby Grand Piano<br />
<input type="checkbox" name="mini" />Mini Piano Stool
```

> If you find that the label for an input element is displayed too close to the element, just add a space between the close of the <input /> tag and the start of the label text, like this:
>
> ```
> <input type="checkbox" name="mini" /> Mini Piano Stool
> ```

The check box labeled Baby Grand Piano is checked in this example. (The user would have to click it to turn it off if he didn't want a piano.) The one marked Mini Piano Stool would be unchecked to begin with, so the user would have to click it to turn it on.

When the form is submitted, selected check boxes appear in the form result:

```
baby=on
```

Blank (*deselected*) check boxes do not appear in the form output at all.

Watch Out!

> XHTML requires all attributes to have an equal sign followed by a value. This explains why I've used checked="checked" to indicate that a check box is checked, as opposed to just checked. This rule applies to all Boolean (true/false, on/off, yes/no, and so on) attributes that you may come across in HTML.

Did you
Know?

You can use more than one check box with the same name, but with different values, as in the following code:

```
<input type="checkbox" name="pet" value="dog"> dog<br />
<input type="checkbox" name="pet" value="cat"> cat<br />
<input type="checkbox" name="pet" value="iguana"> iguana
```

If the user checks both Cat and Iguana, the submission result includes the following:

```
pet=cat
pet=iguana
```

Radio Buttons

Radio buttons, for which only one choice can be selected at a time, are almost as simple to implement as check boxes. Just use `type="radio"` and give each of the options its own `<input />` tag, but use the same name for all the radio buttons in a group:

```
<input type="radio" name="card" value="v" checked="checked" /> Visa<br />
<input type="radio" name="card" value="m" /> MasterCard
```

The `value` can be any name or code you choose. If you include the `checked` attribute, that button is selected by default. (No more than one radio button with the same name can be checked.)

If the user selects `MasterCard` from the preceding radio button set, the following is included in the form submission to the server script:

```
card=m
```

If the user doesn't change the default `checked` selection, `card=v` is sent instead.

Selection Lists

Both *scrolling lists* and *pull-down pick lists* are created with the `<select>` tag. You use this tag together with the `<option>` tag, as this example reveals:

```
<select name="extras" size="3" multiple="multiple">
  <option selected="selected">Electric windows</option>
  <option>AM/FM Radio</option>
  <option>Turbocharger</option>
</select>
```

No HTML tags other than `<option>` and `</option>` should appear between the `<select>` and `</select>` tags.

Unlike the `text` input type, the `size` attribute here determines how many items show at once on the selection list. If `size="2"` were used in the preceding code, only the first two options would be visible, and a scrollbar would appear next to the list so that the user could scroll down to see the third option.

Including the `multiple` attribute allows users to select more than one option at a time, and the `selected` attribute makes an option initially selected by default. The actual text that accompanies selected options is returned when the form is submitted. If the user selected `Electric windows` and `Turbocharger`, for instance, the form results would include the following lines:

```
extras=Electric windows
extras=Turbocharger
```

(As I cautioned you earlier with regard to the `checked` attribute, XHTML requires you to use `multiple="multiple"` and `selected="selected"`.)

If you leave out the `size` attribute or specify `size="1"`, the list will create a pull-down pick list. Pick lists cannot allow multiple choices; they are logically equivalent to a group of radio buttons. For example, another way to choose between credit card types follows:

```
<select name="card">
  <option>Visa</option>
  <option>MasterCard</option>
</select>
```

Text Areas

The `<input type="text">` attribute mentioned earlier allows the user to enter only a single line of text. When you want to allow multiple lines of text in a single input item, use the `<textarea>` and `</textarea>` tags instead. Any text you include between these two tags is displayed as the default entry. Here's an example:

```
<textarea name="comments" rows="4" cols="20">Please send more information.
</textarea>
```

As you probably guessed, the `rows` and `cols` attributes control the number of rows and columns of text that fit in the input box. The `cols` attribute is a little less exact than `rows`, and approximates the number of characters that fit in a row of text. Text area boxes do have a scrollbar, however, so the user can enter more text than fits in the display area.

Submitting Form Data

Every form must include a button that submits the form data to the server. You can put any label you like on this button with the value attribute:

```
<input type="submit" value="Place My Order Now!" />
```

A gray button will be sized to fit the label you put in the value attribute. When the user clicks it, all data items on the form are sent to the email address or program script specified in the form action attribute.

You can also include a button that clears all entries on the form so that users can start over if they change their minds or make mistakes. Use the following:

```
<input type="reset" value="Clear This Form and Start Over" />
```

If the standard Submit and Reset buttons look a little bland to you, you'll be glad to know that there is an easy way to substitute your own graphics for these buttons. Type the following to use an image of your choice for a Submit button:

```
<input type="image" src="button.gif" alt="Order Now!" />
```

The image named button.gif will appear on the page, and the form will be submitted whenever someone clicks the button.gif image. You can also include any attributes normally used with the <img /> tag, such as alt and style. (Hour 8, "Putting Graphics on a Web Page," introduces the <img /> tag.)

The exact pixel coordinates where the mouse clicked an image button are sent along with the form data. For example, if someone entered sol@shoesandglasses.net in the form as shown in Figure 18.3, the resulting form data might look like the following:

```
anotherone=sol@shoesandglasses.net_&x=75_&y=36
```

Normally you should ignore the x and y coordinates, but some server scripts use them to turn the button into an imagemap.

By the Way

Listing 18.2 and Figure 18.3 show a very simple form that uses a customized Submit button. (You saw how to make graphics similar to the signup.gif button in Hour 7, "Creating Your Own Web Page Graphics.")

LISTING 18.2   This Page Uses an <input /> Tag as a Custom Graphical Submit Button

```
<?xml version="1.0" encoding="UTF-8"?>
<!DOCTYPE html PUBLIC "-//W3C//DTD XHTML 1.1//EN"
  "http://www.w3.org/TR/xhtml11/DTD/xhtml11.dtd">
```

LISTING 18.2   Continued

```
<html xmlns="http://www.w3.org/1999/xhtml" xml:lang="en">
  <head>
    <title>FREE!</title>
  </head>

  <body>
    <h1>Free Electronic Junk Mail!</h1>
    <form method="post" action="mailto:you@youremail.com" enctype="text/plain">
      <p>
        To start receiving junk e-mail from us daily*, enter your e-mail address
        below and click on the <em>SignUP!</em> button.
      </p>
      <p>
        <input type="text" name="anotherone" size="25" />
        <input type="image" src="signup.gif" alt="Sign Up Now!"
        style="vertical-align:middle" />
      </p>
      <p>
        By clicking the above button, you also agree to the terms of our
Marketing
        Agreement, which is available upon request at our offices in Bangkok,
        Thailand. A fee may be charged for removal from our list if you elect at
a
        later date not to receive additional sales literature.
      </p>
    </form>
  </body>
</html>
```

FIGURE 18.3
Forms don't need to be complex to be effective. (They might need to be a little less blunt, though.)

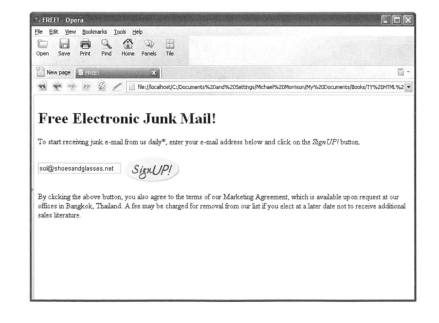

You can make a button that cancels the form and proceeds to another page (ignoring all information the user has entered so far) simply by linking to that other page. Here is an example:

```
<a href="nodice.html">Click here to cancel.</a>
```

There is no specific form type for a graphical reset button, but you can achieve the same effect by putting an image link to the current page, like this:

```
<a href="thispage.html"><img src="cancel.gif" alt="Cancel" /></a>
```

Using a PayPal Buy Now Button

One of the most common usages of forms is to carry out e-commerce, which typically involves a form that serves as a web-based shopping cart. Full-blown shopping cart forms can be very complex, but there is a simple alternative if you don't want to tackle developing a shopping cart of your own.

I'm referring to a PayPal Buy Now button, which takes advantage of the popular PayPal electronic payment service to provide a "buy now" link for your own products and services. If you haven't heard of or used PayPal before, take a moment to visit the PayPal site (http://www.paypal.com/) and take a look around.

PayPal was purchased by eBay a couple of years ago, and is now the preferred payment method for eBay auctions. Needless to say, PayPal is here to stay as an online method of payment.

PayPal makes use of forms in somewhat of an unconventional way—you use a form to create a customized button that appears simply as an image on a page. When the user clicks the image, the form data is passed along to PayPal to provide specifics about the item being purchased. By using a form to submit purchase data, a PayPal Buy Now button allows PayPal to offer a customized shopping experience without much technical mess. More important, PayPal Buy Now buttons make it very easy for web page developers to sell products and services without having to spend lots of money on expensive shopping cart applications and credit processing services.

To get started using PayPal Buy Now buttons, you first need a PayPal account. If you don't already have a PayPal account, you can create one by clicking Sign Up in the upper-left corner of the main PayPal web page (http://www.paypal.com/).

After you have an account created, log in and visit the Buy Now Buttons web page at https://www.paypal.com/us/cgi-bin/webscr?cmd=p/xcl/rec/singleitem-intro. Click the Get Started! link to start creating a PayPal Buy Now button. Figure 18.4 shows the next page that appears, which prompts you to enter information about the product or service you intend to offer for sale.

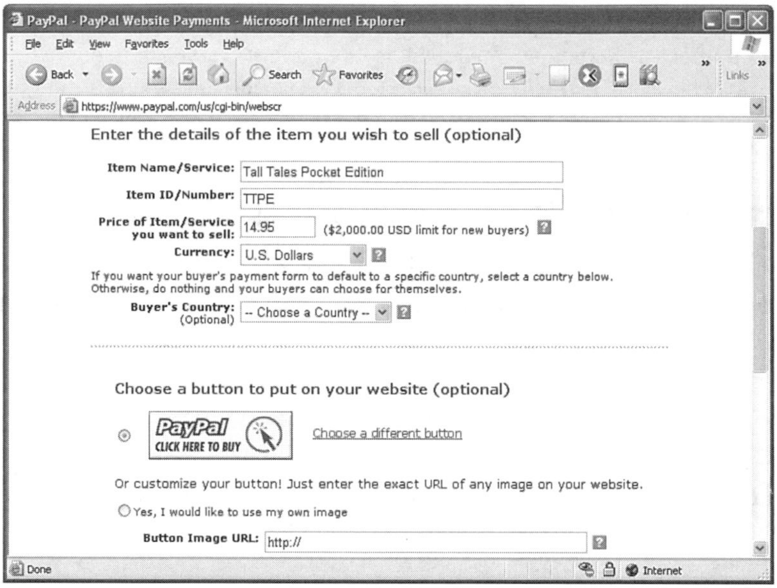

FIGURE 18.4
The PayPal Buy
Now Button tool
prompts you for
details about
the item you
want to sell.

In this example, I've entered information pertaining to a trivia game that I created for my company, Stalefish Labs. As you can see in the figure, I had to enter the name of the product, an item number, and a price; the item number can be anything you want it to be. You must also set the currency for the transaction, as in U.S. Dollars, Canadian Dollars, and so forth. You can also set the country for the buyer, which I don't recommend doing unless you have very specific requirements for the location of buyers.

Click Choose a Different Button to change the appearance of the PayPal button that will appear on your page. In the example, I opted to use a larger button that will be more prominent on the page. You can also use your own button image if you so choose.

The last option you must enter, which isn't visible in Figure 18.4, is whether you want the HTML code for the PayPal button to be encrypted for security purposes. This ensures that if someone hacks your site they'll have a much more difficult time attempting to change the price or other details of your item that is for sale. Whether to use this setting is entirely up to you—I opted not to in order to keep the code simpler for this example.

> Click the Add More Options button to set additional options for the Buy Now button—custom option fields, multiple item purchase, and an optional buyer note, to name a few. Using an encrypted Buy Now button limits some of these advanced options you can set for the button.

Figure 18.5 shows the page that is displayed after the Create Button Now button is clicked.

The figure reveals that the PayPal Buy Now Button page generates the code for a complete HTML form that you can cut and paste directly into your own pages. Just highlight the code in the first edit box, copy it, and then paste it into your page. Listing 18.3 shows an example of a web page that includes the automatically generated PayPal Buy Now button form code.

LISTING 18.3 The Tall Tales Sample Page Now Includes a PayPal Buy Now Button for Buying a Copy of the Game Through PayPal

```
<?xml version="1.0" encoding="UTF-8"?>
<!DOCTYPE html PUBLIC "-//W3C//DTD XHTML 1.1//EN"
  "http://www.w3.org/TR/xhtml11/DTD/xhtml11.dtd">

<html xmlns="http://www.w3.org/1999/xhtml" xml:lang="en">
  <head>
    <title>Tall Tales - The Game of Legends and Creative One-Upmanship</title>
```

LISTING 18.3   Continued

```
    <style type="text/css">
    ...
    </style>
  </head>

  <body>
    ...
    <p>
      To learn more about Tall Tales, visit the Tall Tales Web site at <a
      href="http://www.talltalesgame.com/">www.talltalesgame.com</a>. Or to buy
      the game just click the button below:
    </p>
    <form action="https://www.paypal.com/cgi-bin/webscr" method="post">
      <p style="text-align:center">
        <input type="hidden" name="cmd" value="_xclick" />
        <input type="hidden" name="business" value="michael@stalefishlabs.com"
/>
        <input type="hidden" name="item_name" value="Tall Tales Pocket Edition"
/>
        <input type="hidden" name="item_number" value="TTPE" />
        <input type="hidden" name="amount" value="14.95" />
        <input type="hidden" name="no_note" value="1" />
        <input type="hidden" name="currency_code" value="USD" />
        <input type="hidden" name="bn" value="PP-BuyNowBF" />
        <input type="image"
        src="https://www.paypal.com/en_US/i/btn/x-click-but5.gif"
        style="border-style:none" name="submit" alt="Make payments with
        PayPal - it's fast, free and secure!" />
      </p>
    </form>
  </body>
</html>
```

You may recognize this page from earlier in the book. In this example, an otherwise interesting promotional page is made considerably more valuable by becoming a simplified shopping cart of sorts. In other words, now visitors to the Tall Tales page can not only learn about the game, but also buy a copy by clicking the Buy Now button and paying through PayPal (see Figure 18.6).

By the Way

It's worth mentioning that I had to make some slight changes to the code generated by PayPal. Unfortunately, PayPal doesn't crank out XHTML-compatible code. I had to place the <input /> tags within a parent <p> tag, as well as altering the border code for the button image so that it uses CSS instead of the deprecated border attribute.

Clicking the Buy Now button near the bottom of the screen shown in Figure 18.6 links you to a Checkout page on the PayPal web site, where the item details are presented before the purchase is confirmed (see Figure 18.7).

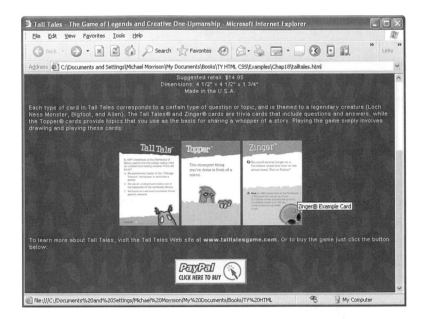

FIGURE 18.6
The PayPal form code in Listing 18.3 produces this form, which is really just a button that links to a PayPal purchase page.

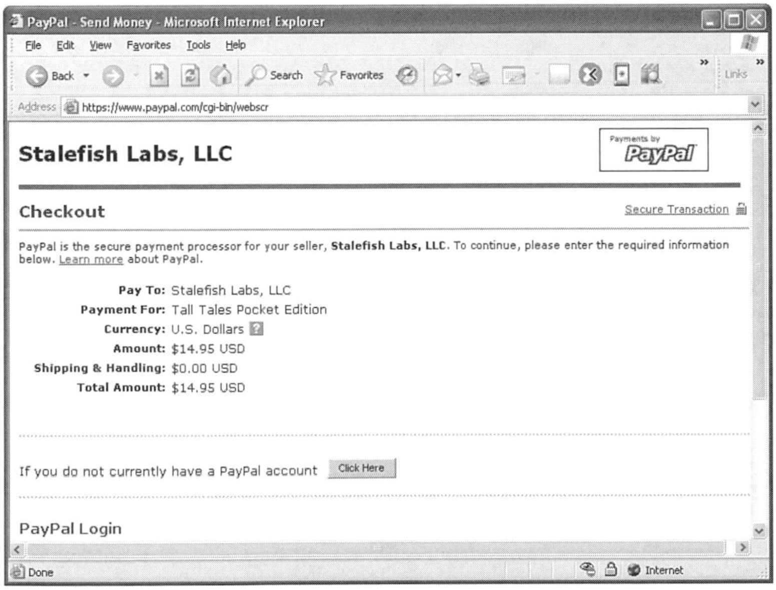

FIGURE 18.7
When the user clicks the Buy Now button, the form takes you to a PayPal purchase page where the purchase is carried out.

From here on, the transaction is purely in the hands of PayPal. The funds for purchases through a PayPal Buy Now button are automatically deposited into your PayPal account, and you receive a notification of the purchase to the email address associated with your PayPal account. Don't forget that it's still up to you to deliver the product or service to the customer—PayPal just handles the payment side of the equation.

Summary

This hour demonstrated how to create HTML forms, which allow visitors to your web pages to enter specific information and send it back to you via email. You also found that you can set up a script or program on your web server to process form data. Your ISP, web server administrator, or server software vendor can help you do this. You even learned how to make a PayPal Buy Now button that allows people to purchase and pay for items directly from your web pages, which is especially useful in a web site that accepts online orders for products. You can be doing business online and making money in just a few minutes using nothing more than the HTML form code generated for you by PayPal.

Table 18.1 summarizes the HTML tags and attributes covered in this hour.

TABLE 18.1   HTML Tags and Attributes Covered in Hour 18

Tag/Attribute	Function
`<form>...</form>`	Indicates an input form.
Attributes	
`action="scripturl"`	The address of the script to process this form input.
`method="post/get"`	How the form input will be sent to the server. Normally set to `post`, rather than `get`.
`<input />`	An input element for a form.
Attributes	
`type="controltype"`	The type for this input widget. Possible values are `checkbox`, `hidden`, `radio`, `reset`, `submit`, `text`, and `image`.
`name="name"`	The unique name of this item, as passed to the script.
`value="value"`	The default value for a text or hidden item; for a check box or radio button, the value to be submitted with the form; for reset or submit buttons, the label for the button itself.
`src="imageurl"`	The source file for an image.
`checked="checked"`	For check boxes and radio buttons, indicates that this item is checked.
`size="width"`	The width, in characters, of a text input region.

TABLE 18.1   Continued

Tag/Attribute	Function
maxlength="*maxlength*"	The maximum number of characters that can be entered into a text region.
<textarea>... </textarea>	Indicates a multiline text entry form element. Default text can be included.
Attributes	
name="*name*"	The name to be passed to the script.
rows="*numrows*"	The number of rows this text area displays.
cols="*numchars*"	The number of columns (characters) this text area displays.
<select>...</select>	Creates a menu or scrolling list of possible items.
Attributes	
name="*name*"	The name that is passed to the script.
size="*numelements*"	The number of elements to display. If size is indicated, the selection becomes a scrolling list. If no size is given, the selection is a pop-up menu.
multiple="multiple"	Allows multiple selections from the list.
<option>...</option>	Indicates a possible item within a <select> element.
Attributes	
selected="selected"	With this attribute included, the option will be selected by default in the list.
value="*value*"	The value to submit if this option is selected when the form is submitted.

Q&A

Q *I've heard that it's dangerous to send credit card numbers over the Internet. Can't thieves intercept form data on its way to me?*

A It is possible to intercept form data (and any web pages or email messages) as it travels through the Internet. If you ask for credit card numbers or other sensitive information on your forms, you should ask the company who runs your web server about secure forms processing. There are several reliable technologies for eliminating the risk of high-tech eavesdroppers, but you typically must pay for them—you will usually need to obtain a security certificate from a secure services provider such as Thawte (http://www.thawte.com/) or VeriSign (http://www.verisign.com/).

To put the amount of risk in perspective, remember that it is much more difficult to intercept information traveling through the Internet than it is to look over someone's shoulder in a restaurant or retail store. Even so, you should always utilize secure pages anytime you're handling sensitive financial information such as credit card numbers, especially when someone else is trusting you to handle theirs.

Q *Can I put forms on a CD/DVD-ROM, or do they have to be on the Internet?*

A You can put a form anywhere you can put a web page. If it's on a disk or CD-ROM instead of a web server, it can be filled out by people whether or not they are connected to the Internet. Of course, they must be connected to the Internet (or your local intranet) when they click the Submit button, or the information won't get to you.

Q *I still don't quite understand when to use a script to process forms and when to use email. What gives?*

A The decision to use a server script to process form data primarily has to do with whether you have access to such a script. A form processing script is almost always a better approach than simply receiving raw form data in an email message, and it's smoother on the user side of the equation as well. However, you may not have access to your web server, and even if you do, you may not be able to find a script that does exactly what you want. This is a situation in which you should ask some questions of your ISP or web server administrator to find out what your form processing options are.

Workshop

The workshop contains quiz questions and activities to help you solidify your understanding of the material covered. Try to answer all questions before looking at the "Answers" section that follows.

Quiz

1. Write the HTML code to create a guestbook form that asks someone for his or her name, sex, age, and email address. Assume that you have a form-processing script set up at /cgi/generic and that you need to include the following hidden input element to tell the script where to send the form results:

```
<input type="hidden" name="mailto" value="you@yoursite.com" />
```

2. If you created an image named `sign-in.gif`, how would you use it as the Submit button for the guestbook in question 1?

Answers

1.
```
<html>

  <head>
    <title>My Guestbook</title>
  </head>

  <body>
    <h1>My Guestbook: Please Sign In</h1>
    <form method="post" action="/cgi/generic">
      <p>
        <input type="hidden" name="mailto" value="you@yoursite.com" />
        Your name: <input type="text" name="name" size="20" /><br />
        Your sex: <input type="radio" name="sex" value="male" /> male
        <input type="radio" name="sex" value="female" /> female<br />
        Your age: <input type="text" name="age" size="4" /><br />
        Your e-mail address: <input type="text" name="email" size="30" />
        <br />
        <input type="submit" value="sign in" />
        <input type="reset" value="erase" />
      </p>
    </form>
  </body>
</html>
```

2. Replace
```
<input type="submit" value="Sign In" />
```

with
```
<input type="image" src="sign-in.gif" lat="Sign In" />
```

Exercises

▶ Try creating a form using all the different types of input elements and selection lists to make sure you understand how each of them works.

▶ Create a PayPal Buy Now button to offer something for sale on your web site. You could have the world's most high-tech lemonade stand!

Embedding Multimedia in Web Pages

Multimedia is a popular buzzword for sound, motion video, and interactive animation. This hour shows you how to include multimedia in your web pages.

The first thing you should be aware of is that Internet multimedia is still an evolving technology. Computer multimedia in general is actually relatively new, but Internet multimedia is even newer, and is therefore in a more noticeable state of change. The rapid pace of growth for Internet multimedia creates three obstacles for anyone who wants to include audiovisual material in a web page:

- ▶ There are many incompatible multimedia file formats from which to choose, and none has yet emerged as a singular industry standard.

- ▶ Some people do not have Internet connections fast enough to receive high-quality audiovisual data without a long wait.

- ▶ HTML tags for including multimedia in web pages have been notoriously inconsistent; XHTML offers a standard approach that is helping to set everything straight.

The moral of the story: Whatever you do today to implement a multimedia web site, be prepared for inevitable changes as multimedia file formats and technologies continue to evolve.

The good news is that you can sidestep these obstacles to some extent today, and they are all likely to become even easier to overcome in the near future. This hour first shows you how to put multimedia on your web pages for maximum compatibility with all web browsers, both new and old. It also introduces you to the standard XHTML approach to placing multimedia on web pages, which provides a clear roadmap to the future of multimedia on the web.

▼

Try It Yourself

Before you see how to place multimedia on your web pages in any way, you need to have some multimedia content to start with.

Creating multimedia of any kind can be a challenging and complicated task. If you're planning to create your own content from scratch, you'll need far more than this book to become the next crackerjack multimedia developer. After you have some content, however, this hour will show you how to place your new creations into your web pages.

For those of us who are artistically challenged, several alternative ways to obtain useful multimedia assets are available. Aside from the obvious (such as hiring an artist), here are a few suggestions:

1. The Web itself is chock-full of useful content of all media types, and stock media clearinghouses of all shapes and sizes now exist online. See the hotlist at the *Sams Publishing* website—for links to some of the best stock media sources on the Web.

2. Don't feel like spending any money? Much of the material on the Internet is free. Of course, it's still a good idea to double-check with the author or current owner of the content; you don't want to be sued for copyright infringement. In addition, various offices of the U.S. government generate content which, by law, belongs to all Americans. (Any NASA footage found online, for instance, is free for your use.)

3. Many search engines (google.com, yahoo.com, lycos.com, and so on) have specific search capabilities for finding multimedia files. As long as you are careful about copyright issues, this can be an easy way to find multimedia related to a specific topic.

4. Check out the online forums, Usenet newsgroups, and RSS news feeds that cater to the interests of videographers. As clearly as possible, describe your site and what you want to do with it. Chances are you'll find a few up-and-coming artists who'd be more than happy to let thousands of people peruse their work online.

▲

Placing Multimedia Content on a Web Page

The following sections show you how to add some audio and video to a web page in two ways:

▶ The "old way" for maximum compatibility with all web browsers, including very old ones

▶ The "new way" that works only with the latest versions of web browsers, but serves as the official standard technique for the present and future

I use QuickTime video (.mov), Windows Media Video (.wmv), streaming RealAudio (.ra, .ram), and MIDI (.mid) sound files in this hour's sample pages. I've done this primarily for better compatibility with non-Windows computers. However, you could just as easily use Windows AVI or MPEG video files, as well as MP3, Windows Media Audio, or even AAC (iTunes) audio files. The good news is that the procedures shown in this hour for incorporating multimedia into your web pages are the same, no matter which media format you choose.

By the Way

Linking to Multimedia Files

The simplest and most reliable option for incorporating a video or audio file into your web site is to simply link it in with `<a href>`, exactly as you would link to another HTML file. (See Hour 3, "Linking to Other Web Pages," for coverage of the `<a>` tag.)

For example, the following line could be used to offer an AVI video of a hockey game:

```
<a href="hockey.mov">View the hockey video clip.</a>
```

When the user clicks the words View the hockey video clip., the hockey.mov QuickTime video file is transferred to her computer. Whichever helper application or plug-in she has installed automatically starts as soon as the file has finished downloading. If no AVI-compatible helper or plug-in can be found, the web browser offers her a chance to download the appropriate plug-in or save the video on the hard drive for later viewing.

> In case you're unfamiliar with *helper applications* (*helper apps* for short), they are the external programs that a web browser calls on to display any type of file it can't handle on its own. Generally, the helper application associated with a file type is called on whenever a web browser can't display that type of file on its own.
>
> *Plug-ins* are a special sort of helper application installed directly into a web browser, and they allow you to view multimedia content directly within the browser window.

Listing 19.1 contains the code for a web page that uses a simple image link to play a QuickTime video. The page is a modified version of the familiar pond example from Hour 9, "Custom Backgrounds and Colors."

LISTING 19.1   The <a> Tag Is Used to Link an Animated GIF Image to a QuickTime Video

```
<?xml version="1.0" encoding="UTF-8"?>
<!DOCTYPE html PUBLIC "-//W3C//DTD XHTML 1.1//EN"
  "http://www.w3.org/TR/xhtml11/DTD/xhtml11.dtd">

<html xmlns="http://www.w3.org/1999/xhtml" xml:lang="en">
  <head>
    <title>Michael's Pond</title>
  </head>

  <body style="background-image:url(water.jpg)">
    <p style="text-align:center">
      <img src="pondtitle.png" alt="Michael's Pond" />
    </p>
    <p>
      My backyard pond is not only a fun hobby but also an ongoing home
      improvement project that is both creative and relaxing. I have numerous
      fish in the pond, all Koi from various places as far as Japan, Israel,
      and Australia. Although they don't bark, purr, or fetch anything other
      than food, these fish are my pets, and good ones at that. The pond was
      built in a matter of weeks but has evolved over several years through
      a few different improvements and redesigns. I still consider it a work in
      progress, as there are always things to improve upon as I continue to
      learn more about how the pond ecosystem works, how to minimize
      maintenance, and how to get a more aesthetically pleasing look.
    </p>
    <p style="text-align:center">
      <a href="pond1.jpg"><img src="pond1_sm.jpg"
      alt="The Lotus, Floating Hyacinth, Japanese Lantern, and Waterfall All
      Add to the Drama of the Pond" style="border-style:none" /></a>
      <a href="pond2.jpg"><img src="pond2_sm.jpg"
      alt="Feeding Time is Always Full of Excitement"
      style="border-style:none" /></a>
      <a href="pond3.jpg"><img src="pond3_sm.jpg"
      alt="One of the Larger Fish Cruises for Dinner"
      style="border-style:none" /></a>
      <a href="pond4.jpg"><img src="pond4_sm.jpg"
      alt="A Dragonfly Hovers Over the Lotus for a Quick Drink"
      style="border-style:none" /></a>
    </p>
```

LISTING 19.1 Continued

```
    <p style="text-align:center">
      To view a video of my fish playing in the pond, click the video below:
      <br />
      <a href="pond.mov"><img src="projector.gif" alt="Pond Video"
      style="border-style:none" /></a>
    </p>
  </body>
</html>
```

Most of the code in the listing is from the original pond example. However, the following code in particular is new:

```
<a href="pond.mov"><img src="projector.gif" alt="Pond Video"
style="border-style:none" /></a>
```

This code uses the `projector.gif` animated GIF image as a link to the `pond.mov` QuickTime video clip. Figure 19.1 shows the pond sample page with the projector image in view.

FIGURE 19.1
The `projector.gif` animated GIF image is used as an image link to a QuickTime movie.

All you must do to view the video is click the animated projector. This results in the browser either playing the video with the help of a plug-in, if one is found that can play the clip, or deferring to a suitable helper application. Figure 19.2 shows Mozilla Firefox playing the QuickTime movie using a plug-in.

If your browser has no support for QuickTime, you can download the QuickTime player free from Apple at http://www.apple.com/quicktime/. Even if you do have QuickTime installed, some browsers may still play QuickTime movies differently based on whether a plug-in is installed. For example, on my Windows computer Internet Explorer and Firefox both play QuickTime movies directly in the browser window via a plug-in, whereas Opera launches QuickTime as a helper application.

FIGURE 19.2
When you follow the image link, the pond.mov QuickTime movie is played using the QuickTime browser plug-in.

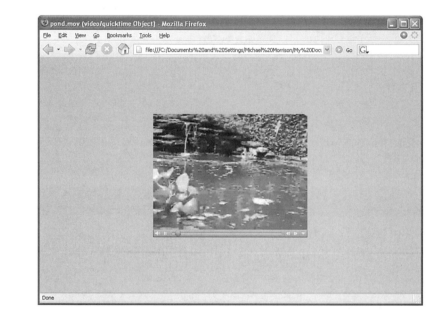

As you might have guessed, this approach of using a simple link to play multimedia files offers the best backward compatibility because it puts all the responsibility of figuring out how to play a multimedia clip on the browser. The downside to this is that you don't have much control over how a clip is played, and you definitely can't play a clip directly in the context of a page.

Embedding Video with Windows Media Player

Over the past few years, browser vendors have offered various conflicting solutions to the problem of how to put multimedia on a web page. Some of these, such as Microsoft's proprietary extensions to the <img> tag, are now completely obsolete.

Another nonstandard tag is Netscape's <embed /> tag, which became quite popular but was eventually replaced by the standard <object>, which is now the preferred way to embed multimedia of any kind in a web page. The <object> tag is also part of the XHTML standard, so you should use it instead of the <embed /> tag if you plan on creating valid HTML web pages. However, not all browsers fully support the <object> tag, so it's not a bad idea to use a combination of the <object> and <embed /> tags for the time being for maximum browser compatibility.

Part of the problem with the <object> tag historically is that it was slow to be adopted in web browsers. supported consistently across different browsers. This mainly had to do with the fact that Internet Explorer supported the <object> tag for quite some time before it was standardized, and included several proprietary attributes that weren't supported in Netscape Navigator or other browsers at the time. Although some of these inconsistencies have been ironed out, it's still not possible to use the <object> tag alone and achieve consistency across different browsers—more on how to solve this problem in a moment.

Following is code to embed the pond video, which you saw earlier, using the <object> tag by itself:

```
<object classid="CLSID:6BF52A52-394A-11d3-B153-00C04F79FAA6" width="320"
height="305">
  <param name="type" value="video/x-ms-wmv" />
  <param name="URL" value="pond.wmv" />
  <param name="uiMode" value="full" />
  <param name="autoStart" value="true" />
</object>
```

This code isn't too terribly complicated when you consider that it is literally embedding a video directly into your web page (see Figure 19.3). The messiest part of the code is the classid attribute of the <object> tag, which is set to a big long alphanumeric code. This code is the "global ID" for Microsoft Windows Media Player, which means that you're telling the <object> tag to embed Windows Media Player on the page to play the video clip. You can just copy and paste this code into your own web pages.

It's important to note that Windows Media Player is a sophisticated enough media player that it automatically *streams* multimedia files, which means that it begins playing them after loading only the first few seconds of content. The idea is that the rest of the content is loaded in the background while you're watching or listening to earlier portions. The result is that visitors don't have to wait through long download times when viewing or listening to your multimedia clips.

By the Way

The width and height attributes of the <object> tag determine the size of the embedded Windows Media Player window. Some browsers will automatically size the embedded player to fit the content if you leave these attributes off, whereas others won't show anything at all—play it safe and set them to a size that suits the multimedia content being played.

There are four <param> tags within the <object> tag that are responsible for additional details about how the clip is to be played. Each of these tags has two attributes, name and value, which are responsible for associating data (value) with a particular setting (name). In this example, the URL for the media clip is set to pond.wmv. The third parameter, uiMode, determines which buttons and user interface options are made available by Windows Media Player—full indicates that all user interfaces features are enabled, such as the control buttons and volume slider. And finally, the autoStart parameter is set to true so that the video clip automatically starts playing when the page is opened in a browser.

I saved the trickiest parameter for last—the type parameter identifies the type of media being displayed, which in this case is a Windows Media Video (WMV) file. This media type must be specified as one of the standard Internet MIME types, which you might have heard of. Following are the MIME types for several popular sound and video formats you might want to use in your web pages:

- ▶ WAV Audio—audio/x-wav

- ▶ AU Audio—audio/basic

- ▶ MP3 Audio—audio/mpeg

- ▶ MIDI Audio—audio/midi

- ▶ WMA Audio—audio/x-ms-wma

- ▶ RealAudio—audio/x-pn-realaudio-plugin

- ▶ AVI—video/x-msvideo

- ▶ WMV—video/x-ms-wmv

- ▶ MPEG Video—video/mpeg

- ▶ QuickTime—video/quicktime

A MIME type is an identifier for uniquely identifying different types of media objects on the Internet. MIME stands for Multipurpose Internet Mail Extensions, and this name comes from the fact that MIME types were originally used to identify email attachments. These MIME types should be used in the type attribute of the <object> tag to identify what kind of multimedia object is being referenced in the data attribute.

Listing 19.2 shows the relevant code for the pond web page, where you can see the <object> tag as it appears in context.

LISTING 19.2   A WMV Video Clip Is Embedded Directly in the Pond Page via the <object> Tag

```
<?xml version="1.0" encoding="UTF-8"?>
<!DOCTYPE html PUBLIC "-//W3C//DTD XHTML 1.1//EN"
  "http://www.w3.org/TR/xhtml11/DTD/xhtml11.dtd">

<html xmlns="http://www.w3.org/1999/xhtml" xml:lang="en">
  <head>
    <title>Michael's Pond</title>
  </head>

  <body style="background-image:url(water.jpg)">
    ...
    <p style="text-align:center">
      Following is a video of my fish playing in the pond:
    </p>
    <p style="text-align:center">
      <object classid="CLSID:6BF52A52-394A-11d3-B153-00C04F79FAA6" width="320"
      height="305">
        <param name="URL" value="pond.wmv" />
```

LISTING 19.2   Continued

```
        <param name="uiMode" value="full" />
        <param name="autoStart" value="true" />
        <embed width="320" height="305" type="video/x-ms-wmv"
        src="pond.wmv" controls="All" loop="false" autostart="true"
        pluginspage="http://www.microsoft.com/windows/windowsmedia/" />
      </object>
    </p>
  </body>
</html>
```

> Because the <embed /> tag is not supported in XHTML, it will prevent your pages from validating. Unfortunately, there really is no workaround for this problem—we'll just have to wait for browsers to fully support the <object> tag by itself.

Wait a minute, there's some extra code that didn't appear in the earlier <object> tag example. Unfortunately, as I alluded to earlier in the lesson, not all web browsers are entirely consistent in their support of the <object> tag. In fact, Opera simply won't show anything if you use the <object> tag to embed the media player. For this reason, it is necessary to include an <embed /> tag within the <object> tag to account for browser inconsistencies. This isn't an ideal solution but it's all we have while browser vendors continue to lag behind prevailing standards. If you pay close attention, you'll notice that the <embed /> tag contains all the same information as the <object> tag.

> I continue to use the <embed /> tag throughout the remainder of the lesson to help ensure maximum compatibility across all major browsers. At some point in the near future, hopefully we'll be able to use the <object> tag exclusively and do away with the <embed /> tag once and for all.

I haven't entirely let on that the <object> tag is a bit more complex than I've revealed here. The reason is that you don't need to know how to use the more advanced facets of the <object> tag just to play multimedia content. In other words, it isn't important for you to become a multimedia guru in order to share some multimedia clips on your web pages.

Embedding Audio with RealPlayer

The preceding section showed you how the <object> tag can be used to embed Windows Media Player into a web page so that a video clip could be played. But what if visitors to your web site are using some other media player such as

RealPlayer? Changing the `<object>` tag to use a different player is primarily a matter of providing the appropriate `classid` for the desired player.

RealAudio is a streaming audio format that was popularized by the RealPlayer media player. To download a free version of RealPlayer, visit http://www.real.com/player/.

By the
Way

The following code shows how to play a RealAudio audio clip using RealPlayer:

```
<object classid="clsid:CFCDAA03-8BE4-11cf-B84B-0020AFBBCCFA" width="290"
height="65">
  <param name="type" value="audio/x-pn-realaudio-plugin" />
  <param name="src" value="http://wiredforbooks.org/alice/chapter1.ram" />
  <param name="controls" value="All" />
  <param name="loop" value="false" />
  <param name="autostart" value="true" />
  <embed width="290" height="65" type="audio/x-pn-realaudio-plugin"
  src="http://wiredforbooks.org/alice/chapter1.ram" controls="All"
  loop="false" autostart="true" pluginspage="http://www.real.com/player/" />
</object>
```

In this example, the RealAudio clip `chapter1.ram` is played using an embedded RealAudio player. Several `<param>` tags are required in order to get the player properly initialized. For example, the `type` parameter sets the standard MIME type for RealAudio, which helps the player know what type of media is being played.

You've probably noticed that the remaining parameters don't all match exactly with the earlier parameters you saw for the embedded Windows Media Player object. This is because each media player is free to define its own parameters. Fortunately, the parameters across media players are reasonably similar.

The `src` parameter for RealPlayer identifies the URL of the multimedia content, and `controls` is similar to `uiMode` in the Windows Media Player control. The `loop` and `autostart` parameters control whether the clip loops repeatedly, as well as whether it immediately starts playing when the page is opened.

I'm sure you also noticed that I included an `<embed />` tag within the `<object>` tag to accommodate older and inconsistent web browsers.

Listing 19.3 shows the RealPlayer control as it appears within a real web page.

LISTING 19.3   The `<object>` Tag Is Used to Embed a RealAudio Audio
Clip Directly in a Page

```
<?xml version="1.0" encoding="UTF-8"?>
<!DOCTYPE html PUBLIC "-//W3C//DTD XHTML 1.1//EN"
  "http://www.w3.org/TR/xhtml11/DTD/xhtml11.dtd">
```

LISTING 19.3   Continued

```
<html xmlns="http://www.w3.org/1999/xhtml" xml:lang="en">
  <head>
    <title>Alice's Adventures in Wonderland</title>
  </head>

  <body>
    <div>
      <h1>Alice's Adventures in Wonderland</h1>
      <h2>By Lewis Carroll</h2>
      <p>
        This audio production of Lewis Carroll's "Alice's Adventures in
        Wonderland" was made possible by <a href="http://wiredforbooks.org/">
        Wired for Books</a>. To listen to the complete recording, visit the
        <a href="http://wiredforbooks.org/alice/">Alice page</a> at the Wired
        for Books Web site.
      </p>
      <p>
        <object classid="clsid:CFCDAA03-8BE4-11cf-B84B-0020AFBBCCFA"
        width="290" height="65">
          <param name="type" value="audio/x-pn-realaudio-plugin" />
          <param name="src" value="http://wiredforbooks.org/alice/chapter1.ram"
/>
          <param name="controls" value="All" />
          <param name="loop" value="false" />
          <param name="autostart" value="true" />
          <embed width="290" height="65" type="audio/x-pn-realaudio-plugin"
          src="http://wiredforbooks.org/alice/chapter1.ram" controls="All"
          loop="false" autostart="true"
          pluginspage="http://www.real.com/player/" />
        </object>
      </p>
    </div>
  </body>
</html>
```

Figure 19.4 shows the Alice in Wonderland RealAudio clip as it is being played via the embedded RealPlayer control. This clip is made available by Ohio University's Wired for Books web site, which is located at http://www.wiredforbooks.org/.

This example shows how a web page can be used as the basis for listening to an audio book, which is possibly something you've never considered. You could even record and place your own audio clips on a site and play them back in this manner. Many businesses and organizations are using such an approach to post regularly scheduled audio messages on their web sites.

Did you Know?

Whenever you set up a web page to play a sound automatically, it's a good idea to give people some way to turn the sound off. (There's nothing more annoying than surfing the Web with your favorite CD on and hitting a musical web page that can't be turned off!) In the Alice in Wonderland example, the RealPlayer media controls are fully accessible, giving the user plenty of options for controlling how the audio is played.

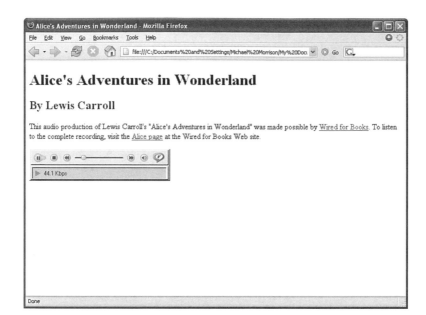

FIGURE 19.4
Playing embed-
ded audio is
possible with a
combination of
the <object>
and <embed />
tags, including
such interesting
audio as a pop-
ular book being
read aloud.

Automatically Embedding the Appropriate Player

Thus far you've seen how to use the <object> tag (plus the <embed /> tag) to embed a media player in a web page. The problem is that you've had to make an assumption regarding which player a typical user has at his disposal. By and large, Windows users tend to have Windows Media Player installed, whereas Apple users tend to have QuickTime, RealPlayer, or both installed.

One way to help tailor your media pages to fit each user is to attempt to use the appropriate media player based on the user's operating system. One reasonable assumption is to go with Windows Media Player for Windows computers and RealPlayer for everything else (Mac, Linux, and so on). Fortunately, there is a simple line of JavaScript code you can use to make this operating system check. Hour 17, "Web Page Scripting for Nonprogrammers," covers JavaScript and how to use it in your web pages.

The following line of JavaScript code checks to see whether the user's operating system is Windows:

```
navigator.appVersion.indexOf("Win")
```

This line of code is either true or false, and can therefore be placed into a conditional *if* statement, like this:

```
if (navigator.appVersion.indexOf("Win") != -1)
  // Play a media file using Windows Media Player
else
  // Play a media file using RealPlayer
```

I used code very similar to this JavaScript code in the Guess That Groove online music game that I developed (http://www.guessthatgroove.com/), which relies heavily on embedded media.

You now have the script code necessary to switch between media players. Listing 19.4 uses this code in the context of a page that plays an Amazon.com music sampling using a media player as determined by the user's operating system.

LISTING 19.4   JavaScript Code Intelligently Chooses between Windows Media Player or RealPlayer to Play an Amazon.com Song Sampling

```
<?xml version="1.0" encoding="UTF-8"?>
<!DOCTYPE html PUBLIC "-//W3C//DTD XHTML 1.0 Transitional//EN"
  "http://www.w3.org/TR/xhtml1/DTD/xhtml1-transitional.dtd">

<html xmlns="http://www.w3.org/1999/xhtml" xml:lang="en">
  <head>
    <title>Tom Waits on Amazon.com</title>
  </head>

  <body>
    <div style="text-align:center">
      <h1>Tom Waits - The Heart of Saturday Night</h1>
      <p>
        This song is titled "New Coat of Paint," and appears on the Tom Waits
        CD, "The Heart of Saturday Night."<br />
        This CD is available on Amazon.com via the following link:
      </p>
      <p>
        <iframe src="http://rcm.amazon.com/e/cm?t=michaelmorris-20&o=1&p=8&
        l=as1&asins=B000002GXS&fc1=000000&=1&lc1=0000ff&bc1=ffffff&&#108;&
        #116;1=_top&IS2=1&bg1=ffffff&f=ifr" style="width:120px;height:240px;"
        scrolling="no" marginwidth="0" marginheight="0" frameborder="0"
        style="text-align:center"></iframe>
      </p>
      <p>
        <script type="text/javascript">
          <!-- Hide the script from old browsers
```

LISTING 19.4   Continued

```
        if (navigator.appVersion.indexOf("Win") != -1)
          document.write("<object
            classid='CLSID:6BF52A52-394A-11d3-B153-00C04F79FAA6' width='290'
            height='65'><param name='type' value='audio/x-ms-wma' />
            <param name='URL' value='http://www.amazon.com/exec/obidos/
            clipserve/B000002GXS001001/0/104-1401177-1194303' /><param
            name='uiMode' value='full' /><param name='autoStart'
            value='true' /><embed width='290' height='65'
            type='audio/x-ms-wma' src='http://www.amazon.com/exec/obidos/
            clipserve/B000002GXS001001/0/104-1401177-1194303' controls='All'
            loop='false' autostart='true'
            pluginspage='http://www.microsoft.com/windows/windowsmedia/' />
            </object>");
        else
          document.write("<object
            classid='clsid:CFCDAA03-8BE4-11cf-B84B-0020AFBBCCFA' width='290'
            height='65'><param name='type'
            value='audio/x-pn-realaudio-plugin' /><param name='src'
            value='http://www.amazon.com/exec/obidos/clipserve/
            B000002GXS001001/1/104-1401177-1194303' /><param name='controls'
            value='All' /><param name='loop' value='false' /><param
            name='autostart' value='true' /><param name='prefetch'
            value='false' /><embed width='290' height='65'
            type='audio/x-pn-realaudio-plugin' src='http://www.amazon.com/
            exec/obidos/clipserve/B000002GXS001001/1/104-1401177-1194303'
            controls='All' loop='false' autostart='true'
            pluginspage='http://www.real.com/player/' /></object>");
        // Stop hiding the script -->
      </script>
    </p>
  </div>
 </body>
</html>
```

This code looks a lot messier than it really is. The first bit of messiness comes from a chunk of code that was generated automatically by Amazon.com. I'm referring to the code appearing within the `<iframe>` tag, which was generated by the Amazon.com Build-A-Link tool at https://associates.amazon.com/gp/associates/network/build-links/main.html. This tool is very handy, and allows you to quickly and easily create links to Amazon.com products. The tool generates HTML code that you can just cut and paste into your web pages. In this case, I used the tool because the audio clip played by the page is a track on a CD that is available on Amazon.com.

The `<iframe>` tag serves as somewhat of a floating window that can be used to contain HTML code from another page. Frames are covered in more detail in Hour 16, "Multipage Layout with Frames." All you really need to know here is that the `<iframe>` tag is being used to insert a "page" containing the link to a CD on Amazon.com.

By the Way

The other source of messiness in the Amazon.com music player example is the code that dynamically selects a different media player based on the operating system. The JavaScript code has to generate the HTML code for the appropriate media player, which looks jumbled because all the code must be packed into a continuous run of text. The end result is an embedded media player object, as shown in Figure 19.5.

FIGURE 19.5
The media player in this example was selected and used based on the operating system being Windows, as opposed to some other operating system.

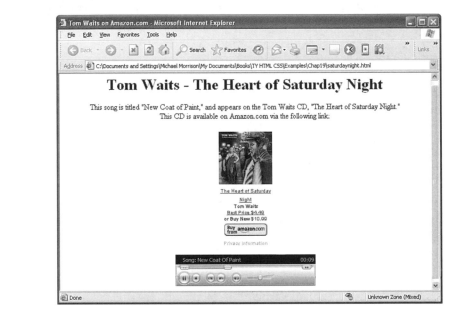

Now is probably a good time to explore Amazon.com and how it uses streaming audio within its music web pages. Visit http://www.amazon.com/ and do a search for some music that you like. Pay close attention to how the site allows you to listen to clips of individual tracks on a CD. This is an excellent example of how multimedia content not only makes a web page more interesting but actually plays a significant role in helping people to shop on Amazon.com.

Summary

In this hour, you've seen how to embed video and sound into a web page. You saw how to use a simple link to a multimedia clip, which is the most broadly supported but least flexible option for playing media content. You then learned how to use the

`<object>` tag to embed a media player directly in a web page. Not only that, but you found out that for maximum browser compatibility it helps to assist the `<object>` tag with the `<embed />` tag. The `<object>` and `<embed />` tags can be used to include a vast array of media types, including WAV, MP3, RealAudio, and MIDI files, not top mention AVI, WMV, and QuickTime videos, to name just a few. Table 19.1 summarizes the tags discussed in this hour.

TABLE 19.1 HTML Tags and Attributes Covered in Hour 19

Tag/Attribute	Function
`<embed />`	Embeds a multimedia file to be read or displayed by a plug-in application; this tag is technically deprecated but still useful due to browsers not fully supporting the `<object>` tag yet.
Attributes	
`width="width"`	The width of the embedded object in pixels.
`height="height"`	The height of the embedded object in pixels.
`type="mimetype"`	The MIME type of the multimedia content.
`src="mediaurl"`	The URL of the file to embed.
`controls="controls"`	The configuration of the user input controls for the media player; use All to enable all controls.
`loop="loop"`	Whether to play the media clip once or loop it repeatedly; set to true or false.
`autostart="autostart"`	Whether to start playing the media clip upon opening the page; set to true or false.
`pluginspage="pluginurl"`	The URL of the plug-in required to play the media clip.
`<object>...</object>`	Inserts images, videos, Java applets, ActiveX controls, or other objects into a document. (See Hour 18 for attributes of the `<object>` tag.)
`<param>...</param>`	Runtime settings for an object, such as the width and height of the area it occupies on a page.
Attributes	
`name="name"`	A named parameter property.
`value="value"`	The value associated with a named parameter property.

Q&A

Q *I hear a lot about streaming video and audio. What does that mean?*

A In the past, video and audio files took minutes and sometimes hours to retrieve through most modems, which severely limited the inclusion of video and audio on web pages. The goal that everyone is moving toward is streaming video or audio, which plays while the data is being received. In other words, you don't have to completely download the clip before you can start to watch it or listen to it.

Streaming playback is now widely supported through most media players, in both standalone versions and plug-ins. When you embed a media object using the `<object>` tag, the underlying media player will automatically stream the media clip if streaming is supported in the player.

Q *How do I choose among audiovisual file formats such as QuickTime, Windows AVI/WAV, RealVideo/RealAudio, and MPEG? Is there any significant difference among them?*

A QuickTime is the most popular video format among Macintosh users, though QuickTime players are available for Windows as well. Similarly, AVI/WMV and WAV/WMA are the video and audio formats of choice for Windows users, but you can get players for the Macintosh that support these formats. MPEG is another popular audio and video standard. MPEG-3, or MP3 for short, is already extremely popular as the high-fidelity audio standard of choice. One other audio format that is based on MPEG is Apple's AAC format, which may be more familiar to you as the native iTunes music format.

How do you choose? If most of your audience uses Windows, pick AVI/WMV for video, or WAV/WMA or MP3 for audio. If your audience includes a significant number of Macintosh users, pick QuickTime or RealVideo/RealAudio, or at least offer it as an alternative; MP3 is also a viable option for Mac audio. If cross-platform compatibility is essential, consider going specifically with MP3 for audio, or RealVideo/RealAudio—although only those who download special software from http://www.real.com/player/ will be able to see RealVideo/RealAudio clips.

Workshop

The workshop contains quiz questions and activities to help you solidify your understanding of the material covered. Try to answer all questions before looking at the "Answers" section that follows.

Quiz

1. What's the simplest way to let the widest possible audience see a video on your web site?

2. Write the HTML to embed a video file named `myvideo.avi` into a web page so that the users of all major web browsers will be able to see it. The video requires an area on the page that is 320×305 pixels in size.

3. How would you code a `<param>` tag within an `<object>` tag so that a media clip is played repeatedly?

Answers

1. Just link to it:

```
<a href="myvideo.avi">my video</a>
```

2. Because the video clip is in a Microsoft format (AVI), it makes sense to embed a Windows Media player object. Use the following HTML code:

```
<object classid="CLSID:6BF52A52-394A-11d3-B153-00C04F79FAA6"
width="320" height="305">
  <param name="type" value="video/x-ms-avi" />
  <param name="URL" value="myvideo.avi" />
  <param name="uiMode" value="full" />
  <param name="autoStart" value="true" />
  <embed width="320" height="305" type="video/x-ms-avi"
  src="myvideo.avi" controls="All" loop="false" autostart="true"
  pluginspage="http://www.microsoft.com/windows/windowsmedia/"></embed>
</object>
```

3. `<param name="loop" value="true" />`

Exercises

▶ Try your hand at creating your own video clip and embedding it in a web page. If you're a Windows user, you might try using the free Windows Movie Maker software, available online at http://www.microsoft.com/windowsxp/moviemaker/. If you're on a Mac computer, try using iMovie, which is part of the iLife suite of applications (http://www.apple.com/ilife/).

▶ The techniques and tags covered in this hour for embedding media also work with Macromedia Flash files. To find out how you can use Flash to put interactive animations in your web pages, check out the Flash home page at http://www.macromedia.com/software/flash/.

HOUR 20

Jazz Up Your eBay Auctions with HTML and CSS

Since its inception in 1995, eBay has grown to become one of the most recognized and heavily trafficked web sites in existence. Serving as the ultimate online marketplace, eBay allows you to buy and sell just about anything short of alcohol, tobacco, and human organs. Entire towns have been sold on eBay, not to mention a Grumman Gulfstream II jet for a mere $4.9 million. Although there are certainly unusual items listed on eBay, the vast majority of items sold consist of popular mass-market products such as sporting goods and electronics.

This hour shows you how to incorporate HTML and CSS into eBay auction listings, effectively spicing up an otherwise mundane sales pitch. You'll even learn how to create a slide show within an auction listing so that you can display multiple item photos without taking up too much screen space.

Try It Yourself ▼

Before you can apply HTML and CSS to an auction listing, you need something to sell. It shouldn't be too difficult to rummage through your attic or closets and find something worth selling. Generally speaking, it's probably not worth the hassle if you can't get at least $5 or $10 for an item on eBay. It's a good idea to do your own "comparative market analysis" by searching eBay for products similar to what you're selling. That will help you gauge a starting price and a hoped-for closing price, not to mention possibly helping you figure out a shipping cost estimate.

After you've found a suitable item to sell, follow these steps to get prepared for listing it on eBay:

1. Take several pictures of the item, ideally at various angles. If it is a boxed product and the box isn't factory sealed, open it up and take pictures of what comes in the box. It's hard to provide too much information to prospective buyers.

2. See whether the manufacturer of the item has a web site, and visit it to see whether you can find additional information about the product. This information would make a great addition to the item description that you'll be coding in HTML and CSS.

▼

3. Search eBay for similar items, paying close attention to how the items are presented, as well as their starting price and condition. Make notes if your item is a collectible and is in noticeably better condition than any of the other items currently listed.

Did you Know?

A good trick to help to determine what an item is worth on eBay is to perform a search, click Completed Listings on the left side of the screen, and then click the Show Items button below it. The search results will change to show only those auctions that have already ended. Prices in green are for items that actually sold, and prices in red are for items that did not sell—just focus on the green prices to help get a feel for what price items have been selling for.

4. If you have a scale, go ahead and box and weigh the item. Then visit the U.S. Postal Service web site at http://www.usps.com/ to get an estimate on how much it costs to ship the item.

Why Use HTML and CSS on eBay?

When it comes to listing items for sale on eBay, you may wonder how HTML and CSS even enter the picture. eBay is simply an auction site, and it certainly has nothing directly to do with creating your own web pages. That's only because you've probably gotten comfortable thinking in terms of your web pages being created entirely by you. In fact, it is possible to create a portion of a page within someone else's web page, which is exactly what takes place on eBay.

By the Way

If you have no experience at all with eBay, I encourage you to visit the eBay web site at http://www.ebay.com/ and spend some time exploring it. If you want more of a guided tour of how eBay works and how to use it, check out eBay's Learning Center at http://pages.ebay.com/education/.

When you list an item for sale on eBay, you have a great deal of control over the description, which is the portion of the auction listing that describes your item. Every eBay auction listing has standard boilerplate information that appears on the page before the description, as shown in Figure 20.1.

The information at the beginning of an eBay item page is gathered when you first list the item, and cannot be edited or modified via HTML or CSS. HTML and CSS enter the picture with the item description, which appears just below the standard auction information (see Figure 20.2).

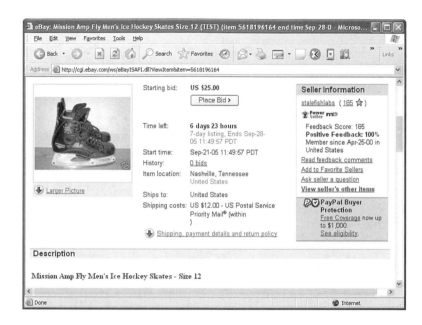

FIGURE 20.1
Every eBay item page begins with boilerplate auction information that cannot be directly modified.

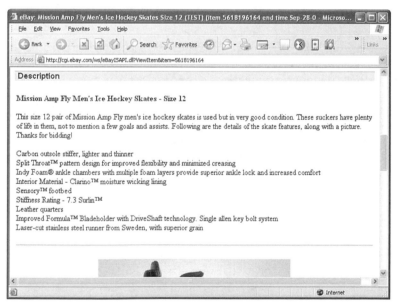

FIGURE 20.2
The item description is where you get an opportunity to jazz things up with HTML and CSS.

In this example, you see perhaps the most boring item description possible, consisting solely of a bold heading and unstyled text. An image does appear below the description, but it doesn't include a caption or border to help dress it up.

Now flip ahead to Figure 20.6 to see how HTML and CSS can liven up an item listing to give it a bit more marketing appeal. This is the same auction listing with the careful addition of HTML and CSS code to make it more exciting. You build the item listing in Figure 20.6 as you progress through this lesson.

Understanding How HTML Fits into eBay

When you're creating a new item listing on eBay using HTML and CSS, it's important to understand what you can and cannot do. The good news is that you have pretty much the entire arsenal of HTML and CSS tags, attributes, and styles at your disposal for creating slicked-out item pages. However, there are a few things you must know when it comes to writing HTML code that ultimately won't reside on your web site.

First off, understand that any code you write will live within the body of the item page on eBay and nowhere else. This means you can't use <meta> tags or any other tags that can appear only in the head of a web page. This also means that you're limited to using inline styles, as opposed to internal style sheets, because the <style> tag can be placed only in the head of a web page.

By the Way

> Some web browsers will allow you to get away with placing an internal style sheet directly in the body of a web page, but I don't recommend doing it.

Because the item page will be hosted on eBay's web servers, not yours, you must always use full URLs when referencing images or pages of your own. For example, any item images that are stored on your web server must be given full URLs (starting with http://) in the src attribute of any <img /> tags. If you plan on linking to any other pages for additional product information, be sure to include the full URLs in the href attribute of the <a> tag.

Because eBay pages are designed as frameless web pages, you can't use frames. This makes sense when you consider that the <frameset> tag effectively replaces the <body> tag in pages that use frames. In an eBay item listing, you have the ability to make changes only between the <body> and </body> tags, so frames clearly aren't an option. Frames are covered in Hour 16, "Multipage Layout with Frames."

Speaking of limitations associated with the <body> tag, because you don't have access to the <body> tag itself, it can be challenging making page-wide style changes to item pages. For example, the background of a page is typically set using the background-color and/or background-image style properties with the <body> tag. Because this approach isn't an option, you have to consider other ways of getting the same effect. You'll learn how to pull off this feat with JavaScript later in this hour, in the section "Altering the Background of an Item Page." For a refresher on how JavaScript is used in web pages, check out Hour 17, "Web Page Scripting for Nonprogrammers."

Creating an eBay Item Listing in HTML

Creating an item listing for eBay using HTML and CSS is surprisingly similar to creating any other web page. In fact, it's a good idea to first create the listing as a normal web page, and then incorporate it into the eBay item description when you list the item for auction.

> eBay allows you to create test auction listings if you just want to test the layout of an item page. Unfortunately, eBay listing fees still apply to test auctions, so don't get too carried away with them. To create a test auction, select Everything Else, Test Auctions, General as the category for the item, and then be sure to clearly indicate that the listing is a test in both the title and the description.

Listing 20.1 contains the code for an eBay item skeleton web page that you can use to create and test item pages for eBay.

LISTING 20.1   The HTML Code for an eBay Item Skeleton Web Page

```
<?xml version="1.0" encoding="UTF-8"?>
<!DOCTYPE html PUBLIC "-//W3C//DTD XHTML 1.1//EN"
  "http://www.w3.org/TR/xhtml11/DTD/xhtml11.dtd">

<html xmlns="http://www.w3.org/1999/xhtml" xml:lang="en">
<head><title></title></head>

<body>
<!-- EBAY HTML CODE STARTS HERE -->

<!-- EBAY HTML CODE ENDS HERE -->
</body>
</html>
```

As you can see, this code is extremely minimal, consisting only of a couple of comments in the body of the page that are used to help call out where the eBay item code goes. When you develop a page using this template, be sure never to place any code outside of these comments because you won't be allowed to do so in the actual eBay listing page. This is a good way to simulate the limitations of an actual eBay listing.

Listing 20.2 contains the code for a web page that contains a suitable item description for a pair of ice hockey skates that I listed for sale on eBay.

LISTING 20.2   A Very Basic Example of Using HTML and CSS to Describe an eBay Item

```
<?xml version="1.0" encoding="UTF-8"?>
<!DOCTYPE html PUBLIC "-//W3C//DTD XHTML 1.1//EN"
  "http://www.w3.org/TR/xhtml11/DTD/xhtml11.dtd">

<html xmlns="http://www.w3.org/1999/xhtml" xml:lang="en">
<head><title></title></head>

<body>
<!-- EBAY HTML CODE STARTS HERE -->
<h2 style="text-align:center">Mission Amp Fly Men's Ice Hockey Skates - Size 12
</h2>
<div>
  This size 12 pair of Mission Amp Fly men's ice hockey skates is used but in
  very good condition. These suckers have plenty of life in them, not to
  mention a few goals and assists. Following are the details of the skate
  features, along with a picture. Thanks for bidding!
  <ul>
    <li>Carbon outsole stiffer, lighter and thinner</li>
    <li>Split Throat&#153; pattern design for improved flexibility and
    minimized creasing</li>
    <li>Indy Foam&#174; ankle chambers with multiple foam layers provide
    superior ankle lock and increased comfort</li>
    <li>Interior Material - Clarino&#153; moisture wicking lining</li>
    <li>Sensory&#153; footbed</li>
    <li>Stiffness Rating - 7.3 Surlin&#153;</li>
    <li>Leather quarters</li>
    <li>Improved Formula&#153; Bladeholder with DriveShaft technology. Single
    allen key bolt system</li>
    <li>Laser-cut stainless steel runner from Sweden, with superior grain</li>
  </ul>
</div>
<div style="text-align:center">
  <img src="http://www.michaelmorrison.com/ebay/skates1.jpg" alt="Mission Amp
  Fly Ice Hockey Skates" style="border:5px solid black" /><br />
  <div style="text-align:center; font-size:16pt; font-weight:bold">Side view of
  skates, some scuffs but overall good shape.</div>
</div>
<!-- EBAY HTML CODE ENDS HERE -->
</body>
</html>
```

This code uses HTML and CSS to improve on the plain-text version of the same item that was shown in Figure 20.2. Figure 20.3 shows the item description in Listing 20.2 as it appears in an actual eBay listing page.

You will typically host your auction images yourself and then reference them in the eBay HTML code directly from your own Web site. Be sure to change the URL of the auction image in the sample code to reference the location of the image file on your Web server—you'll also need to upload the image file to your Web server. You may also be able to host auction images directly on eBay, but you'll still need to find out the full URL of each image to reference in your HTML code.

By the Way

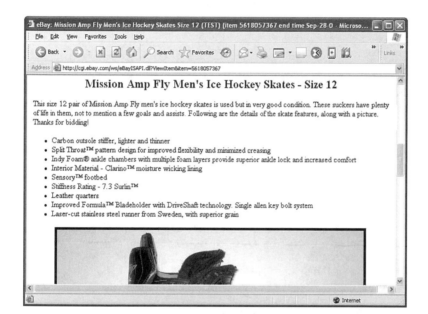

FIGURE 20.3
HTML and CSS are used to improve the layout and appearance of the eBay item listing.

Admittedly, this is a fairly tame example of using HTML and CSS to jazz up the look of an eBay auction. Don't worry, upcoming sections build on this code to make the item listing considerably more compelling to potential buyers.

Figure 20.4 shows the hockey skates eBay listing as it appears in my list of eBay items for sale.

Figure 20.4 reveals how any HTML and CSS code that you inject into an eBay listing has no visible effect on anything but the item description. In other words, a potential buyer has to click the item and view its detailed listing in order to see your code. This means that it's still very important to do a good job of coming up with a catchy and accurate item description, as well as using pertinent eBay listing features such as a gallery image or bold title.

FIGURE 20.4
The hockey
skates eBay
item listing
appearance in
my list of items
for sale.

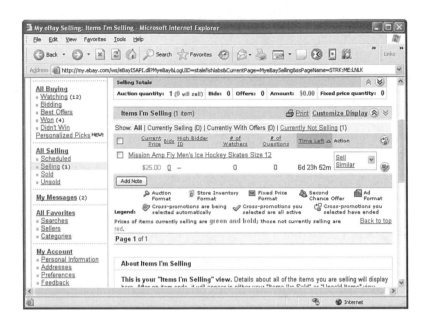

Try as you may, it's unlikely that you'll be able to stir up a bidding frenzy anywhere near what took place when NASCAR driver Robby Gordon put his storied helmet up for auction in September of 2005. Gordon threw the helmet at Michael Waltrip after a race in which they were both involved in an accident. Gordon then placed the helmet up for auction on eBay with the proceeds set to go to charity, but after the bidding topped the $10 million mark, eBay halted the auction. It seems the auction was inflated by "bogus bids" from excited NASCAR fans.

Providing a Link to Your About Me Page

You may not realize it but eBay supports an About Me feature that allows you to include information about yourself or your business. Your About Me page is associated with your eBay User ID, and can be accessed through a simple URL, like this: http://members.ebay.com/aboutme/*UserID*/.

Go ahead and try this link by inserting your own eBay User ID into the *UserID* part of the URL. Either you will see your own About Me page or you'll be given an opportunity to create one.

I mention the About Me page because it provides a good way for potential buyers to learn about you or your business when viewing one of your items for sale. All you have to do is use HTML to provide a link to your About Me page in the code for the item listing. Following is an example of how you might code such a link:

```
<p>
  To learn more about me, just click <a
  href="http://members.ebay.com/aboutme/stalefishlabs/"><img
  src="http://pics.ebay.com/aw/pics/aboutme-small.gif" alt="About Me"
  style="border-style:none" /></a>.
</p>
```

About the only unusual thing about this code is the image that it references, which is a small picture of the word "me" using eBay's trademarked multicolored letters. This image is hosted by eBay at http://pics.ebay.com/aw/pics/aboutme-small.gif, so all you have to do to use it is specify this URL in the src attribute of an <img /> tag.

> Generally speaking, using an image hosted by someone else on your web pages is highly discouraged. However, in this case eBay is the host of the auction page that contains your code, so it's okay.

Figure 20.5 shows the hockey skates eBay item page with the About Me page link visible at the bottom of the item description.

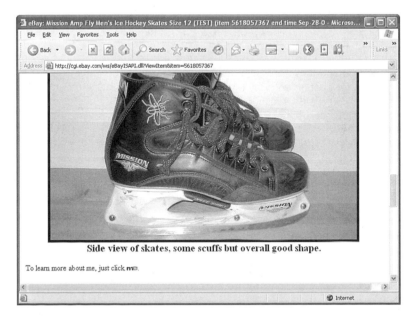

FIGURE 20.5
The image link to the About Me page uses a standard eBay image.

Clicking "me" in the figure takes users to your About Me page, where they can learn more about you or your business.

Altering the Background of an Item Page

If you recall from examples throughout the book, not to mention Hour 9, "Custom Backgrounds and Colors," web page backgrounds are set via the background-color and background-image style properties. For these properties to apply to an entire page, they must be set in the <body> tag. This isn't possible with eBay auction item pages, so you have to resort to some JavaScript trickery to get the desired effect.

The JavaScript trick to which I'm referring involves dynamically setting the value of the document.body.background property, which happens to store the background of a page. Following is an example of how to set this property using a single line of JavaScript code:

```
document.body.background = "http://www.yourwebsite.com/background.jpg";
```

Notice in this sample code that I've provided the full URL for the background.jpg image. This is very important because the auction item page will be hosted on eBay, while the background image will likely be stored somewhere on your web server. Therefore, you must spell out the full address in order for the image to be located.

Listing 20.3 contains the code for a modified hockey skates auction page that now includes a dynamically altered background image.

LISTING 20.3   This Code Dynamically Sets the Background Image Within the <body> Tag

```
<?xml version="1.0" encoding="UTF-8"?>
<!DOCTYPE html PUBLIC "-//W3C//DTD XHTML 1.1//EN"
  "http://www.w3.org/TR/xhtml11/DTD/xhtml11.dtd">

<html xmlns="http://www.w3.org/1999/xhtml" xml:lang="en">
<head><title></title></head>

<body>
<!-- EBAY HTML CODE STARTS HERE -->
<script type="text/javascript">
  <!-- Hide the script from old browsers
  // Set the background image
  document.body.background =
    "http://www.michaelmorrison.com/ebay/missionback.jpg";
  // Stop hiding the script -->
</script>

<h2 style="text-align:center; color:white">Mission Amp Fly Men's Ice Hockey
Skates - Size 12</h2>
<div style="color:white">
```

LISTING 20.3   Continued

```
This size 12 pair of Mission Amp Fly men's ice hockey skates is used but in
very good condition. These suckers have plenty of life in them, not to
mention a few goals and assists. Following are the details of the skate
features, along with a picture. Thanks for bidding!
<ul>
  <li>Carbon outsole stiffer, lighter and thinner</li>
  <li>Split Throat&#153; pattern design for improved flexibility and
  minimized creasing</li>
  <li>Indy Foam&#174; ankle chambers with multiple foam layers provide
  superior ankle lock and increased comfort</li>
  <li>Interior Material - Clarino&#153; moisture wicking lining</li>
  <li>Sensory&#153; footbed</li>
  <li>Stiffness Rating - 7.3 Surlin&#153;</li>
  <li>Leather quarters</li>
  <li>Improved Formula&#153; Bladeholder with DriveShaft technology. Single
  allen key bolt system</li>
  <li>Laser-cut stainless steel runner from Sweden, with superior grain</li>
  </ul>
</div>
<div style="text-align:center; color:white">
  <img src="http://www.michaelmorrison.com/ebay/skates1.jpg" alt="Mission Amp
  Fly Ice Hockey Skates" style="border:5px solid black" /><br />
  <div style="text-align:center; font-size:16pt; font-weight:bold">Side view of
  skates, some scuffs but overall good shape.</div>
</div>
<p style="color:white">
  To learn more about me, just click <a
  href="http://members.ebay.com/aboutme/stalefishlabs/"><img
  src="http://pics.ebay.com/aw/pics/aboutme-small.gif" alt="About Me"
  style="border-style:none" /></a>.
</p>
<!-- EBAY HTML CODE ENDS HERE -->
</body>
</html>
```

The key to this code is the `<script>` tag that appears at the start of the body.
Within this tag, the `document.body.background` property is set to an image that
provides a considerable amount of sizzle to the hockey skates page (see Figure 20.6).

You may have also caught on that I had to add some CSS style properties to this version of the hockey skates item page so that the text is more visible on top of the
dark background. I set all the text on the page to white via the `color` style property.

Now's probably a good time to take a relaxing break and spend some time
exploring eBay for unusual finds. Here's a web site that chronicles some of the
more unusual items to pass through the eBay marketplace: http://www.
weirdauctions.com/. Enjoy!

Coffee Break

FIGURE 20.6
Dynamically set-
ting a back-
ground image
for an auction
item page can
have a dramatic
effect.

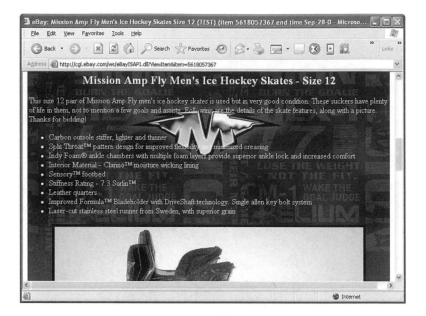

FIGURE 20.6
Dynamically set-
ting a back-
ground image
for an auction
item page can
have a dramatic
effect.

Creating a Slide Show Item Listing

If you really want to add some punch to your eBay auction listings, you can inject
some JavaScript code that turns a static image into an ever-changing slide show.
This allows you to incorporate multiple images of an auction item without having
to clutter up the page. Additionally, you can add a caption to each image that
includes some descriptive text about the item.

Listing 20.4 contains the code for the final version of the hockey skates eBay auction
page, which takes advantage of JavaScript to incorporate a slide show into the item
description.

LISTING 20.4   This Web Page Uses JavaScript Code to Present a
Dynamic Slide Show of Item Images

```
<?xml version="1.0" encoding="UTF-8"?>
<!DOCTYPE html PUBLIC "-//W3C//DTD XHTML 1.1//EN"
  "http://www.w3.org/TR/xhtml11/DTD/xhtml11.dtd">

<html xmlns="http://www.w3.org/1999/xhtml" xml:lang="en">
<head><title></title></head>

<body>
<!-- EBAY HTML CODE STARTS HERE -->
<script type="text/javascript">
  <!-- Hide the script from old browsers
  var slide_wait = 3; // in seconds
  var slide_text = ["Side view of skates, some scuffs but overall good shape.",
```

LISTING 20.4   Continued

```
                    "Front view, toes are solid and intact.",
                    "Other side view, normal wear and plenty of life left.",
                    "Rear view, practically brand new condition."];
  var cur_slide = 1;
  var timer = 0;

  // Preload the images
  for(var i = 0; i < slide_text.length; i++) {
    var image = new Image();
    image.src = "http://www.michaelmorrison.com/ebay/skates" + i + ".jpg";
  }

  // Start the initial timer
  timer = setTimeout("nextImage();", slide_wait * 1000);

  // Set the background image
  document.body.background =
    "http://www.michaelmorrison.com/ebay/missionback.jpg";

  function nextImage() {
    // Clear the timer and set a new one
    if (timer != 0)
      clearTimeout(timer);
    timer = setTimeout("nextImage();", slide_wait * 1000);

    // Advance to the next slide image
    if (++cur_slide > slide_text.length)
      cur_slide = 1;
    var img_element = document.getElementById('slide');
    img_element.setAttribute("src",
      "http://www.michaelmorrison.com/ebay/skates" + cur_slide + ".jpg");
    img_element.setAttribute("alt", slide_text[cur_slide - 1]);

    // Update the slide description
    document.getElementById('caption').innerHTML = slide_text[cur_slide - 1];
  }
  // Stop hiding the script -->
</script>

<h2 style="text-align:center; color:white">Mission Amp Fly Men's Ice Hockey
Skates - Size 12</h2>
<div style="color:white">
  This size 12 pair of Mission Amp Fly men's ice hockey skates is used but in
  very good condition. These suckers have plenty of life in them, not to
  mention a few goals and assists. Following are the details of the skate
  features, along with a few pictures. Thanks for bidding!
  <ul>
    <li>Carbon outsole stiffer, lighter and thinner</li>
    <li>Split Throat&#153; pattern design for improved flexibility and
    minimized creasing</li>
    <li>Indy Foam&#174; ankle chambers with multiple foam layers provide
    superior ankle lock and increased comfort</li>
    <li>Interior Material - Clarino&#153; moisture wicking lining</li>
    <li>Sensory&#153; footbed</li>
    <li>Stiffness Rating - 7.3 Surlin&#153;</li>
    <li>Leather quarters</li>
    <li>Improved Formula&#153; Bladeholder with DriveShaft technology. Single
```

LISTING 20.4   Continued

```
    allen key bolt system</li>
    <li>Laser-cut stainless steel runner from Sweden, with superior grain</li>
  </ul>
</div>
<div style="text-align:center; color:white">
  <img id="slide" src="http://www.michaelmorrison.com/ebay/skates1.jpg"
  alt="Mission Amp Fly Ice Hockey Skates" style="border:5px solid black"
  onclick="nextImage();" /><br />
  <div id="caption" style="text-align:center; font-size:16pt;
  font-weight:bold">Side view of skates, some scuffs but overall good
  shape.</div>
</div>
<p style="color:white">
  To learn more about me, just click <a
  href="http://members.ebay.com/aboutme/stalefishlabs/"><img
  src="http://pics.ebay.com/aw/pics/aboutme-small.gif" alt="About Me"
  style="border-style:none" /></a>.
</p>
<!-- EBAY HTML CODE ENDS HERE -->
</body>
</html>
```

It isn't terribly important for you to understand the script code that makes this page
tick. All you really need to be aware of is how the slide captions are created, as well
as how to change the names of the slides themselves. The following code is what
establishes the captions for the slides:

```
var slide_text = ["Side view of skates, some scuffs but overall good shape.",
                  "Front view, toes are solid and intact.",
                  "Other side view, normal wear and plenty of life left.",
                  "Rear view, practically brand new condition."];
```

This code creates an array of captions that have a one-to-one relationship with each
slide image in the slide show. The number of captions must match the number of
slide images.

Did you Know?

To speed up or slow down the slide show, change the value of the `slide_wait`
variable in the JavaScript code. This variable controls the amount of time each
slide is displayed before moving to the next one. As an example, the following
code slows down the slide show by increasing the slide delay to 5 seconds per
slide:

```
var slide_wait = 5; // in seconds
```

The slide images themselves enter the code in a few places. The following line of
code shows how the URL of each slide image is calculated based on the current slide:

```
img_element.setAttribute("src",
  "http://www.michaelmorrison.com/ebay/skates" + cur_slide + ".jpg");
```

The main thing you need to take from this code is that you must change the URL to accommodate your own specific images. For example, if your auction item images are named `putter1.jpg`, `putter2.jpg`, and so on, and are located at http://www.mygolfstuff.com/images/, the following JavaScript code would correctly set the slide image:

```
img_element.setAttribute("src",
  "http://www.mygolfstuff.com/images/putter" + cur_slide + ".jpg");
```

There are actually a few places in the code where you'll need to make changes based on your specific item images. Just look for the word "skates" and make changes accordingly.

Figure 20.7 shows the completed hockey skates auction item page with the slide show running.

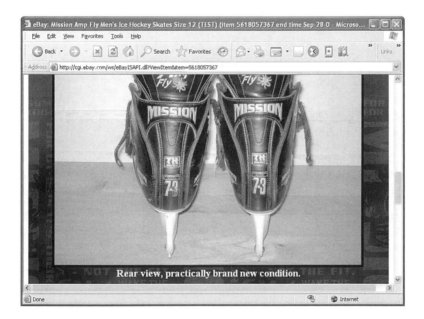

FIGURE 20.7
The hockey skates eBay auction item page now takes advantage of a carefully timed slide show to display a succession of item images.

Not too many eBay auctions are interesting enough to include a dynamic slide show that cycles through item images. By blending JavaScript, HTML, and CSS, you'll hopefully be able to rack up some solid eBay sales numbers!

Summary

This hour ventured into some highly practical territory by showing you how HTML and CSS can be used to create stylized auction item pages on eBay. eBay is the ultimate online marketplace, and you now know how to squeeze the most out of eBay item listings by applying what you've learned about web page design. Not only did you find out how to do some cool things strictly with HTML and CSS, but you also saw how to use JavaScript to add some dynamic features to your auction item pages, such as a slide show.

Q&A

Q *eBay offers templates for creating interesting-looking web pages. Why not just use those?*

A Ah, looking for the easy way out, huh? Although it's true that you can get a decent look out of the standard eBay templates, you'll ultimately end up with an item page that looks a whole lot like a bunch of other item pages. Why bother learning HTML and CSS if you don't use them to put your own unique stamp on the Web? Perhaps more important, you probably know better than anyone else what is unique about the items you sell on eBay. Use that insider knowledge combined with your newly honed HTML and CSS skills to craft some eye-popping auction pages.

Q *It's a pain creating my own item images. Can I just use images of similar items that other people have already listed?*

A Technically, yes. Ethically, probably not. Although you do occasionally see some stock item images that were likely acquired from a manufacturer's web site, many of the item images on eBay are photographs that were taken by the seller of the item. In both cases, the photographs are properties of their respective owners, and are therefore off-limits for you to "borrow" and use. If you should get permission or otherwise decide to use a stock image, be sure to copy the image and host it on your own web server.

Workshop

The workshop contains quiz questions and activities to help you solidify your understanding of the material covered. Try to answer all questions before looking at the "Answers" section that follows.

Quiz

1. When writing HTML and CSS code for including in an eBay item listing, which part of the eBay item page are you allowed to modify?

2. What code would you use to dynamically set the background of an item page to the image `background.gif`, which is stored at http://www.ilovepez.com/pics/?

3. How much would a Grumman Gulfstream II jet set you back on eBay?

Answers

1. You are allowed to place HTML and CSS code only in the description of an auction item, which is automatically placed inside the `<body>` and `</body>` tags of the eBay item page; you have no access to the head of an eBay item page.

2. `document.body.background =`

   `"http://www.ilovepez.com/pics/background.gif";`

3. About $4.9 million—just wanted to make sure you were paying attention!

Exercises

▶ Right now, find an item and list it for sale on eBay. Take a few photos of the item, and then modify the JavaScript code in the hockey skates sample page to create a listing page with a slide show of the item images. Then sit back and watch the bids roll in!

▶ Experiment with going beyond the examples in this lesson to make your auction item pages even more spectacular. For example, consider embedding a video in your auction item page that shows the item in use (assuming that it is used). Or maybe use a table to break out the various attributes of the item, or even do a feature comparison against competitive products.

HOUR 21

Create Your Own Blog

If you recall any of the hoopla from the U.S. Presidential Election of 2004, for the first time in history, the Internet played a vital role in fleshing out the political debate of who should be President. Much of this debate was carried out through blogs, which are themed online publications whose content changes regularly. By themed, I mean that a blog typically focuses on the opinion of a single group or person, or on a narrowly focused topic.

This lesson explores hosted blogs, which are blogs stored on someone else's web server. Hosted blogs have some advantages over "homemade" blogs in that they typically rely on powerful blog software that automates the updating and publishing process. Don't worry, you'll still get to tinker with some code in this lesson as you find out how to customize the appearance of a hosted blog using CSS.

What's a Blog?

Back in Hour 14, "Using Style Sheets for Page Layout," you learned how to create a style sheet template for a basic blog web page. Although this template certainly served its purpose, it didn't address the main allure of blogs: publishing ease. But before I address the publishing side of blogs in more detail, let's take a quick step back and make sure that you understand what a blog is, along with what it isn't.

First off, the word *blog* came from "web log" or "weblog," as in an online log of someone's thoughts or activities. Blogs have been around for a few years but reached a critical mass of sorts in the past year or two. It's important for you to understand that at its core a blog is really just a web page. As such, a blog consists of HTML and CSS code, and can include any content you might normally place on a web page. What constitutes calling a web page a blog is primarily the fact that it contains a stream of regularly updated content that is organized in a consistent, typically sequential manner.

Although blogs can certainly contain images, most of them focus more on text content, often in the form of relatively short articles on a given subject. Some blogs offer a comment feature that allows visitors to leave their own comments in response to a blog entry. It's also common for blogs to provide a unique URL for each blog entry so that visitors can return to an older blog entry later. Such links are known as *permalinks* because they serve as a permanent link to an individual blog entry.

By the
Way

There are blogs called photoblogs that deal primarily with images. Instead of regularly posting text content, in a photoblog you regularly post images such as photographs of places you've been. To learn more about photoblogs, visit http://www.photoblogs.org/.

Figure 21.1 shows an example of a professional-caliber blog that includes most of the bells and whistles you would expect in a top-notch blog.

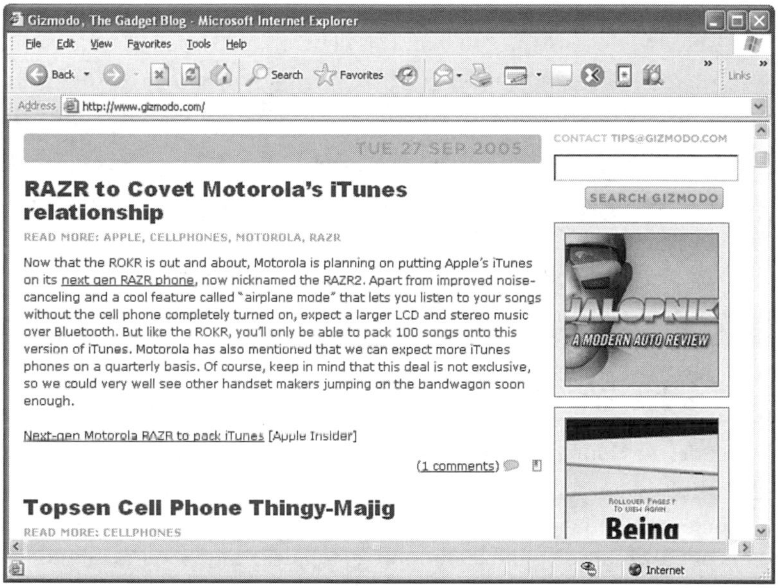

FIGURE 21.1
The Gizmodo blog offers regularly updated information about new electronic gadgets.

The blog in the figure is Gizmodo, which happens to be one of my favorite blogs. It is self-described as The Gadget Blog, and it is a great example of a full-featured blog. If you pay close attention to the figure, you'll notice a comment link to the lower right of the blog entry, along with a tiny permalink icon next to that. The blog also sports a prominent title, cleanly formatted blog text, and the date on which it was posted.

One of the interesting technological advances that really propelled blogging into the mainstream was RSS (Really Simple Syndication), which allows people interested in a blog to receive regular notifications of new blog entries. RSS allows you to use news-feed syndication software such as Feed Demon (http://www.feeddemon.com/) to track and stay abreast of new content on many different blogs at once. If you don't want to install special software, you can use an online RSS reader such as

Bloglines (http://www.bloglines.com/) that works entirely within your web browser. The efficiency made possible by RSS in terms of keeping tabs on your favorite blogs has had a significant effect on the popularity of blogs. Hour 24, "Beyond Traditional Web Sites," explores RSS in a bit more detail, and gives you some ideas about how to go about syndicating web sites (such as blogs) that support RSS.

Getting back to the management side of the blog equation, the killer feature of most blogs is ease of publication. The blog page you developed in Hour 14 is a perfectly acceptable blog by any standard. Where it is limited, however, is in how you update it. For a web site that needs to change regularly, such as daily or even several times a week, it can be a drag manually editing HTML code and publishing pages via FTP. Visual web development tools such as FrontPage and Dreamweaver certainly can ease the pain, but you still have to manually edit HTML code. Don't get me wrong, this whole book is about editing HTML code, but there are times when a little automation can go a long way.

There are quite a few blog services and software packages out there that help streamline the blogging process by allowing you to edit and update your blog via a web interface. In other words, you simply log in to a web site and enter the blog content, after which it is immediately posted to your blog—no FTP, no special web development tool, and in many cases no HTML code. So how could I be recommending a tool that foregoes HTML code in a book about HTML? Because it can make your life easier.

When it comes to the issue of publication ease and blogs, I know what I'm talking about. My personal web site originally had a primitive blog of sorts that I found myself neglecting simply because of the hassle of having to edit raw HTML code and manually publish the files via FTP. When I switched over to using blog software that automated the publishing process, I found myself much more willing to keep the content fresh. Not only that, but because the blog has a web-based interface, I can add and edit blog entries from anywhere without any special software.	**By the** Way

The good news is that this hour isn't abandoning HTML and CSS entirely for the sake of a blog service or specialized blog software. It turns out that you still need a healthy understanding of HTML and CSS in order to customize the appearance of a blog to fit in with the rest of your site. Using this approach, it's possible to link your existing web pages to a blog hosted somewhere else, yet retain a common look across all the pages. This is perhaps the best of both worlds because you have complete control over most of your pages yet you get to enjoy the automation benefits of a blog service.

Creating a Blog on Blogger.com

People who contribute to their own blog are often referred to as *bloggers*. This term also serves as the basis for a popular blog service called Blogger, located at http://www.blogger.com/. This is the service I focus on throughout the remainder of this hour as I show you how to create your own hosted blog, customize it, and then link it in to your existing web pages. Incidentally, I'm not in any way connected to the folks at Blogger—I just happen to find it to be one of the better blog services out there. You may also want to consider one of the following blog services, which all are also free and offer generally similar features as Blogger:

▶ TypePad—http://www.typepad.com/

▶ Bloglines—http://www.bloglines.com/

▶ LiveJournal—http://www.livejournal.com/

▶ MySpace—http://www.myspace.com/

▶ MSN Spaces—http://spaces.msn.com/

By the Way

Blogger was one of the first mainstream blog services to offer free hosted blogs to the public. The Blogger service was gobbled up by Google in early 2003, and it still remains a team within Google that focuses on the organization of personal information.

Getting back to Blogger, you can use the service to create a free blog that is entirely hosted by Blogger. You don't have to create or otherwise publish any pages of your own to use a blog on Blogger. The first step in using Blogger is to create an account by visiting http://www.blogger.com/signup.g—be sure to include the .g at the end of the URL. Follow the instructions to create your free account. Figure 21.2 shows how to enter the basic account information in Blogger.

Click Continue to continue along in the blog creation process. Figure 21.3 shows how you enter the title of the new blog, along with the name that is used in the URL of the blog—this address is what you enter into a web browser to access the blog.

By the Way

If you find that your blog name is already taken, just keep trying variations on the name until you arrive at a URL that Blogger accepts. Be sure to use a name that results in a URL that isn't too difficult to remember or too long to type.

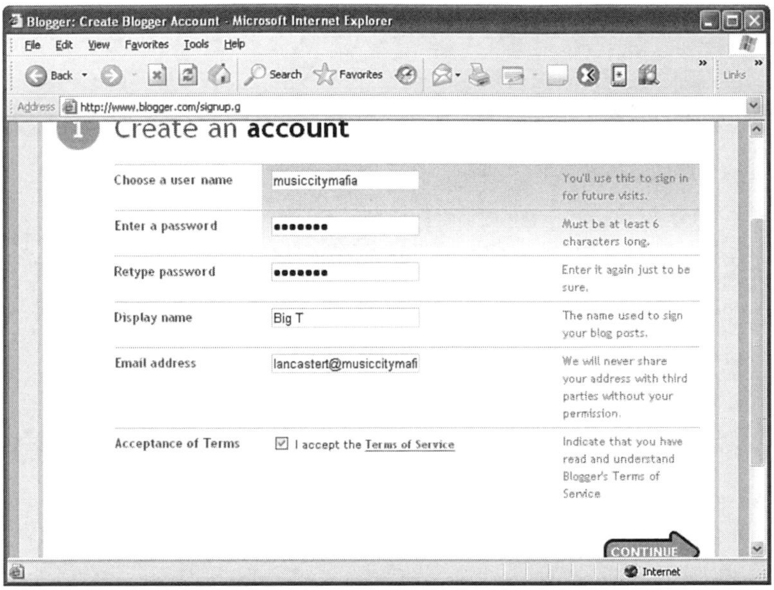

FIGURE 21.2
Creating a Blogger account primarily involves establishing a username and password, and providing your email address.

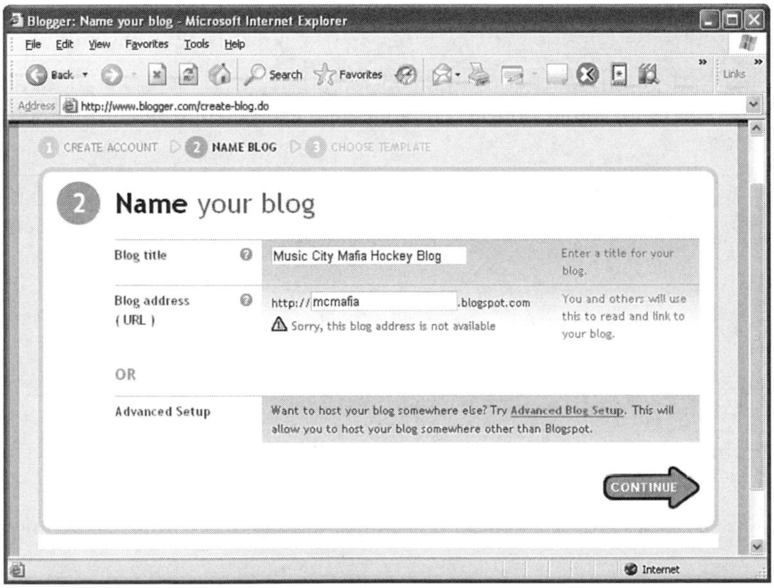

FIGURE 21.3
Specifying the blog title and address is an important part of the blog creation process.

Click Continue once more to proceed to the next step in the blog creation process. Figure 21.4 shows the selection of the blog template, which is required initially even though you will be changing the template code later in the hour.

FIGURE 21.4
You must initially select a blog template, although you'll be customizing the CSS template code a little later in the lesson.

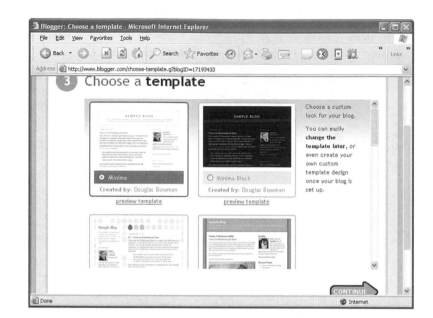

Click Continue to accept the template and move on to wrap up the creation of the blog. You'll see a confirmation screen with a Start Posting link that you can click to post your first blog entry.

Creating Your First Blog Entry

Ah, finally your chance to share your thoughts with the world via your own hosted blog. Figure 21.5 shows the Blogger blog entry page, which includes a large edit box where you enter the content for your new blog entry.

As you can see in the figure, the edit box in the Posting area of Blogger includes several formatting controls along the top that allow you to carry out common formatting tasks such as altering the font and alignment of text. You can also insert images and even spell-check the page content.

From an HTML perspective, the most interesting part of the Blogger Posting area is the Edit Html tab in the upper-right corner of the page. Click this tab to view the blog entry as pure HTML code. Figure 21.6 shows the HTML code for the blog entry that appears in Figure 21.5.

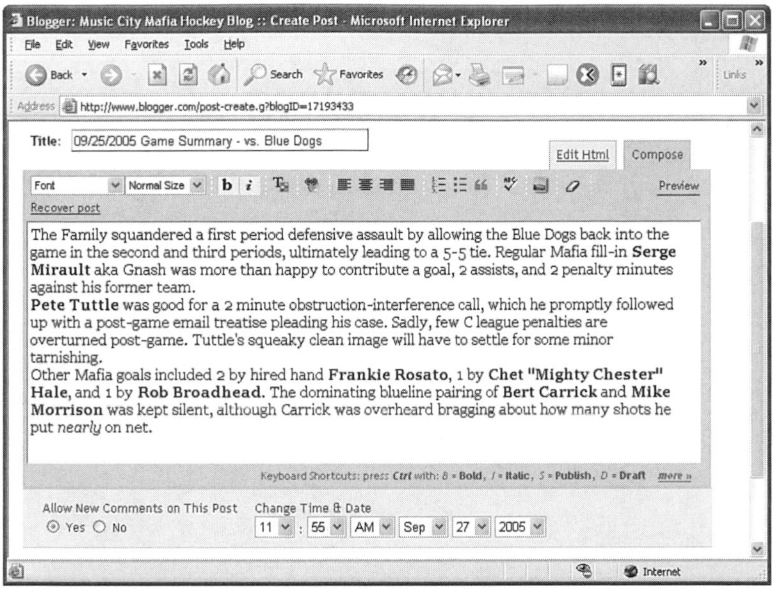

FIGURE 21.5
The Posting area of Blogger includes an edit box where you enter the content for a blog entry.

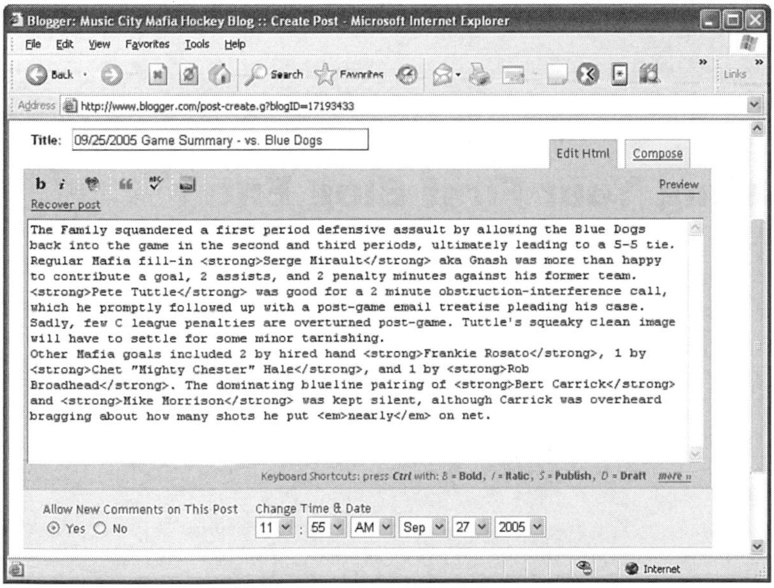

FIGURE 21.6
The Edit Html tab of the Blogger Posting area allows you to edit a blog entry as straight HTML code.

The figure reveals how you can now see the bold and italicized text coded using the <strong> and <em> tags.

The <strong> and <em> tags can be used to apply bold and italicized styles to text, although there is no true guarantee that the text will truly end up bold or italicized. This is because <strong> and <em> are intended more to convey the meaning of text, not how it is to be rendered. So, if a visually impaired person is listening to a web page through a special aural browser, he might hear <strong> text as yelling or <em> text with a different inflection. It just so happens that normal web browsers happen to render <strong> and <em> as bold and italicized text. If you want to guarantee a certain look for text in a blog, use CSS styles instead.

What the blog's HTML code doesn't show is how CSS styles enter the blog picture. You could certainly enter inline styles directly in the HTML code, but that isn't really necessary because your blog is already using a CSS style sheet via its template. The trick is to focus your attention on modifying the template to change the overall look of your blog to match your web site.

But before you do that, go ahead and click Publish Post to finish publishing your first blog entry.

Using CSS to Dress Up Your Blog

To view your new blog entry, just click View Blog in Blogger or navigate to the address of your blog, which is http://*yourblogname*.blogspot.com/. In the example, the address of the blog is http://mcmafia.blogspot.com/—this page is shown in Figure 21.7.

Notice that the URLs of blogs on Blogger are specified relative to blogspot.com, not blogger.com. This is an important detail that you don't want to miss.

You'll notice in the figure that the blog assumes the look of the default template that was selected earlier when you first created the blog. Surprisingly enough, the default template isn't a terrible match for the hockey player page you've seen a few times throughout the book. However, it is still helpful to fine-tune the template to get exactly the look you want.

Click the Template tab on the Blogger page to get started altering the CSS style sheet for the blog. Figure 21.8 shows the Template area of Blogger with the Music City Mafia blog template in view.

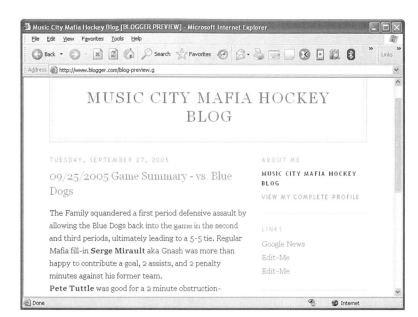

FIGURE 21.7
The Music City
Mafia blog
shows the blog
entry that was
just created.

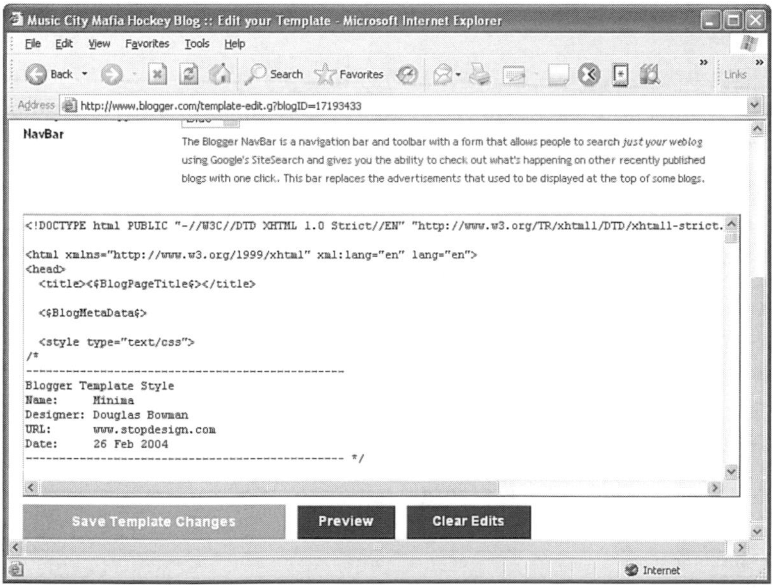

FIGURE 21.8
The Template
area of Blogger
provides access
to the layout
and formatting
of your blog via
HTML and CSS
code.

If you pay close attention to the code shown in the Template area of Blogger, you'll notice that it doesn't just contain CSS code; it's actually a complete XHTML-compliant web page with special Blogger-specific tags that insert blog content. More important, it includes a hefty internal style sheet that serves as the template for the blog. You can make changes to this style sheet to change the look of your blog.

As an example, the following code contains the CSS style rule for the blog's body element:

```
body {
  background:#fff;
  margin:0;
  padding:40px 20px;
  font:x-small Georgia,Serif;
  text-align:center;
  color:#333;
}
```

The first change to the blog style sheet involves altering the font of the body to match the hockey player style sheet, which relies on the Verdana font. If that font isn't available, the style sheet falls back on the Arial font. Here is the new body style rule with the font change:

```
body {
  background:#fff;
  margin:0;
  padding:40px 20px;
  font:x-small Verdana, Arial;
  text-align:center;
  color:#333;
}
```

If you recall, the hockey player style sheet also used special formatting for links. Following is the link formatting code that is present by default in the blog template:

```
a:link {
  color:#58a;
  text-decoration:none;
}
a:visited {
  color:#969;
  text-decoration:none;
}
a:hover {
  color:#c60;
  text-decoration:underline;
}
```

And here are the modified link styles borrowed straight from the hockey player style sheet:

```
a:link, a:visited, a:active {
  color:#19619A;
  font-weight:bold;
  text-decoration:none;
}
a:hover {
  background-color:gold;
  font-weight:bold;
  text-decoration:none;
}
```

The new link styles no longer show an underline for links. Additionally, a light shade of blue is used for the link text, and a gold background is drawn when the user hovers over a link.

In an effort to tie a bit more gold into the blog, it might add some punch to change the blog title so that it has a gold background with navy text. Following is the original CSS code for the header of the blog:

```
#header {
  width:660px;
  margin:0 auto 10px;
  border:1px solid #ccc;
}
```

And here is the modified header that sports a gold background:

```
#header {
  background-color:gold;
  width:660px;
  margin:0 auto 10px;
  border:1px solid #ccc;
}
```

The navy color for the blog title is specified in a separate style rule, #blog-title, shown here:

```
#blog-title {
  margin:5px 5px 0;
  padding:20px 20px .25em;
  border:1px solid #eee;
  border-width:1px 1px 0;
  font-size:200%;
  line-height:1.2em;
  font-weight:normal;
  color:#666;
  text-transform:uppercase;
  letter-spacing:.2em;
}
```

This code is for the default blog title style rule. Following is the modified version with navy text and small caps, which is consistent with the style of the hockey player style sheet:

```
#blog-title {
  margin:5px 5px 0;
  padding:20px 20px .25em;
  border:1px solid #eee;
  border-width:1px 1px 0;
  font-size:200%;
  line-height:1.2em;
  font-weight:normal;
  color:navy;
  font-variant:small-caps;
  letter-spacing:.2em;
}
```

The last section of style code to take a look at is the title of each blog entry, which could also benefit from a navy color and small-caps font. Following is the original style rule for this element:

```
.post-title {
  margin:.25em 0 0;
  padding:0 0 4px;
  font-size:140%;
  font-weight:normal;
  line-height:1.4em;
  color:#c60;
}
```

The modified version of this style rule simply adds the `color` and `font-variant` properties to the end of the rule:

```
.post-title {
  margin:.25em 0 0;
  padding:0 0 4px;
  font-size:130%;
  font-weight:normal;
  line-height:1.4em;
  color:navy;
  font-variant:small-caps;
}
```

Figure 21.9 shows the hockey blog with the new style modifications applied.

If you compare this page with the page shown in Figure 21.7, you'll notice that the changes have a significant effect. Perhaps more important is how the blog page now matches up stylistically with the hockey player page that will link to it. Look ahead to Figure 21.10 to see this page.

FIGURE 21.9
The hockey blog with a modified template now more closely matches the hockey player pages.

Tying Your Blog to Your Web Site

So at this point you hopefully have a collection of web pages and a blog hosted separately on Blogger.com or some other similar blog service. The question now is how to tie the two online components together. As you may already be guessing, this is simply a matter of adding a link to your web pages that connect them to the blog.

Following is an example of how to wire the hockey blog on Blogger.com to the hockey player page for Terry Lancaster via an <a> tag:

```
<a href="http://mcmafia.blogspot.com/" rel="external">View blog</a>
```

Notice that the URL specified in the href attribute is the same URL you established when first creating the blog on Blogger. Also, if you recall, the rel attribute of the <a> tag is used to sidestep a limitation of current browsers so that you can open a link in a separate browser window without invalidating a page as an XHTML page. This trick was covered back in Hour 3, "Linking to Other Web Pages," when you were shown how to open a link in a new browser window.

Figure 21.10 shows the new and improved hockey player page with the blog link highlighted near the bottom of the page.

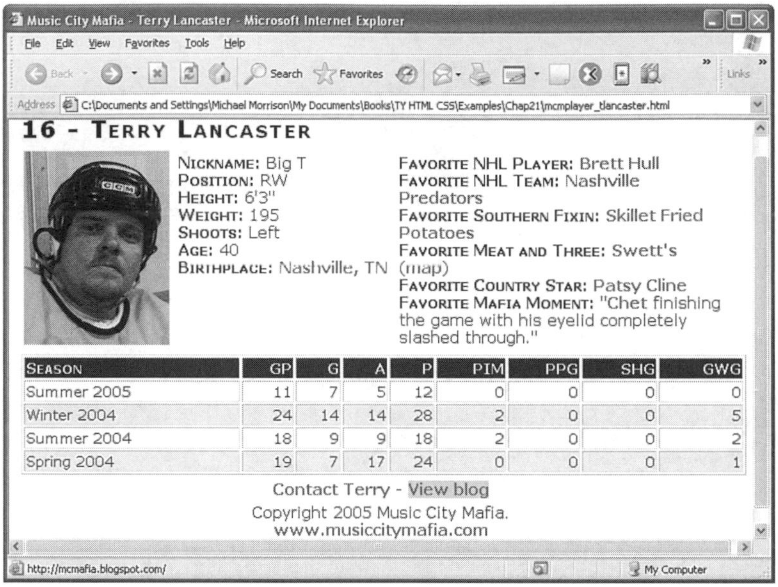

FIGURE 21.10
The blog link is now plainly visible near the bottom of the hockey player web page.

If you click the View Blog link, the Music City Mafia blog opens in a new browser window, and looks just like what you saw in Figure 21.9.

Updating Your Blog

To update your blog and add new entries to it, you must return to the main Blogger site at http://www.blogger.com/. If you aren't automatically logged in, be sure to log back in using the username and password you created earlier in the hour. You'll then be taken to the Blogger Dashboard, where you can see all the blogs you currently have set up. Figure 21.11 shows the Dashboard with the Music City Mafia blog in view.

Coffee Break

> For an extremely practical example of a blog that can really help you out, check out HTML Dog at http://www.htmldog.com/. This blog focuses on HTML and CSS, and is an excellent online source for web page development information.

Out beside the blog name in the figure, you'll notice a plus sign and a gear icon. The plus sign is what you click to create a new blog entry, and the gear icon allows you to change the settings for the blog. Clicking the blog name directly will take you to a listing of all the blog entries for the blog, where you can view, edit, delete, and otherwise manage them.

FIGURE 21.11
The Blogger Dashboard provides access to all the blogs you've created.

Summary

This hour took a slight break from the tedium of hacking out HTML and CSS code by stepping through the creation of a hosted blog. Unlike a blog that you create manually with your own HTML and CSS code, a hosted blog offers publication and automation benefits that are hard to argue. For this reason, I learn toward using a blog service or special blog software as opposed to creating and managing your own blog from scratch. This lesson introduced Blogger as an example of a free blog service that is both easy and fun to use. There are certainly other blog services out there, some of which I mentioned in the lesson. Feel free to explore all of your options before diving into your own blog. The main thing to keep in mind as you enter the blogosphere is that you have a golden opportunity to share your viewpoint with the world—make it count!

Q&A

Q *I hear about people getting rich off of their blogs. How can I cash in?*

A It is true that some people make a decent living off of their blogs thanks to ads that are displayed alongside their blog entries. You can incorporate advertisements into your own blog, in which case you make money each time someone visits your blog and clicks an ad. The Blogger blog service includes built-in support for Google AdSense, which is a great ad program for making money on ads placed on your pages. Hour 17, "Web Page Scripting for Nonprogrammers," covered the basics of Google AdSense. You can also access and enable AdSense within the Blogger site by clicking the Template area followed by AdSense.

Q *How often should I update my blog?*

A Keep in mind that the fresher the content, the more likely people are to visit your blog. And if you're trying to make a few bucks off of your blog via ad revenue, you want to use everything at your disposal to keep people coming back. Having said all that, I recommend adding a new blog entry at least a couple of times a week. If you don't find it to be too much of a drain on your time, adding a new entry daily is even better. Some full-time bloggers are known to update their blogs numerous times a day, although at some point it becomes difficult to post quality content at too small an interval.

Workshop

The workshop contains quiz questions and activities to help you solidify your understanding of the material covered. Try to answer all questions before looking at the "Answers" section that follows.

Quiz

1. What is the significance of a blog's permalink?

2. How does CSS enter the blog picture on the Blogger service?

3. How do you link to a blog named `saltyblog` that is hosted on Blogger, and that links through the link text "Here's the Salty Blog!"?

Answers

1. A permalink is a permanent link to a blog entry, and it is important because it allows you to later reference the specific blog entry via a URL that won't be lost after the entry is no longer visible on the main blog page.

2. CSS enters the Blogger picture because it allows you to customize the template for a blog to use your own fonts, your own colors, and even your own page layout. You can customize just about anything associated with a Blogger template using CSS and even HTML if you have the confidence to learn how the special Blogger tags work.

3. `<a href="http://saltyblog.blogspot.com/" rel="external">Here's the Salty Blog!</a>`

Exercises

▶ If you haven't already created your own hosted blog, by all means do so now. Trust me, you'll find yourself having some fun as you pour your thoughts onto the online page on a regular basis. If you have a favorite hobby, sport, or other interest, consider focusing the blog on that interest.

▶ Encourage your friends, family, and co-workers to visit and participate in your blog. Even though a blog typically presents the viewpoint of a single group or person, in many ways it can serve as an online community. You might be surprised by some of the comments you receive on your blog...hopefully pleasantly surprised!

▶ Try subscribing to your own blog's news feed using news feed aggregator software such as Feed Demon (http://www.feeddemon.com). Your blog's news feed has the same URL as the blog but with atom.xml attached to the end. So the Music City Mafia sample blog from this lesson could be syndicated via http://mcmafia.blogspot.com/atom.xml.

PART V

Building a Web Site

Organizing and Managing a Web Site

The first 21 hours of this book led you through the design and creation of your own web pages and the graphics to put on those pages. Now it's time to take a bigger-picture view of your work and stop thinking about individual web pages; it's time to start thinking about your web site as a whole.

This hour shows you how to organize and present multiple web pages so that people will be able to navigate among them without confusion. You'll also learn about ways to make your web site memorable enough to visit again and again. Web developers use the term "sticky" to describe pages that people don't want to leave. Hopefully this chapter will help you to make your web sites downright gooey!

Because web sites can be (and usually should be) updated frequently, creating pages that can be easily maintained is essential. This hour shows you how to add comments and other documentation to your pages so that you—or anyone else on your staff—can understand and modify your pages.

Try It Yourself ▼

By this point in the book, you should have enough HTML knowledge to produce most of your web site. You probably have made a number of pages already, and perhaps even published them online.

As you read this hour, think about how your pages are organized now and how you can improve that organization. Don't be surprised if you decide to do a redesign that involves changing almost all of your pages—the results are likely to be well worth the effort!

Did you know?

If you have been using a simple text editor such as Windows Notepad or Macintosh SimpleText to create your HTML pages, this is an excellent time to consider trying out an interactive web site development tool, such as Microsoft FrontPage or Macromedia Dreamweaver. Aside from helping you write HTML and CSS code quickly and intuitively, these programs offer time-saving ways to modify and keep track of many pages at once.

▼

On the other side of the coin, these programs aren't free and are not absolutely necessary for managing a small- to medium-sized web site. Unless you plan to have at least 50 web pages on your site, or unless you were planning to buy a version of Microsoft Office that includes FrontPage anyway, you may save the most time and money by using the simple text editor and/or a shareware HTML editor, along with file transfer software you already know how to use.

When One Page Is Enough

Building and organizing an attractive and effective web site doesn't always need to be a complex task. In some cases, you can effectively present a great deal of useful information on a single page, without a lot of flashy graphics. In fact, there are several advantages to a single-page site:

- ▶ All the information on the site downloads as quickly as possible.

- ▶ The whole site can be printed on paper with a single print command, even if it is several paper pages long.

- ▶ Visitors can easily save the site on their hard drive for future reference, especially if it uses a minimum of graphics.

- ▶ Links between different parts of the same page usually respond more quickly than links to other pages.

Figure 22.1 shows the first part of a web page that serves its intended audience better as a single lengthy page than it would as a multipage site. It contains about eight paper pages worth of text explaining how to participate in a popular email discussion list.

The page begins, as most introductory pages should, with a succinct explanation of what the page is about and who would want to read it. A detailed table of contents allows readers to skip directly to the reference material in which they are most interested. (Refer to Hour 6, "Creating Text Links," for a refresher on how to build a table of contents.)

As Figure 22.2 shows, each short section of the page is followed by a link back up to the table of contents, so navigating around the page feels much the same as navigating around a multipage site. Because the contents of the page are intended as a handy reference, readers will definitely prefer the convenience of being able to bookmark or save a single page instead of 8 or 10 separate pages.

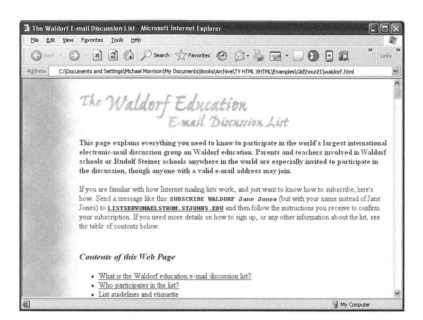

FIGURE 22.1
A good table of contents can make a lengthy page easy to navigate.

Having seen all the fancy graphics and layout tricks in the book, you may be tempted to forget that a good old-fashioned outline is often the clearest and most efficient way to organize a web site. Even if your site does require multiple pages, a list like the table of contents shown in Figure 22.1 may be the best way to guide people through a relatively small web site—or subsections of a larger one.

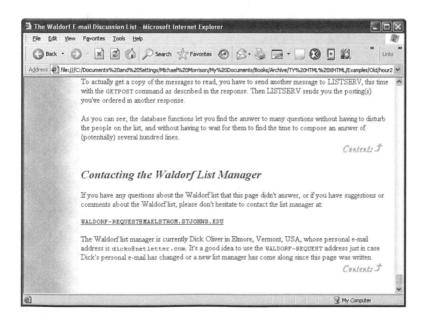

FIGURE 22.2
Always provide a link to the table of contents after each section of a long web page.

Organizing a Simple Site

Although single-page sites have their place, most companies and individuals serve their readers better by dividing their site into short, quick-read pages with graphical navigation icons to move between the pages. That way, the entire site doesn't have to be downloaded by someone seeking specific information. Furthermore, it minimizes having to scroll around a bunch on the page, which can be especially bothersome for people who are using mobile devices to view the site, or who have relatively low-resolution monitors (less than 800×600).

The goal of the home page shown in Figure 22.3, like the goal of many web sites today, is simply to make the organization "visible" on the Internet. Many people today immediately turn to the World Wide Web when they want to find out about an organization, or find out whether a particular type of organization exists at all. A simple home page should state enough information that someone can tell whether she wants to find out more. It should then provide both traditional address and telephone contact information and an electronic mail address, either directly on the home page or via a prominent link (like the About Us button in the upper-right corner of the page in Figure 22.3).

FIGURE 22.3
This small-business home page uses distinctive graphics and no-nonsense text to quickly convey the intended mood and purpose.

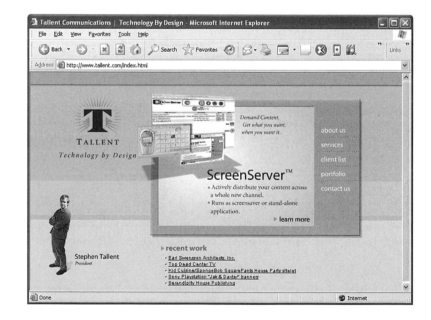

One of the most common mistakes beginning web site developers make is having each page on the site look different than the one before. Another equally serious mistake is using the same, publicly available clip art that thousands of other web authors are also using. Remember that on the Internet, one click can take you around the world. The only way to make your pages memorable and recognizable as a cohesive site is to make all your pages adhere to a unique, unmistakable visual theme. In other words, strive for uniqueness as compared to other web sites, yet uniformity within the site itself.

Regardless of how large your site is, it's a good idea to carefully organize your resources. For example, I always place the images for my web pages in a separate folder named images. Similarly, if you have files that are available for download, you could place them in a folder called downloads. This makes it much easier to keep track of web page resources based on their particular type (HTML page, GIF image, and so on). In the image example, you would refer to images in the images folder like this:

```
<img src="images\myimage.gif" alt="" />
```

As an example of how uniformity can help make a site more cohesive, take a look at what happens when someone clicks the About Us link in Figure 22.3. The user is taken to the page shown in Figure 22.4, which has a very similar feel to the previous page. The visual reiteration of the link as a title and the repetition of the background, logo, and link graphics all make it immediately obvious that this page is part of the same site as the other page. (Reusing as many graphics from the home page as possible also speeds display because these images are already cached by the web browser on the visitor's computer.) Another helpful little detail on this page is the highlighting of the About Us menu icon near the upper-left of the page—a small pointer is aimed at the About Us selection. (If you would like to view this site online, go to http://www.tallent.com/.)

By the Way

Although I'm using the tallent.com web site as an example of a "simple" site, in reality it is a surprisingly thorough site for a web consulting company. In some ways this makes the site an even better example because it maintains a simplistic feel while presenting a considerable amount of information. We should all set a goal of creating a "simple" web site no matter how much information we have to share.

By the Way

It's worth clarifying that the tallent.com sample web site uses Flash, which is an animation technology that allows you to carry out some very interesting visual effects that aren't possible with HTML and CSS. Flash is a bit beyond the scope of this book, and its usage in the sample site really has no bearing on the style and uniformity of the pages themselves, which is the point of this discussion. The tallent.com developers could have foregone some of the fancy interactive animations and achieved the same look and feel purely with HTML and CSS. In fact, some users prefer such a simplified browsing experience.

FIGURE 22.4
Clicking About
Us in the
screen shown in
Figure 22.3
takes you here.
The graphical
theme makes it
instantly clear
that this is part
of the same
site.

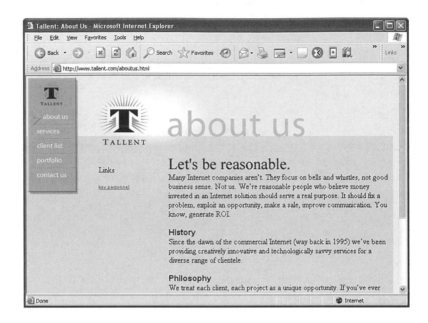

Did you Know?

The page shown in Figure 22.4 avoids another common disease that beginning
web authors too often catch; I call it the "construction site" syndrome. If you've
looked around the Internet very much, I'm sure you're as sick as I am of cute little
road worker icons and dead-end pages that say nothing but Under Construction.
Remember that when you put your pages on the Internet, you are publishing them
just as surely as if a print shop was running off 10,000 copies. No publisher
would ever annoy readers by printing a brochure, book, or newspaper with useless
pages saying only "Under Construction." Don't annoy your readers either: If a page
isn't ready to go online, *don't put it online* until it is ready, and don't put any links
to it on your other pages yet. Don't be afraid to start simple and add depth to
your site only as you get it ready.

Organizing a Larger Site

For complex sites, sophisticated layout and graphics can help organize and improve
the looks of your site when used consistently throughout all of your pages. To see
how you can make aesthetics and organization work hand-in-hand, let's look at a
site that needs to present a large volume of information to several different audi-
ences.

Figure 22.5 shows the main page for my personal web site at http://www.michael-
morrison.com/. I know that this seems like shameless self-promotion, but my site is

actually a good example of a reasonably sophisticated site in terms of layout and organization. My site includes individual pages for more than 40 computer books, as well as magazine articles, downloadable code and games, news feeds, a blog, discussion forums, and much more. It would be impossible to include all of that information on my site without a well-planned overall web site design that is efficient and consistent.

FIGURE 22.5
The links on the left side of my personal web site lead to a surprising wealth of information.

The first page a visitor sees should always begin by explaining what the site is about and provide enough introductory information to "hook" the intended audience. In my case, I include a quick news blurb followed by the latest blog entries on the main page. This keeps the main page fresh with content that changes frequently, thereby encouraging visitors to return to the site regularly. Granted, not every visitor is interested in knowing what the weather is like where I live, but then again, it's okay to have fun with your site and include some content just to liven things up a bit.

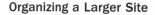

By the Way

My web site uses a splash page, which is an initial page that shows a title or some other introductory information, and then redirects to the main portion of the web site. Along with serving as a brief introduction, my splash page serves an important practical purpose because it allows me to keep the old version of my site online, along with a new version (the one you see in the figure). To "activate" the new version of the site, I simply changed the redirection of the splash page.

One criticism you could make about my site is the lack of emphasis on benefits to the visitor. It is absolutely essential—especially for commercial sites or any site intending to serve the needs of some audience—to make the very first words on the page explain *why* it would benefit a visitor to look further. Research shows that you have 3 to 5 seconds to convince visitors that your site is worth their attention before they head elsewhere, possibly never to return. Use those seconds wisely! (Hint: Is the phrase "Welcome to the Home Page of..." worth wasting two of those precious seconds on?) Of course, in my case most visitors arrive at the site from one of my books, such as this one, and therefore already have a motivation to poke around and see what's on there.

My site shown in Figure 22.5 and Figure 22.6 is organized into seven main categories (not counting Home or Administrator), accessible through the menu link icons that appear on the left side of each page. It's important to notice that these icons were chosen to quickly give visitors access to resources that meet their needs. Always organize the main links on your site according to the questions or desires of your visitors, not necessarily the structure of the information itself. For example, you can navigate to a specific discussion forum directly from the detail page on one of my books, as well as view all the forums at once by clicking Forums on the main menu. This redundancy is important because it allows visitors multiple navigation paths to arrive at information without wading through material they aren't interested in.

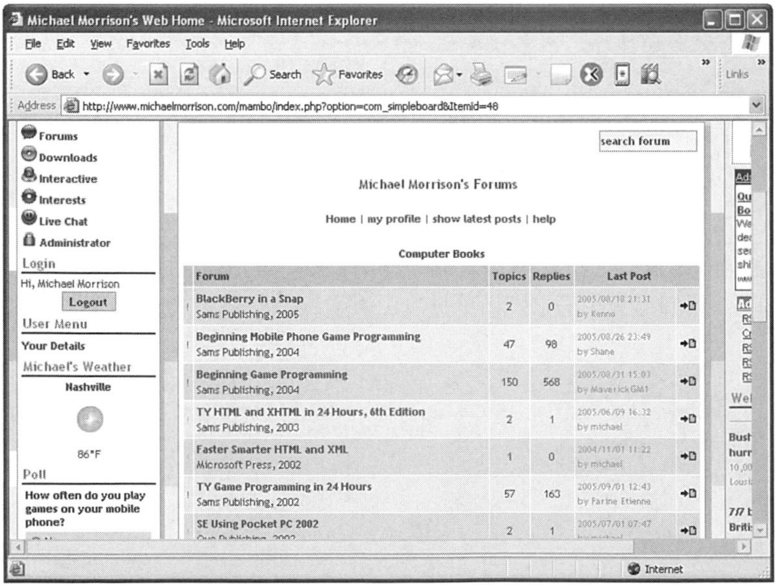

FIGURE 22.6
You get this page when you click Forums in the screen shown in Figure 22.5.

Figure 22.6 is the page you would see if you clicked Forums in the screen shown in Figure 22.5. The graphics and color theme are consistent with the home page, and the menu along the left edge of the page remains consistent with the main menu (the figure shows the page scrolled a bit to reveal more of the forums). Basically the entire framework of the page is the same on all pages of the site, with the main content area in the middle being the only part of each page that changes significantly. Visitors never have to back out of a dead-end page or feel as if they've gotten lost within a messy hierarchy of unorganized pages.

My personal web site is built using a combination of HTML, CSS, a programming language called PHP, and a database called mySQL. These technologies come together to form a software package known as a content management system. I elected to use such a system because my old site, which was pure HTML and CSS, was difficult to maintain given that I needed a great deal of interactivity with readers via discussion forums. I explain the basics of content management systems and whether or not you might consider using them for your own web sites in Hour 24, "Beyond Traditional Web Sites."

Getting back to general site design, keep in mind the following fact: Studies have repeatedly shown that people become confused and annoyed when presented with more than seven choices at a time, and people feel most comfortable with five or fewer choices. Therefore, you should avoid presenting more than five links (either in a list or as graphical icons) next to one another if at all possible, and definitely avoid presenting more than seven at once. When you need to present more than seven links in a navigation list, break them into multiple lists with a separate heading for each five to seven items.

It will also help your readers navigate your site without confusion if you avoid putting any page more than two (or at most three) links away from the home page, and always send readers back to a main category page (or the home page) after they've read a subsidiary page. In other words, try to design somewhat of a flat link structure in which most pages are no more than one or two links deep as compared to the home page. You don't want visitors to have to rely heavily on their browser's Back button to navigate through your site.

Clicking Home at the top of the menu in any of the pages on my site will take the reader back to the home page (see Figure 22.5). The link uses an absolute address (http://www.michaelmorrison.com/) instead of a relative address (index.html) so that anyone who saves the page on his hard drive can still go to the online site by clicking this link. See Hour 3, "Linking to Other Web Pages," for a review of absolute and relative addresses.

Writing Maintainable HTML Code

If you've ever done any programming, you already know how important it is to write code that can be maintained. If you don't have any programming background, understand that what I'm talking about is the ability for you or someone else to look at your code later and not be utterly confused by it. The challenge is to make your code as immediately understandable as possible. Trust me, there will come a time when you'll look back on a page that you wrote and you won't have a clue what you were thinking or why you wrote the code the way you did. Fortunately, there is a way to combat this problem of apparent memory loss!

Documenting Code with Comments

Whenever you develop an HTML page, keep in mind that you or someone else will almost certainly need to make changes to it someday. Simple text web pages are usually fairly easy to read and revise, but complex pages with graphics, tables, and other layout tricks can be quite difficult to decipher.

To see what I'm talking about, visit just about any page in a web browser and view its source code by clicking the View menu followed by Source (Internet Explorer) or View and then Page Source (Firefox). You'll likely see a jumbled bunch of code that is tough to decipher as pure HTML. This largely has to do with the fact that the code for large commercial web pages is generated dynamically by content management software systems, and is therefore more cryptic in structure. For the sake of maintaining your own pages, I encourage you to try to impose a little more order on your web page code.

As you saw in Hour 17, "Web Page Scripting for Nonprogrammers," you can enclose comments to yourself or your co-authors between <!-- and --> tags. These comments will not appear on the web page when viewed with a browser but can be read by anyone who examines the HTML code with a text editor, a word processor, a web development tool, or a web browser's View Source command. The following example provides a little refresher just to show you how a comment is coded:

```
<!-- This image needs to be updated daily. -->
<img src="headline.jpg" alt="Today's Headline" />
```

As this code reveals, the comment just before the <img /> tag provides a clue as to how the image is used. When someone reads this code, they know immediately that this is an image that must be updated every day. The text in the comment is completely ignored by web browsers.

By the Way

To include comments in a JavaScript script, put // at the beginning of each comment line. (No closing tag is needed for JavaScript comments.) In style sheets, start comments with /* and end them with */.

The HTML <!-- and --> tags will not work properly in scripts or style sheets!

You can and should, however, include one <!-- tag just after a <script> or <style> tag, with a --> tag just before the matching </script> or </style>. This hides the script or style commands from older browsers that would otherwise treat them as regular text and display them on the page.

Did you Know?

One handy usage of comments is to hide parts of a web page that are currently under construction. Rather than making the text and graphics visible and explaining that they're under construction, you can hide them from view entirely with some carefully placed comments. This is a great way to work on portions of a page gradually and show only the end result to the world when you're finished.

Try It Yourself ▼

It will be well worth your time now to go through all the web pages, scripts, and style sheets you've created so far and add any comments that you or others might find helpful when revising them in the future. Here's what to do:

1. Put a comment explaining any fancy formatting or layout techniques before the tags that make it happen.

2. Use a comment just before an <img /> tag to briefly describe any important graphic whose function isn't obvious from the alt message.

3. Consider using a comment (or several comments) to summarize how the cells of a <table> are supposed to fit together visually.

4. If you use hexadecimal color codes (such as <div style="color: #8040B0">), insert a comment indicating what the color actually is (bluish-purple).

5. Indenting your comments helps them stand out and makes both the comments and the HTML easier to read. Don't forget to use indentation in the HTML itself to make it more readable, too.

▲

Indenting Code for Clarity

I have a confession. Throughout the book I've been carefully indoctrinating you into an HTML code development style without really letting on. It's time to spill the beans. You've no doubt noticed a consistent pattern with respect to the indentation of all the HTML code in the book. More specifically, each child tag is indented to the right two spaces from its parent tag. Furthermore, content within a tag that spans more than one line is indented within the tag.

The best way to learn the value of indentation is to see some HTML code without it. You know how the song goes—"you don't know what you've got [']til it's gone." Anyway, here's a very simple table coded without any indentation:

```
<table>
<tr><td>Cell One</td>
<td>Cell Two</td></tr>
<tr><td>Cell Three</td>
<td>Cell Four</td></tr>
</table>
```

Not only is there no indentation but there also is no delineation between rows and columns within the table. Now compare this code with the following code, which describes the exact same table:

```
<table>
  <tr>
    <td>Cell One</td>
    <td>Cell Two</td>
  </tr>
  <tr>
    <td>Cell Three</td>
    <td>Cell Four</td>
  </tr>
</table>
```

This heavily indented code makes it plainly obvious how the rows and columns are divided up via `<tr>` and `<td>` tags.

In my opinion, consistent indentation is even more important than comments when it comes to making your HTML code understandable and maintainable. And you don't have to buy into my specific indentation strategy. If you'd rather use three or four spaces instead of two, that's fine with me. And if you want to tighten things up a bit and not indent content within a tag, I don't have a problem with that. The main thing to take from this is that it's important to develop a coding style of your own and then ruthlessly stick to it.

Did you Know?

If you work with other people or plan on working with other people developing web pages, you should consider getting together as a group to formulate a consistent coding style. That way everyone is on the same page, pun intended.

Summary

This hour has given you examples and explanations to help you organize your web pages into a coherent site that is informative, attractive, and easy to navigate. Web users have grown to become quite savvy in terms of expecting well-designed web sites, and they will quickly abandon your site if they experience a poor design that is difficult to navigate.

This hour also discussed the importance of making your HTML code easy to maintain by adding comments and indentation. Comments are important not only as a reminder for you when you revisit code later but also as instruction if someone else should inherit your code. Indentation may seem like an aesthetic issue, but it can truly help you to quickly analyze and understand the structure of a web page at a glance.

Q&A

Q *I've seen pages that ask viewers to change the width of their browser window or adjust other settings before proceeding beyond the home page. Why?*

A The idea is that the web page author can offer a better presentation if she has some control over the size of readers' windows or fonts. Of course, few people ever bother to change their settings, so these sites often look weird or unreadable. You'll be much better off using the tips you learn in this book to make your site readable and attractive at any window size and a wide variety of browser settings. The better organized your site is, the more usable it will be for visitors.

Q *Won't lots of comments and spaces make my pages load slower when someone views them?*

A The size of a little extra text in your pages is negligible when compared to other, chunkier web page resources such as images. Besides, slower dial-up modem connections typically do a decent job of compressing text when transmitting it, so adding spaces to format your HTML doesn't usually change the transfer time at all. You'd have to type hundreds of comment words to cause even one extra second of delay in loading a page. And keep in mind that with the broadband connections (cable, DSL, and so on) that many people now have, text travels extremely fast. It's the graphics that slow pages down, so squeeze your images as tightly as you can (refer to Hour 7, "Creating Your Own Web Page Graphics"), but use text comments freely.

Q *Will you look at my site and give me some suggestions on how to improve it?*

A I'd like to, really. Truly I would. If I looked at all my readers' sites and offered even a tiny bit of wisdom for each, however, I would be at it for hours every day. I have looked at hundreds of reader sites, and my advice usually amounts to this: Your site looks pretty or ugly and you have the basic idea of HTML, but you need to make it clearer, first, who your site is intended for, in the first sentence or heading; second, what earthly good your site is going to do them; and third, what you want them to do as a result of visiting your site. All the great graphics and HTML-manship in the world can't substitute for clearly and consistently answering those three questions for yourself and for your site's visitors. In other words, it's all about the content! Focus on the big picture and then use HTML to methodically bring it into view.

Workshop

The workshop contains quiz questions and activities to help you solidify your understanding of the material covered. Try to answer all questions before looking at the "Answers" section that follows.

Quiz

1. What are three ways to help people stay aware of the fact that all your pages form a single cohesive web site?

2. What two types of information should always be included in the home page that people encounter at your site?

3. If you want to say, "Don't change this image of me. It's my only chance at immortality," to future editors of a web page, but you don't want people who view the page to see that message, how would you do it?

Answers

1. (a) Use consistent background, colors, fonts, and styles.

   (b) Repeat the same link words or graphics on the top of the page that the link leads to.

   (c) Repeat the same small header, buttons, or other element on every page of the site.

2. (a) Enough identifying information so that she can immediately see the name of the site and what it is about.

(b) Whatever the most important message you want to convey to your intended audience is, stated directly and concisely. Whether it's your mission statement or trademarked marketing slogan, make sure that it is in plain view here.

3. Put the following comment immediately before the `<img />` tag:

```
<!-- Don't change this image of me.
     It's my only chance at immortality. -->
```

Exercises

Grab a pencil (the oldfangled kind) and sketch out your web site as a bunch of little rectangles with arrows between them. Sketch a rough overview of what each page will look like by putting squiggles where the text goes and doodles where the images go. Each arrow should start at a doodle icon that corresponds to the navigation button for the page the arrow leads to. Even if you have the latest whiz-bang web site management tools, sketching your site by hand can give you a much more intuitive grasp of which pages on your site will be easy to get to and how the layout of adjacent pages will work together—all before you invest time in writing the actual HTML to connect the pages together. Believe it or not, I still sketch out web sites like this when I'm first designing them. Sometimes you can't beat a pencil and paper!

Helping People Find Your Web Pages

Your web pages are ultimately only as useful as they are accessible—if no one can find your pages, your hard work coding them will be for naught. The HTML tags and techniques you'll discover in this hour won't make any visible difference in your web pages, which may come as a surprise. However, they are extremely important in that they will help make your web pages much more visible to your intended audience. For most web authors, this may be the easiest—but most important—hour in the book. You'll learn how to make links to your pages appear at all the major Internet search sites whenever someone searches for words related to your topic or company. There are no magic secrets that guarantee you'll be at the top of every search list, but there are many reliable and effective techniques you can employ to make sure that your site is as easy to find as possible.

In addition to revealing some tricks to improve the "searchability" of your pages, this hour also shows you how to make one page automatically load another, how to forward visitors to pages that have moved, and how to document a page's full Internet address.

Publicizing Your Web Site

Presumably, you want your web pages to attract someone's attention, or you wouldn't bother to create them. If you are placing your pages only on a local network or corporate intranet or are distributing your pages exclusively on disk or by email, helping people find your pages may not be much of a problem. If you are adding your pages to the millions upon millions of others on the Internet, however, bringing your intended audience to your site is a very big challenge indeed.

To tackle this problem, you need a basic understanding of how most people decide which pages they will look at. There are basically three ways people can become aware of your web site:

▶ Somebody tells them about it and gives them the address; they enter that address directly into their web browser.

▶ They follow a link to your site from someone else's site.

▶ They find your site listed in a search site such as Google, Yahoo!, or MSN Search.

You can make all three of these happen more often if you invest some time and effort. To increase the number of people who hear about you through word-of-mouth, well, use your mouth—and every other channel of communication available to you. If you have an existing contact database or mailing list, announce your web site to those people. Add the site address to your business cards or company literature. Heck, go buy TV and radio ads broadcasting your Internet address if you have the money. In short, do the marketing thing. Good old-fashioned word-of-mouth marketing is still the best thing going, even on the Internet.

Getting links to your site from other sites is also pretty straightforward—though that doesn't mean it isn't a lot of work. Find every other web site related to your topic and offer to add a link to those sites if they add one to yours. If there are specialized directories on your topic, either online or in print, be sure you are listed. There's not much I can say in this book to help you with that, except to go out and do it.

The main thing I can help you with is the third item: being visible at the major Internet search sites. I'm sure you've used at least one or two of the big search sites: Google, Yahoo!, MSN Search, AllTheWeb, Alta Vista, Ask Jeeves, and Teoma. (The addresses of these sites are google.com, yahoo.com, search.msn.com, alltheweb.com, altavista.com, askjeeves.com, and teoma.com.)

By the Way

> The popularity and usefulness of search engines are not etched in stone. In other words, you'll find that search engines come in and out of vogue according to the whims of the web community, as well as the technical details of how they perform searches. For this reason, you might want to visit http://www.searchenginewatch.com/ for a recent assessment of the most popular search engines.

These sites are basically huge databases that attempt to catalog as many pages on the Internet as possible. They all use automated processing to build the databases, although some (such as Yahoo!) emphasize quality by having each listing checked by a human. Others (such as Teoma) prefer to go for quantity and rely almost entirely on robots or spiders. A robot or spider is an automated computer program that spends all day looking at web pages all over the Internet and building a database of the contents of the pages it visits. Still others (such as Google) use highly sophisticated techniques of ranking pages based on how they are linked to from other pages, in addition to using robot techniques.

As the spiders and humans constantly add to the database, another automated program, called a search engine, processes requests from people who are looking for web pages on specific topics. The search engine looks in the database for pages that contain the key words or phrases that someone is looking for and sends that person a list of all the pages that contain those terms. Some people use the term *Internet directory* to indicate a search engine whose database was built mostly by people instead of robots.

Some search engines are known as *portals*, which means that they go far beyond offering a search facility. Portals such as Yahoo! typically offer news, weather, shopping, and other kinds of information in addition to a basic search feature. Many web users have grown to appreciate the simplicity of search engines such as Google that aren't encumbered with portal features.

Listing Your Pages with the Major Search Sites

If you want people to find your pages, you absolutely must submit a request to each of the major search sites to index your pages. Each of these sites has a form for you to fill out with the address, a brief description of the site, and in some cases a category or list of keywords with which your listing should be associated. These forms are easy to fill out; you can easily do all of them in an hour with time left over to list yourself at one or two specialized directories you might have found as well. (How do you find the specialized directories? Through the major search sites, of course!)

Even though listing with the major search engines is easy and quick, it can be a bit confusing: Each of them uses different terminology to identify where you should click to register your pages. Table 23.1 may save you some frustration; it includes the address of each major search engine, along with the exact wording of the link you should click to register.

TABLE 23.1   Registering Your Site with a Search Engine

Search Engine	How to Register Your Page Address
Google	Visit http://www.google.com/addurl/, enter the address of your site and a brief description, and then enter the squiggly verification text shown on the page. Then click the Add URL button to add your site to Google.
Yahoo! Search	Visit http://submit.search.yahoo.com/free/request, enter the address of your site, and then click the Submit URL button.
Yahoo! Directory	Visit http://dir.yahoo.com/, navigate to the specific directory where your site should be listed, and click Suggest a Site in the upper-right corner of the browser window. Follow the directions to submit your site; be sure to choose the free option if applicable to your site.

TABLE 23.1   Continued

Search Engine	How to Register Your Page Address
MSN Search	Visit http://search.msn.com/docs/submit.aspx, enter the verification text followed by the address of your site, and then click the Submit URL button.
AllTheWeb	AllTheWeb search results are provided by Yahoo! Search, so just be sure to submit your site to Yahoo! Search, as explained previously.
AltaVista	AltaVista search results are also provided by Yahoo! Search, so just be sure to submit your site to Yahoo! Search, as explained previously.
Ask Jeeves	Send an email message to url@askjeeves.com requesting an evaluation of your site.
Teoma	Teoma and Ask Jeeves utilize the same search index, so your Ask Jeeves request also applies to Teoma.

URL stands for Uniform Resource Locator, which is just a fancy name for the address of a web page.

Did you Know?

There are sites that provide one form that automatically submits itself to all the major search engines, plus several minor ones. (http://www.scrubtheweb.com/, http://www.submitexpress.com/, and http://www.hypersubmit.com/ are popular examples.) Many of these sites attempt to sell you a premium service that lists you in many other directories and indexes as well. Depending on your target audience, these services may or may not be of value, but I strongly recommend that you go directly to the major search sites listed earlier and use their own forms to submit your requests to be listed. That way you can be sure to answer the questions (which are slightly different at every site) accurately, and you will know exactly how your site listing will appear at each of them.

Wait! Before you rush off this minute to submit your listing requests, read the rest of this hour. Otherwise, you'll have a very serious problem, and you will have already lost your best opportunity to solve it.

To see what I mean, imagine this scenario: You publish a page selling automatic cockroach flatteners. I have a roach problem, and I'm allergic to bug spray. I open my laptop, brush the roaches off the keyboard, log on to my favorite search site, and enter *cockroach* as a search term. The search engine promptly presents me with a list of the first 10 out of 10,254 Internet pages containing the word *cockroach*. You have submitted your listing request, so you know that your page is somewhere on that list.

Did I mention that I'm rich? And did I mention that two roaches are mating on my foot? You even offer same-day delivery in my area. Do you want your page to be number 3 on the list, or number 8,542? Okay, now you understand the problem. Just getting listed in a search engine isn't enough—you need to work your way up the rankings.

Providing Hints for Search Engines

Fact: There is absolutely nothing you can do to guarantee that your site will appear in the top 10 search results for a particular word or phrase in any major search engine (short of buying ad space from the search site, that is). After all, if there were, why couldn't everyone else who wants to be number 1 on the list do it, too? What you can do is avoid being last on the list and give yourself as good a chance as anyone else of being first.

Each search engine uses a different method for determining which pages are likely to be most relevant and should therefore be sorted to the top of a search result list. You don't need to get too hung up about the differences, though, because they all use some combination of the same basic criteria. The following list includes almost everything any search engine considers when trying to evaluate which pages best match one or more keywords. The first three of these criteria are used by almost every major search engine, and most of them also use at least one or two of the other criteria.

▶ Do the keywords appear in the `<title>` tag of the page?

▶ Do the keywords appear in the first few lines of the page?

▶ How many times do the keywords appear in the entire page?

▶ Do the keywords appear in a `<meta />` tag in the page?

▶ Do the keywords appear in the names of image files and `alt` text for images in the page?

▶ How many other pages in my web site link to the page?

▶ How many other pages in other web sites link to the page? How many other pages link to those pages?

▶ How many times have people chosen this page from a previous search list result?

▶ Is the page rated highly in a human-generated directory?

By the Way

> Yahoo! and Ask Jeeves are unique among search engines in that real people analyze and categorize web sites that are added to its directory.

Clearly, the most important thing you can do to improve your position is to consider what word combinations your intended audience is most likely to enter. I'd recommend that you not concern yourself with common single-word searches; the lists they generate are usually so long that trying to make it to the top is like playing the lottery. Focus instead on uncommon words and two- or three-word combinations that are most likely to indicate relevance to your topic. Make sure that those terms and phrases occur several times on your page, and be certain to put the most important ones in the `<title>` tag and the first heading or introductory paragraph.

By the Way

> Some over-eager web page authors put dozens or even hundreds of repetitions of the same word on their pages, sometimes in small print or a hard-to-see color, just to get the search engines to sort that page to the top of the list whenever someone searches for that word. This practice is called *search engine spamming*.
>
> Don't be tempted to try this sort of thing—all the major search engines are on to this practice, and immediately delete any page from their database that sets off a "spam detector" by repeating the same word or group of words in a suspicious pattern. It's still fine (and quite beneficial) to have several occurrences of important search words on a page. Make sure, however, that you use the words in normal sentences or phrases, and the spam police will leave you alone.

Of all the search engine evaluation criteria just listed, the use of `<meta />` tags is probably the most poorly understood. Some people rave about `<meta />` tags as if using them could instantly move you to the top of every search list. Other people dismiss `<meta />` tags as ineffective and useless. Neither of these extremes is true.

A `<meta />` tag is a general-purpose tag you can put in the `<head>` portion of any document to specify some information about the page that doesn't belong in the `<body>` text. Most major search engines look at `<meta />` tags to provide them with a short description of your page and some keywords to identify what your page is about. For example, your automatic cockroach flattener order form might include the following two tags:

```
<meta name="description"
content="Order form for the SuperSquish cockroach flattener." />
<meta name="keywords"
content="cockroach,roaches,kill,squish,supersquish" />
```

Always place `<meta />` tags *after* the `<head>`, `<title>`, and `</title>` tags but *before* the closing `</head>` tag.

According to XHTML standards, `<title>` must be the very first tag in the `<head>` section of every document.

The first tag in this example ensures that the search engine has an accurate description of the page to present on its search results list. The second `<meta />` tag slightly increases your page's ranking on the list whenever any of your specified keywords are included in a search query.

You should always include `<meta />` tags with `name="description"` and `name="keywords"` attributes in any page that you want to be indexed by a search engine. Doing so may not have a dramatic effect on your position in search lists, and not all search engines look for `<meta />` tags, but it can only help.

The previous cockroach example aside, search engine experts suggest that the ideal length of a page description in a `<meta />` tag is in the 100- to 200-character range. For keywords, the recommended length is in the 200- to 400-character range. Experts also suggest not wasting spaces in between keywords, which is evident in the cockroach example. And finally, don't go crazy repeating the same keywords in multiple phrases in the keywords—some search engines will penalize you for attempting to overdo it.

In the unlikely event that you don't want a page to be included in search engine databases at all, you can put the following `<meta />` tag in the `<head>` portion of that page:

```
<meta name="robots" content="noindex" />
```

This causes some search robots to ignore the page. For more robust protection from prying robot eyes, ask the person who manages your web server to include your page address in the server's `robots.txt` file. (She will know what that means and how to do it.) All major search spiders will then be sure to ignore your pages. This might apply to internal company pages that you'd rather not be readily available via public searches.

To give you a concrete example of how to improve search engine results, consider the page listed in Listing 23.1 and shown in Figure 23.1. This page should be fairly easy to find because it deals with a specific topic and includes several occurrences of some uncommon technical terms for which people interested in this subject would be likely to search. However, there are several things you could do to improve the chances of this page appearing high on a search engine results list.

LISTING 23.1   A Page That Will Present Some Problems During an
                   Internet Site Search

```
<?xml version="1.0" encoding="UTF-8"?>
<!DOCTYPE html PUBLIC "-//W3C//DTD XHTML 1.1//EN"
  "http://www.w3.org/TR/xhtml11/DTD/xhtml11.dtd">

<html xmlns="http://www.w3.org/1999/xhtml" xml:lang="en">
  <head>
    <title>Fractal Central</title>
  </head>

  <body style="background-image:url(fractalback.jpg); color:#003399">
    <div style="text-align:center">
      <img src="fractalaccent.gif" alt="" />
    </div>
    <div style="width:133px; float:left; padding:6px; text-align:center;
    border-width:4px; border-style:ridge">
      Discover the latest software, books and more at our online store.<br />
      <a href="orderform.html"><img src="orderform.gif" alt="Order Form"
      style="border-style:none" /></a>
    </div>
    <div style="float:left; padding:6px">
      <h2>A Comprehensive Guide to the<br />
      Art and Science of Chaos and Complexity</h2>
      <p>What's that? You say you're hearing about "fractals" and "chaos" all
      over the place, but still aren't too sure what they are? How about a
      quick summary of some key concepts:</p>
      <ol>
        <li><p>Even the simplest systems become deeply complex and richly
        beautiful when a process is "iterated" over and over, using the
        results of each step as the starting point of the next. This is how
        Nature creates a magnificently detailed 300-foot redwood tree from a
        seed the size of your fingernail.</p></li>
        <li><p>Most "iterated systems" are easily simulated on computers,
        but only a few are predictable and controllable. Why? Because a tiny
        influence, like a "butterfly flapping its wings," can be strangely
        amplified to have major consequences such as completely changing
        tomorrow's weather in a distant part of the world.</p></li>
        <li><p>Fractals can be magnified forever without loss of detail, so
        mathematics that relies on straight lines is useless with them.
        However, they give us a new concept called "fractal dimension" which
        can measure the texture and complexity of anything from coastlines to
        storm clouds.</p></li>
        <li><p>While fractals win prizes at graphics shows, their chaotic
        patterns pop up in every branch of science. Physicists find beautiful
        artwork coming out of their plotters. "Strange attractors" with
        fractal turbulence appear in celestial mechanics. Biologists diagnose
        "dynamical diseases" when fractal rhythms fall out of sync. Even pure
        mathematicians go on tour with dazzling videos of their
        research.</p></li>
      </ol>
      <p>Think all these folks may be on to something?</p>
    </div>
    <div style="text-align:center">
      <a href="http://netletter.com/nonsense/"><img src="findout.gif"
      alt="Find Out More" style="border-style:none" /></a>
    </div>
  </body>
</html>
```

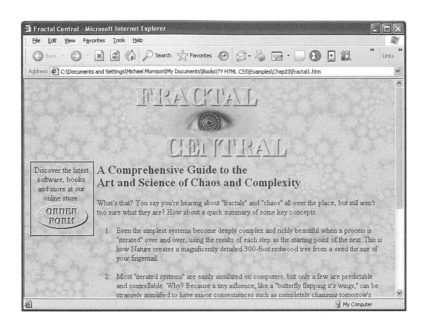

FIGURE 23.1
The first part of the page shown in Listing 23.1, as it appears in a web browser.

The contents of the page in Listing 23.2 and Figure 23.2 look to a human being almost the same as those of the page in Listing 23.1 and Figure 23.1. To search robots and search engines, however, these two pages appear quite different. The following list summarizes the changes and explains why I made each modification:

▶ I added some important search terms to the `<title>` tag and the first heading on the page. The original page didn't even include the word *fractal* in either of these two key positions.

▶ I added `<meta />` tags to assist search engines with a description and keywords.

▶ I added a very descriptive `alt` attribute to the first `<img />` tag. Not all search engines read and index `alt` text, but some do.

▶ I took out the quotation marks around technical terms (such as `"fractal"` and `"iterated"`) because some search engines consider *"fractal"* to be a different word than *fractal*. I replaced the quotation marks with the character entity `&quot;`, which search robots simply disregard. This is also a good idea because XHTML urges web developers to use the `&quot;` entity instead of quotation marks anyway.

▶ I added the keyword *fractal* twice to the text in the order-form box.

It is impossible to quantify how much more frequently people searching for information on fractals and chaos were able to find the page shown in Listing 23.2 versus the page shown in Listing 23.1, but it's a sure bet that none of the changes could do anything but improve the page's visibility to search engines. As is often the case, the improvements made for the benefit of the search spiders probably made the page's subject easier for humans to recognize and understand as well. This makes optimizing a page for search engines a win-win effort!

LISTING 23.2   An Improvement on the Page in Listing 23.1

```
<?xml version="1.0" encoding="UTF-8"?>
<!DOCTYPE html PUBLIC "-//W3C//DTD XHTML 1.1//EN"
  "http://www.w3.org/TR/xhtml11/DTD/xhtml11.dtd">

<html xmlns="http://www.w3.org/1999/xhtml" xml:lang="en">
  <head>
    <title>Fractal Central: A Guide to Fractals, Chaos, and Complexity</title>
    <meta name="description" content="A comprehensive guide to fractal
    geometry, chaos science and complexity theory." />
    <meta name="keywords"  content="fractal, fractals, chaos science, chaos
    theory, fractal geometry, complexity, complexity theory" />
  </head>

  <body style="background-image:url(fractalback.jpg); color:#003399">
    <div style="text-align:center">
      <img src="fractalaccent.gif" alt="Fractal Central: A Guide to Fractals,
      Chaos, and Complexity" />
    </div>
    <div style="width:133px; float:left; padding:6px; text-align:center;
    border-width:4px; border-style:ridge">
      Discover the latest fractal software, books and more at the
      <span style="font-weight:bold">Fractal Central</span> online store.<br />
      <a href="orderform.html"><img src="orderform.gif" alt="Order Form"
      style="border-style:none" /></a>
    </div>
    <div style="float:left; padding:6px">
      <h2>A Comprehensive Guide to Fractal Geometry,<br />
      Chaos Science, and Complexity Theory</h2>
      <p>What's that? You say you're hearing about &quot;fractals&quot; and
      &quot;chaos&quot; all over the place, but still aren't too sure what
      they are? How about a quick summary of some key concepts:</p>
      <ol>
        <li><p>Even the simplest systems become deeply complex and richly
        beautiful when a process is &quot;iterated&quot; over and over, using
        the results of each step as the starting point of the next. This is
        how Nature creates a magnificently detailed 300-foot redwood tree from
        a seed the size of your fingernail.</p></li>
        <li><p>Most &quot;iterated systems&quot; are easily simulated on
        computers, but only a few are predictable and controllable. Why?
        Because a tiny influence, like a &quot;butterfly flapping its
        wings,&quot; can be strangely amplified to have major consequences
        such as completely changing tomorrow's weather in a distant part of
        the world.</p></li>
        <li><p>Fractals can be magnified forever without loss of detail, so
        mathematics that relies on straight lines is useless with them.
```

LISTING 23.2   Continued

```
        However, they give us a new concept called &quot;fractal
        dimension&quot; which can measure the texture and complexity of
        anything from coastlines to storm clouds.</p></li>
        <li><p>While fractals win prizes at graphics shows, their chaotic
        patterns pop up in every branch of science. Physicists find beautiful
        artwork coming out of their plotters. &quot;Strange attractors&quot;
        with fractal turbulence appear in celestial mechanics. Biologists
        diagnose &quot;dynamical diseases&quot; when fractal rhythms fall out
        of sync. Even pure mathematicians go on tour with dazzling videos of
        their research.</p></li>
      </ol>
      <p>Think all these folks may be on to something?</p>
    </div>
    <div style="text-align:center">
      <a href="http://netletter.com/nonsense/"><img src="findout.gif"
      alt="Find Out More" style="border-style:none" /></a>
    </div>
  </body>
</html>
```

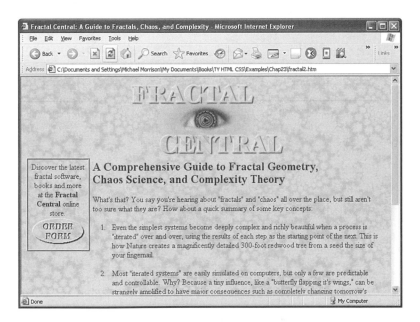

FIGURE 23.2
The first part of the page in Listing 23.2, as it appears in a web browser.

If you've read any popular computer magazines in the past few years, you've probably found claims that XML, the "HTML of the future," will make it much easier to find what you're looking for on the Internet. You might be wondering how to get the web pages you create hooked up to this magical new searching miracle.

The good news is that XML will indeed eventually make online searching easier and more efficient. The bad news is that neither XML nor its offspring, XHTML, can make it any easier for people to find your pages today or even in the very near future. The technologies that will rely on XML to improve web searching are still under development, and may not reach the mainstream for years to come. Having said that, using XHTML and CSS in lieu of old-style HTML is a step in the right direction toward a more organized, and therefore more searchable, Web.

While you're waiting for The Next Big Thing to hit, you might want to keep an eye on future developments in web searching by stopping by the Search Engine Watch site at http://searchenginewatch.com/ every month or so.

Auto Loading Another Web Page

When you are managing a web site, it may become necessary to move some pages from one address to another. You might decide, for example, to change the service provider or your whole site's domain name. You might just reorganize things and move some pages into a different directory folder.

What happens, then, when someone visits his or her favorite web page on your site after you've moved it? If you don't want your visitor to be stranded with a Not Found error message, you should put a page at the old address that says This page has moved to... with the new address (and a link to it).

Chances are you've encountered similar messages on the Internet yourself. Some of them probably employed the neat trick you're about to learn; they automatically transferred you to the new address after a few seconds, even if you didn't click a link.

In fact, you can make any page automatically load any other page after an amount of time you choose. The secret to this trick is another variation of the <meta /> tag, which goes in the <head> section of a page and looks like the following:

```
<meta http-equiv="refresh" content="5; url=nextpage.html" />
```

Replace 5 with the number of seconds to wait before loading the next page, and replace nextpage.html with the address of the next page to load.

In addition to routing a visitor to a new page location, the automatic page-loading trick can be used to display a web page title that appears for a moment and then leads a visitor into the main area of a site. For example, take a look at the code in Listing 23.3, which looks as shown in Figure 23.3 when viewed in Mozilla Firefox. After 5 seconds, the <meta /> tag causes the page at http://www.stalefishlabs.com/news.html (given in Listing 23.4 and shown in Figure 23.4) to appear.

For the impatient, I also included a link to the news.html page, which someone could click before the five seconds is up.

By the Way

LISTING 23.3 The `<meta />` Tag Causes the Web Browser to Automatically Load the Page Shown in Figure 23.4 After 5 Seconds

```
<?xml version="1.0" encoding="UTF-8"?>
<!DOCTYPE html PUBLIC "-//W3C//DTD XHTML 1.1//EN"
  "http://www.w3.org/TR/xhtml11/DTD/xhtml11.dtd">

<html xmlns="http://www.w3.org/1999/xhtml" xml:lang="en">
  <head>
    <title>Stalefish Labs. Dead Serious About Fun.</title>
    <meta name="description" content="Stalefish Labs.
    Dead Serious About Fun." />
    <meta name="keywords" content="games, toys, fun, social, entertainment,
    tall tales, tall tale, topper, zinger" />
    <meta http-equiv="refresh"
    content="5; url=http://www.stalefishlabs.com/news.html" />
    <base href="http://www.stalefishlabs.com/" />
  </head>

  <body style="text-align:center">
    <div style="width:100%; margin-top:100px; text-align:center">
      <a href="news.html"><img src="images/entertitle.gif" alt="Stalefish Labs.
      Dead Serious About Fun." style="border-style:none" /></a>
    </div>
    <div style="width:100%; text-align:center">
      <a href="news.html"><img src="images/enter.gif" alt="Click to enter."
      style="border-style:none" /></a>
    </div>
  </body>
</html>
```

The Stalefish Labs intro page includes a few other little HTML tricks that are worth pointing out before you move on. First off, the description and keyword `<meta />` tags you learned about earlier are used here to help prep the site for search engines. Also, the `margin-top` style property is used in the first `<div>` tag to help provide some vertical space before the title image is displayed on the page. This improves the overall appearance of the page regardless of how large the browser window is sized.

The last trick on the page involves the usage of the `<base />` tag, which appears in the `<head>` of the page. Read on to learn why this tag is important.

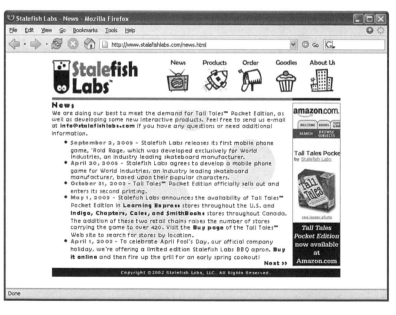

Documenting the Full Address of a Page

Suppose you create a web page advertising your business, and a customer likes your page so much that she saves it on her hard drive. A couple of days later, she wants to show a friend your cool site, but guess what? She forgot to bookmark it, and of course the page doesn't contain a link to itself. She clicks the links to your order form, but they are only filename links (such as `<a href="orderform.html">`); they don't work from her hard drive unless the order form is on her hard drive too. You have lost two eager customers.

One way to avoid this scenario is to always use complete addresses starting with http:// in all links. However, this makes your pages difficult to test and maintain. If you ever move your site or change the domain name, all of your links are suddenly broken.

You could also include a link to your home page's full address on every page, including the home page itself. Yet there's a more elegant way to make a page remember where it came from.

The `<base />` tag lets you include the address of a page within the `<head>` section of that page, like this:

```
<html>
  <head>
    <title>My Page</title>
    <base href="http://www.myplace.com/" />
  </head>
  <body>
    ...The actual page goes here...
  </body>
</html>
```

For the HTML authors whose job is to maintain this page, the `<base />` tag provides convenient documentation of where this page should be put.

Even more important, all links within the page behave as if the page were at the `<base />` address—even if it isn't. For example, if you had the page in Listing 23.3 on your hard drive and you opened it with a web browser, all images on the page would be loaded from the online site at http://www.stalefishlabs.com/ rather than from the hard drive. In fact, the images are actually stored in a folder called `images` beneath the root web folder, which explains why the links in the listing begin with `images/` before the image filename. The link to the news.html page also leads to a page in the root folder at http://www.stalefishlabs.com/, instead of a local page on the hard drive.

> The `<base />` tag has no effect on the URL of pages specified in the `<meta />` tag that are automatically loaded after a certain delay. This explains why the full URL for the news.html page is provided in the `<meta />` tag in Listing 23.3.

Watch Out!

By the
~~Way~~

> Few web page authors use (or even know about) the <base /> tag. Many who do know about it don't like the hassle of changing it when they want to test a page (including images and links) on their hard drive. I've tried to give you enough information in this hour to choose for yourself whether the <base /> tag is worthwhile for you—you may very well decide that it's not.
>
> If you do choose to use the <base /> tag, don't put it in your pages until you're ready to upload them to the web server. That way you can test them with all the images and link pages on your hard drive and then add the <base /> tag at the last minute, to enjoy the benefits it offers after your pages are online.

Summary

This hour covered some extremely important territory by exploring how to provide hints to search engines (such as Google, Yahoo!, MSN Search, Alta Vista, Ask Jeeves, and Teoma) so that people can find your pages more easily on the Internet. You also found out how to make a page remember its own address and how to make a page load another page automatically. Table 23.2 lists the tags and attributes covered in this hour.

TABLE 23.2   HTML Tags and Attributes Covered in Hour 23

Tag/Attribute	Function
<meta />	Indicates meta-information about this document (information about the document itself). Most commonly used to add a page description, to designate keywords, and to make a page automatically load another page or reload itself. Used in the document <head>.
Attributes	
http-equiv= "servercmd"	Gives a command to the web browser or server. For example, http-equiv="refresh" causes a new page to load automatically.
name="name"	Can be used to specify which type of information about the document is in the content attribute. For example, name="keywords" means that keywords for the page are in content.
content="value"	The actual message or value for the information specified in http-equiv or name. For example, if the http-equiv attribute is set to refresh, the content attribute should be set to the number of seconds to wait, followed by a semicolon and the address of the page to load.
<base />	Indicates the base URL of the current document's location on a web server. This optional tag is used within <head>.
Attributes	
href="url"	The base URL of this document.

Q&A

Q *I have lots of pages in my site. Do I need to fill out a separate form for each page at each search site?*

A No. If you submit just your home page (which is presumably linked to all the other pages), the search spiders will crawl through all the links on the page (and all the links on the linked pages, and so on) until it has indexed all the pages on your site.

Q *I submitted a request to be listed with a search engine but my page never comes up, even when I enter my company's unique name. What can I do?*

A Most of the big search engines offer a form you can fill out to instantly check whether a specific address is included in their database. If you find that it isn't, you can submit another request form. Sometimes it takes days or even weeks for the spiders to get around to indexing your pages after you submit a request. Yahoo! is particularly infamous for being way behind on index requests because they employ human beings to check every page they list.

Q *When I put keywords in a `<meta />` tag, do I need to include every possible variation of spelling and capitalization?*

A Don't worry about capitalization; almost all searches are entered in all lower-case letters. Do include any obvious variations or common errors in spelling as separate keywords. Although simple in concept, there are more advanced strategies available when it comes to manipulating the `<meta />` tag than I've been able to cover in this hour. Visit http://www.selfpromotion.com/ for a deeper discussion of the `<meta />` tag and web site promotion in general.

Q *Can I use the `<meta />` tag to make a page automatically reload itself every few seconds or minutes?*

A Yes, but there's no point in doing that unless you have some sort of program or script set up on your web server computer to provide new information on the page. This technique can be useful in special scenarios, however. As an example, sites that display live information such as sports scores often use this technique to automatically reload themselves and show updated scores every few seconds.

Workshop

The workshop contains quiz questions and activities to help you solidify your understanding of the material covered. Try to answer all questions before looking at the "Answers" section that follows.

Quiz

1. If you publish a page about puppy adoption, how could you help make sure that the page can be found by people who enter *puppy*, *dog*, and/or *adoption* at all the major Internet search sites?

2. Suppose you recently moved a page from http://mysite.com/oldplace/ thepage.html to http://mysite.com/newplace/thepage.html, but you're not quite sure whether you're going to keep it there yet. How would you automatically send people who try the old address to the new address, without any message telling them there was a change?

3. What are three ways to make sure that people who save one of your pages on their hard drive can find your site online from it, even if they forget to add it to their Bookmarks or Favorites list?

Answers

1. First, make sure that *puppy*, *dog*, and *adoption* all occur frequently on your main page (as they probably already do), and title your page something along the lines of Puppy Dog Adoption. While you're at it, put the following `<meta />` tags in the `<head>` portion of the page:

```
<meta name="description"
content="dog adoption information and services" />
<meta name="keywords" content="puppy, dog, adoption" />
```

Finally, publish your page online and visit the site submittal page for the major search engines (listed earlier in the lesson) to fill out each of their site submission forms.

2. Put the following page at http://mysite.com/oldplace/thepage.html:

```
<html>
  <head>
    <meta http-equiv="refresh" content="0;
    http://mysite.com/newplace/thepage.html">
  </head>
  <body>
  </body>
</html>
```

3. (a) Include a link to the site, using the full Internet address, on every page. Here is an example:

```
The address of this page is:
<a href="http://www.mysite.com/home.html">
http://www.mysite.com/home.html</a>
```

(b) Use full Internet addresses in all links between your pages. Here is an example:

```
This is my home page. From here you can
<a href="http://mysite.com/personal.html">
find out about my exciting personal life</a>, or
<a href="http://mysite.com/work.html">
find out about my boring work life</a>.
```

(c) Use the <base /> tag to specify the base Internet address of a page. Here is an example:

```
<head>
  <title>My Home Page</title>
  <base href="http://mysite.com/" />
</head>
```

Exercises

Can you think of some fun and useful ways to employ automatically changing pages (with the <meta http-equiv="refresh"> tag)? I'll bet you can.

HOUR 24

Beyond Traditional Web Sites

Everything you've learned in this book is likely to work flawlessly with HTML-compatible software for many years to come. There are tens of millions of pages of information written in standard HTML, and even as that standard evolves, tomorrow's web browsers and business software will retain the capability to view today's web pages. This book has focused on the most recent version of HTML, XHTML, which is well on its way to supplanting HTML as the language of choice for web page creation.

Some of the most exciting cutting-edge applications of HTML, however, are still rapidly developing. This hour introduces the latest HTML extensions and helps you understand what these new capabilities will enable you to do.

Try It Yourself ▼

Web technology is constantly changing, which means that you shouldn't rely solely on the printed word to stay up-to-date with the latest goings-on in the HTML/XHTML world. For this reason, I encourage you to make an effort to keep tabs on the latest web technologies with the help of the following web sites:

▶ Your best two sources for the latest HTML standards (and proposed future standards) are the World Wide Web Consortium site (http://www.w3.org/) and the HTML Compendium (http://www.htmlcompendium.org/).

▶ To see how the standards are actually implemented in the latest web browsers, and to see what nonstandard HTML extensions might be available, visit the Microsoft (http://www.microsoft.com/), Mozilla Firefox (http://www.getfirefox.com/), and Opera (http://www.opera.com/) web sites. Macintosh users may also want to visit the Apple web site (http://www.apple.com/) for the latest news on the Safari web browser.

You can also get copies of the latest web browser updates from these web sites. ▲

HTML Beyond the Web

The intimate familiarity with HTML you gained from reading this book will be one of the most important (and profitable) skills that anyone can have both in the present and in coming years. However, most of the HTML pages you'll create in your lifetime probably will not be web pages.

To understand why, and to see the big picture of where HTML is headed, consider the following features of the latest HTML (XHTML) standard:

▶ Through style sheets and scripting, HTML gives you precise control over the appearance and functionality of virtually any textual and graphical information.

▶ All major programming languages, interactive media, and database formats can also be seamlessly integrated with HTML.

▶ HTML's extended character sets and fonts can be used to communicate in the native script of almost any human language in the world.

▶ Data security standards make it practical to carry out financial and other sensitive transactions with HTML, and to manage confidential or restricted-access information.

▶ All future versions of the Microsoft Windows operating system will continue to use HTML as a fundamental part of the user interface. Nearly all current versions of office productivity software also support HTML, with some of them highly reliant on HTML (and XML) as a standard data format.

All this adds up to a very near future in which HTML will, without a doubt, play a central role—it might even be accurate to say *the* central role—in the display and exchange of almost all information across all computers and computer networks on earth. This sounds important because it is important. However, this hour will make a case that HTML will have an even more important role than that to play. To understand how that can be so, we'll need to take another step back to see an even bigger picture: the changing role of the computer itself in our society.

From Calculators to Wireless Communicators

The computer was once considered a device for accounting and number crunching. Then it evolved into a device for crunching all types of information, from words and numbers to graphics and sounds. Today and tomorrow, the computer is above all a communications device; its primary use is the transmission of information between people.

In most workplaces today, you can use a computer to access business information without knowing much more than how to click links and scroll through pages—and you can do so without knowing which information is coming from your computer, which is coming from the server down the hall, and which is coming from other servers perhaps thousands of miles away.

Users who become accustomed to seeing highly readable and attractive pages of information on their computer screens are losing the tiny bit of tolerance they have left for cryptic icons, unadorned text messages, and idiosyncratic menu mazes. They have grown to expect their computer screens to always be as easy to read and interact with as is the Web.

Those who make their millions supplying computer software are well aware of that expectation, and are expending an unprecedented amount of research and development effort toward fulfilling it. Along the way, the central metaphor for interacting with computers changed from the "window" of the 1980s "desktop" to the "page" of the 1990s "World Wide Web." This metaphor is already changing to accommodate the needs and capabilities of users in this first decade of the new millennium, in which wireless handheld devices and networks are rapidly becoming a standard part of daily life.

HTML as the New User Interface

As the role of the computer evolves, HTML is becoming more and more central to nearly everything we do with computers. HTML is the de facto global standard for connecting all types of information in a predictable and presentable way.

HTML gives you a painless and reliable way to combine and arrange text, graphics, sound, video, and interactive programs. Unlike older proprietary page layout standards, HTML was originally designed for efficient communication among all kinds of computers worldwide.

The prominence of HTML, however, does not mean that web browsers will be a major category of software application in the coming years. In fact, the web browser as a distinct program has already nearly disappeared. Microsoft Internet Explorer, for instance, does much more than retrieve pages from the World Wide Web. It lets you use HTML pages as the interface for organizing and navigating through the information on your own computer, including directory folders and the Windows desktop itself. In conjunction with HTML-enabled software such as Microsoft Office, HTML becomes the common standard interface for word processing, spreadsheets, and databases. Mozilla Firefox is also much more than a web browser. It uses HTML to integrate all types of media into email, discussion groups, schedule management, business documents, and collaborative project management.

The newest Windows operating system, Windows Vista, seamlessly blends a web browser into the desktop computing experience. In other words, the concept of a web browser as a distinct application may be a thing of the past as web pages are incorporated into every nook and cranny of the computing experience.

Meanwhile, HTML support is being included in virtually every major software release so that most programs on your computer can import and export information in the form of HTML pages. In a nutshell, HTML is the glue that holds together all the diverse types of information on our computers and ensures that it can be presented in a standard way that will look the same to anyone in the world.

In situations in which HTML doesn't provide enough structure to accurately describe information, XML is filling in as a universal data format. So while HTML may suffice to serve as the glue for different kinds of visual information, XML serves as the glue for information that isn't so easily seen: electronic orders, automatic funds transfers, news feeds, mobile phone settings, and so forth. XML provides a highly structured alternative to HTML for representing information on the Web.

In a business world that now sees fast, effective communication as the most common and most important task of its workers, the "information glue" of HTML and XML has the power to connect more than just different types of media. It is the hidden adhesive that connects a business to its customers and connects individual employees to form an efficient team. Knowing how to apply that glue—the skills you gained from this book—puts you in one of the most valuable roles in any modern organization.

The Digital Media Revolution Will Not Be Televised

The most important changes in the next few years might not be in HTML itself, but in the audience you can reach with your HTML pages. Many web site developers are banking on Internet-based content gaining the appeal to become the mass-market successor to television and radio. Less optimistic observers note that the global communications network has a long way to go before it can even deliver widespread television-quality video, or reach a majority of the world's populace at all. However, the rapid proliferation of high-speed wireless networks, many of them free, is beginning to support the notion of widespread high-speed Internet access for everyone who wants it.

All communication industries, from television to telephony, are moving rapidly toward exclusively digital technology. As they do so, the lines between communication networks are blurring. New Internet protocols promise to optimize multimedia trans-missions at the same time new protocols allow wireless broadcasters to support two-way interactive transmissions. The same small satellite dish can give you both Internet access and high-definition TV.

Add to this the fact that HTML is the only widely supported worldwide standard for combining text with virtually any other form of digital medium. Whatever surpris-ing twists and turns digital communication takes in the future, it's difficult to imag-ine that HTML won't be sitting in the driver's seat, with XML riding shotgun!

Millions of people can already access the Internet without a "real computer"—via TV set-top boxes and specialized Internet "appliances," not to mention all the mobile phones and pagers that are web-enabled. These devices are only the first wave of much more ubiquitous appliances that provide HTML content to people who wouldn't otherwise use computers. Full-blown handheld computers such as Treo, BlackBerry, and Pocket PC devices allow you to surf the Web from anywhere wirelessly. And for those less gadget-savvy, popular home video-game systems such as Xbox 360 provide web access in addition to their online gaming services.

By the Way

The prospect of mass-market HTML access is obviously a great opportunity for HTML page authors. However, it can also present a number of challenges when you're designing HTML pages because many people might see your pages on low-resolution TV screens or on small handheld devices. See the next section, "Preparing Yourself for Tomorrow," for some pointers on making sure that your HTML pages can be enjoyed and understood by the widest possible audience.

Preparing Yourself for Tomorrow

If you've made your way through most of this book's hours, you already have one of the most important ingredients for future success in the new digital world: a solid working knowledge of HTML, XHTML, and CSS.

Chances are that your primary reason for learning HTML at this time was to create some web pages, but I hope this hour has convinced you that you'll be using XHTML for far more than that in the future. Here are some of the factors you should consider when planning and building your web site today so that it will also serve you well tomorrow:

► Whenever you run into something that you'd like to do on a web page, but can't with HTML as it stands today, include a comment in the page so that you can add that feature when it becomes possible in the future. The multime-dia and interactive portions of your site are likely to need more revisions to keep up with current technology than will the text and graphics portions. When possible, keep the more cutting-edge elements of your site separate and take especially good care to document them well with the `<!--` and `-->` comment tags.

▶ Although high-bandwidth interactive media may be the wave of the future, be careful not to go overboard with it. Even people with fast Internet connections may not want to wait for a streaming video to start playing. Be sure to give your site visitors options when it comes viewing or listening to interactive media.

▶ Because style sheets give you complete control over the choice and measurements of type on your web pages, it is a good idea to study basic typography now if you aren't familiar with it. Understanding and working with things such as *leading*, *kerning*, *em spaces*, and *drop caps* has long been essential for producing truly professional-quality paper pages. It will soon be essential for producing outstanding web pages too.

▶ When you design your pages, don't always assume that everyone who sees them will be using a computer with a full-size monitor. Televisions, mobile phones, game consoles, and many other devices might have access to them as well. Some of these devices have very low-resolution screens (with 200×200 pixels or even less on some phones). Although it's difficult to design a web page to look good at that resolution, you'll reach the widest possible audience if you do.

By the *Way*

> It's not wrong if you decided not to worry about trying to design your pages for devices with very small screens. In fact, it's usually not realistic to design a single page that can look good at both 200×200 and 1280×1024 resolutions. However, you may consider offering an alternative version of your pages that can be viewed on devices with small screens. A bit later in the hour you'll learn about XHTML Mobile, which offers exactly that option.

▶ Several relatively new standards have been issued by the World Wide Web Consortium that will increasingly impact the Web as time goes by. These include the following:

XHTML Mobile

Portable Network Graphics (PNG)

Really Simple Syndication (RSS)

Synchronized Multimedia Interface Language (SMIL)

Scalable Vector Graphics (SVG)

Mathematics Markup Language (MathML)

eXtensible Style Sheet Language (XSL)

On the privacy and security front, new standards include these:

Platform for Internet Content Selection (PICS)

Platform for Privacy Preferences (P3P)

Digital Signature standard (Dsig)

Because these advances are likely to both expand the potential capabilities of your web site and change some of the methods you currently use to build web pages, you should visit the w3.org site and take the time to learn a little about each of them.

By the Way

You'll find links to several online reference and learning resources at the *Sams Publishing* website at http://www.samspublishing.com/.

In addition to providing an easy way to review all the sample pages and HTML techniques covered in this book, this site offers many sample pages this book didn't have room for.

You'll also find links to hundreds of web sites created by this book's readers. You're sure to pick up some great ideas for your own pages!

The Future of HTML Applications

The near-universal compatibility of HTML and XML provides a big incentive to format any important document as a web page—even if you have no immediate plans for putting it on the World Wide Web. You can create a single page that can be printed on paper, sent as an email message, displayed during a board meeting presentation, and posted for reference on the company intranet. You can also take the traditional route and format the page separately for each of these applications—and edit each file with a different software program when the information needs to be updated. Now that most business software supports the HTML standards, many organizations are trying to get employees to consistently use it for all important documents.

Yet the great migration to HTML goes beyond what you might have thought of as "documents" in the old days. Combined with XML, style sheets, JavaScript, and other technologies, HTML-based presentations can in many cases replace what was once done with proprietary data formats, specialized software, or more traditional programming languages. Here are a few of the other areas where HTML is finding application beyond the Web:

▶ *Kiosks* with HTML-based interactive content are popping up everywhere. They look like ATMs on steroids, and they're helping sell records and movie tickets, expand department store displays, and even automate the paying of parking tickets.

▶ Information-rich CD-ROM/DVD-ROM titles are fast migrating to HTML. *Encyclopaedia Britannica* is entirely HTML-based, which enables the company to offer the content on CD-ROM, the Web, or a combination of both for maximum speed and up-to-the-minute currency. Because CD-ROM drives display multimedia so much faster than most Internet connections, dynamic HTML presentations that are too media intensive to be done on today's World Wide Web become possible. DVD-ROM drives are even faster and hold much more information, making them ideally suited to large multimedia "sites."

By the Way

Of course, HTML is also rendering even the CD-ROM–based encyclopedia obsolete. Back in Hour 6, "Creating Text Links," you learned how to link your pages to Wikipedia, which is an online publicly editable encyclopedia that in my opinion is fundamentally changing the way information is managed. Wikipedia is literally allowing us (all of us!) to use HTML to write history as it unfolds. If you've already forgotten how cool it is, check it out online at http://www.wikipedia.org/.

▶ Corporate HTML-based newsletters are now often created in HTML for the company intranet, and printed on paper for delivery to employees or customers who won't see them on the Web. The traditional difference between online and paper presentations was that graphics needed to be high-resolution black-and-white for printing and low-resolution color for computer screens. Today's inexpensive color printers, however, do a great job making low-res color images look great in an HTML-based newsletter.

▶ Teachers are finding that tests and educational worksheets are easier to administer as HTML pages and can include many types of interactive content that isn't possible on paper. Simple HTML documents can be passed out on writable CDs or memory cards for students who lack access to the Internet.

▶ Hour 21, "Create Your Own Blog," introduced you to blogging and how to create your very own blog. Blogging has grown to become a powerful force in American culture as more and more people rely on blogs created from HTML to share information and debate various topics ranging from politics to technology to sports.

▶ Similar to blogs, online photo-sharing services built around HTML, such as Flickr (http://www.flickr.com/) and Google's Hello (http://www.hello.com/), are allowing people to provide friends, family, and the general public with an unprecedented glimpse into their lives.

▶ Vertical market users often buy a computer specifically to run a certain custom-designed application or set of applications. The value-added resellers and systems integrators that provide these systems are delivering machines configured to start displaying HTML pages. This can help step users through the use of the machine or replace old-fashioned *idiot menus* with a more attractive and sophisticated interface without sacrificing ease of use.

▶ Google shocked the online world when it released its unbelievably high-powered online mapping application, Google Maps, which is built from HTML, XML, and JavaScript. You learned how to link your own pages to Google Maps in Hour 3, "Linking to Other Web Pages." To show how far-reaching such technologies can be, a spin-off application of Google Maps known as Google Earth was used by major news networks such as CNN and MSNBC to show detailed aerial satellite imagery from Hurricane Katrina as the tragic events unfolded in the Gulf of Mexico.

I could list many more creative and beneficial uses of HTML beyond run-of-the-mill web pages, but the point is clear: If you need to present any type of information, seriously consider HTML as an alternative to the specialized software or programming tools you would have used for the job a couple of years ago.

The remainder of this hour focuses on some specific web technologies that allow you to build web pages that go beyond the confines of basic HTML. Although these technologies certainly go beyond HTML, they all rely on HTML at their core.

RSS and Web Page Syndication

Really Simple Syndication (RSS) is a technology that allows you to create and syndicate news feeds using an XML markup language. There are various ways in which you can use RSS. You can display RSS feeds from other web sites on your web site, you can build your own library of RSS feeds and view them regularly using special software called a news aggregator, or you can syndicate your own site using RSS so that other people can view your feeds.

When I say that RSS allows you to syndicate web content, I mean that you can subscribe to web sites and easily find out about new changes to a site without actually having to visit the site. Using special software called a news aggregator, you can monitor news feeds from multiple sites and effectively keep tabs on a wide range of information without having to stop by every different site on a regular basis. You can think of RSS as providing somewhat of a "stock ticker" for web page data—it allows you to keep constant tabs on when your favorite sites post something new.

The easiest way to learn how RSS works is by installing news aggregator software and exploring feeds for yourself. One of the most popular news aggregators available now is FeedDemon, which is available in a free trial version online at http://www.feeddemon.com/. FeedDemon is a standalone desktop application that is completely independent of your web browser.

By the Way

> Some other popular online news aggregators include Bloglines (http://www. bloglines.com/), NewsIsFree (http://www.newsisfree.com/), and Microsoft's experimental start.com (http://www.start.com/). Google News (http://news.google. com/) can even be considered an aggregator of sorts, although it doesn't provide as much flexibility as a true RSS feed manager. Google News is perhaps more powerful as a feed generator because you can use it to easily syndicate Google News categories and even Google searches.

Figure 24.1 shows the FeedDemon desktop aggregator used to view a news feed.

FIGURE 24.1
FeedDemon is one of the leading desktop news aggregators, and it's reasonably priced.

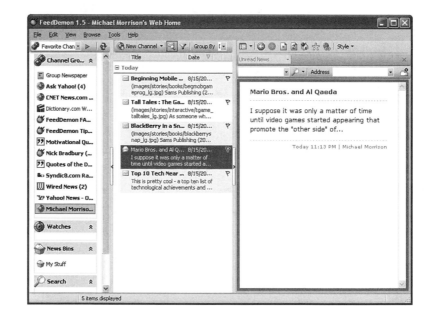

If you pay close attention to the figure, you'll notice that the news feed being accessed is my very own news feed as syndicated from michaelmorrison.com. FeedDemon makes it possible to easily manage quite a few feeds without feeling as if you're totally overburdened with information. After you get comfortable using a news aggregator such as FeedDemon, you'll quickly realize how much more efficiently you can access and process web content. I rarely find myself hopping from site to site now that I can conveniently keep tabs on favorites via news feeds.

Unfortunately, the details of how to create your own RSS news feeds are beyond the scope of this book. However, I encourage you to learn more if you're interested by visiting the Really Simple Syndication entry on Wikipedia at http://en.wikipedia.org/wiki/Really_Simple_Syndication.

Using a Content Management System

You've no doubt visited web sites that had a surprising amount of user interaction in the form of discussion groups, private messages, polls, and other forms of dynamic web content and communications capabilities. As you've probably figured out by now, it is difficult to create such web sites using pure HTML alone. Even XHTML combined with CSS and JavaScript has its limitations in terms of dynamic data management, which is typically required of sites that have a great deal of two-way user interaction.

Creating a site with high-powered interactive features typically involves a fair amount of high-powered development work. More specifically, most of these kinds of sites require a database management system (DBMS) along with a server-side scripting technology such as Microsoft's Active Server Pages (ASP) or PHP (PHP Hypertext Preprocessor). In short, you need a lot more skills than this book has to offer, not to mention a fair amount of time and resources to develop such a site.

Or you can download some free software and do it the easy way—take advantage of someone else's hard work. The software for creating highly interactive, data-driven web sites is known as a content management system, or CMS. Although expensive commercial options exist, there are plenty of open-source (free) content management systems available for you to use. To use such a system, you first download the software and install it to your web server. You then must work through an installation procedure to make sure that the CMS can successfully connect to your database. From there, you spend most of your time organizing the site and developing its content, often entirely through a web-based user interface.

Some popular CMS software packages include Mambo (http://www.mamboserver. com/), Drupal (http://drupal.org/), and e107 (http://e107.org/). I've experimented with many of these packages, and in fact used Mambo to build my personal web site at http://www.michaelmorrison.com/. Moving from a traditional web site to a CMS site has paid off in a big way for me because of how much I need to be able to interact with readers via discussion forums, live chats, polls, and my regularly updated blog.

CMS has some significant advantages over traditional web sites because CMS web sites are typically driven entirely by data in a database. For example, most of the pages in a CMS web site are generated dynamically from code stored in a database. This allows you to edit and create web pages directly from within a web browser, and at any location. I regularly update my web site while traveling by using nothing more than Internet Explorer to log in and access the administration area of the site. You really have to think of a CMS as more of a live web publishing system than a static collection of HTML pages.

So why have you spent an entire book learning about HTML if a CMS is what you really need? Because a CMS is not for everyone. If you don't need a great deal of user interaction via discussion forums and things of that nature, a CMS may not be all that beneficial to you. Furthermore, CMS web sites can be difficult to "decorate" in terms of giving them a unique look and feel. Many CMS web sites look exactly alike, which is a bummer. If you do take the time and energy to give your CMS site a unique look and feel, you'll need a very good knowledge of HTML and CSS to do so.

And this brings me to the final issue related to CMS web sites. Even if you decide to switch gears and go with a CMS software package for your web site, as opposed to creating traditional HTML pages yourself, it's still extremely important to know HTML/XHTML and CSS. You will undoubtedly want to create some unusual pages within the CMS site and possibly even tinker with the overall look and feel of the site. Every CMS software package I've seen relies heavily on CSS to establish a layout and color scheme for its pages. And, obviously, all the pages are HTML or XHTML at their core. So, to make a long story slightly shorter, your HTML/XHTML and CSS knowledge will never go to waste as long as you're dealing with the Web.

If you'd like to experiment with some CMS software packages and see how they work, take a look at http://www.opensourcecms.com/. This site has live installations of numerous open-source CMS packages, and they are set up so that you can log in and try them all out. Additionally, my personal site at http://www.michaelmorrison. com/ is an example of a Mambo CMS site, while http://www.musiccitymafia.com/ is an example of an e107 CMS site.

Web Pages to Go with XHTML Mobile

Although I've generally referred to the language that runs the Web as HTML, you've actually been learning XHTML as you've progressed through the book. You may be surprised to learn that there is another version of XHTML that I haven't mentioned. I'm referring to XHTML Mobile, which is a scaled-down version of XHTML that is geared toward the limited needs of mobile devices. Mobile devices include any hand-held or easily portable technology—cell phones, pagers, connected organizers, hand-held PCs, and potentially others. Such devices typically have much smaller screens, less memory, and more confined user interfaces (often no keyboard or mouse) than their desktop counterparts.

Before XHTML Mobile came along, there were two primary mobile web services, WAP and iMode. iMode was created by NTTDoCoMo, and is popular in Japan and parts of Europe. WAP was created by a group of mobile industry leaders, and is the predominant standard for serving up mobile web pages worldwide. This version of WAP is known as WAP 1.0, and it has taken a fair amount of criticism despite its success. WAP 1.0 and iMode rely on their own markup languages for coding pages served on each. More specifically, WAP 1.0 is based on WML (Wireless Markup Language) and iMode is based on cHTML (Compact HTML). These languages have both worked as basic markup languages for mobile web pages, but they are lacking in many ways as we move to a more powerful XML-based wireless web.

Many of the core features in WML and cHTML converged in XHTML Mobile. Most current mobile browsers support XHTML Mobile, which fortunately supports the usage of CSS. As you've seen several times throughout the book, CSS provides a great deal of control over the formatting and display of web pages. When I refer to CSS as it applies to XHTML Mobile, I'm actually referring to a subset of CSS known as WCSS (Wireless CSS), which is somewhat of a scaled-down CSS. In other words, WCSS is to XHTML Mobile what CSS is to XHTML.

The great thing about XHTML Mobile is that it is no different than XHTML, except that it is more limited. So if you know XHTML, you already know XHTML Mobile. At worst, you'll just have to learn to live with a smaller set of tools because XHTML Mobile is a bit more limited than XHTML. Generally speaking, you'll find that XHTML Mobile can do just about anything markup-wise that you will want to do on a mobile web page.

As an example of how XHTML Mobile can be used in the context of a wireless application, Listing 24.1 contains the code for a mobile movie description web page that you might view on your mobile phone when trying to decide whether to go see the movie *King Kong*.

LISTING 24.1   The XHTML Mobile *King Kong* Movie Page

```
 1: <?xml version="1.0" encoding="UTF-8"?>
 2:
 3: <html>
 4:   <head>
 5:     <link rel="stylesheet" type="text/css" href="movie.css" />
 6:   </head>
 7:
 8:   <body>
 9:     <h1 align="center">King Kong</h1>
10:     <p>This remake of the 1933 classic follows an expedition to the
11:       mysterious Skull Island, where a legend of a giant gorilla draws
12:       explorers and filmmakers. The legend, however, is both real and
13:       dangerous, living in a massive jungle that has protected him and
14:       other prehistoric creatures for decades. Kong finds solace in a
15:       beautiful woman (Naomi Watts), and is subdued enough to be captured
16:       and brought back to New York. However, as the captors and the public
17:       will learn, it takes a lot more shackles to hold back an animal of
18:       such monstrous size.</p>
19:   </body>
20: </html>
```

This code is very similar to that of the XHTML web pages you've seen throughout the book. The first line declares the version of XML being used, and then a WCSS style sheet is associated with the page in line 5. The `movie.css` style sheet specifies colors and more exacting fonts for the *King Kong* movie content. The remainder of the document is fairly straightforward in terms of following normal XHTML syntax. For example, the body of the document consists of run-of-the-mill XHTML code with familiar <h1> and <p> tags.

Listing 24.2 contains the code for the `movie.css` style sheet that is used to format the King Kong movie XHTML Mobile document.

LISTING 24.2   The WCSS Style Sheet for the *King Kong* Movie Page

```
 1: body {
 2:   background: #FFFFFF;
 3: }
 4:
 5: h1 {
 6:   font-size: x-large;
 7:   color: #660000;
 8:   text-align: center;
 9:   text-decoration: underline;
10: }
11:
12: p {
13:   display: block;
14:   border: 1px #330000 solid;
15:   background: #660000;
16:   color: #FFFFFF;
```

LISTING 24.2   Continued

```
17:   text-align: left;
18:   font-size: medium;
19:   padding: 4px;
20: }
```

Figure 24.2 shows the results of viewing the *King Kong* XHTML Mobile page in the Opera web browser's "small screen" view.

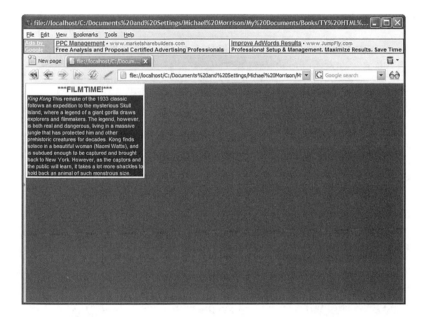

FIGURE 24.2
XHTML Mobile allows you to create mobile web pages that can be viewed on devices such as mobile phones and handheld computers.

The Opera web browser is unique in that it supports a "small screen" mode that allows you to simulate a much smaller screen within a desktop browser. You can activate small-screen mode by selecting Small Screen from the View menu in Opera. Opera's small-screen mode allows you to test XHTML Mobile pages without having to use a real mobile device. However, it is very important to eventually use a real mobile device to test your XHTML Mobile web pages.

> The Opera web browser is available free at http://www.opera.com/.

By the Way

XHTML Mobile is a technology that is relatively new but that will continue to rise in importance as more and more web browsing takes place on mobile devices.

Summary

This hour provided a bird's-eye view of the future of HTML. It discussed the new roles that HTML will play in global communications and briefly introduced how HTML relates to some emerging technologies that are based on HTML and the closely related XML standard. The lesson also offered some advice for planning and constructing web pages today that will continue to serve you well into the future.

Q&A

Q *What is the difference between digital communication and other communication, anyway? Does digital mean it uses HTML?*

A When information is transferred as distinct bits of information, which are essentially numbers, it's called *digital*. It's much easier to store, retrieve, and process information without losing or changing it when it is transferred digitally. Any information from a computer (including HTML) is by its nature digital, and in the not-too-distant future, all telephone, television, radio, and even motion picture production will be digital. Many mobile phone networks are already digital, and high-definition (HD) television is digital.

Q *How soon can I start designing Internet web pages that aren't limited by what people can transfer over a dial-up modem?*

A That depends on who you want to read your pages. Unfortunately, there will be quite a few 56Kbps dial-up modems in use for several years to come. The good news is that the number of people with 1Mbps (1,000Kbps) or faster cable, copper-optic, and wireless broadband connections is growing rapidly. That difference of 18× in speed will lead more and more web page publishers to offer separate high-speed and low-speed sites; many are already offering media content in varying sizes for each connection speed. As long as you provide users with the ability to bypass bandwidth-hungry content such as video and music, you shouldn't have anything to worry about.

Q *How do I convert a normal XHTML document to XHTML Mobile?*

A Because the syntax is identical between the two languages, the main trick is to eliminate features that aren't supported in XHTML Mobile, such as frames. Beyond that, your main challenge is in scaling down any images and simplifying styles so that pages look good on a small display that has potentially fewer colors to work with.

Workshop

The workshop contains quiz questions and activities to help you solidify your understanding of the material covered. Try to answer all questions before looking at the "Answers" section that follows.

Quiz

You've taken 23 quizzes in 24 hours! Instead of taking another, may I suggest that you congratulate yourself for a job well done, take a break, and treat yourself to something special? You deserve it.

Exercises

Back from your break yet? Now that you've learned HTML, XHTML, and CSS and have your web site online, this book can still help you make your site better and better. You may want to review the Q&A sections throughout the book and Appendix A, "Readers' Most Frequently Asked Questions." Be sure to also stick a bookmark at the beginning of Appendix C, the "Complete XHTML 1.1 and CSS 2 Quick Reference." Exploring the "Exercises" sections that you might have skipped the first time around will help build your HTML skills as well.

I'm sure you haven't yet explored all the oodles and oodles of entertaining examples and tutorial tips at the *Sams Publishing* website. That's www. samspublishing.com, where the JavaScript is hot and the HTML never stops flowing. See you there!

PART VI

Appendixes

Readers' Most Frequently Asked Questions

I have read and carefully collated more than 1,000 questions and suggestions sent to me by readers of this book's previous editions. This feedback has influenced everything in this edition, from the overall outline to the specific notes, tips, and quiz questions. I've tried to incorporate the answers to readers' questions into the text at just the point in each hour when you would have found yourself asking those questions.

This appendix is for those times when you may have overlooked or forgotten a key point in the book. It's also a chance for me to answer those questions that just didn't fit under any particular topic. These questions are presented in order of frequency: Number 1 is the most commonly asked question, number 2 is the next, and so on down to number 24. (A good number. I had to stop somewhere!)

In cases in which the answer is clearly explained in the book, I just refer you to the relevant part of that hour. In cases in which you might need a little more from me, I provide a succinct answer here and may also refer to an online resource that can help.

The 24 Top Questions from Readers of *Sams Teach Yourself HTML and CSS in 24 Hours*

1. **What should I read next?**

   Try *Sams Teach Yourself JavaScript in 21 Days* or *Web Site Design Goodies*, which are available at most bookstores, including online at http://www.amazon.com.

2. **I'm stuck on my first page. It didn't work. What did I do wrong?**

   The first page is always the hardest. If you see all the HTML code when you try to view the file (by selecting File, Open in your web browser) or if you see some weird characters at the top of the page, you haven't saved the file in plain-text or ASCII text format. If you can't figure out how to do that in your word processor, use the Notepad or TextEdit editor that came with your computer instead. (WordPad is especially problematic in this regard.) Also make sure that you've saved the file with a .html or .htm file extension.

For more guidance on making your first page, carefully go over the first "Try It Yourself" section and "Getting Started with a Simple Web Page" in Hour 2, "Create a Web Page Right Now."

Also, remember that you don't have to be connected to the Internet to edit and view web pages on your hard drive. (If your web browser tries to connect to the Internet every time you start it, change the home page in your browser settings to a page on your hard drive.)

3. **Graphics or media files don't work/don't show online.**

There are several common pitfalls you may encounter when putting graphics on a web page:

- Make sure that the graphics file is in the same folder as the HTML document that refers to it. (If you're trying to refer to it in a different folder, review the "Addressing Web Pages" section of Hour 3, "Linking to Other Web Pages.")

- Make sure that the graphics file is saved in GIF, JPEG, or PNG format. Open the file with Paint Shop Pro, Picasa, or another graphics program, and use File, Save As to save it again just to be sure.

- Make sure that the capitalization of the filename and the `src=` attribute in the `<img />` tag match. `MyImage.gif` and `myimage.GIF` are not the same to most web servers!

- To get rid of the blue line around a graphic, put `style="border:none"` in the `<img />` tag.

- This one's unlikely, but possible: Do you have Load Images turned off under Tools, Options, Web Features in Mozilla Firefox, or Show Pictures turned off under Tools, Internet Options, Advanced in Microsoft Internet Explorer?

- True story: One reader spent four days trying to figure out why none of his images worked. He was typing `<img scr=` instead of `<img src=` every single time. Don't laugh—just check *your* page for typos.

Refer to Hour 8, "Putting Graphics on a Web Page." If you're having trouble arranging graphics on the page, you'll find many helpful hints not only in Hour 8 but in Hour 9, "Custom Backgrounds and Colors," and Hour 10, "Graphical Links and Imagemaps," as well.

Audio and video files are trickier and more prone to problems. There's no practical way to make them work in every version of every popular browser, but refer to Hour 19, "Embedding Multimedia in Web Pages," for as much help as I can give.

4. How do I get forms to work on my server?

Ask your ISP to help you set up a forms-processing script. If your ISP can't do it, you either need to find one that is willing to actually provide some service or use a third-party form-processing service, such as http://www.freedback.com. You can also simply have form information sent to your email address, but this approach is a little unreliable because it is dependent on all users having their email properly configured through their web browser.

5. How do I put a counter on my page?

You probably don't truly need one because most ISPs offer a detailed statistical report each week, summarizing exactly how many times each of your pages was accessed. You should expect (read: demand) this service, but some web hosting services (especially free ones, or those outside North America) just won't provide it. In that case, you need to set up a CGI script on your server. That isn't terribly difficult, and you'll find the code and some advice on how to do it at http://www.developer.com and other web development sites.

6. I'm confused about frames. Mine don't work, and I don't understand why. Do you?

Frames are tricky. It may take a couple readings of Hour 16, "Multi-Page Layout with Frames," and some experimentation before everything clicks and you see how the whole thing works. Here are some tips that may help:

- Remember that you can right-click in any frame and pick This Frame, View Frame Source in Mozilla Firefox or View Source in Microsoft Internet Explorer to see the HTML for that frame. Selecting View, Source from the main menu shows you the HTML for the frameset document.

- The only way to make a link change the contents of two or more frames at once is to link to a new frameset and include target="_top" in the <a> link tag.

- You also use target="_top" when you want to break out of all the frames and go back to a regular single-page document.

7. **How do I pursue a career in web page design, and how much should I charge to make someone a web page?**

As in any competitive business (and web page design is a very competitive business), you need a solid marketing plan to be successful. If you've already found some clients, the amount you charge them is obviously up for negotiation. As a general rule, the going rate for experienced web developers is between $25 and $50 per hour. If you are still learning, expect to charge less than that, unless you are already a professional graphics or publications designer with a loyal client base.

8. **How do I make password-protected pages?**

Consult your ISP to see what kinds of security options they have available. For true password protection, you will need to utilize secure pages, or at least a script of some sort that limits access to users who can enter a verified password.

9. **Where can I find Java applets/prewritten JavaScript?**

Try http://www.developer.com, http://www.javascript.com, and http://javascript.internet.com, or look in any of the major Internet search sites under "Java" or "JavaScript."

10. **I can't get a link to work. What could be wrong?**

Check the spelling and capitalization of the `href` link and the file to which you're trying to link. Some links will work on your hard drive, but fail on the web server if the capitalization doesn't match. (This is because Windows doesn't care about capitalization of filenames, but UNIX does.) Also, review Hour 3, "Linking to Other Web Pages," and Hour 6, "Creating Text Links," to make sure that you understand the finer points of relative and absolute addressing and link anchors.

11. **I am having trouble getting JavaScript code to work, even though I'm pretty sure I got the syntax right.**

Please don't imagine for a moment that Microsoft and Netscape could possibly have bugs in their web browsers, especially in the sacred JavaScript module. You are the problem. To redeem yourself, you must build a shrine next to your computer, paste gilt-edged pictures of Bill Gates and Marc Andreessen to it, and humbly offer it cold pizza thrice daily. If you do this with a clean heart and a pure mind, all problems with code implementation will still be your own darn fault, but at least Microsoft may decide not to take legal action against you for it.

Seriously, you may want to consider using a JavaScript debugger to try to solve JavaScript problems that have you at your wit's end. Mozilla offers a free debugger called Venkman (someone at Mozilla is a Ghostbuster's fan!) that integrates into Firefox; to learn more, visit http://www.mozilla.org/projects/venkman/. A script debugger is built in to Internet Explorer, and you can activate it by disabling the browser setting Disable Script Debugging (Internet Explorer) from the Advanced tab in the Internet Options dialog box.

12. Where can I get more help creating graphics and multimedia?

If you use Paint Shop Pro for graphics, try the online tutorials at the Web Graphics on a Budget web site (http://mardiweb.com/web/). If you're using Picasa, Google offers a decent "Getting Started Guide" in the Support area of the Picasa web site (http://picasa.google.com/support/). For stylistic design help with your web graphics, take a look at the book *Web Graphics for Non-Designers* at a major bookstore. Another option is to use an online media gallery, or clip art site, such as Microsoft's Design Gallery Live (http://dgl.microsoft.com).

13. How do I put more "bells and whistles" (a chat room, a hit counter, password protection, interactive sound, a pull-down list of links, and things of that nature) on my site?

Most of those involve JavaScript or CGI scripting (advanced stuff) to make them work. To help you go beyond what this book teaches, I've assembled a list of advanced developer resources at http://www.samspublishing.com/.

14. How do I get a message to scroll along the bottom?

You'll find JavaScript for that at both http://www.developer.com and http://www.javascript.com.

15. How do I put files on a web site for download?

Just upload the file in the same place you put your web pages and use a regular HTML link, like the following:

```
<a href="bigfile.zip">Click here to download bigfile.zip.</a>
```

Keep in mind that an image linked in this manner will likely open up within the browser window, which may not be the desired effect if you're placing the image online for download. The solution is for the users to save the image to their local computer after it is opened in the browser.

16. **How do I put a browser on a memory card or CD-ROM? Do I need to if I publish web pages to portable media?**

   Most people have a web browser on their computer these days, but if you want to provide one just in case, you need permission from the browser company. I recommend Opera (http://www.opera.com), which takes up very little space and allows distribution of free time-limited evaluation copies.

17. **When I try to download Paint Shop Pro or the FTP software you recommended, the download is deathly slow or stops altogether. Can you help?**

   I'm afraid there's not much I (or you) can do, except recommend that you try again later. And you thought you needed a car to get in a traffic jam?

18. **Should I use Java applets and other advanced stuff?**

   Not unless you need to do something you can't do any other way. Basic HTML is faster, more widely compatible, and easier to maintain.

19. **How do I make a form for people to fill out and print?**

   They can fill out and print any HTML form. Just tell them to do it. See the "Q&A" section at the end of Hour 18, "Gathering Information with HTML Forms." Make sure that the form elements are still placed within a <form> tag, even if you don't plan on having the form submitted electronically.

20. **How do I justify text so that it lines up with both margins?**

   If you have a flat-panel screen, you could try scissors and glue. Or just use the text-align CSS style like this: style="text-align:justify".

21. **How do I publicize my site, and how do I find advertisers for my site?**

   The first section of Hour 23, "Helping People Find Your Web Pages," will help some, but mostly you'll need to come up with your own marketing/PR plan tailored to your specific situation.

   There are many web advertising services and companies that will pay independent web publishers like you to run ads or affiliate with them in other potentially profitable ways. Most pay you a small amount each time a visitor clicks one of their ads; see http://www.sitecash.com/guide.htm for some possibilities. An even better option involves Google Ad Sense, which is a program Google offers in which context-sensitive ads are displayed on your site, and you make money anytime someone clicks one of the ads. To learn more, visit the Google AdSense web site at https://www.google.com/adsense/.

22. How do I create HTML pages or links within email messages?

Just type regular HTML as you would to make a web page. Most advanced email programs nowadays allow you to create and view mail in HTML. You format it just as you would a document—no HTML experience required. Generally speaking, if a web address is preceded by http:// in an email, most email programs will automatically convert it into a link.

23. How do I open a link in a new window?

Use `target="_blank"` in your a `href` link tag. Keep in mind that this approach is technically not XHTML 1.1 compatible. For a workaround that is XHTML 1.1 compliant, read the section in Hour 3 titled "Opening a Link in a New Browser Window."

24. How do I link to a database and let people search my site?

You'll probably need to give a software company some money for a good answer to that one. More than likely your web hosting service already supports a particular kind of database, and might be able to provide you with guidance for building pages that are capable of accessing a database. You may also want to look into learning PHP and mySQL, which are two popular technologies that allow you to add database features to web sites.

APPENDIX B

HTML and CSS Resources on the Internet

General HTML, XHTML, and CSS Information

The *Sams Publishing* website—the companion site to *Sams Teach Yourself HTML and CSS in 24 Hours*, including an online version of this appendix:

http://www.samspublishing.com/

The World Wide Web Consortium (W3C):

http://www.w3.org/

Microsoft Internet Explorer web browser:

http://www.microsoft.com/windows/ie/

Mozilla Firefox web browser:

http://www.getfirefox.com/

Opera web browser:

http://www.opera.com/

The HTML Writer's Guild:

http://www.hwg.org/

The Web Developer's Virtual Library:

http://www.wdvl.com/

XHTML.org:

http://www.xhtml.org/

Wireless Developer Network—Wireless web pages:

http://www.wirelessdevnet.com/

HTML on Wikipedia:

http://en.wikipedia.org/wiki/Html

XHTML on Wikipedia:

http://en.wikipedia.org/wiki/XHTML

CSS on Wikipedia:

http://en.wikipedia.org/wiki/Cascading_Style_Sheets

Web Page Design

Creating Graphics for the Web:

http://www.widearea.co.uk/designer/

The WDVL Style Guide:

http://www.wdvl.com/Authoring/Style/Guides/WDVL.html

Web Pages That Suck:

http://www.webpagesthatsuck.com/

HTML Help (Web Design Group):

http://www.htmlhelp.com/

Web Monkey:

http://webmonkey.wired.com/webmonkey/

Software

FrontPage—Microsoft's web publishing tool that integrates with Office:

http://www.microsoft.com/frontpage/

Dreamweaver—Macromedia's high-end web development tool:

http://www.macromedia.com/software/dreamweaver/

TopStyle—An excellent XHTML editor and web publishing tool:

http://www.bradsoft.com/topstyle/

Paint Shop Pro—A highly recommended Windows graphics and animation editor:

> http://www.corel.com/

Picasa—Google's creative answer to photo management and editing:

> http://picasa.google.com/

GIF Construction Set—Another alternative for creating animated graphics:

> http://www.mindworkshop.com/alchemy/gcsdemo.html

Adobe Photoshop Elements—Consumer version of Adobe's industry-leading photo editing tool:

> http://www.adobe.com/products/photoshopel/main.html

Mapedit— A tool for Windows and X11 for creating imagemap map files:

> http://www.boutell.com/mapedit/

Shareware.com—Best source for almost any type of free or inexpensive software for all types of computers:

> http://shareware.cnet.com/

WinSite Windows Software Archive:

> http://www.winsite.com/

Graphics

Microsoft Design Gallery Live:

> http://dgl.microsoft.com/

Barry's Clipaart Server:

> http://www.barrysclipart.com/

HTML color picker:

> http://www.pagetutor.com/pagetutor/makapage/picker/

RGB Triplet Color Chart:

> http://quasar.unl.edu/tutorials/rgb.html

Color Blender:

> http://www.meyerweb.com/eric/tools/color-blend/

Color Schemer Online:

> http://www.colorschemer.com/online.html

Multimedia

Windows Media:

> http://www.windowsmedia.com/

Windows Movie Maker:

> http://www.microsoft.com/windowsxp/using/moviemaker/default.mspx

Apple QuickTime:

> http://www.apple.com/quicktime/

RealAudio and RealVideo:

> http://www.real.com/

Macromedia's Shockwave Player:

> http://www.macromedia.com/software/shockwaveplayer/

Macromedia's Flash Player:

> http://www.macromedia.com/software/flashplayer/

Sound Central—Free sound files in various formats:

> http://www.soundcentral.com/

MIDIworld—Music files:

> http://www.midiworld.com/

Stock video/film footage:

> http://www.cinema-sites.com/Cinema_Sites_PROD4.html

Multimedia Authoring:

> http://www.mcli.dist.maricopa.edu/authoring/

Advanced Developer Resources

WebReference—Tutorials and references to HTML and related technologies:

> http://www.webreference.com/

JavaScript.com—The Definitive JavaScript Resource:

> http://www.javascript.com/

EarthWeb WebDeveloper:

> http://webdeveloper.earthweb.com/

Microsoft Developer Network (MSDN) developer network:

> http://msdn.microsoft.com/

Search Engine Submission Tips:

> http://searchenginewatch.com/webmasters/

Microsoft's TrueType typography pages:

> http://www.microsoft.com/truetype/

HTML Validators

W3C Markup Validation Service:

> http://validator.w3.org/

HTML-Kit and HTML Tidy—Web page editor that also converts to XHTML 1:

> http://www.chami.com/html-kit/

Directories with HTML Information

HTML Goodies:

> http://www.htmlgoodies.com/

Yahoo! World Wide Web:

> http://www.yahoo.com/Computers/Internet/World_Wide_Web/

Cool Site of the Day:

> http://cool.infi.net/

Web Site Services

The List—The Definitive ISP Buyer's Guide:

http://thelist.internet.com/

freedback.com—Free form processing service:

http://www.freedback.com/

The Counter—Free web counter/tracker:

http://www.thecounter.com/

TrainXchange—Advertise your site/exchange ads with other sites:

http://www.ntwp.net/trainxchange/

Microsoft Small Business Center's Submit It!—Register your pages with hundreds of search sites, paid service:

http://www.submit-it.com/

Open Directory Project—The largest, most comprehensive human-edited directory of the Web:

http://dmoz.org/about.html

Free Web Site Hosting

Yahoo! Geocities:

http://geocities.yahoo.com/

Angelfire:

http://www.angelfire.lycos.com/

Cyber Cities:

http://www.cybercities.com/

Tripod:

http://www.tripod.lycos.com/

MySpace:

http://www.myspace.com/

APPENDIX C

Complete XHTML 1.1 and CSS 2 Quick Reference

XHTML 1.1 represents a modern reformulation of HTML as an XML application, allowing extensions to the language to be more easily defined and implemented. This appendix provides a quick reference to all the elements and attributes of XHTML 1.1, as well as the style properties that CSS 2 comprises.

To make the information readily accessible, this appendix organizes HTML elements by their function in the following order:

- ▶ Structure
- ▶ Text phrases and paragraphs
- ▶ Text formatting elements
- ▶ Lists
- ▶ Links
- ▶ Tables
- ▶ Frames
- ▶ Embedded content
- ▶ Style
- ▶ Forms
- ▶ Scripts

The elements are listed alphabetically within each section, and the following information is presented:

- ▶ Usage—Gives a general description of the element.
- ▶ Start/End Tag—Indicates whether these tags are required, optional, or illegal.
- ▶ Attributes—Lists the attributes of the element with a short description of their effect.
- ▶ Empty—Indicates whether the element can be empty.
- ▶ Notes—Relates any special considerations for using the element.

The CSS style properties follow a similar arrangement except that they are listed with acceptable values, as opposed to attributes.

By the Way

XHTML 1.1 includes several fundamental attributes that apply to a significant number of elements. These are referred to within each element listing as `core`, `i18n`, and `events`. These attribute groups are covered in detail after all the XHTML elements are presented. There you'll find the specific attributes associated with each of these attribute groups.

XHTML Structure

XHTML relies on several elements to provide structure to a document (as opposed to structuring the text within) as well as to provide information that is used by the browser or search engines.

<bdo>...</bdo>

Usage	The bidirectional algorithm element used to selectively turn off the default text direction.
Start/End Tag	Required/Required.
Attributes	`core`.
	`lang="language"`—The language of the document.
	`dir="direction"`—The text direction (`ltr`, `rtl`). Mandatory attribute.
Empty	No.

<body>...</body>

Usage	Contains the document's content.
Start/End Tag	Optional/Optional.
Attributes	`core`, `i18n`, `events`.
	`onload="eventcode"`—Intrinsic event triggered when the document loads.
	`onunload="eventcode"`—Intrinsic event triggered when document unloads.
Empty	No.
Notes	There can be only one `<body>`, and it must follow the `<head>`. The `<body>` element can be replaced by a `<frameset>` element.

Comments `<!-- ... -->`

Usage	Used to insert notes or scripts that are not displayed by the browser.
Start/End Tag	Required/Required.
Attributes	None.
Empty	Yes.
Notes	Comments are not restricted to one line and can be any length. The end tag is not required to be on the same line as the start tag.

`<div>...</div>`

Usage	The division element is used to add structure to a block of text.
Start/End Tag	Required/Required.
Attributes	core, i18n, events.

> **By the Way**
>
> You may run across HTML web pages that use the `<div>` element with an attribute named align. This attribute was removed in XHTML, with the new approach to alignment involving the text-align CSS style property. This style property is covered later in this appendix.

Empty	No.
Notes	Cannot be used within a p element.

`<!doctype...>`

Usage	Version information appears on the first line of an HTML document and is an SGML declaration rather than an element.

`<h1>...</h1>` Through `<h6>...</h6>`

Usage	The six headings (h1 is uppermost, or most important) are used in the body to structure information in a hierarchical fashion.
Start/End Tag	Required/Required.

Attributes	core, i18n, events.
Empty	No.
Notes	Visual browsers will display the size of the headings in relation to their importance, <h1> being the largest and <h6> being the smallest.

<head>...</head>

Usage	This is the document header and it contains other elements that provide information to users and search engines.
Start/End Tag	Optional/Optional.
Attributes	i18n.
	profile="*url*"—URL specifying the location of meta data.
Empty	No.
Notes	There can be only one <head> per document. It must follow the opening <html> tag and precede the <body>.

<hr />

Usage	Horizontal rules are used to separate sections of a web page.
Start/End Tag	Required/Illegal.
Attributes	core, events, i18n.
Empty	Yes.

<html>...</html>

Usage	The html element contains the entire document.
Start/End Tag	Optional/Optional.
Attributes	i18n.
Empty	No.
Notes	The version information is duplicated in the <!doc-type...> declaration and is therefore not essential.

`<meta />`

Usage	Provides information about the document.
Start/End Tag	Required/Illegal.
Attributes	i18n.
	http-equiv="*servercmd*"—HTTP response header name.
	name="*name*"—Name of the meta information.
	content="*value*"—Content of the meta information.
	scheme="*scheme*"—Assigns a scheme to interpret the meta data.
Empty	Yes.

`<span>...</span>`

Usage	Organizes the document by defining a span of text.
Start/End Tag	Required/Required.
Attributes	core, i18n, events.
Empty	No.

`<title>...</title>`

Usage	The name you give your web page. The <title> tag is placed in the <head> tag and is displayed in the browser window title bar.
Start/End Tag	Required/Required.
Attributes	i18n.
Empty	No.
Notes	Only one title allowed per document.

XHTML Text Phrases and Paragraphs

Text phrases (or blocks) can be structured to suit a specific purpose, such as creating a paragraph. This should not be confused with modifying the formatting of the text.

`<abbr>...</abbr>`

Usage	Used to define abbreviations.
Start/End Tag	Required/Required.
Attributes	core, i18n, events.
Empty	No.
Notes	The material enclosed by the tag is the abbreviated form, whereas the long form is defined by attributes within the tag.

`<acronym>...</acronym>`

Usage	Used to define acronyms.
Start/End Tag	Required/Required.
Attributes	core, i18n, events.
Empty	No.

`<address>...</address>`

Usage	Provides a special format for author or contact information.
Start/End Tag	Required/Required.
Attributes	core, i18n, events.
Empty	No.
Notes	The ` ` element is commonly used inside the `<address>` element to break the lines of an address.

`<blockquote>...</blockquote>`

Usage	Used to display long quotations.
Start/End Tag	Required/Required.
Attributes	core, i18n, events.
	cite="*url*"—The URL of the quoted text.
Empty	No.

`<br />`

Usage	Forces a line break.
Start/End Tag	Required/Illegal.
Attributes	core, i18n, events.
Empty	Yes.

`<cite>...</cite>`

Usage	Cites a reference.
Start/End Tag	Required/Required.
Attributes	core, i18n, events.
Empty	No.

`<code>...</code>`

Usage	Identifies a code fragment for display.
Start/End Tag	Required/Required.
Attributes	core, i18n, events.
Empty	No.

`<del>...</del>`

Usage	Shows text as having been deleted from the document since the last change.
Start/End Tag	Required/Required.
Attributes	core, i18n, events.
	cite="url"—The URL of a linked document explaining the change.
	datetime="datetime"—Indicates the date and time of the change.
Empty	No.

\<dfn>...\</dfn>

Usage	Defines an enclosed term.
Start/End Tag	Required/Required.
Attributes	core, i18n, events.
Empty	No.

\<h1>...\</h1> **Through** \<h6>...\</h6>

Usage	Text heading.
Start/End Tag	Required/Required.
Attributes	core, i18n, events.
Empty	No.

\<ins>...\</ins>

Usage	Shows text as having been inserted in the document since the last change.
Start/End Tag	Required/Required.
Attributes	core, i18n, events.
	cite="*url*"—The URL of a linked document explaining the change.
	datetime="*datetime*"—Indicates the date and time of the change.
Empty	No.

\<kbd>...\</kbd>

Usage	Indicates text a user would type.
Start/End Tag	Required/Required.
Attributes	core, i18n, events.
Empty	No.

`<p>`...`</p>`

Usage	Defines a paragraph.
Start/End Tag	Required/Optional.
Attributes	core, i18n, events.
Empty	No.

`<pre>`...`</pre>`

Usage	Displays preformatted text.
Start/End Tag	Required/Required.
Attributes	core, i18n, events.
Empty	No.

`<q>`...`</q>`

Usage	Used to display short quotations that do not require paragraph breaks.
Start/End Tag	Required/Required.
Attributes	core, i18n, events.
	cite="*url*"—The URL of the quoted text.
Empty	No.

`<samp>`...`</samp>`

Usage	Identifies sample output.
Start/End Tag	Required/Required.
Attributes	core, i18n, events.
Empty	No.

`<strong>`...`</strong>`

Usage	Stronger emphasis.
Start/End Tag	Required/Required.
Attributes	core, i18n, events.
Empty	No.

_{...\}

Usage	Creates subscript.
Start/End Tag	Required/Required.
Attributes	core, i18n, events.
Empty	No.

\^{...\}

Usage	Creates superscript.
Start/End Tag	Required/Required.
Attributes	core, i18n, events.
Empty	No.

\<var>...\</var>

Usage	A variable.
Start/End Tag	Required/Required.
Attributes	core, i18n, events.
Empty	No.

XHTML Text Formatting Elements

General text characteristics such as the size, weight, and style can be modified using these elements, but the preferred approach is to use CSS style properties. Later in the appendix you'll find a complete reference for these properties, which provide an incredible amount of control over text formatting.

\...\

Usage	Bold text.
Start/End Tag	Required/Required.
Attributes	core, i18n, events.
Empty	No.

\<big>...\</big>

Usage	Large text.
Start/End Tag	Required/Required.
Attributes	core, i18n, events.
Empty	No.

\<i>...\</i>

Usage	Italicized text.
Start/End Tag	Required/Required.
Attributes	core, i18n, events.
Empty	No.

\<small>...\</small>

Usage	Small text.
Start/End Tag	Required/Required.
Attributes	core, i18n, events.
Empty	No.

\<tt>...\</tt>

Usage	Teletype (or monospaced) text.
Start/End Tag	Required/Required.
Attributes	core, i18n, events.
Empty	No.

XHTML Lists

You can organize text into a more structured outline by creating lists. Lists can be nested.

`<dd>...</dd>`

Usage	The definition description used in a `<dl>` (definition list) element.
Start/End Tag	Required/Optional.
Attributes	core, i18n, events.
Empty	No.
Notes	Can contain block-level content, such as the `<p>` element.

`<dl>...</dl>`

Usage	Creates a definition list.
Start/End Tag	Required/Required.
Attributes	core, i18n, events.
Empty	No.
Notes	Must contain at least one `<dt>` or `<dd>` element in any order.

`<dt>...</dt>`

Usage	The definition term (or label) used within a `<dl>` (definition list) element.
Start/End Tag	Required/Optional.
Attributes	core, i18n, events.
Empty	No.
Notes	Must contain text (which can be modified by text markup elements).

`<li>...</li>`

Usage	Defines a list item within a list.
Start/End Tag	Required/Optional.
Attributes	core, i18n, events.
Empty	No.

`<ol>...</ol>`

Usage	Creates an ordered list.
Start/End Tag	Required/Required.
Attributes	`core`, `i18n`, `events`.
Empty	No.
Notes	Must contain at least one list item.

`<ul>...</ul>`

Usage	Creates an unordered list.
Start/End Tag	Required/Required.
Attributes	`core`, `i18n`, `events`.
Empty	No.
Notes	Must contain at least one list item.

XHTML Links

Hyperlinking is fundamental to XHTML. These elements enable you to link to other documents, other locations within a document, or external files.

`<a>...</a>`

Usage	Used to define links and anchors.
Start/End Tag	Required/Required.
Attributes	`core`, `i18n`, `events`.
	`charset="encoding"`—Character encoding of the resource.
	`name="name"`—Defines an anchor.
	`href="linkurl"`—The URL of the linked resource.
	`rel="linktype"`—Forward link types.
	`rev="linktype"`—Reverse link types.
	`shape="value"`—Enables you to define client-side imagemaps using defined shapes (`default`, `rect`, `circle`, `poly`).
	`coords="values"`—Sets the size of the shape using pixel or percentage lengths.
Empty	No.

`<base />`

Usage	All other URLs in the document are resolved against this location.
Start/End Tag	Required/Illegal.
Attributes	`href="linkurl"`—The URL of the linked resource.
Empty	Yes.
Notes	Located in the document `<head>`.

`<link />`

Usage	Defines the relationship between a link and a resource.
Start/End Tag	Required/Illegal.
Attributes	`core, i18n, events.`
	`charset="encoding"`—The character encoding of the resource.
	`href="linkurl"`—The URL of the resource.
	`rel="linktype"`—The forward link types.
	`rev="linktype"`—The reverse link types.
	`type="contenttype"`—The Internet content type.
	`media="media"`—Defines the destination medium (`screen, print, projection, braille, speech, all`).
	`target="placement"`—Determines where the resource is displayed (user-defined name, `blank, parent, self, top`).
Empty	Yes.
Notes	Located in the document `<head>`.

XHTML Tables

Tables are meant to display data in a tabular format. Prior to XHTML, tables were widely used for page layout purposes, but with the advent of style sheets, this is officially discouraged by the W3C.

`<caption>...</caption>`

Usage	Displays a table caption.
Start/End Tag	Required/Required.
Attributes	core, i18n, events.
Empty	No.
Notes	Optional.

`<col />`

Usage	Groups individual columns within column groups in order to share attribute values.
Start/End Tag	Required/Illegal.
Attributes	core, i18n, events.
	span="*numcols*"—The number of columns the group contains.
	width="*width*"—The column width as a percentage, pixel value, or minimum value.
	align="*alignment*"—Horizontally aligns the contents of cells (left, center, right, justify, char).
	char="*charalignment*"—Sets a character on which the column aligns.
	charoff="*charoffset*"—Offset to the first alignment character on a line.
	valign="*verticalalignment*"—Vertically aligns the contents of a cell (top, middle, bottom, baseline).
Empty	Yes.

`<colgroup>...</colgroup>`

Usage	Defines a column group.
Start/End Tag	Required/Optional.
Attributes	core, i18n, events.
	span="*numcols*"—The number of columns in a group.
	width="*width*"—The width of the columns.
	align="*alignment*"—Horizontally aligns the contents of cells (left, center, right, justify, char).

char="*charalignment*"—Sets a character on which the column aligns.

charoff="*charoffset*"—Offset to the first alignment character on a line.

valign="*verticalalignment*"—Vertically aligns the contents of a cell (top, middle, bottom, baseline).

Empty   No.

`<table>...</table>`

Usage	Creates a table.
Start/End Tag	Required/Required.
Attributes	core, i18n, events.

width="*width*"—Table width.

cols="*numcols*"—The number of columns.

border="*borderwidth*"—The width in pixels of a border around the table.

frame="*frame*"—Sets the visible sides of a table (void, above, below, hsides, lhs, rhs, vsides, box, border).

rules="*rules*"—Sets the visible rules within a table (none, groups, rows, cols, all).

cellspacing="*cellspacing*"—Spacing between cells.

cellpadding="*cellpadding*"—Spacing in cells.

summary="*description*"—Provides a text description of the table for accessibility purposes.

Empty   No.

`<tbody>...</tbody>`

Usage	Defines the table body.
Start/End Tag	Optional/Optional.
Attributes	core, i18n, events.

align="*alignment*"—Horizontally aligns the contents of cells (left, center, right, justify, char).

char="*charalignment*"—Sets a character on which the column aligns.

charoff="*charoffset*"—Offset to the first alignment character on a line.

valign="*verticalalignment*"—Vertically aligns the contents of cells (top, middle, bottom, baseline).

Empty	No.

<td>...</td>

Usage	Defines a cell's contents.
Start/End Tag	Required/Optional.
Attributes	core, i18n, events.

abbr="*name*"—Abbreviated name.

axis="*axisnames*"—axis names listing row and column headers pertaining to the cell.

rowspan="*numrows*"—The number of rows spanned by a cell.

colspan="*numcols*"—The number of columns spanned by a cell.

align="*alignment*"—Horizontally aligns the contents of cells (left, center, right, justify, char).

char="*charalignment*"—Sets a character on which the column aligns.

charoff="*charoffset*"—Offset to the first alignment character on a line.

valign="*verticalalignment*"—Vertically aligns the contents of cells (top, middle, bottom, baseline).

headers="*headers*"—Header information for a cell.

scope="*scope*"—Indicates whether a cell provides header information for other cells.

Empty	No.

`<tfoot>...</tfoot>`

Usage	Defines the table footer.
Start/End Tag	Required/Optional.
Attributes	core, i18n, events.
	align="*alignment*"—Horizontally aligns the contents of cells (left, center, right, justify, char).
	char="*charalignment*"—Sets a character on which the column aligns.
	charoff="*charoffset*"—Offset to the first alignment character on a line.
	valign="*verticalalignment*"—Vertically aligns the contents of cells (top, middle, bottom, baseline).
Empty	No.

`<th>...</th>`

Usage	Defines the cell contents of the table header.
Start/End Tag	Required/Optional.
Attributes	core, i18n, events.
	axis="*name*"—Abbreviated name.
	axes="*axisnames*"—axis names listing row and column headers pertaining to the cell.
	rowspan="*numrows*"—The number of rows spanned by a cell.
	colspan="*numcols*"—The number of columns spanned by a cell.
	align="*alignment*"—Horizontally aligns the contents of cells (left, center, right, justify, char).
	char="*charalignment*"—Sets a character on which the column aligns.
	charoff="*charoffset*"—Offset to the first alignment character on a line.
	valign="*verticalalignment*"—Vertically aligns the contents of cells (top, middle, bottom, baseline).

headers="*headers*"—Header information for a cell.

scope="*scope*"—Indicates whether a cell provides header information for other cells.

Empty	No.

<thead>...</thead>

Usage	Defines the table header.
Start/End Tag	Required/Optional.
Attributes	core, i18n, events.
	align="*alignment*"—Horizontally aligns the contents of cells (left, center, right, justify, char).
	char="*charalignment*"—Sets a character on which the column aligns.
	charoff="*charoffset*"—Offset to the first alignment character on a line.
	valign="*verticalalignment*"—Vertically aligns the contents of cells (top, middle, bottom, baseline).
Empty	No.

<tr>...</tr>

Usage	Defines a row of table cells.
Start/End Tag	Required/Optional.
Attributes	core, i18n, events.
	align="*alignment*"—Horizontally aligns the contents of cells (left, center, right, justify, char).
	char="*charalignment*"—Sets a character on which the column aligns.
	charoff="*charoffset*"—Offset to the first alignment character on a line.
	valign="*verticalalignment*"—Vertically aligns the contents of cells (top, middle, bottom, baseline).
Empty	No.

XHTML Frames

Frames create new "panels" in the Web browser window that are used to display content from different source documents; frames allow you to build a Web page composed of several other web pages. Frames are not supported in XHTML 1.1 but can still be used via the XHTML 1.0 Frameset DTD and XHTML 1.0 Transitional DTD (iframes).

<frame />

Usage	Defines a frame.
Start/End Tag	Required/Illegal.
Attributes	core.
	name="*name*"—The name of a frame.
	src="*sourceurl*"—The source to be displayed in a frame.
	frameborder="*border*"—Toggles the border between frames (0, 1).
	marginwidth="*width*"—Sets the space between the frame border and content.
	marginheight="*height*"—Sets the space between the frame border and content.
	noresize="noresize"—Disables sizing.
	scrolling="*scrolling*"—Determines scrollbar presence (auto, yes, no).
	longdesc="*descurl*"—A URL to a long description of the frame; for browsers without frames.
Empty	Yes.
Notes	XHTML 1.0 Frameset DTD.

<frameset>...</frameset>

Usage	Defines the layout of frames within a window.
Start/End Tag	Required/Required.
Attributes	core.
	rows="*numrows*"—The number and size/proportion of rows.

cols="*numcols*"—The number and size/proportion of columns.

onload="*eventcode*"—The intrinsic event triggered when the document loads.

onunload="*eventcode*"—The intrinsic event triggered when the document unloads.

Empty	No.
Notes	XHTML 1.0 Frameset DTD. Framesets can be nested.

`<iframe>`...`</iframe>`

Usage	Creates an inline frame.
Start/End Tag	Required/Required.
Attributes	core.

name="*name*"—The name of the frame.

src="*sourceurl*"—The source to be displayed in a frame.

frameborder="*border*"—Toggles the border between frames (0, 1).

marginwidth="*width*"—Sets the space between the frame border and content.

marginheight="*height*"—Sets the space between the frame border and content.

scrolling="*scrolling*"—Determines scrollbar presence (auto, yes, no).

height="*height*"—Height.

width="*width*"—Width.

longdesc="*descurl*"—A URL to a long description of the frame; for browsers without frames.

Empty	No.
Notes	XHTML 1.0 Transitional DTD.

`<noframes>`...`</noframes>`

Usage	Alternative content when frames are not supported.
Start/End Tag	Required/Required.
Attributes	core, i18n, events.
Empty	No.
Notes	XHTML 1.0 Frameset DTD.

XHTML Embedded Content

Also called *inclusions*, embedded content applies to images, imagemaps, Java applets, Flash animations, and other multimedia or programmed content that is placed in a Web page to provide additional functionality.

`<area />`

Usage	The `<area>` element is used to define links and anchors.
Start/End Tag	Required/Illegal.
Attributes	core, i18n, events.
	shape="*value*"—Enables you to define client-side imagemaps using defined shapes (default, rect, circle, poly).
	coords="*values*"—Sets the size of the shape using pixel or percentage lengths.
	href="*linkurl*"—The URL of the linked resource.
	nohref="*nohref*"—Indicates that the region has no action.
	alt="*alttext*"—Displays alternative text.
	onfocus="*eventcode*"—The event that occurs when the element receives focus.
	onblur="*eventcode*"—The event that occurs when the element loses focus.
Empty	Yes.

`<img />`

Usage	Includes an image in the document.
Start/End Tag	Required/Illegal.
Attributes	`core`, `i18n`, `events`.

`src="`*`sourceurl`*`"`—The URL of the image.

`alt="`*`alttext`*`"`—Alternative text to display.

`height="`*`height`*`"`—The height of the image.

`width="`*`width`*`"`—The width of the image.

`border="`*`border`*`"`—Border width.

`hspace="`*`horizontalspace`*`"`—The horizontal space separating the image from other content.

`vspace="`*`verticalspace`*`"`—The vertical space separating the image from other content.

`usemap="`*`mapurl`*`"`—The URL to a client-side imagemap.

`ismap="ismap"`—Identifies a server-side imagemap.

`longdesc="`*`descurl`*`"`—A URL to a long description of the image; for browsers that don't display images.

Empty	Yes.

`<map>`...`</map>`

Usage	When used with the `<area>` element, creates a client-side imagemap.
Start/End Tag	Required/Required.
Attributes	`core`, `i18n`, `events`.

`name="`*`name`*`"`—The name of the imagemap to be created.

Empty	No.

`<object>`...`</object>`

Usage	Includes an object.
Start/End Tag	Required/Required.
Attributes	`core`, `i18n`, `events`.

`declare="declare"`—A flag that declares but doesn't create an object.

classid="*objecturl*"—The URL of the object's location.

codebase="*codebaseurl*"—The URL for resolving URLs specified by other attributes.

data="*dataurl*"—The URL to the object's data.

type="*datatype*"—The Internet content type for data.

codetype="*codetype*"—The Internet content type for the code.

standby="*waitmsg*"—Show message while loading.

height="*height*"—The height of the object.

width="*width*"—The width of the object.

border="*border*"—Displays the border around an object.

hspace="*horizontalspace*"—The space between the sides of the object and other page content.

vspace="*verticalspace*"—The space between the top and bottom of the object and other page content.

usemap="*mapurl*"—The URL to an imagemap.

shapes="*shapes*"—Enables you to define areas to search for hyperlinks if the object is an image.

name="*nameurl*"—The URL to submit as part of a form.

Empty	No.

\<param />

Usage	Initializes an object.
Start/End Tag	Required/Illegal.
Attributes	name="*name*"—Defines the parameter name.
	value="*value*"—The value of the object parameter.
	valuetype="*valuetype*"—Defines the value type (data, ref, object).
	type="*contenttype*"—The Internet medium type.
Empty	Yes.

XHTML Style

Style sheets (both inline and external) are incorporated into an HTML document through the use of the `<style>` element.

`<style>`...`</style>`

Usage	Creates an internal style sheet.
Start/End Tag	Required/Required.
Attributes	i18n.
	type="*contenttype*"—The Internet content type.
	media="*media*"—Defines the destination medium (screen, print, projection, braille, speech, all).
	title="*title*"—The title of the style.
Empty	No.
Notes	Located in the `<head>` element.

XHTML Forms

Forms create an interface for the user to select options, enter information, and return data to the Web server for processing.

`<button>`...`</button>`

Usage	Creates a button.
Start/End Tag	Required/Required.
Attributes	core, i18n, events.
	name="*name*"—The button name.
	value="*value*"—The value of the button.
	type="*type*"—The button type (button, submit, reset).
	disabled="disabled"—Sets the button state to disabled.
	onfocus="*eventcode*"—The event that occurs when the element receives focus.
	onblur="*eventcode*"—The event that occurs when the element loses focus.
Empty	No.

`<fieldset>...</fieldset>`

Usage	Groups related controls.
Start/End Tag	Required/Required.
Attributes	`core`, `i18n`, `events`.
Empty	No.

`<form>...</form>`

Usage	Creates a form that holds controls for user input.
Start/End Tag	Required/Required.
Attributes	`core`, `i18n`, `events`.
	`action="`*`actionurl`*`"`—The URL for the server action.
	`method="`*`post/get`*`"`—The HTTP method (get, post). get is deprecated.
	`enctype="`*`mediatype`*`"`—Specifies the MIME (Internet media) type.
	`onsubmit="`*`eventcode`*`"`—The intrinsic event that occurs when the form is submitted.
	`onreset="`*`eventcode`*`"`—The intrinsic event that occurs when the form is reset.
	`accept="`*`contenttypes`*`"`—The list of content types acceptable by the server.
	`accept-charset="`*`encodings`*`"`—The list of character encodings.
Empty	No.

`<input />`

Usage	Defines controls used in forms.
Start/End Tag	Required/Illegal.
Attributes	`core`, `i18n`, `events`.
	`type="`*`controltype`*`"`—The type of input control (text, password, checkbox, radio, submit, reset, file, hidden, image, button).
	`name="`*`name`*`"`—The name of the control (required except for submit and reset).

value="*value*"—The initial value of the control (required for radio and check boxes).

checked="checked"—Sets the radio buttons to a checked state.

disabled="disabled"—Disables the control.

readonly="readonly"—For text password types.

size="*size*"—The width of the control in pixels except for text and password controls, which are specified in number of characters.

maxlength="*maxlength*"—The maximum number of characters that can be entered.

src="*imageurl*"—The URL to an image control type.

alt="*alttext*"—An alternative text description.

usemap="*mapurl*"—The URL to a client-side imagemap.

onfocus="*eventcode*"—The event that occurs when the element receives focus.

onblur="*eventcode*"—The event that occurs when the element loses focus.

onselect="*eventcode*"—An intrinsic event that occurs when the control is selected.

onchange="*eventcode*"—An intrinsic event that occurs when the control is changed.

accept="*filetypes*"—File types allowed for upload.

Empty   Yes.

`<label>`...`</label>`

Usage   Labels a control.

Start/End Tag   Required/Required.

Attributes   core, i18n, events.

for="*control*"—Associates a label with an identified control.

onfocus="*eventcode*"—The event that occurs when the element receives focus.

onblur="*eventcode*"—The event that occurs when the element loses focus.

Empty   No.

`<legend>...</legend>`

Usage	Assigns a caption to a `fieldset`.
Start/End Tag	Required/Required.
Attributes	core, i18n, events.
Empty	No.

`<optgroup>...</optgroup>`

Usage	Used to group form elements within a `<select>` element.
Start/End Tag	Required/Required.
Attributes	core, i18n, events.
	`disabled="disabled"`—Not used.
	`label="label"`—Defines a group label.
Empty	No.

`<option>...</option>`

Usage	Specifies choices in a `<select>` element.
Start/End Tag	Required/Optional.
Attributes	core, i18n, events.
	`selected="selected"`—Specifies whether the option is selected.
	`disabled="disabled"`—Disables control.
	`label="label"`—Defines a label for the group of options.
	`value="value"`—The value submitted if a control is submitted.
Empty	No.

`<select>...</select>`

Usage	Creates choices for the user to select.
Start/End Tag	Required/Required.
Attributes	core, i18n, events.
	`name="name"`—The name of the element.

size="*size*"—The width in number of rows.

multiple="multiple"—Allows multiple selections.

disabled="disabled"—Disables the control.

onfocus="*eventcode*"—The event that occurs when the element receives focus.

onblur="*eventcode*"—The event that occurs when the element loses focus.

onselect="*eventcode*"—An intrinsic event that occurs when the control is selected.

onchange="*eventcode*"—An intrinsic event that occurs when the control is changed.

Empty   No.

`<textarea>`...`</textarea>`

Usage   Creates an area for user input with multiple lines.

Start/End Tag   Required/Required.

Attributes   core, i18n, events.

name="*name*"—The name of the control.

rows="*numrows*"—The width in number of rows.

cols="*numcols*"—The height in number of columns.

disabled="disabled"—Disables the control.

readonly="readonly"—Sets the displayed text to read-only status.

onfocus="*eventcode*"—The event that occurs when the element receives focus.

onblur="*eventcode*"—The event that occurs when the element loses focus.

onselect="*eventcode*"—An intrinsic event that occurs when the control is selected.

onchange="*eventcode*"—An intrinsic event that occurs when the control is changed.

Empty   No.

Notes   Text to be displayed is placed within the start and end tags.

XHTML Scripts

Scripts make it possible to process data and perform other dynamic events. Scripts are included in web pages thanks to the `<script>` element, which also identifies the specific scripting language being used (JavaScript, VBScript, and so on.).

`<noscript>`...`</noscript>`

Usage	Provides alternative content for browsers unable to execute a script.
Start/End Tag	Required/Required.
Attributes	core, i18n, events.
Empty	No.

`<script>`...`</script>`

Usage	The `<script>` element contains client-side scripts that are executed by the browser.
Start/End Tag	Required/Required.
Attributes	`type="scripttype"`—Script language Internet content type.
	`src="scripturl"`—The URL for the external script.
	`defer="defer"`—Indicates that the script doesn't alter document content.
Empty	No.
Notes	You can set the default scripting language in the `<meta />` element.

XHTML Common Attributes and Events

The following six attributes are abbreviated as `core` in the preceding sections:

▶ `id="id"`—A global identifier.

▶ `class="styleclasses"`—A list of classes separated by spaces.

▶ `style="styles"`—Style information.

▶ title="*title*"—Provides more information for a specific element, as opposed to the <title> element, which titles the entire Web page.

▶ accesskey="*shortcut*"—Sets the keyboard shortcut used to access an element.

▶ tabindex="*taborder*"—Sets the tab order of an element.

The following two attributes for internationalization are abbreviated as i18n in the preceding sections:

▶ lang="*lang*"—The language identifier.

▶ dir="*textdir*"—The text direction (ltr, rtl).

The following intrinsic events are abbreviated events:

▶ onclick="*eventcode*"—A pointing device (such as a mouse) was single-clicked.

▶ ondblclick="*eventcode*"—A pointing device (such as a mouse) was double-clicked.

▶ onmousedown="*eventcode*"—A mouse button was clicked and held down.

▶ onmouseup="*eventcode*"—A mouse button that was clicked and held down was released.

▶ onmouseover="*eventcode*"—A mouse moved the cursor over an object.

▶ onmousemove="*eventcode*"—The mouse was moved.

▶ onmouseout="*eventcode*"—A mouse moved the cursor off an object.

▶ onkeypress="*eventcode*"—A key was pressed and released.

▶ onkeydown="*eventcode*"—A key was pressed and held down.

▶ onkeyup="*eventcode*"—A key that was pressed has been released.

CSS Dimension Style Properties

Quite a few CSS style rules rely on dimensional properties in one form or another. It would be difficult to size elements with them.

height

Usage	Sets the height of an element.
Values	auto, *length*, %.

line-height

Usage	Sets the distance between lines of elements.
Values	normal, *length*, %.

max-height

Usage	Sets the maximum height of an element.
Values	none, *length*, %.

max-width

Usage	Sets the maximum width of an element.
Values	none, *length*, %.

min-height

Usage	Sets the minimum height of an element.
Values	*length*, %.

min-width

Usage	Sets the minimum width of an element.
Values	*length*, %.

width

Usage	Sets the width of an element.
Values	auto, *length*, %.

CSS Text and Font Style Properties

The heart of CSS styling lies in the text and style properties, which give you an incredible amount of control over the appearance of Web page text.

color

Usage	Sets the color of text.
Values	*color*.

direction

Usage	Sets the direction of text, as in left-to-right or right-to-left.
Values	`ltr, rtl`.

font

Usage	A shorthand property that allows you to set all the font properties in one declaration.
Values	*font-style, font-variant, font-weight, font-size/line-height, font-family*.

font-family

Usage	A prioritized list of font family names and/or generic family names for an element.
Values	*family-name, generic-family*.

font-size

Usage	Sets the size of a font.
Values	`xx-small, x-small, small, medium, large, x-large, xx-large, smaller, larger,` *length*, `%`.

font-style

Usage	Sets the style of the font.
Values	`normal, italic, oblique`.

font-variant

Usage	Displays text in a small-caps font or a normal font.
Values	`normal`, `small-caps`.

font-weight

Usage	Sets the weight (boldness) of a font.
Values	`normal`, `bold`, `bolder`, `lighter`, `100`, `200`, `300`, `400`, `500`, `600`, `700`, `800`, `900`.

letter-spacing

Usage	Increase or decrease the space between characters of text.
Values	`normal`, *length*.

text-align

Usage	Aligns the text within an element.
Values	`left`, `right`, `center`, `justify`.

text-decoration

Usage	Applies a decoration to text.
Values	`none`, `underline`, `overline`, `line-through`, `blink`.

text-indent

Usage	Indents the first line of text in an element.
Values	*length*, %.

text-transform

Usage	Controls the capitalization of letters of text.
Values	`none`, `capitalize`, `uppercase`, `lowercase`.

white-space

Usage	Establishes the handling of white space within an element.
Values	normal, pre, nowrap.

word-spacing

Usage	Increases or decreases the space between words.
Values	normal, *length*.

CSS Background Style Properties

There are several CSS style properties that can be used to alter the background of pages and individual elements on pages.

background

Usage	A shorthand property that allows you to set all the background properties in one declaration.
Values	*background-color*, *background-image*, *background-repeat*, *background-attachment*, *background-position*.

background-attachment

Usage	Determines whether a background image is fixed or scrolls with the rest of the page.
Values	scroll, fixed.

background-color

Usage	Sets the background color of an element.
Values	*color-rgb*, *color-hex*, *color-name*, transparent.

background-image

Usage	Sets an image as the background.
Values	*url*, none.

background-position

Usage	Sets the starting position of a background image.
Values	`top left`, `top center`, `top right`, `center left`, `center center`, `center right`, `bottom left`, `bottom center`, `bottom right`, *x-% y-%*, *x-pos y-pos*.

background-repeat

Usage	Sets whether and how a background image is repeated.
Values	`repeat`, `repeat-x`, `repeat-y`, `no-repeat`.

CSS Border Style Properties

Every block element has a border that can be styled. Although you can certainly leave borders invisible, there are several styles that can be applied to element borders.

border

Usage	A shorthand property that allows you to set all the properties for the four borders in one declaration.
Values	*border-width*, *border-style*, *border-color*.

border-bottom

Usage	A shorthand property that allows you to set all the bottom border properties in one declaration.
Values	*border-bottom-width*, *border-style*, *border-color*.

border-bottom-color

Usage	Sets the color of the bottom border.
Values	*border-color*.

border-bottom-style

Usage	Sets the style of the bottom border.
Values	*border-style*.

border-bottom-width

Usage	Sets the width of the bottom border.
Values	thin, medium, thick, *length*.

border-color

Usage	Sets the color of the four borders.
Values	*color*.
Notes	Can be specified using from one to four colors.

border-left

Usage	A shorthand property that allows you to set all the left border properties in one declaration.
Values	*border-left-width*, *border-style*, *border-color*.

border-left-color

Usage	Sets the color of the left border.
Values	*border-color*.

border-left-style

Usage	Sets the style of the left border.
Values	*border-style*.

border-left-width

Usage	Sets the width of the left border.
Values	thin, medium, thick, *length*.

border-right

Usage	A shorthand property that allows you to set all the right border properties in one declaration.
Values	*border-right-width*, *border-style*, *border-color*.

border-right-color

Usage	Sets the color of the right border.
Values	border-color.

border-right-style

Usage	Sets the style of the right border.
Values	*border-style*.

border-right-width

Usage	Sets the width of the right border.
Values	thin, medium, thick, *length*.

border-style

Usage	Sets the style of the four borders.
Values	none, hidden, dotted, dashed, solid, double, groove, ridge, inset, outset.
Notes	Can be specified using from one to four styles.

border-top

Usage	A shorthand property that allows you to set all the top border properties in one declaration.
Values	*border-top-width, border-style, border-color*.

border-top-color

Usage	Sets the color of the top border.
Values	*border-color*.

border-top-style

Usage	Sets the style of the top border.
Values	*border-style*.

border-top-width

Usage	Sets the width of the top border.
Values	thin, medium, thick, *length*.

border-width

Usage	A shorthand property for setting the width of the four borders in one declaration.
Values	thin, medium, thick, *length*.
Notes	Can be specified using from one to four widths.

CSS Margin Style Properties

Margins allow you to add a bit of spacing around the outer edge of an element, outside of the element's border.

margin

Usage	A shorthand property that allows you to set all the margin properties in one declaration.
Values	*margin-top*, *margin-right*, *margin-bottom*, *margin-left*.

margin-bottom

Usage	Sets the bottom margin of an element.
Values	auto, *length*, %.

margin-left

Usage	Sets the left margin of an element.
Values	auto, *length*, %.

margin-right

Usage	Sets the right margin of an element.
Values	auto, *length*, %.

margin-top

Usage	Sets the top margin of an element.
Values	auto, *length*, %.

CSS Padding Style Properties

Padding allows you to add space around an element, inside of the element's border.

padding

Usage	A shorthand property that allows you to set all the padding properties in one declaration.
Values	*padding-top, padding-right, padding-bottom, padding-left.*

padding-bottom

Usage	Sets the bottom padding of an element.
Values	*length*, %.

padding-left

Usage	Sets the left padding of an element.
Values	*length*, %.

padding-right

Usage	Sets the right padding of an element.
Values	*length*, %.

padding-top

Usage	Sets the top padding of an element.
Values	*length*, %.

CSS Layout and Display Style Properties

The layout and display properties in CSS play an extremely important role in determining how elements are laid out and arranged on the page.

bottom

Usage	Sets the offset between the bottom edge of the element and the bottom edge of its parent element.
Values	auto, *length*, %.

clear

Usage	Determines the sides of an element where other floating elements are not allowed.
Values	left, right, both, none.

clip

Usage	Sets the shape of an element.
Values	auto, *shape*.
Notes	The element is clipped to this shape when displayed.

cursor

Usage	Specifies the type of mouse cursor to be displayed.
Values	*url*, auto, crosshair, default, pointer, move, e-resize, ne-resize, nw-resize, n-resize, se-resize, sw-resize, s-resize, w-resize, text, wait, help.

display

Usage	Sets whether and how an element is displayed.
Values	none, inline, block, list-item, run-in, compact, marker, table, inline-table, table-row-group, table-header-group, table-footer-group, table-row, table-column-group, table-column, table-cell, table-caption.

float

Usage   Sets where an image or text will appear relative to another element.

Values   `left, right, none.`

left

Usage   Sets the offset between the left edge of the element and the left edge of its parent element.

Values   `auto,` *`length`*`, %.`

overflow

Usage   Determines what happens if the content of an element overflows its area.

Values   `auto, visible, hidden, scroll.`

position

Usage   Specifies the layout of an element as using static, relative, absolute, or fixed positioning.

Values   `static, relative, absolute, fixed.`

right

Usage   Sets the offset between the right edge of the element and the right edge of its parent element.

Values   `auto,` *`length`*`, %.`

top

Usage   Sets the offset between the top edge of the element and the top edge of its parent element.

Values   `auto,` *`length`*`, %.`

vertical-align

Usage	Sets the vertical alignment of an element.
Values	baseline, sub, super, top, text-top, middle, bottom, text-bottom, *length*, %.

visibility

Usage	Determines whether an element should be shown (visible) or hidden (invisible).
Values	visible, hidden, collapse.

z-index

Usage	Sets the z-order (stacking order) of an element.
Values	auto, *number*.

CSS List and Marker Style Properties

You may not have realized how much flexibility there is when it comes to the styling of lists via CSS. Several CSS styles apply to lists and the list-item markers, or bullets, within the lists.

list-style

Usage	A shorthand property that allows you to set all the list properties in one declaration.
Values	*list-style-type*, *list-style-position*, *list-style-image*.

list-style-image

Usage	Sets an image as the list-item marker (bullet) for the list.
Values	none, *url*.

list-style-position

Usage	Sets where the list-item marker (bullet) is placed in the list.
Values	inside, outside.

list-style-type

Usage	Sets the type of the list-item marker (bullet).
Values	none, disc, circle, square, decimal, decimal-leading-zero, lower-roman, upper-roman, lower-alpha, upper-alpha, lower-greek, lower-latin, upper-latin, hebrew, armenian, georgian, cjk-ideographic, hiragana, katakana, hiragana-iroha, katakana-iroha.

CSS Table Style Properties

There are a few advanced table properties that enable you to fine-tune the manner in which tables are rendered and displayed.

border-collapse

Usage	Sets the border model of a table.
Values	collapse, separate.

border-spacing

Usage	Sets the distance between the borders of adjacent cells.
Values	*length length*.

caption-side

Usage	Sets the position of the caption relative to the table.
Values	top, bottom, left, right.

empty-cells

Usage	Determines whether cells with no visible content should have borders.
Values	show, hide.

table-layout

Usage	Determines how the table is laid out.
Values	auto, fixed.
Notes	Speeds up browser rendering for fixed-size tables if you set it to fixed.

APPENDIX D

Migrating from HTML to XHTML

Although the relationship between HTML and XHTML has been covered in several places throughout the book, I felt it would be beneficial to have all the information in one place. This appendix serves as a reference for quickly obtaining the information regarding the differences between HTML 4 and XHTML 1.1, which are the primary two web standards involved in web page creation.

Differences Between XHTML 1 and HTML 4

XHTML 1.1 is an improved version of HTML 4 that plays by the more rigid rules of XML. Fortunately, most of the differences between XHTML and HTML don't dramatically impact the overall structure of HTML documents. Migrating an HTML document to XHTML is more a matter of cleaning and tightening up the code than converting it to a new language.

Following is a list of the primary differences between XHTML and HTML, with a focus on what XHTML requires that HTML doesn't:

- ▶ Element and attribute names must be in lowercase (`<a href="index.html">`).

- ▶ End tags are required for non-empty elements (`<p>Howdy!</p>`).

- ▶ Empty elements must consist of a start-tag/end-tag pair or an empty element (`<br />`).

- ▶ Attribute values must always be quoted (`href="index.html"`).

- ▶ Attribute names cannot be used without a value (`ismap="ismap"`).

- ▶ The XHTML namespace must be declared in the `html` element.

- ▶ The `head` and `body` elements cannot be omitted.

- ▶ The `title` element must be the first element in the `head` element.

- ▶ Documents must use the `id` attribute to uniquely name elements on the page; the `name` attribute can no longer be used in XHTML for this purpose.

Based on your newfound knowledge of XML, none of these differences should come as too much of a surprise, especially because you've been following the rules of XHTML throughout the book. Fortunately, they are all pretty easy to find and fix in HTML documents, which makes the move from HTML to XHTML relatively straightforward.

XHTML and Document Validity

All XHTML documents must specify a document type definition, or DTD, which is used to identify XHTML as the language for the web page. In XHTML 1.0, the W3C developed three different DTDs, which are all included in the XHTML specification. These DTDs provided varying levels of detail for XHTML, which resulted in three different classifications of XHTML documents. The idea was that you could use a more minimal XHTML DTD if you didn't need to use certain XHTML language features, or you could use a more thorough DTD if you needed additional features. The three XHTML 1.0 DTDs were classified as shown here, in order of increasing features:

▶ *Strict*—No HTML presentation elements are available (font, table, and so on.); style sheets must be used to format documents for display.

▶ *Transitional*—HTML presentation elements are available for formatting documents.

▶ *Frameset*—Frames are available, as well as HTML presentation elements.

The Strict DTD was a minimal DTD that was used to create very clean XHTML documents without any presentation tags. Documents created from this DTD required style sheets in order to be formatted for display. Not surprisingly, this is the DTD that would later form the basis of XHTML 1.1; more on that subject in a moment. The Transitional DTD built on the Strict DTD by adding support for presentation tags. This DTD was useful in performing a quick conversion of HTML documents when you didn't want to take the time to develop style sheets. The Frameset DTD was the broadest of the three DTDs, and included support for creating web pages with frames.

XHTML 1.1 did away with the three different DTDs and instead went with a single DTD that is very similar to the XHTML 1.0 Strict DTD. The idea is that you should be focused on separating content from formatting in XHTML 1.0, which means you should be using style sheets instead of the old HTML presentation tags. This book focuses solely on XHTML 1.1 and its strict approach to creating highly structured web pages.

You must declare the DTD for all XHTML documents in a document type declaration at the top of the document. A Formal Public Identifier (FPI) is used in the document type declaration to reference the standard XHTML 1.1 DTD. Following is an example of how to declare the Strict DTD in a document type declaration:

```
<!DOCTYPE html PUBLIC "-//W3C//DTD XHTML 1.1//EN"
  "http://www.w3.org/TR/xhtml11/DTD/xhtml11.dtd">
```

It isn't terribly important that you understand the details of the FPI in this code. The main point is that it identifies the XHTML 1.1 DTD, which is required of all XHTML 1.1 web pages. You should hopefully recognize this code because it appears at the start of every sample web page in this book. Keep in mind that the significance of the document type declaration is that you must place it at the top of every XHTML web page that you create in order for it to qualify as a valid XHTML document.

Declaring XHTML Namespaces

In addition to declaring an appropriate DTD in a document type declaration, a valid XHTML document must also declare an XHTML namespace in the html element. Following is the XHTML 1.1 namespace, which is associated with the DTD you just learned about:

```
http://www.w3.org/1999/xhtml
```

The xmlns namespace declaration attribute is used to declare the XHTML namespace in the html element of an XHTML 1.1 document. Following is an example of how to specify the XHTML 1.1 namespace:

```
<html xmlns="http://www.w3.org/1999/xhtml">
...
</html>
```

Converting HTML Documents to XHTML

Although it's great to focus on creating new web pages from scratch using XHTML, the reality is that at some point you are likely to encounter HTML documents that you will want to convert to XHTML. Fortunately, it isn't too terribly difficult to bring HTML 4 documents up to par with the XHTML 1.1 specification. You've already learned about the ways in which XHTML documents differ from HTML documents. These differences become your guide to converting HTML to XHTML.

Following is a checklist to use as a guide while performing the conversion from HTML to XHTML:

1. Add a document type declaration that declares the XHTML 1.1 DTD.

2. Declare the XHTML 1.1 namespace in the html element that matches the DTD.

3. Convert all element and attribute names to lowercase.

4. Match every start tag with an end tag.

5. Replace > with /> at the end of all empty tags.

6. Enclose all attribute values in quotes (").

7. Make sure that all elements and attributes are defined in the XHTML 1.1 DTD; use CSS styles to replace deprecated presentation tags.

8. Convert special characters to entity references; for example, " becomes " (see Table D.1 for more details).

TABLE D.1   Characters to Avoid Using in XHTML Pages

Replace This...	With This...
& (ampersand)	& or &
" (quotation/inch mark)	" or "
< (open angle bracket)	< or <
> (close angle bracket)	> or >
[(open square bracket)	&#91;
] (close square bracket)	&#93;
' (apostrophe/single quote)	&#39;

Did you Know?

If you have a number of HTML pages that you'd like to convert to XHTML-compatible format, I strongly recommend that you download the free HTML-Kit software from http://www.chami.com/html-kit/. This free program includes a module called HTML-Tidy, which automatically changes HTML to conform to the rules mentioned here and also reports any other problems or incompatibilities it finds. HTML-Kit is also a friendly and well-designed text editor with many handy features for writing new XHTML pages. (One caveat: HTML-Tidy changes the line breaks and spacing of your code, so you may have to do some reformatting by hand if you like to neatly indent your code.)

After you've converted your pages over to XHTML, you will want to validate them to make sure that the conversion was a complete success. The W3C provides a free online validation service you can use to see whether your pages adhere completely to the official XHTML standard. The validation service, located at http://validator.w3.org/, allows you to browse XHTML files on your own computer for validation, as well as files that are already published on the Web. I strongly encourage you to try out the validation service because it represents the final word on the accuracy of XHTML code.

The good news in regard to XHTML document conversion is that this book has already taught you good enough coding habits that conversion shouldn't be a problem for your new web pages. And even when tackling existing pages that don't conform to XHTML, you should be able to methodically tackle the conversion by following the steps mentioned in this appendix. If you carry out each of these steps, you should arrive at a legitimate XHTML document that conforms to all the rules of the XHTML 1.1 standard.

Index

X

Y-Z